I0882368

Regulating Fair Competition Toward Sustainable Development Goals

Siti Fazilah Abdul Shukor
University of Tunku Abdul Rahman, Malaysia

Farahdilah Ghazali
University of Malaysia Terengganu, Malaysia

Nur Yuhanis Ismon
University of Tun Hussien Onn, Malaysia

Aerni Isa
Taylor's University, Malaysia

A volume in the Advances in Public Policy and Administration (APPA) Book Series

IGI Global
PUBLISHER of TIMELY KNOWLEDGE

Published in the United States of America by
IGI Global
Information Science Reference (an imprint of IGI Global)
701 E. Chocolate Avenue
Hershey PA, USA 17033
Tel: 717-533-8845
Fax: 717-533-8661
E-mail: cust@igi-global.com
Web site: http://www.igi-global.com

Copyright © 2024 by IGI Global. All rights reserved. No part of this publication may be reproduced, stored or distributed in any form or by any means, electronic or mechanical, including photocopying, without written permission from the publisher. Product or company names used in this set are for identification purposes only. Inclusion of the names of the products or companies does not indicate a claim of ownership by IGI Global of the trademark or registered trademark.

Library of Congress Cataloging-in-Publication Data

Names: Siti Fazilah Abdul Shukor, 1986- editor.
Title: Regulating fair competition toward sustainable development goals / edited by Siti Fazilah Abdul Shukor, Farahdilah Ghazali, Nur Ismon, Aerni Isa.
Description: Hershey, PA : Information Science Reference, [2024] | Includes bibliographical references and index. | Summary: "This book aims to explore the interaction between competition law and policy and the Sustainable Development Goals (SDGs)"-- Provided by publisher.
Identifiers: LCCN 2023038652 (print) | LCCN 2023038653 (ebook) | ISBN 9798369303900 (hardcover) | ISBN 9798369303917 (paperback) | ISBN 9798369303924 (ebook)
Subjects: LCSH: Sustainable development--International cooperation. | Competition, Unfair.
Classification: LCC HC79.E5 R44627 2024 (print) | LCC HC79.E5 (ebook) | DDC 338.9/27--dc23/eng/20230817
LC record available at https://lccn.loc.gov/2023038652
LC ebook record available at https://lccn.loc.gov/2023038653

This book is published in the IGI Global book series Advances in Public Policy and Administration (APPA) (ISSN: 2475-6644; eISSN: 2475-6652)

British Cataloguing in Publication Data
A Cataloguing in Publication record for this book is available from the British Library.

All work contributed to this book is new, previously-unpublished material. The views expressed in this book are those of the authors, but not necessarily of the publisher.

For electronic access to this publication, please contact: eresources@igi-global.com.

Advances in Public Policy and Administration (APPA) Book Series

ISSN:2475-6644
EISSN:2475-6652

Mission

Proper management of the public sphere is necessary in order to maintain order in modern society. Research developments in the field of public policy and administration can assist in uncovering the latest tools, practices, and methodologies for governing societies around the world.

The **Advances in Public Policy and Administration (APPA) Book Series** aims to publish scholarly publications focused on topics pertaining to the governance of the public domain. APPA's focus on timely topics relating to government, public funding, politics, public safety, policy, and law enforcement is particularly relevant to academicians, government officials, and upper-level students seeking the most up-to-date research in their field.

Coverage

- Government
- Law Enforcement
- Political Economy
- Politics
- Public Administration
- Public Funding
- Public Policy
- Resource allocation
- Urban Planning

IGI Global is currently accepting manuscripts for publication within this series. To submit a proposal for a volume in this series, please contact our Acquisition Editors at Acquisitions@igi-global.com or visit: http://www.igi-global.com/publish/.

The Advances in Public Policy and Administration (APPA) Book Series (ISSN 2475-6644) is published by IGI Global, 701 E. Chocolate Avenue, Hershey, PA 17033-1240, USA, www.igi-global.com. This series is composed of titles available for purchase individually; each title is edited to be contextually exclusive from any other title within the series. For pricing and ordering information please visit http://www.igi-global.com/book-series/advances-public-policy-administration/97862. Postmaster: Send all address changes to above address. Copyright © 2024 IGI Global. All rights, including translation in other languages reserved by the publisher. No part of this series may be reproduced or used in any form or by any means – graphics, electronic, or mechanical, including photocopying, recording, taping, or information and retrieval systems – without written permission from the publisher, except for non commercial, educational use, including classroom teaching purposes. The views expressed in this series are those of the authors, but not necessarily of IGI Global.

Titles in this Series

For a list of additional titles in this series, please visit: www.igi-global.com/book-series

Using Crises and Disasters as Opportunities for Innovation and Improvement
Saeed Siyal (School of Economics and Management, Beijing University of Chemical Technology, hina)
Information Science Reference • © 2024 • 323pp • H/C (ISBN: 9781668495223) • US $240.00

Cognitive Governance and the Historical Distortion of the Norm of Modern Development A Theory of Political Asymmetry
Renny Rueda (American University in the Emirates UAE)
Information Science Reference • © 2024 • 254pp • H/C (ISBN: 9781668497944) • US $215.00

Financial Evaluation and Risk Management of Infrastructure Projects
Kleopatra Petroutsatou (Aristotle University of Thessaloniki, Greece) and Constantin Zopounidis (Technical University of Crete, Greece & Audencia Business School, France)
Information Science Reference • © 2024 • 248pp • H/C (ISBN: 9781668477861) • US $225.00

Policies, Practices, and Protocols for International Commercial Arbitration
Basheer Ahmed Mohammed Khan (Supreme Court of India Bar Association, India) and Kaushal Kishore (Supreme Court of India Bar Association, New Delhi, India)
Information Science Reference • © 2023 • 271pp • H/C (ISBN: 9781668440407) • US $225.00

Governmental Power Market-Ing in the VU-CHAOS World
Kittisak Jermsittiparsert (University of City Island, Cyprus) Srirath Gohwong (Universitas Muhammadiyah Sidenreng Rappang, Indonesia) Shayut Pavapanunkul (Universitas Muhammadiyah Sidenreng Rappang, Indonesia) and Nasaran Mahittichatkul (Universitas Muhammadiyah Sidenreng Rappang, Indonesia)
Information Science Reference • © 2023 • 296pp • H/C (ISBN: 9781668472804) • US $205.00

Historical and Political Analysis on Power Balances and Deglobalization
Emily Brynn Stacey (Rose State College, USA)
Information Science Reference • © 2023 • 253pp • H/C (ISBN: 9781668456330) • US $205.00

Juvenile Justice in African and Western Criminal Justice Systems
Simeon Peter Sungi (United States International University-Africa, Kenya) George Rugaimukamu Kakoti (Tennessee State University, USA) and Deneil D. Christian (Tennessee State University, USA)
Information Science Reference • © 2024 • 300pp • H/C (ISBN: 9781668493434) • US $215.00

IGI Global
PUBLISHER of TIMELY KNOWLEDGE

701 East Chocolate Avenue, Hershey, PA 17033, USA
Tel: 717-533-8845 x100 • Fax: 717-533-8661
E-Mail: cust@igi-global.com • www.igi-global.com

Editorial Advisory Board

Hartinie Abd Aziz, *University of Sultan Zainal Abidin, Malaysia*
Siti Suraya Abd Razak, *University of Technology, Malaysia*
Hamizah Abdul Rahman, *University of Sultan Zainal Abidin, Malaysia*
Nasarudin Bin Abdul Rahman, *International Islamic University, Malaysia*
Miroslava Marinova, *Department of Law, Policing and Justice, University of East London, UK*
Choong Yuen Onn, *University of Tunku Abdul Rahman, Malaysia*
Ng Lee Peng, *University of Tunku Abdul Rahman, Malaysia*
Tilottama Raychaudhuri, *West Bengal National University of Juridical Sciences, Kolkata*
Wan Mohd Zulhafiz Wan Zahari, *International Islamic University, Malaysia*
Mailinda Eka Yuniza, *University of Gadjah Mada, Indonesia*

Table of Contents

Detailed Table of Contents

The significance of consumer protection in achieving sustainable development goals is a critical element in stimulating a more dynamic and competitive digital economy. Consumers are the major economic participants in the economy with an active role in the digital marketplace, the participation of responsible platforms' businesses, and the empowerment of responsible consumers contribute directly toward achieving sustainable development goals. Consumer protection and competition law are intertwined with both focusing on consumers as the key stakeholder. This chapter focuses on the interplay between consumer protection law and competition law in the e-commerce platforms economy, highlighting the trade-off for e-commerce in sustainable consumption and production, and how reconsidering competition law in e-commerce platforms could enhance sustainable consumption and production.

As of June 2023, the percentage of Tanzanians who had access to a telephone was more than one hundred per cent. However, this has not always been so. For example, in 1997, there was a telephone density of 0.32 per cent. This average was much lower than those of neighbouring Kenya (0.92), the Southern African Development Community (SADC) (3.4), Asia (3.86), and Europe (35.36). Fast forward a little over twenty years and practically everyone in Tanzania now has access to a telephone. This chapter, among other things, argues that establishing favourable legislative and regulatory frameworks that encourage the competitive provision of telecommunication services has directly contributed to these developments.

As a result, the chapter's primary argument is that the implementation of these frameworks has directly contributed to increased access to telecommunications services, which in turn has contributed to the achievement of the SDGs.

This chapter delves into the intricate interplay between competition law and sustainable development goals (SDGs), uncovering their interplay by unravelling how competition law's principles of fair play, economic efficiency, consumer protection, and prevention of market power abuse align seamlessly with multiple SDGs in Malaysia. It investigates the similarities between the objectives of competition law in Malaysia and the UN SDGs. It dissects how competition law fosters economic growth, innovation, and access to essential goods and services, aligning with SDGs that seek to eradicate poverty, enhance industry, promote inclusive societies, and ensure responsible consumption. The chapter will show the symbiotic relationship between competition law and SDGs, where principles of fair competition align harmoniously with broader development goals. Thus, the enforcement of competition law just like the pursuit of the SDGs should be seen as a dynamic force for societal progress, economic equity, and global betterment.

Some studies have found that liberalized electricity market led to acceleration of the development of renewable energy sector, particularly with community-based financing for local renewable projects in place. The idea of liberalization of electricity market focuses on the fair competition especially among the key players which subsequently entice more investment on infrastructures and reduce electricity tariff. Energy liberalization has dramatically enhanced monopoly utility governance, competition, innovation prospects, and the policy for environmental emissions management by creating trading mechanisms. This chapter discusses the practices of power liberalization, especially in Europe, regarding the benefits and challenges. Moreover, the chapter examines Malaysian practices in pursuing renewable energy programs to attain sustainability and energy security goals, which is also vital to support a more competitive energy sector.

This chapter investigates the possibility of policy in support of low carbon transition under the competition law. It is true that competition law and environmental policies are key drivers of innovation, but their interplay is need to be explored more. The main question in this chapter is: does the competition law can help to achieve the Indonesia's Net Zero and sustainability goals? This study uses a qualitative approach that analysis the success of competition law in fighting climate change and boosting the transition to low carbon. Qualitative techniques are carried out through literature studies or references that describe analysing of implementing a competition law on the environment and mitigating climate change caused by carbon emissions.

With the effect of the Covid pandemic, people lost their jobs, and it magnified the rate of workforce turnover in the labour market. It has caused difficulty for employees to find new jobs because the non-compete clause has been incorporated into the employment agreement. The purpose of inserting the clause is to protect the employer's business interest, however, it also gives some difficulties to employees to proceed with new employment. The validity of the non-compete clause in the employment agreement seems reasonable for the employer, however it seems to be a restrictive measure for the employees. The chapter intends to review the impact of non-compete clauses in employment contracts in Malaysia. Besides, the chapter also intends to review the cases related to a non-compete clause in Malaysia and provide legal protections to protect the best interest of both employers and employees. Lastly, this study focuses on promoting decent work opportunities as well as productive employment for all.

The intersection of competition law and data privacy presents a significant challenge in the current legal framework. The connection between data privacy law and competition law lacks clarity and definition, requiring further exploration. The immense scale of data collection poses challenges and gives companies a market advantage, sometimes at the expense of individuals' control over their personal data. The shift from price-focused to data-focused markets complicates the integration of privacy concerns within competition law. This chapter aims to enrich discussions on the intersection of competition law and data protection, highlighting the potential for a mutually beneficial connection between these frameworks. It examines the relationship between competition law and sustainable development goals, with a focus on digital and green market development. This chapter contributes to the understanding of consumer protection in the digital age and the need for a comprehensive approach to address the challenges posed by the data-driven economy.

Competition law plays a significant role in ensuring fair practices in economy market and in protecting consumers' interests. Malaysia has been moving forward in recognizing the essential of competition

Preface

The present trends of global transitions toward population, lifestyle, and economic growth put more pressure on socioeconomic and environmental systems. With that, the cooperation between governments and other sectors is crucial in ensuring humanity's survival amidst the climate change crisis. Thus, the regulation of fair competition is crucial in fostering innovation, enhancing productivity, consumer choice, and economic vitality, as well as mitigating the risks of monopolistic practices. This edited reference book, *Regulating Fair Competition Toward Sustainable Development Goals*, delves into the intricate interplay between competition law and policy and the United Nations' Sustainable Development Goals (SDGs).

The Sustainable Development Goals are a global call and governments playing their role accordingly to end poverty, protect the earth's environment and climate, and ensure that people everywhere can enjoy peace and prosperity. Moreover, the SDGs are primarily concerned with promoting sustainable growth via ensuring social well-being, economic growth, and environmental legislation, and it is interconnected elements that cannot be addressed separately. Furthermore, sustainability remains a vital long-term goal of SDGs, and the Green Economy is describing a pathway to sustainable development.

Competition law and sustainable development intersect in their emphasis on efficient resource allocation, protecting product quality, and promoting technological advancement and innovation. Therefore, the role of competition policy is to promote and enhance sustainability issues. Competition policy relates to green growth, that emphasizes environmental and social priorities, through the substantive competition rules in fostering social and ecological purposes. This book explores the interaction between competition law and policy and sustainability. It emphasizes the three components of sustainability: environmental, economic, and social. The describes how sustainability can be fostered by competition enforcement against practices hindering sustainability and then illustrates the interaction of competition law and business activities where business activity leads to increased sustainability. Competition law and policy can contribute to achieving SDGs especially Target 7 (Affordable and Clean Energy), Target 8 (Decent work and economic growth), Target 9 (Industry, Innovation and Infrastructure), Target 10 (Reduced Inequalities), Target 12 (Responsible consumption and production), Target 13 (Climate action).

The correlation between competition law and policy and the Sustainable Development Goals is unmistakable. Competition law is an important tool for promoting competition and protecting consumers and helps to drive innovation, lower prices, and improve the quality of goods and services for consumers. Competition law and policy, and SDGs are closely related as both aim to create a fair and sustainable world. Competition law can contribute to achieving some of these SDGs by promoting fair competition in the market and preventing anti-competitive practices that can harm consumers and the environment. This book, conceived as an exploration and examination of these connections, is not just an academic exercise but a guide for policymakers, researchers, and industry leaders seeking sustainable and equitable development. We delve into the implementations and limitations of competition law and policy with a keen focus on achieving the United Nation's Sustainable Development Goals.

The pages that follow bring together the expertise of our editors, along with contributions from a diverse array of academics from different countries including Malaysia, India, Indonesia, the United Kingdom and Tanzania. This collaborative effort explores the nuanced dynamics of competition law and policy across various sectors, including the economy, environment, energy, employment, business, and management. Our target audience is broad and diverse, encompassing academics, students, policymakers, government and private research institutions, and industry/business corporations. The thematic scope of this book extends beyond the conventional realms of corporate, contract, and consumer protection law. It spans the critical domains of trade, employment, environment, energy and more.

In the pursuit of understanding the multifaceted relationship between competition regulation and sustainable development, we invite readers to embark on a journey through the comprehensive analyses and insights provided in this volume. Together, let us explore the potential of competition law and policy to facilitate sustainable development, laying the groundwork for a fair, innovative, and prosperous future.

Editors,

Siti Fazilah Abdul Shukor
University of Tunku Abdul Rahman, Malaysia

Farahdilah Ghazali
University of Malaysia Terengganu, Malaysia

Nur Yuhanis Ismon
University of Tun Hussien Onn, Malaysia

Aerni Isa
Taylor's University, Malaysia

Acknowledgment

Writing a chapter is hard. But editing a book is the hardest yet more rewarding than we could have ever imagined. None of this would have been possible without the contribution of our dedicated authors and the opportunities provided by our publisher, IGI Global USA.

We are also eternally grateful to our dedicated Editorial Board Members (EAB) who have assisted us in reviewing the manuscripts. Also, a very special thanks to our external reviewers from various universities, Prof. Dr. Ashgar Ali Muhammed, Assoc. Prof. Elistina Bakar, Dr. Diana Johnson, Dr. Wan Maisara Wan Mohamad, Dr. Ida Shafinaz Mohamed Kamil, Dr. Jeong Chun Phuoc, Dr. Ma Kalthum Ishak, Dr. Md Ashraful Azam Khan, Dr. Rahmawati Mohd Yusoff, Dr. Ridoan Karim, Dr. Mohamad Zreik, Nurul Jannah Mustafa Khan, Sharija Che Shaari and Dr. Zulkefli Muhamad Hanapiyah. Again, thank you for your amazing efforts in helping authors to improve their writings.

We want to thank everyone who ever contributed whether directly or indirectly to this project. Without the experiences and support from all of you, this book would not exist.

Above all, we want to thank God most of all, for granting us patience and determination to do any of this.

Chapter 1
Reconsidering E-Commerce Platforms Competition Law in Enhancing Sustainable Consumption and Production

Tze Chin Ong
https://orcid.org/0000-0003-3602-543X
University of Malaya, Malaysia

Zalina binti Abdul Halim
https://orcid.org/0000-0003-0676-0759
University of Malaya, Malaysia

Sherin Binti Kunhibava
University of Malaya, Malaysia

Sridevi Thambapillay
University of Malaya, Malaysia

Norhoneydayatie binti Abdul Manap
National University of Malaysia, Malaysia

Mei Fei Lee
University of Malaya, Malaysia

ABSTRACT

The significance of consumer protection in achieving sustainable development goals is a critical element in stimulating a more dynamic and competitive digital economy. Consumers are the major economic participants in the economy with an active role in the digital marketplace, the participation of responsible platforms' businesses, and the empowerment of responsible consumers contribute directly toward achieving sustainable development goals. Consumer protection and competition law are intertwined with both focusing on consumers as the key stakeholder. This chapter focuses on the interplay between consumer protection law and competition law in the e-commerce platforms economy, highlighting the trade-off for e-commerce in sustainable consumption and production, and how reconsidering competition law in e-commerce platforms could enhance sustainable consumption and production.

DOI: 10.4018/979-8-3693-0390-0.ch001

Copyright © 2024, IGI Global. Copying or distributing in print or electronic forms without written permission of IGI Global is prohibited.

1. INTRODUCTION

The importance of consumer protection in achieving sustainable development goals (SDG) was highlighted in the 2017 publication of the United Nations Conference on Trade and Development (UNCTAD) entitled "Achieving the Sustainable Development Goals through Consumer Protection." Many studies have demonstrated that consumer protection and competition law policies are interlinked with both focusing on consumers as the key stakeholder. For one, competition law focuses on fair competition in the market for the ultimate benefit of the consumers and likewise, consumer protection law focuses on the protection of consumer rights in a fair levelled-playing market. Further, competition law is centred on the protection of consumer welfare and competition process to prevent market failure while consumer protection law is centred on ensuring the protection of consumers against the effects of market failure due to inefficient competition (OECD, 2023). In other words, consumer protection law is the reaction to market failure that contributes to equity and social justice by enhancing bargaining equality and the interests of both the consumers and market players (OECD, 2008). Both competition and consumer protection laws and policies play critical roles in supporting sustainability initiatives. Hence, to achieve SDG, it is pertinent for two matters to transpire, i.e., the participation of responsible platforms businesses in the ecosystem of the digital economy and the empowerment of responsible consumers. For example, to attain sustainability advantages, businesses will have to innovate production, distribution, and sales processes. On the other hand, for sustainable choices to be preferred by consumers, clear and accurate information must be transmitted to them in a way that they can understand (UNCTAD, 2023). As vital economic participants with an active role in the surge of e-commerce and the acceleration of digital transformation in the digital economy, empowered customers will become the driving force to encourage business innovation, investment, and sustainable competition (UNCTAD, 2023).

The digital economy, in particular the e-commerce platforms market has gained increasing importance in the global economy in recent years. e-commerce's share of the global retail trade increased from 14% in 2019 to about 17% in 2020 amid the global economic slowdown during the Covid-19 pandemic (Popov, 2021). This has further changed consumers' daily lives, shaping, and transforming how consumers consume and businesses do business, thereby contributing significantly to societal and economic transformation at a global scale (Das, Sarkar, & Debroy, 2022). Mercado Libre, Latin America's online marketplace, sold twice as many items per day in the second quarter of 2020 as compared with the previous year. Jumia, an African e-commerce platform, reported an increase of 50% in transactions during the first half of 2020 (UNCTAD, 2021). In Kazakhstan, there was an increase in online share of retail shares from 5% in 2019 to 9.4% in 2020. In East Asia, China reported an increase in its online share of retail sales from 19.4% to 24.6% between August 2019 and August 2020. In Thailand, there was an increase of 60% in the download of shopping apps in just one week in March 2020 (Andrey, 2021). In many ways, the Covid-19 pandemic has been a blessing in disguise for certain consumers and businesses to the rise of e-commerce in the global economy. As for the Malaysian digital economy, the e-commerce market has been increasingly significant with a contribution of more than 37% growth during the Covid-19 pandemic as compared to the previous year (Raj & Gohain, 2021) (Global Data, 2020). With the support of the Malaysian government for local sellers and micro, small and medium Enterprises (MSMEs), Malaysia became the 38th largest market for e-commerce with a revenue of US$4 billion (Raj & Gohain, 2021) (Malaysia - eCommerce, 2019). The acceleration of e-commerce also resulted in an increase in the Malaysian Gross Domestic Product (GDP) with an initial contribution in 2015 of RM 89.15 billion, rising to RM 95.64 billion in 2016, RM 107.3 billion in 2017, RM 117.45 billion in

2018, and RM 129.35 billion in 2019 (Statista, 2023). The gradual increase of approximately 10 billion on a year-by-year rise from 2015 to 2019 rose to an approximate RM 40 billion year-by-year increase in contribution to GDP amid the Covid-19 pandemic with RM 163.84 billion in 2020 and RM 201.08 billion in 2021 (Statista, 2023). The overall increase in contribution to GDP post-pandemic was also endorsed by the Minister of Communications and Digital, YB Fahmi Fadzil, quoting the Information and Communication Technology Satellite Account (ICTSA) of the Department of Statistics Malaysia (DOSM) by stating that e-commerce contribution to the Malaysian GDP from 11.6% in 2020 rose to 13% in 2021 (Chong, 2023).

Sustainability has been on the international agenda for some time but many of the SDG remains behind schedule despite many efforts and progress to improve sustainability (United Nations, 2023). Since the unprecedented Covid-19 pandemic, the paramount importance of sustainability has been re-emphasised as evident in amongst others the adoption of the Bridgetown Covenant during the 15th session of the UN Conference on Trade and Development (UNCTAD 15) in 2021. With increasing consumer preferences for online shopping, unsustainability practices are exacerbated thus dramatically increasing its environmental impact including emissions of greenhouse gases and the rise of waste to landfills from overpackaging of goods with non-degradable adhesive tapes, cartons, or plastic fillings (Igini, 2022). This is further aggravated by worsening unsustainable consumption and production patterns in the digital economy that compromise prosperity, and lead to climate change and environmental degradation (UNCTAD, 2021). In this regard, it is widely understood that the enhancement of consumer welfare is crucial either in the context of competition law or consumer protection law. Thus, competition policy and consumer policy now speak the same language; with a common overarching goal (Frederiksson & Korka, 2017). Competition and consumer protection policies can play a decisive role in achieving SDG 12 on ensuring responsible consumption and production patterns. UNCTAD, as the focal point within the United Nations for competition and consumer protection, encourages Governments, international organizations, businesses, consumer groups and academia to continue to reflect on the best ways in which such policies can be used to help improve the sustainability of markets (Kwon & Arnau Izaguerri, 2023). With digitization, new needs for coordination between competition law and other legal regimes emerge, and adjustments and/or re-interpretation of contract law, consumer protection law, or unfair trading law will be part of the shaping of the legal order in reaction to a different economic reality (Crémer, Montjoye, & Schweitzer, 2019).

This chapter focuses on the role of competition law in achieving sustainable development goals, the interplay between consumer protection law and competition law in achieving sustainable consumption and production, and reconsidering competition law to enhance sustainable consumption and production in the e-commerce platforms market.

2. COMPETITION LAW AND SUSTAINABILITY DEVELOPMENT GOALS CONSIDERATIONS

The Organisation for Economic Co-operation and Development (OECD) Competition Committee reported in its 2020 Discussion Paper that many OECD countries are already considering adopting sustainability features in their competitive enforcement practices (OECD, 2020). Despite this, there remains a normative debate among scholars in justifying sustainability considerations in competition law which are hard to reconcile as that depends on the legal framework, constitutional setting, and the goals of the competition law of the specific country (OECD, 2020). UNCTAD has argued that competition laws and policies in ensuring that consumers can make better-informed choices and businesses can innovate production and distribution processes can contribute to greater profitability and sustainability (UNCTAD, 2023). For example, in a market where environmental sustainability is of consumers' priority, businesses are incentivised to offer "*genuinely green*" goods and services in an effective competition that contributes to the environment and business prosperity (Grenfell, 2023). Yet, sustainability is still not considered in competition analysis in many jurisdictions and there is no universally accepted method to incorporate sustainability in competition analysis (UNCTAD, 2023). This is evident from the European Union's issuance of fines amounting to $1 billion against Volkswagen and BMW for emissions cartel to slow the deployment of cleaner emissions technology since the 90s based on anti-competitive practices and not based on the extent of damage to the environment (Bellan, 2021). Another example is the Dutch competition authority's approval of a joint agreement between 4 soft drink suppliers to stop using plastic handles on multipacks in July 2022 not due to the sustainability advantages but because of the lack of effects on market competition (UNCTAD, 2023). While these examples were eventually decided in favour of consumers and the environment, it is important to note that in some jurisdictions, even sustainability agreements are disallowed despite clear environmental sustainability benefits. This is exemplified in the disbanding of a landmark 2014 Indonesia Palm Oil Pledge (IPOP) due to threats of anti-competitive enforcement by the Indonesian Anti-Monopoly Agency (KPPU) despite clear ecological benefits with KPPU declaring that it was a cartel giving rise to monopoly and unhealthy competition in the market which constitute approximately 40% of smallholders managing Indonesia's palm oil plantations that could not meet the IPOP agreement (Vit, 2016).

In the efforts to promote sustainability in the markets, there has been a trend of exempting corporate collaborative initiatives that may traditionally constitute anti-competitive mergers and agreements as they seek to promote and provide environmental sustainability benefits (Grenfell, 2023). In fact, countries like Australia, Austria, China, Netherlands, New Zealand, the United Kingdom and the European Union have incorporated sustainability advantages in competition law analysis (UNCTAD, 2023). For example, in 2018, the Australia Competition and Consumer Commission authorised Tyre Stewardship Australia's scheme which imposed obligations on participants to commit to environmentally sound use of used tyres and to deal only with accredited businesses in the supply chain (ACCA, 2018). It was reported that despite the anti-competitive effects of the scheme, authorisation is granted because the scheme increases the recycling of tyres and the use of products from recycled tyres which ultimately promotes environmentally sustainable initiatives (UNCTAD, 2023). Notwithstanding this, concerns have been raised against the restriction of competition laws and policies in this regard wherein firstly, there have been arguments that businesses already have the incentive to compete effectively on sustainable production and delivery processes with consumers' growing appreciation for sustainability, and thus exemption in competition laws and policies may do little to none to contribute to SDG (Schinkel & Treuren, 2021).

Secondly, exempting sustainability agreements aligned with consumer welfare standards may leave consumers worse off as consumers already have a pre-existing low willingness to pay more for sustainably produced goods in consideration of sustainability advantages albeit the possibility of obtaining a compensating share of the sustainability benefits (Schinkel & Treuren, 2021). For example, in the 1999 EU CECED case, consumers could benefit from lower electricity bills due to sustainability-manufactured washing machines but eventually, consumers would still have to absorb the higher price of goods (Schinkel & Treuren, 2021). Making matters worse, some jurisdictions are broadening the consumer welfare standard to include other stakeholders thus making consumers worse off than the consumer welfare standard as consumers are no longer the crucial stakeholder for consideration (Schinkel & Treuren, 2021).

Thirdly, with high competition on "*green*" in the market, there is also the possibility of greenwashing or "*cartel greenwashing*" being employed by businesses to escape liability from anti-competitive practices (UNCTAD, 2023). In other cases, businesses have resorted to greenwashing to keep up with investors' interest in sustainable business practices (Saini & Rajagopal, 2022). In October 2022, the Canada Competition Bureau launched an investigation into greenwashing allegations against the Royal Bank of Canada for misleading customers on its commitments to climate action in particular its commitment to achieve net-zero financed emissions across its operations by 2050 (Saini & Rajagopal, 2022).

During the UNCTAD 15 in 2021, the member states adopted the Bridgetown Covenant to promote inclusive and resilient economic recovery in developing countries in member states' recovery strategies amid the COVID-19 pandemic crisis (UNCTAD, 2021). Consistently, the overriding objective "*from inequality and vulnerability to prosperity for all*" of UNCTAD 15 is in line with UNCTAD's move to get back on track to meet the 2030 Agenda for Sustainable Development. Amongst others, the Bridgetown Covenant suggests a multilateral dialogue and cooperation in reconsidering competition law to address challenges in e-commerce and the digital economy aligned with the UN's SDG (UNCTAD, 2021). Considering the significant economic impact that e-commerce has on the global economy and the urgent need to address the environmental degradation caused by unsustainable consumption and production patterns in e-commerce and the digital economy, there is a need to further consider the competition law analysis in the context of e-commerce and the digital economy.

As a point of reference, China which is unmatched in its e-commerce success with its courier industry handling a total of 83 billion express parcels in 2020, was reported by the State Administration for Market Regulation to have simultaneously produced approximately 1.8 million tonnes of plastic waste and over 9 million tonnes of paper waste every year (Chen, 2021). With the current rushed online shopping trends prioritising express deliveries and free return shipping, it is also estimated that increased shipping of goods purchased online will lead to an increase of about 6 million tonnes of CO2 emissions by 2030 (Igini, 2022). According to the 2023 UN Sustainable Developments Report, the global material consumption (amount of raw materials used for production processes in a country) between 2000 and 2019 has tripled with an increase of 66% since the 1970s to reach 95.1 billion metric tons (United Nations, 2023). To make matters worse, the environmental degradation caused by unsustainable consumption and production practices in e-commerce and the digital economy is reported to hit hard the most vulnerable segments of the population in developing countries (UNCTAD, 2023). The findings of the 2023 UN Sustainable Developments Report demonstrate the negative effects of e-commerce on environmental degradation and wasteful consumption. It is thus vital that countries shift towards a more circular economy with responsible consumption and production practices in their recovery strategies post the COVID-19 pandemic to ensure a more sustainable and climate-resilient economy.

Studies have identified overpackaging and distribution of goods to be the primary source of contribution to increasing carbon emissions (Revinova, 2021). This is also exemplified in the generation of waste following the e-commerce boom in China. In the context of Southeast Asia, plastic waste generated by the rise of e-commerce is at an estimate of over 31 million tonnes per year with 91% of consumers in the region being concerned about environmental degradation issues as a result (Adilla, 2022). The changing trends in consumers' preference for sustainability practices and ESG strategies also indicate the differential competitive advantage that market players can have in the e-commerce market (Kim et al, 2021). One of the leading e-commerce platforms in Southeast Asia, Lazada announced the launch of its sustainability campaign “LazEarth” as part of its commitment to support sustainable practices in the digital market of e-commerce platforms market by reducing plastic waste reduction (Adilla, 2022) In the long run, sustainable practices in the e-commerce platforms market can lead to the creation of a sustainable platform supply chain, subject to the magnitude of platform fee imposed and consumer preference for sustainability (Wang, Gao, & Wang, 2021).

3. ROLE OF COMPETITION LAW IN ACHIEVING SUSTAINABLE CONSUMPTION AND PRODUCTION

In enhancing sustainable consumption and production, competition law plays a major role in ensuring fair and efficient competition particularly in e-commerce. As e-commerce platforms market is highly relying on innovation and technological advancement, with an ecosystem that involves various industries and participating entities including platform marketplace, software industry, innovation design, advertising, AI tools development, sellers from major brands, individual sellers, third-party sellers, other coordinating businesses such as warehouse services, last mile delivery services, riders and consumers. The large ecosystem when dominated by a few large e-commerce marketplace providers which affects the supplies and demands of production and consumption (OECD, 2018). With the incumbent platforms marketplace players dominating the market and set the industry practices, it is less likely that more sustainable practices would be put in place to encourage fair and efficient competition. The barriers to entry from a new and more sustainable e-commerce marketplace player with the aims to align their business practices to sustainable business practice would be hindered as entries in the market is not possible (Amornkitvikai et al, 2022). As supplies and demands of products and services are dependent on the perceived value of production and consumption, production and consumption convey meanings beyond it and leave traces on the social world (Porter, 2021). For example, product life cycle includes life of the product from manufacture, marketing, sale to consumers and use through to disposal is clearly affected in e-commerce, As the few incumbent dominant players engaging in lower to zero price mechanism in strengthening its market position, recruitment of participating entities, businesses, and sellers without due diligent indirectly caused the businesses participating in e-commerce ecosystem to engage in price competition. Besides, lack of information provided regarding suppliers of raw materials and producers to the consumers in e-commerce hinder sustainable production and consumption (Micklitz, et al., 2020). The risk of green washing and misleading marketing (Kwon & Arnau Izaguerri, 2023) without due diligence in recruiting businesses and sellers in e-commerce platforms to prevent competitive elements distorting competition. With aggressive price matching and comparison attract low value and compromise products quality participating in e-commerce undermine sustainable production. On the consumption side, low value and compromise products quality affects sustainable consumption on products return for various reasons (Micklitz, et al., 2020). Besides, the return policies provided by the incumbant e-commerce platforms do not disclose the transport costs, the mechanism involved in inspecting returned goods and disposal of the return products such practices often discourage return hence unsubstainable. With dominant power of the few platfroms, businesses and sellers in the e-commerce platforms are force to follow the rules set by the platforms for ratings, reviews and listings would choose to discourage returns affecting sustainable consumption. As barries to entry in the e-commerce platforms market due to its competive dynamic and market structure (Stigler Committee on Digital Platforms, 2019), hindering new entrence with more sustainable business model.

Consumer consumption in e-commerce often driven by the role of data and recommendation in e-commerce, the use of unbiased AI tools is crucial. As consumers consumption behaviour influence and affected by the AI formula that recommend to them, specific attention to the predictable characteristics of AI recommendation and reviews may be manipulated by the e-commerce planforms players in the competition for the market rather than in the market (Stigler Committee on Digital Platforms, 2019). Without clear responsibilities and liabilities of e-commerce platforms players in their business strategies, incumbant dominant e-commerce players setting the practices, affecting sustainable production and consumption.

4. THE COMPETITIVE DYNAMIC OF THE E-COMMERCE PLATFORMS MARKET

E-commerce platforms markets are dynamic and thriving, deriving huge profits for the ease of consumers to browse and shop at their fingertips with the advanced payment modes of the cyber age. Reports in 2021 have stated that in 2025, e-retail sales are projected to account for nearly 25% of global retail sales (Lebow, 2021). Currently, 2/3 of e-commerce sales are sold through online marketplaces/platforms and in February 2023, it was reported that the United States e-commerce in 2022 topped $1 trillion for the first time (Digital Commerce 360, 2023). Considering the increasing significance of e-commerce in the global economy, market study on the nature and dynamic of the e-commerce platforms market has been at the forefront in recent years. Thus far, scholarly studies and world competition authorities have identified that online consumer markets differ fundamentally from conventional brick-and-mortar markets (Stigler Committee on Digital Platforms, 2019). This means that the robustness of the market competition regulation and enforcement is vital. As a point of reference, the differences between online and offline markets in the intensity of market competition as encapsulated by a literature review on the competitive pricing in online markets (Gerpott & Berends, 2022) and other studies are set out in Table No. 1 below: -

Table 1. Differences between online and offline markets in the intensity of market competition

	Consumer-related peculiarities (demand side)	**Firm-related peculiarities (supply)**
Online	Low possibility of inspecting goods before buying	High possibility to extensively monitor the prices of competitors
	Easy comparison of products from various sellers	Low costs to change prices swiftly and repeatedly to respond to the price actions of competitors
	Low search costs	High availability of price and demand data
	High price transparency	The high impact of competitor pricing on demand for own product offerings (Brynjolfsson & Smith, 2000)
	High-intensity competition (Balakrishnan, Sundaresan, & Zhang, 2013)	
	Consumer-related peculiarities (demand side)	**Firm-related peculiarities (supply)**
Offline	High possibility to inspect goods before buying	High level of store experience as a lever to build more personal relationships with consumers
	High travel and inconvenience costs	Differentiation through loyalty
	High barriers for consumers to acquire information about other sellers' prices	Low impact of competitor pricing on demand for own product offerings (Penz & Hogg, 2011)
	Low impact of competitor pricing on buying decision (Devaraj, Fan, & Kohli, 2002)	

The OECD also laid out in its 2022 handbook the challenges brought by the digitalisation of the economy and the moving away from conventional offline brick-and-mortar businesses (OECD, 2022). The OECD stated that the digital economy incorporates all economic activity reliant on, or significantly enhanced using digital inputs, including digital technologies, digital infrastructure, digital services, and data. It refers to all producers and consumers, including the Government, that are utilising these digital inputs in their economic activities (OECD, 2022). The OECD also identified that digital specificities of the digital economy can lead to many benefits (OECD Competition Law and Policy, 2023), some of which are listed as follows: -

(a) New markets and opportunities;
(b) Increased choice and reduced information costs to consumers
(c) Low or zero service prices;
(d) Few incumbent online platforms dominating the digital landscape.

According to Antonio Capobianco, the Deputy Head of the Competition Division OECD, online platforms open new markets and opportunities enabling transactions and operations that were impossible in the past (OECD Competition Law and Policy, 2023). With a higher number of players, consumers have more choices and low or zero costs to make informed choices with easy access to further information about the goods and services available in the digital market. Simultaneously, sellers in the digital market can also provide goods and services at low costs. Unfortunately, a more comprehensive study of the digital market also shows the unique combination of features in the dynamic digital economy with strong network effects, extremely high economies of scale and economies of scope, and accumulation of data (Stigler Committee on Digital Platforms, 2019). The digital market characteristics, when combined, lead to a '*tipping effect*' where the market becomes concentrated with a few incumbent platforms that consequently affect market competitiveness and efficiency (Lancieri & Sakowski, 2021). Crucially, the extremely strong network effects in the digital market of e-commerce platforms mean that as the number of users on the platform grows, the value of the platform to the users increases (OECD, 2022). As a result, digital platforms enjoy significant scale and scope advantages that lead to market concentration with a few large incumbent firms.

The e-commerce platforms market is also multi-sided with several interconnected sides. Consumers of content who generate data, suppliers, advertisers, and data aggregators, each with an incentive to contribute to the already extremely strong network effects. In this ecosystem, firms can leverage the accumulation of consumer data from their primary markets that can be difficult to replicate and costly to analyse in another market with additional competitive advantages (Iansiti, 2021). In addition, vertically integrated and conglomerate business models enable digital platforms to act as gatekeepers between downstream firms and their consumers. As a result, nascent and smaller rivals will find it difficult or almost impossible to compete on a fair playing field with the incumbent firm. This also means serious repercussions to privacy and risks of consumer harm in the digital economy (OECD, 2022). Consequently, incumbent platforms and intermediary that matches demand (online consumers) and supply (retailers) in the multi-sided market reap the most reward or rent by charging participating businesses in the online marketplace with commission and other service fees (Hagiu, 2007). Adding to this is the situation where intermediary/platform firms participate as sellers themselves thereby posing direct competition to retailers that do not have the advantage of data that intermediary/platform firms would have (Ryan, Sun, & Zhao, 2012).

In a digitalised environment, digital services such as e-commerce platforms do not work in isolation. In fact, e-commerce platforms create an ecosystem that is an integrated group of systems with various entities interconnected and interdependent functions that work together that provide goods and services electronically (Mahn, 2017). Many types of industries and companies form a network of interconnected functions with participants from both the demand and supply sides of the market that contribute to the full cycle of buying and selling goods and services online (Rachinger et al, 2019). The coincidence of several factors in the e-commerce platforms market makes the market unique and dynamic. E-commerce platforms serve as intermediaries that connect two or more groups of users and encompass multisided aspects, enabling interactions and value creation between different groups of users within the platform (Wismer, Bongard, & Rasek, 2017). This business model of the e-commerce platforms leads to the creation of multi-sided markets with the presence of strong network effects. Besides, e-commerce platforms comprise positive feedback loops due to network effects, and the growing returns in supply which means that greater amounts of users from a platform encourage a greater number of incentives for third-party developers to create more complementary products and services within its ecosystem (McIntyre & Srinivasan, 2017). Imagine, a new e-commerce platform with very few sellers, customers, and third-party partners, would any consumer be willing to switch to a new platform? The more users there are on a network, the richer the users' experience would be. This is because e-commerce platforms rely on customer reviews, ratings, the number of sales on the sellers' record, behavioural data of users from the participation of users and users' experiences etc. When a user opts to switch to a new platform from an incumbent platform, more often or not, due to the lack of personalised and behavioural data that the new platform has on the user who had just registered for an account with it for the first time, the user would eventually find the new platform to be unable to capture their needs with a better suggestion of what they are searching for (OECD, 2021). Even though the switching cost is zero, consumers often find it troublesome to register for a new account and enter the information required to establish an account in the new platform. Further, consumers may find it inconvenient because of the lack of ease and familiarity with the settings of the new platform. Besides, incumbent platforms assert a certain level of trust and confidence among consumers by having affiliation and collaboration with many trusted brands and reputable third-party participation (Jarvenpaa et al, 2000). The badge of credibility of incumbent platforms will further discourage consumers from switching to a new platform unless there are huge incentives for switching. Aside from the role of data and behavioural issues, multi-sided markets with strong network effects have raised concerns among researchers and competition authorities. This market structure with a combination of new characteristics creates various challenges to competition law in regulating the market of the platforms (Stigler Committee on Digital Platforms, 2019). Moreover, the platform's market is highly concentrated with strong economies of scale and scope due to the role of data (Stigler Committee on Digital Platforms, 2019). According to the European Commission Report on Competition Policy for the Digital Era (2019), the cost of production is much less in proportion to the number of users served (Crémer, Montjoye, & Schweitzer, 2019). In the context of e-commerce platform markets in ASEAN, platform providers such as Alibaba, Lazada, and Shopee have been identified as one of the most popular platforms. With strong economies of scale and scope, once the platform is created, the platform can serve hundreds and thousands of users without additional cost. When sales increase, average unit cost decreases, even though there is an increase in cost because the rise of costs will be much slower than the increase of users. Increasing returns to scale leads to companies investing in fixed costs rather than their marginal cost (Sutton, 1991). Benefiting from the larger user base, incumbent platform firms enjoy lower average costs per user served. It is also more profitable to lower their price to poach users of competing platforms as compared to increasing the cost of serving additional users (marginal cost) (Crémer, Montjoye, & Schweitzer, 2019). In the circumstances, nascent platform providers would be reluctant to enter markets already dominated by incumbent platforms, unless it is supported by a large investment to pay for the fixed cost with superior and cheaper technology (Stigler Committee on Digital Platforms, 2019). The presence of large economies of scale also explains how services provided by the platform are usually at zero cost. Since the platforms enjoy the cost advantage of a large number of users served, the platforms would rather choose to increase their income from advertising than charge the users for their service.

Data from the users within the e-commerce platforms ecosystem play an important role in economies of scope. The relationships between the users, brands, advertising services, matching services, and third-party developers offer additional advantages to the incumbent e-commerce platforms (Cozzolino et al, 2021). E-commerce platforms use machine learning and artificial intelligence (AI) coupled with personalised behavioural nudges to improve their services and expand their activities into new markets. Machine learning and AI provide better insights into larger datasets, to this end, incumbent platforms with large amounts of data can easily raise the quality of their services better as compared to a smaller platform. From offering sales of goods to consumers, now e-commerce platforms also offer holiday packages, ticketing, advertising services, cloud services, business analysis to their users, and even financial services in the form of e-wallets (Cuofano, 2023). During the COVID-19 pandemic, major e-commerce platforms in Malaysia even serve as charitable fund collectors for various charitable organizations. For example, Lazada (one of the major e-commerce platforms in ASEAN) through their Stronger Together initiative via "LazadaForGood" collected RM802,574 on 5th April 2020 to aid Malaysian front liners and the less fortunate (Malaysiakini, 2021) (Lazada, 2023). Other reputable organizations such as Mercy Malaysia, Malaysian Red Crescent, Hospis Malaysia, Zoo Negara Malaysia, and even UNICEF also collect donations via Lazada (Lazada, 2023). E-commerce platform services are not just offering new business opportunities and facilitating cross-border trading, it has also extended to social activities by civil participation in charitable funds collection via their platforms.

Despite the benefits and values that e-commerce platforms have brought to the digital economy, they still function as intermediaries, connecting a large number of business users and consumers. Its impact on the domestic market and society raises considerable challenges to competition law in comprehending the competitive dynamic of its ecosystem in the digital environment. The rising concerns of digital platforms have raised much attention in the world competition and antitrust authorities in investigating the market dynamic of digital platforms by conducting studies with expert reports to comprehend new harms and risks that pose to the markets. Among others, the literature and reports are:

(a) European Commission Final Report on the E-commerce Sector Inquiry, May 2017, Report from the Commission to the Council and the European Parliament (European Commission Final Report on the E-commerce Sector Inquiry);
(b) Organisation for Economic Co-operation and Development (OECD), Implications of E-commerce for Competition Policy - Background Note, June 2018. The background note is provided by the OECD roundtable discussion to explore the growing phenomenon of e-commerce in terms of its implications for competition law and policy within the OECD. (OECD Implications of E-commerce for Competition Policy - Background Note 2018);
(c) Unlocking Digital Competition, March 2019 issued by the Digital Competition Expert Panel for the Government of the United Kingdom (Furman Report);

(d) Competition Policy for the Digital Era, May 2019, issued by an expert panel under the Directorate-General for Competition of the European Commission. (European Commission Competition Policy for the Digital Era Report);
(e) Sub-committee on Market Structure and Antitrust Report, September 2019, issued by the Stigler Committee on Digital Platforms - an independent academic committee from the University of Chicago's George J. Stigler Center for the Study of the Economy and the State (Stigler Committee on Digital Platforms, 2019);
(f) Market Study on E-Commerce in India: Key Findings and Observations, January 2020, issued by the Competition Commission of India (Market Study on E-Commerce in India)
(g) E-Commerce Platforms Market Study, issued by the Competition and Consumer Commission of Singapore (CCCS) in September 2020 (Singapore E-Commerce Platforms Market Study Report)

Besides the above-mentioned reports, there are more than fifty documents and reports related to digital markets and competition available in different languages and countries' approaches (Lancieri & Sakowski, 2021). Amongst others, the many notable reports include the Working Paper: Market Power of Platforms and Networks, issued by the German *Bundeskartellamt* in June 2016; OECD, 2018 report on Rethinking Antitrust Tools for Multi-Sided Platforms; Digital Platforms Inquiry–Final Report, July 2019 issued by the Australian Consumer and Competition Commission; Online Platforms and Digital Advertising–Market Study Final Report, July 2020 issued by the British Competition and Market Authority; A New Competition Framework for the Digital Economy, issued by the Competition 4.0 Commission on behalf of the German Federal Ministry of Economic Affairs and Energy in September 2019; US House of Representatives, 116th Cong., Report on Investigation of Competition in Digital Markets: Majority Staff Report and Recommendations, 2020. The wealth of literature clearly indicates the rising and serious concerns about digital markets' power on the competition.

To this end, many jurisdictions have introduced ex-ante regulations to address data-related concerns, for instance, the obligation to grant access to competitors to data sets and ensure data portability between competitors whether at the platform level or retailers' level. This means nascent entrants and rivals of intermediary/platform firms in the digital market could request and have access to the accumulated consumer data in a structured, commonly used, and machine-readable format on an ad-hoc or continuous basis (OECD, 2022). It also ensures the interoperability of different digital services to work together and communicate with one another. As a result, this may prevent the gatekeeper status of incumbent online platforms which limits self-preferencing and bundling (also referred to as tying) where firms require customers to purchase one or more "tied" products if they wish to purchase a "tying" product through technical or contractual means or when a firm offers multiple products together in a single package like a bundle (sometimes at a discount) (OECD, 2022). Simultaneously, this also protects consumers because they will not be forced to purchase a standalone "tying" product which is only available for sale by the incumbent platform on a bundling or tying basis thereby incurring less costs to procure a standalone "tying" product.

Many experts and world competition authorities' reports pointed to the competitive dynamics of the digital markets, whereby platforms serve as intermediaries that directly influence the supply of goods or services (Lancieri & Sakowski, 2021). The platforms generally benefited from direct and indirect network effects. The platform markets are two-sided or multi-sided markets. There are no single characteristics of the platform markets but combinations of multiple characteristics that require different analyses from the conventional market analysis of dominance. The dominance of the platform markets is characterised by strong network effects, economies of scale, economies of scope connected to the role of data as an input, and extremely low marginal costs with global scope (Lancieri & Sakowski, 2021). The markets with such characteristics are prone to tipping with strong competition for the market resulting in winner-take-all or monopolistic in nature. The platform markets are concentrated with few incumbent platforms enjoying considerable market power. Some studies are concerned with the lack of assessment tools in competition to assess the market power and its dominance. The challenges in market definition and the conventional Small but Significant Non-Transitory Increase in Prices ("SSNIP") test also known as the "Hypothetical Monopolist Test" (HMT) is not suitable for assessing platforms market (OECD, 2018). However, some experts are of the opinion that the focus should be on the evidence of market power, theories of harm to competition, and the identification of anticompetitive strategies rather than defining the market (Crémer, Montjoye, & Schweitzer, 2019). The ecosystem of the platforms also plays a role in the competitive dynamics and lock-in consumer effects in the digital market (Crémer, Montjoye, & Schweitzer, 2019). The role of data plays a significant role in platforms' market power. Further, the Report issued by the Stigler Committee on Digital Platforms - an independent academic committee from the University of Chicago's George J. Stigler Center for the Study of the Economy and the State indicated that data resources are a barrier to entry, a side effect of not having the history, scale, or scope of the incumbent, can inhibit entry, expansion, and innovation (Stigler Committee on Digital Platforms, 2019). Consistently, there are three German reports such as Modernising the Law on Abuse of Market Power (2018) issued by Heike Schweitzer, Justus Haucap, Wolfgang Kerber, and Robert Welker for the German Federal Ministry for Economy Affairs and Energy; Competition Law and Data (2016), a joint study issued by the French Autorité de la Concurrence and the German Bundeskartellamt; and Working Paper: Market Power of Platforms and Networks (2016) issued by the German Bundeskartellamt, which all agreed that control over data is a source of market power. The Furrman report (2019) also confirms the same. However, the Singapore E-Commerce Platforms Market Study Report (2020) differs with the view that data is not a barrier to entry at the moment. The wealth of literature pointed to serious competitive concerns despite the disagreement on the concepts, scopes, doctrines, methodological differences, and their nature.

5. INTEGRATING CONSUMER PROTECTION CONSIDERATIONS IN E-COMMERCE

In 2015 the United Nations General Assembly adopted two significant resolutions, namely the Agenda for Sustainable Development 2030, that is, the 17 Sustainable Development Goals, and the revised Guidelines on Consumer Protection (UNCTAD, 2016). It is no coincidence that both these resolutions were adopted within three months of each other since the positive impacts of consumer protection ensure a more inclusive and sustainable development (UNCTAD, 2017). The Organisation for Economic Cooperation and Development (OECD), an intergovernmental organisation comprising 29 member countries, also recognised the ease, swiftness, and borderless nature of e-commerce and the information asymmetry between consumers and businesses in e-commerce. This led to the issuance of the OECD Guidelines for Consumer Protection in 2016 to recommend guidelines that aim to eliminate uncertainties on consumers' and businesses' respective rights and responsibilities in e-commerce for adoption by member states according to their respective socioeconomic circumstances (UNCTAD, 2017). Recently, the European Commission (EC) enacted the Digital Markets Act (DMA) and Digital Services Act (DSA) to address new challenges in the digital market. In particular, the DMA was enacted to protect consumers by addressing all types of misinformation, unfair conduct, and illegal content in the digital market.

The development of consumer protection laws and policies in the e-commerce ecosystem demonstrates that it is widely acknowledged that consumer protection safeguards the consumers of goods and services from harmful and unfair practices in the marketplace. This is necessary as consumers are usually under-informed and in a weaker position than the supplier in an information asymmetry that warrants protection (Howells & Weatherill, 2005). To have a holistic consumer protection framework, various stakeholders must work together, namely the government, businesses, and the consumers themselves (ASEAN, 2020). The government must have in place the right legal framework and infrastructure to prevent and address unfair and harmful practices against consumers, while businesses must abstain and desist from unfair, dishonest, and harmful practices. Consumers must also take reasonable steps to be informed of their rights and avenues for complaints and enforcement of those rights (ASEAN, 2020). This section in this chapter explores the consumer protection laws and policies implemented by the United Nations, OECD, and the European Union.

5.1 UN's Guidelines and OECD Guidelines on Consumer Protection

The UN's Guidelines on Consumer Protection was adopted, inter alia, to assist nations in maintaining ethical standards, curbing unfair and abusive practices by all entities, and protecting their population as consumers. The UN Guidelines also attempt to ensure sustainable consumption, cooperation between countries on consumer protection, and the facilitation and formation of independent consumer groups (UNCTAD, 2016). Reading the UN Guidelines holistically, it is noted that it applies to business-to-consumer (B2C) interactions and is divided into, general principles, principles for good business practices, guidelines, international cooperation, and international institutional machinery. Under the general principles, the UN Guidelines refer to the need of member states to have a strong and adequate consumer protection policy that is in line with the peculiarities and needs of that member state. The general principles also lay down the need for sustainable consumption, ensuring the infrastructure for enforcement of consumer protection, and research by academic institutions on developing consumer protection among others.

For ease of reference, the principles set down in the UN Guidelines for good business practices in ensuring consumer protection are reproduced below: -

i. Fair and equitable treatment of all consumers by businesses
ii. Commercial behaviour by businesses must not include improper behaviour like discrimination, and unethical and deceptive practices.
iii. Disclosure and transparency must be provided by businesses, and false or misleading information on the goods and services must be avoided.
iv. Businesses must ensure that education and awareness are developed amongst consumers so that consumers know of the various risks and pitfalls of the transactions they are entering into and where to obtain independent professional advice.
v. Businesses should ensure the protection of data and the privacy of consumers.
vi. Businesses should put in place proper mechanisms for consumers' complaints and disputes.

The UN Guidelines also contain 11 guiding principles from A to K for member states to consider adoption in their respective countries including strengthening international cooperation in consumer protection guided by international institutional machinery. For ease of reference, the 11 guidelines are explained briefly below wherein member states should ensure that: -

i. National policies on consumer protection are established with good consumer practices.
ii. Appropriate measures are adopted to ensure the physical safety of goods and products.
iii. Proper promotion and protection of the economic interests of consumers are in place including ensuring optimal competition in the markets for consumers to get the widest choice of products and services at a minimal cost.
iv. Adequate standards for the safety and quality of consumer goods and services are in place.
v. Efficient distribution facilities for essential consumer goods and services are adopted.
vi. Fair, impartial, transparent, and effective dispute resolution and redress are in place for consumers' complaints and disputes.
vii. Education and information programmes for consumers are developed including training of educators so consumers are better informed on issues relating to environmental impact, costs, benefits of choice, and change in consumption.
viii. Sustainable consumption is promoted, where sustainable consumption is defined as '*meeting the needs of present and future generations for goods and services in ways that are economically, socially, and environmentally sustainable.*
ix. Consumer confidence in electronic commerce is instilled by developing transparent and effective policies and ensuring equal protection of e-commerce transactions for consumers as compared to other forms of commerce. Member states are also encouraged to review existing consumer protection policies to accommodate the unique characteristics of e-commerce and ensure consumers and businesses are informed and cognisant of their respective rights and obligations in the digital market in line with international guidelines and standards such as the OECD Guidelines for Consumer Protection in the Context of Electronic Commerce, which will be further discussed below.
x. Proper financial consumer protection services are in place.
xi. Measures relating to specific areas given priority, such as food, water, pharmaceuticals, energy, public utilities, and tourism.

Overall, the UN Guidelines centre around the protection, safety, and future by recommending consumer protection at all stages of B2C interaction. In particular, Guideline I on e-commerce places e-commerce interaction on the same footing in terms of fairness with other commercial interactions between B2C. Certainly, the recommendations in the UN Guidelines would protect consumers in the e-commerce environment.

As the UN Guidelines specifically mentioned that member states must be mindful of the OECD Guidelines for Consumer Protection in the Context of Electronic Commerce (1999) revised in 2016 (OECD, 2000), it is necessary to discuss the relevant parts of the OECD Guideline in the next section.

5.2 OECD Guidelines for Consumer Protection in the Context of Electronic Commerce (1999) Revised in 2016

The OECD Guidelines were designed to help ensure that consumers are no less protected when shopping online than they are when they buy in person from a store or in other ways, i.e., from a catalogue (UNCTAD, 2017). It is noted that the OECD Guidelines apply only to B2C transactions and there are 8 core principles which are emphasised in the OECD Guidelines, briefly summarised below:-

i. First Principle: Consumers should have transparent and adequate protection in the e-commerce field like other forms of commerce.
ii. Second Principle: Businesses should have proper regard for consumers and ensure fair business, advertising, and marketing practices.
iii. Third Principle: Businesses should ensure clear, transparent, easily accessible, and accurate online disclosures on all matters including goods and services, and information about businesses and transactions.
iv. Fourth Principle: Consumers should be provided with a proper confirmation process, so they can precisely identify the goods or services they intend to purchase; identify and correct any errors or modify the order; express an informed and deliberate consent to the purchase or cancel the transaction before payment; and retain a complete and accurate record of the transaction.
v. Fifth Principle: Consumers should have secure and easy-to-use payment systems for e-commerce transactions.
vi. Sixth Principle: Consumers should have access to a reasonably fair and prompt dispute resolution and redress mechanism without undue cost or burden for all complaints and disputes in e-commerce transactions that are often cross-border and subject to existing legal frameworks in other countries. In this regard, member states are recommended to consider modifying existing laws to enable fair consumer protection for e-commerce transactions which are on par with the protection afforded to other commerce transactions.
vii. Seventh Principle: E-commerce transactions should be in line with OECD's privacy policies and principles.
viii. Eight Principle: Consumers and businesses should have sufficient education and awareness of the related rights and obligations in e-commerce transactions.

These principles are exclusive for the protection of consumers in e-commerce transactions and therefore address the unique needs of consumers in the e-commerce platforms market. While both the OECD Guidelines and the UN Guidelines generally focus on consumer protection, it is noted that the principles in the OECD Guidelines are more centred on protecting consumers in the e-commerce sphere.

The next international legal framework discussed in this section involves the pioneer legislation enacted to regulate the digital market, that is the European Union's Digital Services Act and Digital Markets Act which aim to protect EU citizens from all types of harmful digital engagement (Schmid & Koehler, 2022) from very large digital platforms that can act as 'gatekeepers' in the digital market.

5.3 EU's Digital Services Act (DSA) and Digital Markets Act (DMA)

At the heart of DSA and DMA is the protection of consumers in the digital ecosphere. It is currently the most comprehensive legal framework in the world to address digital services and markets (Schmid & Koehler, 2022). In particular, the DMA and DSA aim to safeguard consumers while simultaneously ensuring that competition and innovation are facilitated and enhanced. It is also noted that the DSA and DMA apply to EU member states without any further implementation and, it applies to B2C dealings and businesses-to-businesses (B2B) interactions. Since the DSA and DMA both cover all digital types of engagements, only key points are summarised here in this section.

For the DMA, it requires, among other things, transparency, external audits, protection of their platforms from manipulation and user consent before '*processing personal data for targeted advertising*' (Schmid & Koehler, 2022). On the other hand, the DSA 'builds' on the EU Electronic Commerce Directive 2000 while not replacing it (Turillazi, Casolari, Taddeo, & Floridi, 2022). However, due to the DSA's and DMA's twin comprehensiveness and breadth, it would seem that the EU Electronic Commerce Directive 2000 faded into the background overshadowed by the DSA and DMA (Turillazi, Casolari, Taddeo, & Floridi, 2022). Some key points worth highlighting from the DSA are amongst others the following (Schmid & Koehler, 2022): -

i. A digital environment that is safe and free from illegal content, goods, and services.
ii. Increasing accountability, due diligence, and transparency of digital intermediary services.
iii. Protection of consumers, and in particular minors, from online targeted advertising
iv. Facilitating and increasing competition and innovation
v. '*improving legal certainty for providers of digital services, especially for cross-border activities enhancing enforcement.*' (Schmid & Koehler, 2022)

The review of the UN Guidelines, the OECD Guidelines and the EU's DMA and DSA demonstrates the international agenda to set down a common standard for consumer protection in the digital ecosphere, especially in the e-commerce platforms market. This emphasis on the holistic protection of consumers indicates that ensuring consumer protection itself is a crucial element for the efficient, fair, and competitive functioning of the economy. As consumers are the major economic participants in the economy, assuming an active role in the marketplace of the digital economy, the participation of responsible platforms' businesses in the ecosystem of the digital economy and the empowerment of responsible consumers contribute directly toward achieving SDG (UNCTAD, 2016). A crucial connection between consumer protection, SDG and e-commerce is sustainable consumption and production (Micklitz, et al., 2020). As highlighted in the UN Guidelines, sustainable consumption is consuming with the mindful consideration of the needs of future generations. Thus, sustainable consumption involves promoting the efficient use of resources and energy. In this regard, e-commerce can have greater adherence to SDG especially in the labour market with jobs being easier to find since the Internet allows a cross-border working environment, although elements like shipping, packaging, and options to return goods do leave a carbon footprint (Revinova, 2021).

To promote sustainable consumption, consumer education is paramount to empower consumers to make the right choices including environmental impact, costs, benefits of choice and change in consumption as provided by Principle G of the UN Guidelines. Having explored the relevant UN Guidelines, OECD Guidelines and the EU's DMA and DSA on the regulation of consumer protection in the digital ecosphere, the fundamental principles and guidelines of consumer protection and its connection to sustainable consumption, the next section explores competition and consumer protection policies with sustainability.

6. THE INTERPLAY BETWEEN CONSUMER PROTECTION LAW AND COMPETITION LAW IN ACHIEVING SUSTAINABLE DEVELOPMENT GOALS

The 2030 Agenda for Sustainable Development (including its 17 sustainable development goals, SDGs) adopted by the United Nations General Assembly in 2015, provides a shared blueprint—a 'plan of action for people, planet, and prosperity' to guide all countries' policies towards sustainable development until 2030 (Malinauskaite, 2022). The 17 SDG "*recognize that ending poverty and other deprivations must go hand-in-hand with strategies that improve health and education, reduce inequality and spur economic growth*," all while addressing climate change and working to preserve oceans and forests, and the achievement of the SDG requires the participation of responsible and empowered consumers. In this context, UNCTAD published "Achieving the Sustainable Development Goals through Consumer Protection", noting that the only way to unleash the potentially transformative power of consumers in domestic and international trade is by ensuring a high level of consumer protection and fostering good business practices that seek the same goal (Kwon & Izaguerri, 2023). Thus, SDG 12 ensures responsible consumption and production patterns include targets applicable to various stakeholders, including Governments, businesses, and consumers. Sustainability highlights resource efficiency, innovation, and the role of the private sector in achieving the sustainability goals set by the UN. Sustainability requires productive efficiency and dynamic efficiency to achieve and ensure the optimal level of usage of natural resources. Moreover, sustainability is a feature that is valued by consumers. While the value and the willingness to pay for sustainability might differ between consumers, it seems to be a fair assumption that consumers would choose the more sustainable product between two otherwise identical products if offered at the same price. We can therefore see sustainability as a quality element (Nowag, 2021). Competition and consumer protection laws and policies play a crucial role in supporting sustainability initiatives (Fisse, 2019) as they address market failures and help provide a level playing field in which businesses and consumers can make the best choices (Kwon & Izaguerri, 2023). Insofar as competition law enforcement benefits consumers and safeguards the economic freedom of smaller market actors in the face of abusive conduct of powerful rivals, it also benefits social sustainability. Further, competition law naturally benefits environmental sustainability in several ways, including via technological developments or resource efficiency, both of which are typical features of a well-functioning, undistorted competitive market. Some types of sustainability benefits of products or services can furthermore be something that firms directly compete about, provided that enough customers value the characteristics in question. That said, until recently environmental sustainability has hardly ever been an explicit antitrust concern (Uffer, 2023). The increased competition after the antitrust intervention collaterally leads to increased sustainability. This effect can be a more or less accidental spillover effect or the result of more targeted antitrust action with sustainability in mind (Nowag, 2021). Besides that, competition law protects efficient competition and the freedom to pursue professional activities (economic liberty), and thereby also promotes the participation of a plurality of market actors in economic life. In that sense, functioning, competitive markets are democratic institutions. Conversely, high concentrations of market power typically entail significant risks of restrictions of competition and thus of harm to the consumer and social welfare (Uffer, 2023). The idea of sustainability and the concept of sustainable development are typically considered to encompass an environmental, an economic and a social dimension. By promoting economic efficiency and consumer welfare (e.g., quality, lower prices, variety, and innovation), competition law favours economic sustainability (Uffer, 2023).

In the digital economy, effects on quality and especially on innovation are more relevant. This is especially clear in platform-to-consumers ("P2C") platform markets, where services are offered to consumers at zero price, and where, therefore, and obviously, there are no price effects. But it is also true for other parts of the digital economy, for instance, platform-to-business ("P2B") and business-to-business ("B2B") platforms whose degree of innovation determines the productivity of the European economy. In a digital world, where the future is more uncertain and less understood, there will be under-enforcement if we insist that the harm be identified with a high degree of probability. Nonetheless, under-enforcement in the digital era will be of particular concern, even more as the harm will presumably be longer term than in traditional markets because of the stickiness of market power caused by several factors. Therefore, even if consumer harm cannot be precisely measured, strategies employed by dominant platforms aimed at reducing the competitive pressure they face should be forbidden in the absence of clearly documented consumer welfare gains (Crémer, Montjoye, & Schweitzer, 2019). Recent competition cases show that competition law frameworks and enforcement need to be adapted to the features and business models of digital platforms. There is a need, therefore, to adapt the competition framework by broadening the consumer welfare standard beyond price and market share considerations, as consumer welfare involves not only lower prices but also choice, privacy, data protection and innovation (UNCTAD, 2019). Businesses should engage in sustainability initiatives in a responsible manner, such as by developing codes of conduct, self-regulation, and good business practices (Kwon & Izaguerri, 2023). In the ASEAN regional guidelines on competition policy, it is stated that competition policy contributes to economic growth to the ultimate benefit of the consumers, in terms of better choice, better quality and lower prices. Competition policy may serve as a complement to consumer protection policies to address market failures such as information asymmetries, lack of bargaining position, towards producers and high transaction costs.

The role of competition law concerning consumer welfare is about the allocation of available productive forces and materials among the various lines of industry and the effective coordination of various means of production in each industry into such groupings as will produce the greater result. Allocative and productive efficiency together make up the overall efficiency that determines the society's economic wealth, which is termed consumer welfare by the Chicago School economists, - a neoclassical economic school of thought originating from the University of Chicago in the 1930s (Mishan, 1975). Consumer protection laws might not always include specific provisions on sustainable consumption, yet consumer protection authorities have used existing provisions to act in this area, engaging in consumer education and providing guidance to businesses, as well as addressing related cases (Kwon & Izaguerri, 2023). Consumer protection laws, including prohibitions of misleading or deceptive conduct or unconscionable conduct, may be more helpful to small businesses. They are concerned with promoting fair trading, including fair trading by large suppliers with small businesses. They do not require market power or dominant market power. Nor are they defined in the troublesome terms of misuse or abuse of market power (Fisse, 2019). Consumers also must promote sustainable consumption, by refraining from purchasing goods and services that negatively affect their lives and those of future generations. The rights of consumers to safe and effective products and services go together with their responsibility to help preserve the planet (Kwon & Izaguerri, 2023) and increased awareness among consumers and concern about the social, economic and environmental impacts of production and consumption has led to to increased demand for sustainable products (Kwon & Izaguerri, 2023).

As sustainability becomes a priority policy objective for policymakers worldwide, markets will increasingly be expected to deliver sustainable results. Competition and consumer protection policies are conducive to improving the efficiency and fairness of markets and are therefore well placed to serve public policy goals. They can have a positive impact on sustainability, regarding social, economic and/or environmental aspects. Competition law and policy can be aligned with sustainability objectives, although there may be circumstances in which competition and sustainability initiatives conflict (Kwon & Izaguerri, 2023). Governments should enforce consumer protection laws against misleading and unfair commercial practices, particularly related to false environmental claims and greenwashing (Kwon & Izaguerri, 2023).

The primary objective of competition and consumer policies is to improve the welfare of the consumers. The United Nations Guidelines for Consumer Protection emphasises the interconnection between competition and consumer protection, asserting that governments should actively promote fair and efficient competition. By doing so, they can ensure that consumers have access to a wide variety of products and services, while also benefitting from competitive pricing. The ultimate aim is to empower consumers with ample choices and affordable options within the marketplace that fosters fair competition. The presence of increased competition however does not automatically guarantee better outcomes for consumers, especially in information-asymmetric markets where consumers lack the necessary information to make well-informed decisions or switch between traders, particularly, in e-commerce transactions (Stucke, 2013). In such situations, businesses may not be sufficiently motivated to compete based on the quality of their products or services. Instead, they may resort to using complicated pricing strategies, making it difficult for consumers to make accurate comparisons, or engaging in unfair commercial practices, including but not limited to, false/misleading advertising, fake reviews, and dark patterns. Hence, in certain jurisdictions, the explicit objective of competition law includes the welfare and protection of consumer interests. This can be observed in countries such as Australia, India, Indonesia, Japan, Serbia, the United Republic of Tanzania, and Zambia (UNCTAD, 2016). Moreover, some jurisdictions like Canada (Canada Minister of Justice, 2023) and South Africa (South African Government, 2021) have gone a step further by defining the purpose of competition law acts as the promotion and maintenance of competition to ensure competitive prices and a wide range of product choices for consumers. Clearly, these countries recognise that consumer welfare is intricately linked to a competitive market environment.

Different jurisdictions prioritise their regulations based on the level of potential harm inflicted on consumers. For example, the European Commission focuses on addressing exclusionary conduct by dominant companies under Article 82 of the Treaty 29 establishing the European Community (European Commission, 2009) targeting conduct that poses the greatest harm to consumers. Similarly, the Federal Trade Commission in the United States emphasises promoting competition in industries that have significant impact on consumers, such as healthcare, real estate, oil and gas, technology, and consumer goods. These jurisdictions recognise the importance of safeguarding consumer interests and seek to foster competitive markets in sectors directly affecting consumers' wellbeing (Qawaya & Lipimile, 2008). Therefore, policy coordination is essential to tackle the underlying causes of market failures and determine the most suitable combination of policy measures. Irrespective of the specific institutional framework for implementing competition and consumer policies, one effective approach to achieve policy coordination is by prioritising consumer interests in both competition law and consumer protection advocacy and enforcement. By aligning competition law enforcement with consumer empowerment initiatives, policymakers can create a harmonised approach. This involves combining efforts to ensure fair competition with empowering consumers to make informed decisions. Alongside traditional enforcement measures, voluntary solutions and initiatives focused on businesses and consumers' education can complement enforcement efforts. These measures can help raise awareness among businesses and consumers about their rights and responsibilities, promoting fair commercial practices and enhancing consumer protection. Additionally, leveraging social media platforms and communications tools can play a vital role in educating consumers, particularly in regulated markets, and assisting them in switching traders when necessary. Through these channels, consumers can access valuable information, compare opinions, and receive guidance on making choices that align with their needs and preferences, particularly, in e-commerce transactions.

A recent trend has emerged to merge competition law enforcement and consumer protection law into a single institution, aiming to foster collaboration and synergy between these two functions (OECD, 2008). An illustrative case is the establishment of the Netherland Authority for Consumers and Markets in April 2013, which consolidated the Consumer Authority, the Independent Post and Telecommunication Authority, and the Competition Authority (Ottow, 2014). The primary objective of this new authority is to enhance consumer welfare, while promoting opportunities and choices for both businesses and consumers. Similarly, other countries have followed suit by creating authorities with dual responsibilities for enforcing competition law and consumer law. For example, the Australian Competition and Consumer Commission, the newly formed Competition and Markets Authority in the United Kingdom, and the Federal Trade Commission in the United States. These institutions are designed to address both competition and consumer-related issues, recognising the interconnected nature of these areas and the benefits of a comprehensive approach. By integrating competition law and consumer law under a unified enforcement authority, there is an expectation of improved coordination, streamlined process, and a more holistic perspective in addressing challenges and ensuring fair commercial practices in the marketplace. This consolidation acknowledges the mutual benefits of aligning competition and consumer protection objectives and underscores the importance of promoting market efficiency while safeguarding consumer rights (OECD, 2008). It also ensures consumer protection in the context of complex digital marketplace which often presents challenges for consumers to fully understand the quality, safety, and legitimacy of products or services offered online. Unfair commercial practices, such as fake reviews, false/misleading advertising, and dark patterns can mislead or harm consumers. Regulations seek to address these issues, ensuring transparency, accurate information, and fair commercial practices in ecommerce transactions. Moreover, regulating unfair commercial practices in e-commerce transaction helps to maintain fair competition. By prohibiting deceptive or restrictive commercial practices, authorities foster a level playing field for businesses, preventing market distortions, and promoting healthy competition. This, in turn, encourages innovation, efficiency, and a wider range of choices for consumers. Additionally, addressing unfair commercial practices contributes to the overall stability and integrity of the economy. By deterring fraudulent or unethical behaviours, the policymakers help maintain market integrity, investor confidence, and sustainable economic growth.

7. CONCLUSION

E-commerce and the digital economy have gained increasing importance in the global economy with e-commerce gaining an impressive increase in market share year by year even amid the global economic slowdown during the Covid-19 pandemic (Lebow, 2021). With the rapid expansion of e-commerce with its different nature and dynamic as compared to the conventional brick-and-mortar market, the intensity of market competition warrants reconsidering traditional competition laws and policies to address new challenges in the digital market such as prevalent consumer harms arising from the competitive dynamic of the digital market of e-commerce platforms (Gerpott & Berends, 2022). Connecting this with the exacerbated unsustainable consumption and production patterns in the digital economy that cause worsening environmental degradation day by day due to unsustainable production processes, rush shopping and express shipping, the need to review traditional competition laws and policies becomes highly pertinent for the sake of public interest.

With the rapid expansion of e-commerce following the unprecedented COVID-19 pandemic, simultaneously there has been a rapid rise in emissions of greenhouse gases and waste to landfills (UNCTAD, 2023). As a result, shareholders and consumers have now moved to prioritise and prefer sustainable businesses that offer environmentally friendly goods and services thereby gradually placing sustainability at the forefront of the international agenda. Yet, despite much progress in incorporating consumer protection laws and policies in the digital economy, efforts to foster and improve sustainability practices in the digital economy remain behind schedule.

Considering the benefits and risks of incorporating public interest consideration in terms of sustainability in competition law analysis overall, fostering sustainability features in the application of substantive competition law in the e-commerce platforms market whether by using traditional tools in a conventional manner or creative ways would eventually and ultimately benefit consumers (OECD, 2020). To this end, it is timely that competition authorities are encouraged to target enforcement in cases where anti-competitive practices are against public interest, (i.e., environmental degradation) to incentivise businesses to move in a more sustainable direction (OECD, 2020).

8. ACKNOWLEDGMENT

We want to thank the Ministry of Higher Education for the Fundamental Research Grant Scheme (FRGS/1/2022/SSI12/UM/02/8) awarded to Dr Ong Tze Chin. The authors are also extremely thankful to University of Malaya for the technical assistant and for providing the necessary resource facilities for this research.

REFERENCES

ACCA. (2018, May 24). *ACCC re-authorises Tyre Stewardship Scheme*. ACCA. https://www.accc.gov.au/media-release/accc-re-authorises-tyre-stewardship-scheme

Adilla, F. (2022, April 18). Lazada unveils campaign to support sustainable practices in e-commerce. *New Straits Times*. https://www.nst.com.my/business/2022/04/789773/lazada-unveils-campaign-support-sustainable-practices-e-commerce

Amornkitvikai, Tham, S. Y., Harvie, C., & Buachoom, W. W. (2022). Barriers and Factors Affecting the E-Commerce Sustainability of Thai Micro-, Small- and Medium-Sized Enterprises (MSMEs). *Sustainability (Basel)*, *14*(14), 8476. doi:10.3390u14148476

ASEAN. (2020). *Consumer Protection*. Competitive, Innovative and Inclusive Economic Region. https://asean.org/our-communities/economic-community/competitive-innovative-and-inclusive-economic-region/consumer-protection/

Balakrishnan, A., Sundaresan, S., & Zhang, B. (2013, August 30). Browse-and-Switch: Retail-Online Competition under Value Uncertainty. *Production and Operations Management*, *23*(7), 1129–1145. doi:10.1111/poms.12165

Bellan, R. (2021, July 9). *EU fines BMW, VW $1B for running emissions cartel since the 90s*. Tech Crunch. https://techcrunch.com/2021/07/08/eu-fines-bmw-vw-1b-for-running-emissions-cartel-since-the-90s/

Brynjolfsson, E., & Smith, M. D. (2000, April 1). Frictionless Commerce? A Comparison of Internet and Conventional Retailers. *Management Science*, *46*(4), 563–585. doi:10.1287/mnsc.46.4.563.12061

Canada Minister of Justice. (2023, October 5). *Competition Act (R.S.C., 1985, c. C-34)*. Justice Laws Website. https://laws.justice.gc.ca/eng/acts/C-34/index.html

Chen, J. (2021, March 6). *China guides e-commerce sector to greener path of development*. EN. http://en.people.cn/n3/2021/0306/c90000-9825820.html

Chong, S. (2023, July 4). E-Commerce Contribution To Malaysia's GDP Rises To 13%, Said Fahmi. *Business Today*. https://www.businesstoday.com.my/2023/07/04/e-commerce-contribution-to-malaysia-gdp-rises-to-13-said-fahmi/#:~:text=The%20Minister%20Of%20Communications%20And,2020%20to%2013.0%25%20in%202021

O. E. C. D. Law and Policy. (2023, March 20). *Digital challenges for competition policy explained in 9 minutes. Budapest, Central Hungary, Hungary*. [Video]. YouTube. https://www.youtube.com/watch?v=0cN9gkrUuVw

Cozzolino, Corbo, L., & Aversa, P. (2021). Digital platform-based ecosystems: The evolution of collaboration and competition between incumbent producers and entrant platforms. *Journal of Business Research*, *126*, 385–400. doi:10.1016/j.jbusres.2020.12.058

Crémer, J., Montjoye, Y.-A. d., & Schweitzer, H. (2019). *Competition Policy for the digital era*. European Commission.

Cuofano, G. (2023, November 6). *How does Shopee Make Money? The Shopee Business Model in A Nutshell*. Four Week MBA. https://fourweekmba.com/shopee-business-model/#:~:text=Shopee%20employs%20a%20typical%20marketplace,of%20ancillary%20and%20complimentary%20services

Das, D., Sarkar, A., & Debroy, A. (2022). Impact of Covid-19 on changing consumer behaviour: Lessons from an emerging economy. *International Journal of Consumer Studies*, *46*(3), 692–715. doi:10.1111/ijcs.12786 PMID:35602666

Devaraj, S., Fan, M., & Kohli, R. (2002, September 3). Antecedents of B2C Channel Satisfaction and Preference: Validating e-Commerce Metrics. *Information Systems Research*, *13*(3), 316–333. https://www.jstor.org/stable/23015740. doi:10.1287/isre.13.3.316.77

Digital Commerce 360. (2023, February 17). *US ecommerce in 2022 tops $1 trillion for first time*. Digital Commerce 360. https://www.digitalcommerce360.com/article/us-ecommerce-sales/

European Commission. (2009, February 24). *Guidance on the Commission's enforcement priorities in applying Article 82 of the EC Treaty to abusive exclusionary conduct by dominant undertakings*. EC. https://eur-lex.europa.eu/legal-content/EN/ALL/?uri=CELEX%3A52009XC0224%2801%29

Fisse, B. (2019). Facilitating the SDGs by Competition and Consumer Law and Policy Reform: Aspirations and Challenges in Papua New Guinea. In J. Walker, A. Pekmezovic, & G. Walker (Eds.), *Sustainable Development Goals: Harnessing Business to Achieve the SDGs through Finance, Technology, and Law Reform*. John Wiley & Sons Ltd. doi:10.1002/9781119541851.ch18

Frederiksson, T., & Korka, D. (2017). *Harnessing E-Commerce for Sustainable Development*. OECD.

Gerpott, T. J., & Berends, J. (2022, June 14). Competitive pricing on online markets: A literature review. *Journal of Revenue and Pricing Management*, *21*(6), 596–622. doi:10.105741272-022-00390-x

Global Data. (2020, September 8). *COVID-19 accelerates e-commerce growth in Malaysia, says GlobalData*. Global Data. https://www.globaldata.com/media/banking/covid-19-accelerates-e-commerce-growth-malaysia-says-globaldata/

Grenfell, D. M. (2023, March 16). *Can we protect the environment and keep the benefits of competition?* Economist Impact. https://impact.economist.com/sustainability/resilience-and-adaptation/can-we-protect-the-environment-and-keep-the-benefits-of-competition

Howells, G., & Weatherill, S. (2005). *Consumer Protection Law*. Routledge.

Iansiti, M. (2021). The Value of Data and Its Impact on Competition. Harvard Business School, 1 - 26.

Igini, M. (2022, December 15). *The Truth About Online Shopping and Its Environmental Impact*. Earth.org. https://earth.org/online-shopping-and-its-environmental-impact/

Jarvenpaa, Tractinsky, N., & Vitale, M. (2000). Consumer trust in an Internet Store. *Information Technology and Management*, *1*(1/2), 45–71. doi:10.1023/A:1019104520776

Kim, Kim, M., Im, S., & Choi, D. (2021, October 19). Competitiveness of E Commerce Firms through ESG Logistics. *Sustainability (Basel)*, *13*(20), 1–15. doi:10.3390u132011548

Kwon, H., & Izaguerri, A. (2023). *Competition and Consumer Protection Policies for Sustainability*. United Nations.

Lancieri, F., & Sakowski, P. M. (2021). *Competition in Digital Markets: A Review of Expert Reports*. Standford Journal of Law, Business & Finance.

Lazada. (2023, August 28). *LazadaForGood*. Lazada. https://pages.lazada.com.my/wow/camp/lazada/dailycampaign/my/donation/lazadaforgood

Lebow, S. (2021, August 19). *Worldwide ecommerce continues double-digit growth following pandemic push to online*. Insider Intelligence. https://www.insiderintelligence.com/content/worldwide-ecommerce-continues-double-digit-growth-following-pandemic-push-online

Mahn, K. (2017, August 9). *Navigating the E-Commerce Ecosystem for Growth Opportunities*. Smart Trust. https://www.smarttrustuit.com/whitepaperspost/navigating-the-e-commerce-ecosystem-for-growth-opportunities/

Malaysia - eCommerce. (2019, August 19). Export.gov. https://www.export.gov/apex/article2?id=Malaysia-E-Commerce

Malaysiakini. (2021, July 23). *Lazada steps up support for frontliners and Malaysians in need*. Malaysiakini. https://www.malaysiakini.com/announcement/584188

Malinauskaite, J. (2022). Competition Law and Sustainability: EU and National Perspectives. *Journal of European Competition Law & Practice*, 336 - 348.

McIntyre, D. P., & Srinivasan, A. (2017, January). Network, platforms, and strategy: Emerging views and next steps. *Strategic Management Journal*, *38*(1), 141–160. doi:10.1002mj.2596

Micklitz, H. W., Schiefke, N., Liedtke, C., Kenning, P., Specht-Riemenschineider, L., & Baur, N. (2020). *E-commerce and the trade-off between consumer protection and sustainability*. Advisory Council for Consumer Affairs.

Mishan, E. (1975). The Folklore of the Market: An Inquiry into the Economic Doctrines of the Chicago School. *Journal of Economic Issues*, *9*(4), 681–752. https://www.jstor.org/stable/4224459. doi:10.1080/00213624.1975.11503319

Nowag, J. (2021). *Sustainability & Competition Law and Policy - Background Note*. OECD.

OECD. (2000). *Guidelines for Consumer Protection in the Context of Electronic Commerce*. OECD Publishing.

OECD. (2008). Global Forum on Competition: The Interface between Competition and Consumer Policies. OECD.

OECD. (2018). *Implications of e-commerce for competition policy*. OECD. www.oecd.org/daf/competition/e-commerce-implications-for-competition-policy.htm

OECD. (2018). *Rethinking Antitrust Tools for Multi-Sided Platforms*. OECD.

OECD. (2020). *Sustainability and Competition*. OECD.

OECD. (2021). *Data Portability, Interoperability and Digital Platform Competition*. OECD. https://oe.cd/dpic

OECD. (2022). *Handbook on Competition Policy in the Digital Age*. OECD Publishing. https://www.oecd.org/daf/competition-policy-in-the-digital-age

OECD. (2023). *The Consumer Welfare Standard - Advantages and Disadvantages Compared to Alternative Standards, OECD Competition Policy Roundtable Background Note*. OECD. https://www.oecd.org/daf/competition/consumer-welfare-standard-advantages-and-disadvantages-to-alternative-standards-2023.pdf

Ottow, A. T. (2014, April). Erosion or innovation? The institutional design of competition agencies—A Dutch case study. *Journal of Antitrust Enforcement*, *2*(1), 25–43. doi:10.1093/jaenfo/jnt016

Penz, E., & Hogg, M. K. (2011, February 15). The role of mixed emotions in consumer behaviour: Investigating ambivalence in consumers' experiences of approach-avoidance conflicts in online and offline settings. *European Journal of Marketing*, *45*(1/2), 104–132. doi:10.1108/03090561111095612

Popov, A. (2021, March 15). *How COVID-19 triggered the digital and e-commerce turning point.* UNCTAD News. https://unctad.org/news/how-covid-19-triggered-digital-and-e-commerce-turning-point#:~:text=As%20lockdowns%20became%20the%20new,to%20about%2017%25%20in%202020

Porter, E. (2021). *The Consumer Citizen.* Oxford University Press. doi:10.1093/oso/9780197526781.001.0001

Qawaya, H., & Lipimile, G. (2008). *The effects of anti-competitive business practices on developing countries and their development prospects.* UNCTAD.

Rachinger, Rauter, R., Müller, C., Vorraber, W., & Schirgi, E. (2019). Digitalization and its influence on business model innovation. *Journal of Manufacturing Technology Management, 30*(8), 1143–1160. doi:10.1108/JMTM-01-2018-0020

Raj, V., & Gohain, M. (2021). Impact of Covid-19 on Malaysian E-Commerce. *International Journal on Recent Trends in Business and Tourism*, 8 - 10.

Revinova, S. (2021). E-Commerce effects for the sustainable development goals. *SHS Web of Conferences*, 1 - 8.

Ryan, J. K., Sun, D., & Zhao, X. (2012, March 11). Competition and Coordination in Online Marketplaces. *Production and Operations Management, 21*(6), 997–1014. doi:10.1111/j.1937-5956.2012.01332.x

Saini, M., & Rajagopal, D. (2022, October 13). *Canada's watchdog launches investigation into RBC over climate complaints.* (S. Kuber, Editor) Reuters. https://www.reuters.com/world/americas/canadas-watchdog-launches-investigation-into-rbc-over-climate-complaints-2022-10-12/

Schinkel, M. P., & Treuren, L. (2021, March 26). *Green Antitrust: Why Would Restricting Competition Induce Sustainability Efforts?* Promarket. https://www.promarket.org/2021/03/26/green-antitrust-why-would-restricting-competition-induce-sustainability-efforts/

Schmid, D. G., & Koehler, P. (2022, September 19). *Digital Services Act - an overview.* Taylor Wessing. https://www.taylorwessing.com/en/interface/2022/the-eus-digital-services-act/digital-services-act---an-overview

South African Government. (2021, March 31). *The Competition Act of 1998.* The Competition Commission. https://www.compcom.co.za/wp-content/uploads/2021/03/Competition-Act-A6.pdf

Statista. (2023). *Contribution of e-commerce to the gross domestic product (GDP) of Malaysia from 2015 to 2021.* Statista. https://www.statista.com/statistics/956908/e-commerce-contribution-to-gdp-malaysia/

Stigler Committee on Digital Platforms. (2019). *Final Report.* Chicago: The University of Chicago Booth School of Business.

Stucke, M. E. (2013, April). Is Competition always Good? *Journal of Antitrust Enforcement, 1*(1), 162–197. doi:10.1093/jaenfo/jns008

Sutton, J. (1991). *Sunk Cost and Market Structure: Price Competition, Advertising, and the Evolution of Concentration.* MIIT Press.

Turillazi, A., Casolari, F., Taddeo, M., & Floridi, L. (2022). *The Digital Services Act: An Analysis of Its Ethical.* Legal, and Social Implications.

Uffer, M. (2023). Chapter 9 Competition Law: Sustainability Through Competition and Participation. In B. Peters, & E. J. Lohse, Sustainability through Participation: Perspectives from National, European and International Law. Bril / Nijhoff.

UNCTAD. (2016). *United Nations Guidelines for Consumer Protection.* UNCTAD.

UNCTAD. (2017). *Harnessing E-Commerce for Sustainable Development.* OECD Publishing.

UNCTAD. (2019). *Competition issues in the digital economy.* United Nations.

UNCTAD. (2021). *Fifteenth session of the United Nations Conference on Trade and Development (UNCTAD 15).* UNCTAD. https://unctad.org/meeting/fifteenth-session-united-nations-conference-trade-and-development-unctad-15

UNCTAD. (2021, March 15). *How COVID-19 triggered the digital and e-commerce turning point.* Unctad.org. https://unctad.org/news/how-covid-19-triggered-digital-and-e-commerce-turning-point

UNCTAD. (2021). *The Bridgetown Covenant: From inequality and vulnerability to prosperity for all.* United Nations.

UNCTAD. (2023). *Competition and Consumer Protection Policies for Sustainability.* UNCTAD.

United Nations. (2023). *The Sustainable Development Goals Report* (Special Edition). United Nations.

Vit, J. (2016, July 1). *Under gov't pressure, palm oil giants disband green pledge.* Mongabay Indonesia. https://news.mongabay.com/2016/07/under-government-pressure-palm-oil-giants-disband-green-pledge/

Wang, J., Gao, X., & Wang, Z. (2021, April 8). Sustainable Supply Chain Decisions under E-Commerce Platform Marketplace with Competition. *Sustainability (Basel), 13*(8), 1–23. doi:10.3390u13084162

Wismer, S., Bongard, C., & Rasek, A. (2017, April). Multi-Sided Market Economics in Competition Law Enforcement. *Journal of European Competition Law & Practice, 8*(4), 257–262. doi:10.1093/jeclap/lpw082

KEY TERMS AND DEFINITIONS

Circular Economy: The economic system/markets that give incentives to reusing products, rather than scrapping them and then extracting new resources, thus, all forms of waste are returned to the economy or used more efficiently.

Consumer Harm: Consumer harms include the economic harms caused to end users or buyers of e-commerce platforms categorised into primary economic harms caused by defective goods and services and unfair contract terms and secondary harms such as time spent seeking refund or redress.

Digital Platforms: Technically, it is a technological software which has a functionality that serves as a foundation upon which complementary participating entities in the e-commerce platforms market can be developed. Non-technically, it is an intermediary connecting two or more groups of users in the multi-faceted digital market.

E-Commerce: The production, distribution, marketing, sale or delivery of goods and services over any kind of computer network including the internet, extranet (a private platform that uses internet technology), TCP/IP, or electronic data interchange (EDI) network.

Economies of Scale: The situation where with better-quality data (widespread and more actual) collected, platforms can develop and offer better and improved products/services to consumers as compared to their competitors. Platforms collect data (large population datasets and high dimensional datasets from users in their infrastructure. In time, the data collected led to better insights into user behavioural biases and preferences which platforms can use to provide a richer experience for users and different categories of users including potential users with better personalised algorithms.

Economies of Scope: The situation where due to the better-quality data (large population datasets and high dimensional datasets) collected, platforms can enter new markets and offer new and better-personalised products/services at lower costs as compared to their competitors. Platforms' complex ecosystems have multiple sides and various categories of users. With the collection of high-quality user data from one side of the market (retail marketplace), dominant platforms can enter and expand into new or adjacent markets (fulfilment and logistics) and offer new and better-personalised products/services.

Ex Ante Regulation: A mechanism that seeks to prevent harmful conduct from occurring. This is only possible if the regulation is accessible to its users.

Intermediary Platforms: Technological software that brings together or facilitate transactions between third parties on the Internet by giving access to host, transmit and index content, products and services originated by third parties on the Internet-based services to third parties. This includes internet access and service providers, data processing and web hosting providers, internet search engines and portals, e-commerce intermediaries, internet payment systems and participative networking platforms.

Market Power: A tool that is integral to competition law enforcement to assess the market size of a firm. The traditional concept of market power focusing on price has been challenged by the complexity of the digital markets wherein platforms employ emerging business models to gain and maintain monopoly power, including via zero-priced goods and services subsidized by ad revenue generated in the markets. Focusing on behavioural futures markets as the main source of profits and market power, subsided consumption via negative mark-ups or zero prices can no longer be an indicator of low market power in a multi-sided digital market.

Network Effects: The situation where the value of a platform increases when the number of users utilizing the platform increases. As platforms offer better-personalised products and services, the platform becomes more attractive and the number of users on the platform increases. Simultaneously, the more users are on the platform, the higher the value of the platform is.

Chapter 2
The Role of Competition Law in Promoting Access to Telecommunication Services in Tanzania:
Taking Stock of the Developments so Far

Goodluck Temu
https://orcid.org/0000-0003-2936-5102
University of Dar es Salaam, Tanzania

ABSTRACT

As of June 2023, the percentage of Tanzanians who had access to a telephone was more than one hundred per cent. However, this has not always been so. For example, in 1997, there was a telephone density of 0.32 per cent. This average was much lower than those of neighbouring Kenya (0.92), the Southern African Development Community (SADC) (3.4), Asia (3.86), and Europe (35.36). Fast forward a little over twenty years and practically everyone in Tanzania now has access to a telephone. This chapter, among other things, argues that establishing favourable legislative and regulatory frameworks that encourage the competitive provision of telecommunication services has directly contributed to these developments. As a result, the chapter's primary argument is that the implementation of these frameworks has directly contributed to increased access to telecommunications services, which in turn has contributed to the achievement of the SDGs.

INTRODUCTION

In 2015, the United Nations adopted the Sustainable Development Goals (SDGs), a "universal call to action to end poverty, protect the planet, and ensure that by 2030 all people enjoy peace and prosperity" (UNDP, 2023). Adopted by the UN General Assembly on 25th September 2015, the SDGs, also known as the 2030 Agenda for Sustainable Development, is "a plan of action for people, planet and prosperity"

DOI: 10.4018/979-8-3693-0390-0.ch002

Copyright © 2024, IGI Global. Copying or distributing in print or electronic forms without written permission of IGI Global is prohibited.

that seeks to "strengthen universal peace in larger freedom" (UNGA, 2015, p.1) The SDGs contain seventeen interconnected goals whose successful implementation is aimed at seeing a better and developed world by 2030. Overly ambitious, as observed by the adopting heads of state, the SDGs nevertheless convey a bold attempt to create a developed equal, just, fair world.

Goal number nine of SDGs focuses on building resilient infrastructure, promoting inclusive and sustainable industrialization and fostering innovation (United Nations Department of Social and Economic Affairs, 2023). Target 9(c) of the goal seeks to see a significant "increase in access to information and communications technology" and "universal and affordable access to the Internet in least developed countries by 2020" (United Nations Department of Social and Economic Affairs, 2023, p.1). The emphasis on information and communications technology in goal nine was not an accident. It was already acknowledged by the heads of states that ICT "has great potential to accelerate human progress, to bridge the digital divide and to develop knowledge societies" (UNGA, 2015, p. 5).

The United Republic of Tanzania, like other United Nations members, participated in the development of the SDGs in 2015. As a result, it is dedicated to putting them into action and ensuring that Tanzania is free of poverty by 2023. The country's dedication to implementing the SDGs may be seen in the enactment of various laws, policies, and plans of action. The-relevancy of this chapter is the enactment of various laws and regulations aimed at increasing access to information and communication technologies and related services. Tanzania has enacted several laws to regulate the sector, which promote, among other things, fair competition. The central thesis of this chapter is that the introduction of these laws that foster competition in the sector has directly contributed to increased access to telecommunications services, consequently contributing to the achievement of SDGs.

At this point, it becomes important to answer one crucial question in this chapter: what is competition? Competition is a simple but difficult concept to grasp. It is defined as a "process by which two or more parties engage in a contest/rivalry" (Temu, 2021, p. 61). On a technical level, the term has become intricate and a subject of extensive academic devotion (Ezrachi, 2021; Hunt & Morgan, 1995; McNulty, 1968; Stigler, 1972; Vickers, 1995). Generally, competition has been defined as "rivalry in selling goods, in which each selling unit normally seeks maximum net revenue, under conditions such that the price or prices each seller can charge are effectively limited by the free option of the buyer to buy from a rival seller or sellers of what we think of as "the same" product, necessitating an effort by each seller to equal or exceed the attractiveness of the others' offerings to a sufficient number of sellers to accomplish the end in view"(Clark, 1925, p. 243).

In Tanzania, competition is defined in Section 5 (2) of the Fair Competition Act which mean "competition in a market in Tanzania and refers to the process whereby two or more persons: (a) supply or attempt to supply the same or substitutable goods or services to the persons in the same relevant geographical market; or (b) acquire or attempt to acquire the same or substitutable goods or services from the persons in the same relevant geographical market." Competition is said to exist when there are no entry barriers (e.g., no monopolies), no collusive or coordinated behavior/conduct among market participants, and sufficient information in the market, especially to consumers. Overall, consumer welfare is improved because of increased innovation, superior technology, and lower prices.

Having understood what competition is, it is pertinent to move a step further to define competition law. Competition law includes "rules that are intended to protect the process of competition in order to maximize consumer welfare" (Whish & Bailey, 2012). Rules of competition seek to guard against anti-competitive practices such as abuse of dominance, collusive practices and other acts that restrict or lessen competition in markets. They also deal with the regulation of mergers and acquisitions. Additionally, competition law, which is also known as antitrust law in America (Gavil et al., 2022), addresses public restraints of competition, especially by checking against unfettered powers of government authorities (Whish & Bailey, 2012).

It is important to highlight that the legal framework for enforcing competition in the telecommunication sector in Tanzania is slightly different from that applicable to the general sectors of the economy. Whereas general competition enforcement focuses on ex-post enforcement of competition law by prohibiting restrictive trade practices (cartels) and abuse of dominance, the economics of the telecommunication sector and its network effects necessitate the use of ex-ante rules that establish market conditions that serve as the basis for effective competition (see further Schweitzer, 2022; OECD, 2021; Frieden, 2015). For that reason, Tanzania has the Fair Competition Act No. 8 of 2003, which does not apply in the telecommunication sector. On the contrary, there are specific rules of competition that combine both ex-ante and ex-post enforcement as contained in the Electronic and Postal Communications Act (EPOCA) of 2010, now revised as Cap No 346 R.E 2022. Therefore, references to competition law in the telecommunications industry in this chapter will also include both ex-post and ex-ante provisions contained in several sector regulatory laws. For instance, legislation governing competitive licensing, interconnection, and radio spectrum frequency, among others, will be addressed as constituting the competition law ecosystem in Tanzania's telecommunications sector.

The purpose of this chapter is to evaluate developments in the telecommunications sector considering legislative developments meant to promote, among other things, fair competition in markets. It will expressly assess how the application of competition legislation has been crucial in boosting access to communications services, contributing to the achievement of goal number nine of SDGs.

TANZANIA: CONTEXTUAL COUNTRY PROFILE

Officially the United Republic of Tanzania, Tanzania is a country located in the eastern part of the African continent. According to the Ministry of Finance and Planning (2022), Tanzania is home to more than 60 million people. It is bordered by eight countries: Kenya and Uganda to the north, Rwanda, Burundi and DRC Congo to the west, and Malawi, Zambia and Mozambique to the South. On the eastern side, Tanzania boasts about 800 kilometres of coastline alongside the Indian Ocean. Tanzania is also home to UNESCO's protected and renowned world-class sites, such as the Serengeti National Park, Ngorongoro Conservation Area, Mount Kilimanjaro-the tallest mountain in Africa and the tallest free-standing mountain in the world, and the beautiful clove isles of Zanzibar (BBC, 2023).

According to the African Development Bank (2023), Tanzania is classified as a lower-middle-income economy with a GDP of roughly $60 billion. Nearly 40% of its population lives in urban areas. Tanzania's GDP growth rate in 2022 was 4.6 per cent, slightly higher than 4.3 per cent in 2021, according to the World Bank (2023a). The World Bank noted that Tanzania's 2022 economic recovery was broad-based, with most sectors returning to pre-COVID levels of activity. The epidemic, on the other hand, pushed the poverty rate from 26.2 per cent in 2019 to 27 per cent in 2021 (The World Bank, 2023a). Agriculture, mining, and tourism are among the primary economic sectors of the country. The telecommunications sector is not far behind, having recently been claimed to have contributed approximately 5.2 per cent of the national GDP (The Citizen 2023).

THE STATE OF THE TELECOMMUNICATIONS SECTOR IN THE COUNTRY

According to the Tanzania Communications Regulatory Authority (TCRA) report for the second quarter ending June 2023, more than 100 per cent of Tanzanians were recorded to have access to telephone services (TCRA, 2023). However, this fact has never remained constant. For example, according to the Ministry of Communications and Transport (1997), Tanzania had a telephone density of 0.32 per 100 persons in 1997. This average was significantly lower than that of neighbouring Kenya (0.92), the Southern African Development Community (SADC) (3.4), Asia (3.86), and Europe (35.36), while the world rate stood at 10.49 per 100 inhabitants (Ministry of Communications and Transport, 1997). The dismal figures shown above exposed the country's terrible and pathetic state of communications. It was evident that most of rural and urban Tanzanians were "constrained by the lack of communications services" (Ministry of Communications and Transport, 1997, p.1).

To address the country's deplorable state of communication services, policymakers resolved to develop a policy that would ensure "telecommunications services are provided in a liberalized and competitive manner (Ministry of Communications and Transport, 1997, p.1). This would be attainable if at least six out of every hundred people have access to telecommunications services by 2020 (p. 3). It would follow that the policymakers' projections were too pessimistic and uninformed by the sector's [would be] revolutionary changes. At the turn of the millennium, 1% of Tanzanians already had access to telephone services (TCRA, 2010a). This access rose to 10%, 50%, and over 80% in 2005, 2010, and 2020, respectively, as seen in the table below. By June 2023, over 64 million Tanzanians already had access to telecom services, accounting for 100 per cent of all Tanzanians (TCRA, 2023). These figures reflect what the sector has seen in 20 years after Tanzania implemented its Telecommunications Policy.

Table 1. Trend of subscription to telecom services in the past ten years [2013/23]

Year	Subscription %
2013	61
2014	71
2015	79
2016	80
2017	78
2018	81
2019	88
2020	89
2021	91
2022	98
2023	100

Source: TCRA Communications Statistics

Table 2. Trend of internet subscription for the past six years [2018/23]

Year	Number of subscriptions
2018	22,300,588
2019	25,796,579
2020	26,080,526
2021	29,105,503
2022	31,172,544
2023	34,045,384

Source: TCRA Communications Statistics

Data on internet access, on the other hand, presents quite a different picture. Only about 52 per cent had an internet connection as of June 2023 (TCRA, 2023). Of these, 99.7 per cent use their mobile phones while the remaining 0.3 per cent connect to the internet via fixed wired or wireless connections (TCRA, 2023). This trend demonstrates that while telephone ownership in Tanzania has expanded dramatically, the same cannot be said for internet connectivity, with only roughly 52 per cent having access. Even still, practically all Tanzanians use mobile phones to access the internet, with only 65 per cent using 3G or 4G, as shown in the table below (TCRA, 2023).

It is worth noting that Tanzania performs relatively well in the region when compared to its neighbours, ranking second only to Kenya. Kenya had a mobile sim penetration rate of 130.5% as of March 2023, with 94.7 per cent of Kenyans having access to internet services (Communications Authority of Kenya, 2023). Other countries perform far worse than Tanzania. For example, at the end of 2022, Uganda had a telephone density of 77 per cent (Uganda Communications Commission, 2022), Rwanda had a density of 80.7 per cent (Rwanda Utilities Regulatory Authorities, 2022), and Burundi, DRC Congo, and South Sudan had a telephone density of 62, 49 and 30 per cent, respectively (World Bank, 2023b).

DEVELOPMENTS OF TANZANIA TELECOMMUNICATION SECTOR: THE JOURNEY

Telecommunications services have been provided in the country since colonial times. Tanzania (then known as Tanganyika) fell under German control following the infamous Berlin Conference of 1884/85, in which imperial powers split the African continent among themselves (Craven, 2015; Gjersø, 2015; Harlow, 2003). Tanzania, along with Rwanda, Burundi, and a small portion of Mozambique, formed part of what was then known as German East Africa (Deutsch-Ostafrika), initially under the commercial administration of the Germany East African Company (Die Deutsch-Ostafrikanische Gesellschaft), and later under the German imperial government (Amy McKenna, para 1). Germany's supremacy in Africa ended in 1918, following its defeat in World War One where Tanganyika was then placed under British protection as a protectorate, with powers to govern it until it could gain independence (Illife,1979).

During the British administration, traces of telecommunications services surfaced. Tanganyika was administered by the British throughout this period as part of the British East Africa mandate, which also included Kenya and Rwanda. British provided services in the three territories where the then East African High Commission regulated communication and transportation (Dresang & Sharkansky, 1973). The Commission continued to offer telecommunications services, among other things, until the three nations gained independence in the early 1960s [Tanzania in 1961, Uganda in 1962, and Kenya in 1963] (Smith, 1971; East African Community, 2023).

Immediately following independence, the three countries opted to continue having telecommunications services jointly provided by the East African Common Services Organizations, with the hope of eventually becoming a political federation of the three governments (Hazlewood, 1965). By 1967, the three countries had created the first East African Community, with telecommunications services provided jointly under the East African Postal and Telecommunication Corporation, which was founded by Article 71(2) of the East African Community Treaty of 1967. Until now, telecommunications services were only provided by the government and were only available to a small percentage of the population. The East African Community, on the other hand, was short-lived. It disintegrated in 1977 after just ten years, implying that services previously offered jointly under the community would now be delivered by individual countries (Kauzya, 2011; The Daily Monitor, 2011).

Tanzania's Adoption of Socialism and Telecommunications Services

Following the collapse of the East African Community, Tanzania established its own Post and Telecommunications Corporation (TPTC) in 1977 vide the Tanzania Post and Telecommunications Act No 15 of 1977. It is worth noting that Tanzania had already made a significant change in its policy at this point by establishing socialism as its official state policy. Adopted through the famous Arusha Declaration, socialism aimed at ensuring that the state controls all major means of production and that all services are provided equitably by the state (Nyerere, 1977). This meant that no services could be provided in the country unless under or by the state monopoly.

In keeping with the spirit of socialism, Section 59(1) of the 1977 Act granted the corporation a monopoly on telecom services in the country. This remained the case until the 1990s when measures to reinstate a market economy took root. Throughout this time, the doors to private firms' engagement in the economy, particularly the telecommunications industry, remained firmly closed. It is also worth noting that the TPTC served as both the country's regulator and the provider of telecommunications services.

Early Telecom Reforms: 1990's -2000

The adoption of socialism was accompanied by negative economic outcomes (Hunter, 2015). Even the main architect of the policy, the late Mwalimu Julius Kambarage Nyerere, who served as Tanzania's first president, was not happy with the results of the policy (Nyerere, 1977). After ten years had passed since the Arusha Declaration, Mwalimu pointed out that Tanzania was "certainly neither socialist, nor self-reliant" and that many people were still surviving in conditions of great poverty while the country was still reliant on the assistance of other nations (pp.1-2). Other sources demonstrate that the implementation of socialism as a policy in Tanzania resulted in the country's deterioration into a more pitiful state than it was before the policy was introduced (Edwards, 2014). It was now abundantly clear that reforms were going to be required in all sectors of the economy. As for the telecommunications industry, the reforms have been carried out in stages and are still in progress, as will be discussed more below.

First, the government decided to abolish TPTC's monopoly. Tanzania Telecommunication Incorporation Company Act No. 20 of 1993 established a new telecom company, Tanzania Communication Company Limited (TTCL). Despite being completely owned by the government, this corporation did not have a monopoly on mobile telecommunications services. However, TTCL maintained monopoly control over fixed-line services until 2005, when that market was liberalized as well (Temu, 2021). Thus, for the first time in Tanzanian history, private telecommunications enterprises were permitted. The doors to the private sector were now wide open (Mawenya, 1997).

Second, the Tanzania Communications Act No. 18 of 1993 established the Tanzania Communications Commission as a separate regulator of communications services (TCC). In contrast to the previous structure, in which the TPTC was both the regulator and the service provider, the TCC would now regulate both the TTCL and other private firms.

Third, postal and broadcasting services were separated from telecommunications services. The Tanzania Broadcasting Commission, established by the Tanzania Broadcasting Services Act No. 6 of 1993, was now in control of broadcasting services.

These reforms resulted in a significant shift in market participants in the telecom sector. By early 2000, new mobile telecom service providers such as Mobitel (now Tigo), Tritel, Zantel, and Vodacom had been granted licenses (Temu, 2021). This shift was mirrored in the number of subscribers. For example, TCRA (2011) reports that the country had only 37,940 mobile telecommunications subscribers in 1998. In just two years, this figure increased by 13.3 per cent to 284,109 in 2000 (TCRA, 2011).

CONTINUED REFORMS: THE GOLDEN ERA OF 2000-2010

The 2000-2010 decade may be remembered as a golden era of reform in the country's telecommunications sector. Several legislative and policy changes were enacted, significantly altering the country's telecommunications sector. Three major policy changes were implemented, as described in more detail in this section.

First, Tanzania enacted the Tanzania Communications Regulatory Authority Act No 12 of 2023 in 2003. The purpose of the Act was to govern the country's telecommunications, postal, and broadcasting services. The Tanzania Communication Regulatory Authority (TCRA) was established as the sector regulator in Section 4 of the Act. The Act also introduced a new licensing framework, also known as a converged licensing framework (Mfungahema, 2006). This framework adheres to the notion of service and technological neutrality, allowing telecom providers to use any technology they can afford to meet their customers' demands (Temu, 2021). Another distinguishing characteristic of this Act was the emphasis placed on competition promotion. The TCRA was obliged by law to "promote competition and economic efficiency" under Section 5(a). Furthermore, Section 19(1)(a) and (b) require the TCRA, in carrying out its functions, to consider whether the conditions for effective competition exist in the market" and whether the exercise of its mandate "is likely to cause any lessening of competition." whether the conditions for effective competition exist in the market" and whether the exercise of its mandate "is likely to cause any lessening of competition." This Act had the overall effect of establishing a legal framework for the competitive provision of communications services in the country.

Second, the country passed the Universal Communications Services Act, No. 11 of 2016. The conception of the Universal Communications Services Access Fund (the Fund) was central to this Act, with the goal of promoting "social, education and economic development in rural and urban-underserved areas." This would then ensure that all Tanzanians have access to telecommunications services. Section 18 of the Act requires all holders of communication licenses to contribute to the Fund through a universal service levy. The contributions are then used as subsidies for telecom companies to reach and serve underserved areas that could not be saved solely through market forces of demand and supply.

Third, the country enacted the Electronic and Postal Communications Act in 2010, which was later revised as Cap No 346 R.E 2022. The purpose of this Act was to establish a "comprehensive regulatory regime for electronic communications service providers and postal communications service providers." It was thorough, attempting to keep up with the rapid technological developments. The adoption of comprehensive rules that promote competition is central to our subject, including comprehensive rules on licensing (Part II(a) of the Act), rules on interconnection and access (Part II(b) of the Act), and rules on competitive practices and conduct (Part IV of the Act). Overall, the result was substantive telecommunications rules that responded to industry needs at the time and ultimately promoted more competition in the sector.

The three Acts discussed above serve as the foundation for the sector's primary legislation. They brought in reforms that had the effect of completely transforming the sector. These reforms provided, to an appreciable extent, regulatory certainty as well as favorable business environments. The impact of the reforms described above can be measured in terms of the effect brought to the sector. For example, as of December 2010, there were seven (7) active providers of telecommunications services (network services) in the country: Vodacom, Tigo, Airtel, Zantel, TTCL, Benson, and Sasatel (TCRA, 2010b). The number of active subscribers had also skyrocketed to 21.5 million (TCRA, 2010b), accounting for about 50% of the penetration rate compared to 1% at the start of the decade, as shown in the table below (Temu, 2021).

Table 3. Tele density of telecommunication services in the country from 2005 to 2010

Year	Subscription	% of penetration
2005	3,118,157	10%
2006	5,766,566	15%
2007	8,486,126	21%
2008	13,130,602	32%
2009	17,642,408	43%
2020	21,158,364	50%

Source: TCRA Communications Statistics of December 2012

Further Reforms for Modernization: 2011 to Present

In 2011, additional reforms to optimize telecommunications services were spearheaded. Most of these reforms centered on fine-tuning existing laws and enacting regulations to keep up with rapid technological innovation. In terms of primary legislation, two significant pieces of legislation were passed in 2015: the Cybercrimes Act and the Electronic Transactions Act. The Cybercrimes Act No. 14 of 2015 was passed specifically to deal with offences involving computer and electronic services. The overarching goal of the Act is to protect against the dangerous use of computer and telecommunications services. Users of electronic and telecommunications services would now be protected under this Act, and any violation of their rights would result in proportional penalties.

The Electronic Transactions Act No. 13 of 2015, on the other hand, sought to provide for the "legal recognition of electronic transactions, e-government services, the use of Information and Communication Technologies in evidence collection, and the admissibility of electronic evidence" among other things. Users of telecommunications would be assured that their transactions, including voice and text communications, would be legally recognized under this Act.

Specific to the subject at hand, several regulations have been enacted to promote competition in the sector. These include the Electronic and Postal Communications Regulations of 2018 amended in 2022, the Electronic and Postal Communications (Interconnection) Regulations of 2018, the Electronic and Postal Communications (Competition) Regulations of 2018, the Electronic and Postal Communications (Access, Co-Location and Infrastructure Sharing) Regulations of 2018 as amended in 2022) and the Electronic and Postal Communications (Radio Communication and Frequency Spectrum) Regulations of 2018 as amended in 2022. All these Regulations create an environment in which telecom firms can compete freely in the market. Access regulations and co-location, for example, lower entry barriers by encouraging firms with varying financial resources to enter markets at various phases. Similarly, interconnection rules ensure that telecom firms' customers can readily connect with those of other firms, improving competition among those firms.

It can thus be concluded that since 2011, efforts have been taken to further modernize the provision of telecommunication services. These measures are consistent with Tanzania's policy commitments to increase access to communications services. These commitments are clearly stated in the National Telecommunications Policy of 1997 and the National ICT Policy of 2016. Indeed, the impact of these reforms can be seen in the 2023 communications statistics, as shown in the table below. Not only has access to telecom services increased, but there has also been expansion into other related services, such as mobile money, which are directly related to telecom services (Aker & Mbiti, 2010; Bank of Tanzania, 2019; Blechman et al., 2017; CGAP, 2015; Economides & Jeziorski, 2017; GSMA, 2013; Winn & de Koker, 2013). As a result, the gap between telecom and financial services is rapidly closing in Tanzania, promoting ease of transactions, consumer welfare, and overall life improvement in rural and urban areas.

Table 4. Status of telecom services subscription as of June 2023

Service	Subscriptions	% of the population
Telecom subscriptions	64,088,651	101%
Internet services	34,047,407	53.5%
Mobile money	47,275,660	74.3%

Source: TCRA communications statistics as of June 2023

THE ROLE OF COMPETITION IN INCREASING ACCESS TO TELECOMMUNICATIONS SERVICES IN THE COUNTRY

At the centre of this chapter is an argument that the increased access to communications services in the country is strongly charged by improved rules of competition, among other things. It is argued that with a robust competition framework, Tanzania's telecom market attracted telecom firms to provide services, increasing the country's overall access to communication services, as has already been seen. There is sufficient empirical evidence to support the argument that competition contributes to improving services and access, especially through innovation, efficiency, and consumer welfare (Kira et al., 2021). For Tanzania, the role of competition is evident from having 1% subscription at the dawn of the new millennia to over 100% subscriptions slightly over twenty years after. This section illustrates the foregoing conclusion.

Competitive Licensing

Licensing is a very powerful instrument used by governments to control entry into the telecommunications industry. Through licensing, governments dictate who is to enter the market and the terms and conditions of such entry. Licensing provides for authorizations, determining the extent to which licensed firms can operate in the markets (Flanagan, 2018). It is also used to achieve other social and economic objectives, such as distributive justice and collection of revenue (Flanagan, 2018).

The framework of licensing of telecom services in the country is governed by the Electronic and Postal Communications Act of 2010, together with the Licensing Regulations of 2018, as amended in 2022. Through these laws, several licensing principles have been established, the result of which is to facilitate entry. For example, the TCRA has been issuing licenses under a converged framework since 2005 (Mfungahema, 2006). The converged framework observes the principle of service and technology neutrality, allowing telecom firms to adopt whatever type of technology they can afford to meet their customers' demands.

There are three categories of telecommunications licenses available under the law within this framework. These include network facilities licenses (for communication infrastructure), network services licenses (for network connectivity), and network applications services (for application services), as defined in Sections 11, 12, and 14 of the Electronic and Postal Communications Act, respectively. To obtain a license under this system, a company does not need to be tied to a certain type of technology. For example, broadcasting and other technology firms may only obtain application services, whereas firms providing pure telecommunications services will require a network services license. This framework also permits telecom companies to provide virtual services because they are not required to own a communication infrastructure or core network. Similarly, tower companies will just require a network facility license and not the other two. The eventual outcome is that as many market participants as possible are encouraged, access to communication services is increased.

The impact of the existing licensing framework on facilitating access may also be seen in the geographical segmentation of licenses. Because these licenses are so expensive, markets have been fragmented to meet the specific needs of telecom firms. For example, Regulation 9 of the Licensing Regulations allows licenses to be granted at the district (serving up to three districts), regional (serving up to ten regions), national (serving the entire nation), and international levels (licenses with international connectivity). A telecom firm can choose where to begin offering its services based on its financial capabilities. As a result, those enterprises that are unable to start at the national level due to huge sunk costs are given the opportunity to start at a lower level, giving consumers more options. The substantial number of licensed operators as of 2023 is stronger evidence of the impact of the competitive nature of the current licensing framework.

Competitive Allocation of Radio Frequency Spectrum

The licensing framework described above represents only one side of the requirements for the provision of telecommunication services. Another prerequisite for providing telecommunications services is the radio frequency spectrum. The radio frequency spectrum, like wires to fixed-line telecom services, is essential to mobile communications. To comprehend the radio frequency spectrum, we must briefly revisit physics classes, beginning with an understanding of electromagnetic radiation. Electromagnetic radiation is "the flow of energy at the universal speed of light through free space or a material medium in the form of the electric and magnetic fields" (Fritzsche & Phillips, 2017). The radiations can be distributed per frequency or wavelength. Such distribution is known as the electromagnetic spectrum. Thus, when referring to the frequency spectrum, attention is given to different parts of the spectrum, measured in Hertz after Heinrich Hertz, a German physicist who first proved radio waves' existence (Sims et al., 2016).

Because radio frequency is essential to the provision of wireless communications, many governments have come to see the spectrum as a scarce and valuable resource (Haldorai & Kandaswamy, 2019; Levin, 2013; Pandit & Singh, 2017; Prasad et al., 2016; Yi & Cai, 2016). This has led to the enactment of different rules on its proper and effective management. Regrettably, radio frequencies have always been under the monopoly of governments, which means that governments have the power to decide who provides services of this nature. If spectrum is not made accessible on a competitive basis to all firms who are interested in it, then any attempt to boost competition in the industry and consequently improve access to telecommunications services, will be fruitless.

Tanzania has seen the importance of competitive spectrum allocation and has adopted legal and policy measures to guarantee the same. In its ICT Policy of 2016, the government notes that "spectrum is a key scarce public ICT resources that goes to waste if not efficiently used and managed, and therefore there is need to recognize it in the sectoral policies for guaranteeing sustainable future of ICT services provisioning in the country" (Ministry of Works, Transportation and Communications, 2016, p. 24). As such, the policy objective on spectrum management is to "strengthen management and promote efficiency in spectrum allocation and utilization that guarantees availability and competition in both urban and rural areas" (Ministry of Works, Transportation and Communications, 2016, p. 25). This is to be achieved by ensuring the "availability of spectrum for various uses and allocation that favours public interest; promotes innovation, research and development; strengthens competition and attracts foreign direct investment" and also to "ensure that allocation and assignment of commercial spectrum resources that is transparent, competitive, does not confer permanent ownership to users and that sees to it that the allocated resources are used efficiently for sustainable provision of affordable and quality ICT services"(Ministry of Works, Transportation and Communications, 2016, p. 25).

As a result of the above policy statements and objectives, the EPOCA contains extensive provisions from Sections 71-78 that guarantee a coordinated and regulated availability of frequency spectrum. Details of this framework are contained in the Radio Frequency Regulations of 2018, as amended in 2022. In principle, spectrum rights are competitively assigned using what is known as a hybrid tendering process (Mpapalika, 2014). This process involves the TCRA's selection of qualified bidders [pre-qualification process], who are then subjected to the second round of competitive auction. The overarching goal of this process is to ensure that those who can afford it have access to spectrum rights. This, in turn, has enhanced such firms' ability to provide communications services, thereby increasing access to customers throughout the country.

Establishing Rules of Competition in the Sector

The Fair Competition Act of 2003 is the primary legislation in Tanzania that regulates competition in the country's general economic sectors. However, this Act is exempt from application in the regulated sectors such as the telecoms industry. As a result, there are sector-specific laws, such as the Electronic and Postal Communications Act of 2010 and the Competition Regulations of 2018, that govern competition. The purpose of these sector-specific rules is to outlaw anti-competitive behaviours, which, if left unchecked, could have a negative impact on the overall availability of telecommunication services.

It must be understood that competition rules strive to protect the competition process in a specific market rather than competitors (Tanga Fresh v FCC, 2014). The main assumption underpinning this theory is that competition, as opposed to other types of economic structures such as monopoly or oligopoly, is most likely to produce the most welfare (Train, 1991). To get the most out of markets, competition regulations require standards that ensure fair play, such as free entry (absence of entry barriers), unfettered operation, and free exit. As a result, such rules would regulate mergers and acquisitions to prevent the formation of unhealthy market dominance, as well as prohibit restrictive trade practices and collusive practices (cartels).

Part IV (b) of the Electronic and Postal Communications Act set basic rules to govern competition in the sector. Such rules include the prohibition of abuse of dominance in the market, the prohibition of collusive practices, and the regulation of mergers and acquisitions.

Abuse of Dominance

It is critical to recognize that competition law does not restrict firms from gaining a dominant position. There is enough research to show that dominance is not illegal (Raitt, 2019; Schütze, 2018; Ewing, 2006). It is the abuse of that dominance that is illegal. To understand abuse of dominance, one must first define dominance. Dominance is defined in Section 3 of the EPOCA as a position that permits a firm "to operate in a market without being significantly affected by competition, and it engages in conduct that is likely to impede the development or maintenance of effective competition." In Hoffman-La Roche v Commission (1979), the European Court of Justice defined abuse of dominance as "a position of economic strength enjoyed by an undertaking that enables it to prevent effective competition from being maintained on the relevant market by affording it the power to behave to a significant extent independently of its competitors, customers, and ultimately consumers" (p.520). This definition, which is widely accepted by many competition law authors (Albors-Llorens, 2002; Behrens, 2018; Brisimi, 2014; Whish & Bailey, 2012), implies that if left unchecked, a dominant firm is capable of distorting competition (White, 2015). Thus, abuse of dominance refers to the dominant firm's illegal use of its market position to restrict competition (Fox, 2014). Abuse of dominance may include acts "which harm competition" (Monti, 2007, p. 160), "that hinder undistorted competition," or "that deviate from 'normal' or 'fair' or 'undistorted' competition" (Whish & Bailey, 2012, pp. 190-192).

Since abuse of dominance has the potential to distort competition, both the EPOCA and the Competition Regulations of 2018 forbid any act that could result in abuse of dominance. Exclusionary practices such as predatory pricing (see further Elzinga & Mills, 2015; Giocoli, 2014; Wurmnest, 2011), price (margin) squeezing (Orbach & Avraham, 2015; Jones, 2011), price (cross) subsidization (Ritter & Braun, 2005), and price discrimination (Peeperkorn, 2009) are examples of prohibited conducts. Other prohibited conducts include excessively high prices (Botta & Wiedemann, 2019) and uncompetitive tying and bundling (Lorenz, 2013). Furthermore, prohibited practices include conduct that would hinder or diminish competition, such as service bundling, unfair dealing with competitors, and discriminating practices, to name a few.

The argument for regulating abuse of dominance is apparent, especially when considering the need to promote access to telecom services. It is clear from the preceding that a dominant firm will have market control. Without regulation, such firms will most likely abuse their market dominance. Because of such abuse, competition is inhibited, making the dominant firm less motivated to invest, innovate, and expand its service offerings. Tanzania Postal and Telecommunication Corporation's dominance in the country, as seen in the preceding sections of this chapter, demonstrates this conclusion. As a result, it has been stated elsewhere that rules against abuse of dominance must be established and enforced, and that a dominant firm has a "special responsibility not to allow its conduct to damage genuine undistorted competition" (Michelin V Commission, 1983, p. 3511).

Restrictive Trade Practices

Firms frequently engage in tactics that seek to maximize profit, often at the expense of consumers. Adam Smith once noted, "people of the same trade seldom meet together, even for merriment or diversion, but the conversation ends in a conspiracy against the public or in some contrivance to raise prices (Bruneckienė et al., 2015, p. 1). Because the goal of many firms is to maximize profit, the incentive to collude for profit maximization remains valid (Levenstein & Suslow, 2015). For these reasons, restrictive trade practices are prohibited under competition law.

The EPOCA and Competition Regulations of 2018 contain specific provisions against restrictive practices. Section 64 of EPOCA prohibits telecom firms from entering "into any understanding, agreement or arrangement, whether legally enforceable or not, which provides for (a) rate fixing; (b) market sharing; (c) boycott of a supplier of apparatus; or (d) boycott of another competitor." To enforce this prohibition, the TCRA is authorized by Regulation 5(1)(a) of the Competition Regulations to issue additional rules prohibiting such acts. Furthermore, the TCRA has the authority to assess all agreements entered by telecom firms to verify that they do not include price-fixing arrangements, bid-rigging, market allocations, or exclusive dealing.

The prohibitions and rules above are required to create a level playing field for all market participants. In the absence of such rules, firms will do all possible to maximize profits at the expense of consumers. This would most certainly result in expensive, low-quality services, restricting access to communications services.

Regulating of Mergers and Acquisitions

Merger refers to the joining of two or more firms to form a new one, whereas acquisition refers to one company acquiring the interests of another (Jones et al., 2019). Semantics aside, both mergers and acquisitions relate to combining the assets and liabilities of two or more entities into one, strengthening the post-merger/acquisition firm. In general, mergers and acquisitions are not always harmful, and in some circumstances, they might produce greater economic and efficiency benefits (See, for instance, Jones et al., 2019; Paul Healy, 1992; Turner, 1965). Mergers and acquisitions are only prohibited where the post-merger/acquisition entity distorts competition, for example, by eliminating competitors entirely from the market (Hovenkamp, 2016).

In Tanzania, the general law governing mergers and acquisitions is found in Sections 11-14 of the Fair Competition Act of 2003 as well as the Fair Competition Regulations (FCC Regulations) of 2018. This is the only instance where the Fair Competition Commission has the authority to act in the telecommunications industry. Per Section 11 of the Act, a merger is prohibited "if it generates or increases a position of dominance in a market." At the moment, the threshold necessary to notify the FCC of a merger is 3.5 billion Tanzanian shillings (about 1.5 million USD).

Even though the Fair Competition Commission regulates and approves mergers in the country, the TCRA is given oversight authority on the same. In practice, the FCC will not approve a merger application unless it first consults with the TCRA. The rationale is to ensure that the TCRA, as the sector regulator, monitors the process to ensure that the end product does not distort the telecom market. The TCRA's authority stems from Regulations 4 and 5 of the Competition Regulations of 2018. In doing so, the TCRA ensures that no anti-competitive mergers are authorized, which would distort competition.

Despite the existence of explicit competition rules, as explained in this section, the Tanzania Communications Regulatory Authority prioritizes ex-ante competition law enforcement (Temu, 2021). There is no precedent for the TCRA addressing competition law issues ex-post, such as abuse of dominance or restrictive trade practices. TCRA typically operates by issuing directives to which all telecom firms must comply. Nonetheless, these directives are crucial in ensuring that all market participants have a level playing field. The result is the same; competition in the sector has increased, directly contributing to the attainment of SDGs, among other things (Tanzania Telecoms Market Report, 2023; Robb et al., 2020).

As a result, the overall impact of effective competition rules in the sector is to ensure fair play among market participants. Such rules, among other things, encourage entry by lowering entry barriers. Other conditions remaining unchanged, more market participants would suggest increased services and user access. This is demonstrated by the brief history presented in the first sections of this chapter. During the country's monopoly era, access to telecommunications services was less than 0.5 per 100 people. By 2023, that figure has changed, with more than 100 per cent access rate. As a result, competition regulations enable unfettered entry, ensuring that no firm desiring to provide telecom services in the market is prevented because of anticompetitive behavior, whether from other firms or the government. Once entry is guaranteed, the same rules of competition ensure fair play, which means that market entry, existence and exit are determined only by forces of demand and supply, rather than by unfair tactics by competitors.

Interconnection Regulation

Section 3 of the Electronic and Postal Communications Act defines interconnection as "the physical or logical linking of one public electronic communications network to another for the purpose of allowing the persons using one of them to be able to (a) communicate with users of the other network; or (b) make use of services provided by means of the other one." To grasp the importance of interconnection in promoting competition, we must first understand how it works, particularly in the age of mobile telecommunications. We will use two big Tanzanian telecom companies, Vodacom and Tigo, as well as a smaller mobile service provider, TTCL. In the absence of any regulatory requirements, Vodacom and Tigo subscribers have the freedom to call only those who have subscribed to their respective networks. As a result, a Vodacom subscriber may only call other Vodacom subscribers and not otherwise. If we suppose that Vodacom customers have family members who have Tigo subscriptions, then without interconnection rules, Vodacom customers will be unable to call Tigo subscribers.

To get out of the aforesaid morass, Vodacom customers will have to subscribe to other networks to call customers from those networks. Or there is another preferable alternative: Vodacom must enter into an arrangement with Tigo in which Tigo connects Vodacom subscribers to its network when they call, and then terminates the line when the call is over. The two companies may freely enter into such arrangements for mutual benefit, but only if doing so is commercially advantageous to them. To put it another way, if TTCL only has a few clients, Vodacom will have little business motivation to connect with them. This means that firms with many customers will have a monopoly on interconnection services and may decide not to interconnect with smaller or newer firms. As a result, incumbent enterprises will take advantage of such monopoly to solidify their dominance. It is at this time that interconnection rules become mandatory.

Interconnection regulation, therefore, seeks to set favourable conditions of entry for all firms, regardless of their sizes. In the absence of such regulations, firms with market powers will refuse to interconnect with smaller ones, creating strategic entry barriers. Acknowledging this importance, Section 27 of EPOCA sets basic rules of interconnection. Principally, the law empowers the TCRA to regulate interconnection in cases of market failure, to issue interconnection negotiation procedures and guidance, and to arbitrate in cases of interconnection disputes.

Additional details on the interconnection framework are found in the Interconnection Regulations of 2018. These regulations mandate telecommunication licensees to interconnect, meaning that no telecom firm will refuse to interconnect with another. Regulation 4(1) provides that "a network service licensee shall have an obligation to interconnect with the network of any other network service licensee in the United Republic." Upon receiving requests for interconnection, Regulation 4(b) mandates telecom licensees "to interconnect with the interconnection seeker at reasonable terms and conditions set out in the interconnection agreement."

With the interconnection rules described above, anyone wishing to enter the telecom market will encounter no entry barriers due to interconnection constraints. To ensure that telecom firms do not misuse interconnection powers, the TCRA already acts ex-ante by symmetrically fixing interconnection rates for all firms (TCRA, 2004; TCRA, 2007; TCRA 2013; TCRA, 2017). Although this practice has been challenged in court multiple times, it has been determined that it is the best practice for promoting competition and fairness in markets (Vodacom Tanzania PLC v Tanzania Communications Regulatory Authority, 2018; Vodacom Tanzania Limited v Tanzania Communications Regulatory Authority & Six Telecommunications Company Limited, 2007). The two cases have demonstrated that ex-ante interconnection regulation is required to maintain fair play and competition in the market. As a result of these decisions, the TCRA has continued to lower interconnection fees, hence reducing calling rates between different operators. Overall, the effect has been to make telecommunications services more affordable to the public, hence boosting access to telecommunications services (The Citizen, 2021).

From the foregoing, it can be concluded that interconnection regulation encourages entry, increases the availability of service providers, and enhances access to telecom services, both voice and data. It has also been argued that effective interconnection regulation will most likely contribute to reduced communication prices and increased quality of service (Hawthorne, 2018; Manyele & Moyo, 2019; Mothobi, 2017). This, too, has the direct impact of enticing more people to subscribe to telecom services, hence improving access.

Regulation of Access, Co-Location, and Sharing of Infrastructure

The establishment of telecommunications services requires considerable sunk costs (Dkhil, 2014; Elvidge & Martucci, 2003; Franklin, 2015). Firms are typically forced to invest large sums of money that must be recovered over a long period of time. As a result, enterprises that have already established themselves in the market have a competitive advantage in that they have most likely already recouped their investment costs and are now in the process of accumulating profit. This benefit, however, will not be available to newcomers. This truth becomes clear when considering the presence of national monopolies that were practically entirely sponsored by governments. With government support that is expected to continue even after telecom sector liberalization, private enterprises may not be on an equal playing field when it comes to fair competition. To overcome the aforementioned issue, especially in nations with strong incumbent former national monopolies, rules on access, co-location, and infrastructure sharing become important.

Access relates to the requirement of one firm offering its facilities or services to another firm for the provision of telecommunication services (Winkler & Baumgarten, 2009). Access involves offering services to simple transactions, such as roaming services to complex ones, such as access to the whole unutilized network capacity or sharing of the same network (Garcia & Kelly, 2015). Access regulation reduces to "barrier to market entry, so a new operator will not have to replicate every network element that the incumbent has before being able to offer a competing end-to-end service" (Walden, 2018, p. 435). Access is, therefore, a "key element in any strategy to develop competition for local access" (Nikolinakos, 2006, p. 614).

In Tanzania, access is regulated by Section 28 of EPOCA, which provides that access is guaranteed as a matter of right. Every licensee of telecommunications services has the right to request access to elements of an electronic communication network or electronic communication services provided by another licensee. The TCRA is empowered under Section 28(2) to regulate the overall access procedures, including how the licensees will negotiate and enter into access arrangements. Further details are contained in the Access Regulation of 2018 as amended in 2022. Per these Regulations, both tangible and intangible network facilities are subject to access. Tangible facilities, per Regulation 3 of the Regulations, include "lines, cables, or wires whether fibre optic or other, equipment, apparatus, towers, masts, tunnels, ducts, risers, manholes, pits, poles, landing stations, huts, lands, access roads, buildings or facilities." Per the same Regulation, intangible facilities which may be subject of access include "agreements, arrangements, licences, franchises, rights of way, easements and other such interests."

Access regulation also has to do with co-location and sharing of infrastructure. As with access, the sharing of infrastructure is not a novel phenomenon. Literature witnesses this to be a common practice intending to promote entry by reducing barriers, hence increasing providers of telecom services (Gelvanovska et al., 2014; OECD, 2014). Access Regulations define co-location in Regulation 3 as "the accommodation of two or more licensee's switches, antennas or other electronic communications equipment in, or on a single building, tower or other structure." Per these Regulations, co-location can either be physical or remote. On the one hand, physical co-location involves the party controlling the building, tower, or other structure in or on which another party switches, antennas, or other electronic communications equipment are accommodated, also allows the other party to operate those switches, antennas, or other electronic communications equipment." On the other hand, the same Regulations define remote co-location to include "the equipment of the interconnection demanding operator is installed in a location near the premises of the interconnection providing operator and a transmission medium is used to realize the physical interconnection."

Access, co-location, and infrastructure sharing all have the same goal of promoting entry and, thus competition in the sector. Firms are guaranteed at least the following with access regulations: First, entry will not be restricted just because entrants are unable to replicate infrastructure already developed by incumbents. They can already begin to offer services using the incumbents' infrastructures, directly competing with them for increased consumer welfare. Second, telecom companies will focus on making better use of their resources, such as investing in higher-quality services rather than reproducing and replicating infrastructure, which is also increasingly viewed as an environmental hazard, especially in urban areas (Garcia & Kelly, 2015; GSMA, 2012). Third, with guaranteed access and infrastructure sharing, telecom companies can focus on innovation and other services in high demand by consumers. The net effect is more competition among firms, regardless of their financial strength. This translates into increased access because each firm is driven to seek out additional subscribers to remain competitive. Access regulation has already proved to be extremely useful in increasing access, first by reducing costs of communication services and second, by reaching rural and underserved areas (BEREC 2018).

Other Rules and Regulations

The frameworks explained above have just provided how Tanzania has adopted various policies and regulations, which resulted in promoting competition in the sector. Beyond those regulations, several other regulatory steps have also been taken with the same effect of promoting competition in the sector, hence increasing access. For example, the Electronic and Postal Communications (Mobile Number Portability) Regulations of 2018 make it possible for one person to change his or her network without necessarily losing his number. By introducing this flexibility, users of telecom services will benefit from having unfettered choices. Telecom firms will also have to work hard and invest in getting new customers as the locking-in effect has been eroded by this flexibility. Again, the impact is to increase competition among telecom firms, which is a catalyst for increased access.

The same effect is achieved by the Tariff Regulations of 2018. Among other things, these Regulations ensure that telecom firms do not charge unfair prices in the markets. Further, they also guard against the dominant firm's abuse of market powers through unacceptable pricing techniques, promotion, and market strategies. It must be understood that pricing is one of the key instruments which firms, especially those with significant market powers, can apply to restrict competition, thereby increasing dominance. With rules on tariff regulation, firms are now guaranteed to compete on fair ground. This, too, promotes competition, hence increasing access to telecom services.

CONCLUSION: TAKING THE STOCK

Target 9(c) of the Sustainable Development Goal number 9 seeks to "significantly increase access to information and communications technology and strive to provide universal and affordable access to the Internet in the least developed countries by 2020" (Department of Economic and Social Affairs, 2023). The indicator of achieving this goal is the "proportion of population covered by a mobile network, by technology" (Department of Economic and Social Affairs, 2023). Indeed, the UN reports that as of 2023, "Mobile broadband (3G or above) access is available to 95% of the world's population, while 4G coverage has doubled to 88% between 2015 and 2022. However, growth is slowing down, and connecting the remaining 5% is proving difficult. In Sub-Saharan Africa, the gap is 18%, predominantly affecting the population of Central and Western Africa. The coverage gap is almost the same in LDCs and LLDCs." (Department of Economic and Social Affairs, 2023).

Considering the above-reported progress, Tanzania is doing relatively well. The aggregate subscription to telecommunications services exceeds 100%, implying that every Tanzanian has access to at least one type of communication service. Even though this number may not accurately reflect the reality on the ground, since some people may have more than one SIM card, the growth trend represented in the quarterly communications statistics is very encouraging. In terms of broadband connectivity, 3G covers 77 per cent of the whole population, while 4G covers 65 per cent (TCRA, 2023). Furthermore, in terms of geographical coverage, the 3G network covers more than 62 per cent of Tanzania, compared to 50 per cent for the 4G network. 5G is currently in its rolling stage (TCRA, 2023).

While Tanzania has not yet attained the world rate, it can arguably be said that it is heading towards the right direction, thanks to the supportive legal and regulatory environment. The said framework, which also includes rules on competitive provisions of communication services, has contributed to the increased access to communication services in the country, as already justified by the provided statistics.

Considering the growth trend, especially after the reintroduction of competition in the sector, it can thus be concluded that rules of competition have indeed been vital in achieving the SDGs, even though we are yet to achieve the targets at one hundred per cent.

REFERENCES

African Development Bank Group. (2023). *Tanzania.* ADBG. https://www.afdb.org/en/countries/east-africa/tanzania

Aker, J. C., & Mbiti, I. M. (2010). Mobile Phones and Economic Development in Africa. *The Journal of Economic Perspectives*, *24*(3), 207–232. doi:10.1257/jep.24.3.207

Albors-Llorens, A. (2002). *EC competition law and policy*. Willan Pub.

Amy McKenna. (n.d.). German East Africa: Former German dependency, Africa. In *Britannica*. https://www.britannica.com/place/German-East-Africa

Bank of Tanzania. (2019). *Mobile Money Transactions*. Bank of Tanzania.

BBC. (2023, February 5). *Zanzibar Profile*. BBC. https://www.bbc.com/news/world-africa-14115176

Behrens, P. (2018). The Ordoliberal Concept of 'Abuse' of a Dominant Position and its Impact on Article 102 TFEU. In F. Di Porto & R. Podszun (Eds.), *Abusive Practices in Competition Law* (pp. 5–25). Edward Elgar Publishing. doi:10.4337/9781788117340.00008

BEREC (Body of European Regulators for Electronic Communications). (2018). *BEREC Report on infrastructure sharing*. BEREC.

Blechman, J., Odhiambo, F., & Roberts, S. (2017). Competition Dynamics in Mobile Money Markets in Tanzania. Centre for Competition, Regulation and Economic Development, Centre for Competition, Regulation and Economic Development.

Botta, M., & Wiedemann, K. (2019). Exploitative Conducts in Digital Markets: Time for a Discussion after the Facebook Decision. *Journal of European Competition Law & Practice*, *10*(8), 465–478. doi:10.1093/jeclap/lpz064

Brisimi, V. (2014). *The Interface between Competition and the Internal Market: Market Separation under Article 102 TFEU*. Bloomsbury Publishing.

Bruneckienė, J., Pekarskienė, I., Guzavičius, A., Palekienė, O., & Šovienė, J. (2015). *The impact of cartels on national economy and competitiveness: A Lithuanian case study*. Springer International Publishing. doi:10.1007/978-3-319-17287-3

CGAP. (2015, March). *Tanzania's Mobile Money Revolution*. CGAP. https://www.cgap.org/research/infographic/tanzanias-mobile-money-revolution

Communications Authority of Kenya. (2023). *Third Quarter Sector Statistics Report for the Financial Year 2022/2023 (1st January – 31st March 2023)*. Communications Authority of Kenya. https://www.ca.go.ke/sites/default/files/2023-06/Sector%20Statistics%20Report%20Q3%202022-2023.pdf

Craven, M. (2015). Between law and history: The Berlin Conference of 1884-1885 and the logic of free trade. *London Review of International Law*, *3*(1), 31–59. doi:10.1093/lril/lrv002

Department of Economic and Social Affairs. (2023). *Sustainable Development*. UN. https://sdgs.un.org/goals/goal9

Dkhil, I. B. (2014). *Regulation and Investment in Telecom Network Infrastructure Facilities: The Recent Developments and Debates* [MPRA Paper No. 72910]. MPRA. https://mpra.ub.uni-muenchen.de/72910/1/MPRA_paper_72910.pdf

Dresang, D. L., & Sharkansky, I. (1973). Public Corporations in Single-Country and Regional Settings: Kenya and the East African Community. [JSTOR.]. *International Organization*, *27*(3), 303–328. doi:10.1017/S0020818300003520

Economides, N., & Jeziorski, P. (2017). Mobile Money in Tanzania. *Marketing Science*, *36*(6), 815–837. doi:10.1287/mksc.2017.1027

Edwards, S. (2014). *Toxic aid: Economic collapse and recovery in Tanzania* (1st ed.). Oxford University Press. doi:10.1093/acprof:oso/9780198704423.001.0001

Elvidge, A. M., & Martucci, J. (2003). Telecommunications Network Total Cost of Ownership and Return on Investment Modelling. *BT Technology Journal*, *21*(2), 184–190. doi:10.1023/A:1024467706446

Elzinga, K. G., & Mills, D. E. (2015). Predatory Pricing. In R. D. Blair & D. D. Sokol (Eds.), *The Oxford handbook of international antitrust economics* (pp. 40–61). Oxford University Press. doi:10.1093/oxfordhb/9780199388592.013.0002

Ewing, K. P. (2006). *Competition rules for the 21st century: Principles from America's experience* (2nd ed.). Kluwer Law International.

Ezrachi, A. (2021). *Competition and antitrust law: A very short introduction* (1st ed.). Oxford University Press. doi:10.1093/actrade/9780198860303.001.0001

Flanagan, A. (2018). Authorization and Licensing. In I. Walden (Ed.), *Telecommunications Law and Regulation* (5th ed., pp. 285–380). Oxford University Press. doi:10.1093/oso/9780198807414.003.0009

Fox, E. (2014). Monopolization and abuse of dominance: Why Europe is different. *Antitrust Bulletin*, *59*(1), 129–152. doi:10.1177/0003603X1405900106

Franklin, S. L. Jr. (2015). Investment decisions in mobile telecommunications networks applying real options. *Annals of Operations Research*, *226*(1), 201–220. doi:10.100710479-014-1672-9

Frieden, R. (2015). Ex Ante Versus Ex Post Approaches to Network Neutrality: A Comparative Assessment. *Berkeley Technology Law Journal*, *30*(2), 1561–1612. doi:10.15779/Z386Z81

Fritzsche, H., & Phillips, M. (2017). Electromagnetic Radiation. In *Encyclopaedia Britannica*. https://www.britannica.com/science/electromagnetic-radiation

Garcia, J. M., & Kelly, T. (2015). *The Economics and Policy Implications of Infrastructure Sharing and Mutualisation in Africa*. World Bank Publications.

Gavil, A. I., Kovacic, W. E., Baker, J. B., & Wright, J. D. (2022). *Antitrust law in perspective: Cases, concepts, and problems in competition policy* (4th ed.). West Academic Publishing.

Gelvanovska, N., Rogy, M., & Rossotto, C. M. (2014). *Broadband Networks in the Middle East and North Africa: Accelerating High-Speed Internet Access*. World Bank Publications.

Geradin, D., & O'Donoghue, R. (2005). The Concurrent Application of Competition Law and Regulation: The Case of Margin Squeeze Abuses in the Telecommunications Sector. *Journal of Competition Law & Economics*, *1*(2), 355–425. doi:10.1093/joclec/nhi009

Giocoli, N. (2014). *Predatory pricing in antitrust law and economics: A historical perspective*. Routledge. doi:10.4324/9781315832692

Gjersø, J. F. (2015). The Scramble for East Africa: British Motives Reconsidered, 1884–95. *The Journal of Imperial and Commonwealth History*, *43*(5), 831–860. doi:10.1080/03086534.2015.1026131

GSMA. (2012). *Mobile Infrastructure Sharing*. GSMA.

GSMA. (2013). *Tanzania Mobile Money Infographic*. GSMA. https://www.gsma.com/mobilefordevelopment/wp-content/uploads/2014/03/Tanzania-Mobile-Money-infographic-GSMA-MMU.pdf

Haldorai, A., & Kandaswamy, U. (2019). *Intelligent Spectrum Handovers in Cognitive Radio Networks*. Springer Nature Switzerland AG. doi:10.1007/978-3-030-15416-5

Harlow, B. (2003). The Scramble for Africa. In B. Harlow & M. Carter (Eds.), Archives of Empire: Volume 2. The Scramble for Africa (pp. 1–9). Duke University Press.

Hawthorne, R. (2018). The effects of lower mobile termination rates in South Africa. *Telecommunications Policy*, *42*(5), 374–385. doi:10.1016/j.telpol.2018.02.007

Hazlewood, A. (1965). The Territorial Incidence of the East African Common Services1. *Bulletin of the Oxford University Institute of Economics & Statistics*, *27*(3), 161–176. doi:10.1111/j.1468-0084.1965.mp27003001.x

Healy, P. (1992). The Effect of Changes in Corporate Control of Firms Performance. In T. A. Kochan & M. Useem (Eds.), *Transforming Organizations* (pp. 61–79). Oxford University Press. doi:10.1093/oso/9780195065046.003.0005

Hoffmann-La Roche v Commission, [1979] European Court of Justice, Case 85/76. (European Court of Justice).

Hovenkamp, H. (2016). *Federal Antitrust Policy: The Law of Competition and Its Practice* (5th ed.). West Group.

The Citizen. (2019). *How telecoms can boost contribution to the economy. The Citizen*. https://www.thecitizen.co.tz/news/1840340-5031780-format-xhtml-xwxxg8/index.html

Hunt, S. D., & Morgan, R. M. (1995). The Comparative Advantage Theory of Competition. *Journal of Marketing*, *59*(2), 1–15. doi:10.1177/002224299505900201

Hunter, E. (2015). *Political Thought and the Public Sphere in Tanzania*. Cambridge University Press. doi:10.1017/CBO9781316104620

Iliffe, J. (1979). In A Modern History of Tanganyika (African Studies, pp. I-Vi). Cambridge: Cambridge University Press.

Clark, J. (1925). What is Competition? *The University Journal of Business, 3*(3), 217–240. JSTOR.

Jones, A. (2011). *Identifying an Unlawful Margin Squeeze: The Recent Judgments of the Court of Justice in Deutsche Telekom and TeliaSonera. Cambridge Yearbook of European Legal Studies, 13, 161–193*. Cambridge Core. doi:10.5235/152888712801752942

Jones, A., Sufrin, B., & Dunne, N. (2019). *EU Competition Law: Text, Cases and Materials* (7th ed.). Oxford University Press.

Kauzya, J.-M. (2011). Comparative Perspectives of the Challenges and Prospects of the Civil Services Reforms in Kenya, Tanzania and Uganda. In A. Massey (Ed.), *International Handbook on Civil Service Systems* (pp. 178–224). Edward Elgar Publishing. doi:10.4337/9781781001080.00015

Kira, B., Sinha, V., & Srinivasan, S. (2021). Regulating digital ecosystems: Bridging the gap between competition policy and data protection. *Industrial and Corporate Change*, *30*(5), 1337–1360. doi:10.1093/icc/dtab053

Levenstein, M. C., & Suslow, V. Y. (2015). Cartels and Collusion: Economic Theory and Experimental Economics. In R. D. Blair & D. D. Sokol (Eds.), *The Oxford Handbook of international antitrust economics* (pp. 442–463). Oxford University Press. doi:10.1093/oxfordhb/9780199388592.013.0018

Levin, H. J. (2013). *The Invisible Resource: Use and Regulation of the Radio Spectrum*. Routledge. doi:10.4324/9781315064574

Lorenz, M. (2013). *An Introduction to EU Competition Law*. Cambridge University Press. doi:10.1017/CBO9781139087452

Manyele, A., & Moyo, D. (2019). Impacts of the Tanzanian 2013—2017 Glide Path Implementation Phase on Telecom Voice Call Pricing. *International Journal of Scientific and Engineering Research*, *10*(6), 1–5.

Mawenya, A. (1997). Regulating the Communications Sector in Tanzania: Experiences and Lessons. In M. Mwandosya, G. Mbowe, & P. Young (Eds.), *Competition policy and utility regulation* (pp. 111–124). Centre for Energy, Environment, Science and Technology.

McNulty, P. J. (1968). Economic Theory and the Meaning of Competition. *The Quarterly Journal of Economics*, *82*(4), 639. doi:10.2307/1879604

Mfungahema, R. (2006, October 3). *Policy and Regulatory Approach on The Next Generation Networks: The Case of Tanzania*. ITU-Regional Workshop on the Next Generation Networks (NGN), Markham Suite Hotel, Dar es Salaam. https://www.itu.int/ITU-T/worksem/ngn/200610/presentations/npr-p2.pdf

Michelin, V. (1983). *Commission, [1983] European Court of Justice, Case 322/81*. European Court of Justice.

Ministry of Transportation. (1997). *National Telecommunications Policy*. Government Printers.

Ministry of Works, Transportation and Communications. (2016). *National ICT Policy*. Ministry of Works, Transportation and Communications.

Monti, G. (2007). *EC competition law*. Cambridge University Press. doi:10.1017/CBO9780511805523

Mothobi, O. (2017). The Impact of Telecommunication Regulatory Policy on Mobile Retail Price in Sub-Saharan African Countries. *ERSA Working Paper 662*.

Mpapalika, J. (2014, February 11). A Market Led Approach to Digital Dividend Review for Financing Digital Broadcasting Migration. *9th Annual Digital Switchover Forum Africa*. 9th Annual Digital Switchover Forum Africa, Arusha, Tanzania.

Nikolinakos, N. T. (2006). *EU Competition Law and Regulation in the Converging Telecommunications, Media and IT Sectors*. Kluwer Law International B.V.

Nyerere, J. K. (1977). *The Arusha Declaration Ten Years After*. Government Printer.

OECD. (2014). *OECD Review of Telecommunication Policy and Regulation in Colombia*. OECD Publishing.

OECD. (2021). *Ex-Ante Regulation and Competition in Digital Markets – Note by BEUC*. OECD Publishing. https://one.oecd.org/document/DAF/COMP/WD(2021)66/en/pdf

Orbach, B., & Avraham, R. (2015). Squeezing Claims: Refusal to Deal, Essential Facilities, and Price Squeezes. In R. D. Blair & D. D. Sokol (Eds.), *The Oxford Handbook of international antitrust economics* (pp. 120–131). Oxford University Press. doi:10.1093/oxfordhb/9780199388592.013.0006

Pandit, S., & Singh, G. (2017). Spectrum Sharing in Cognitive Radio Networks: Medium Access Control Protocol Based Approach. Springer International Publishing Imprint: Springer. doi:10.1007/978-3-319-53147-2

Peeperkorn, L. (2009). Price Discrimination and Exploitation. In B. E. Hawk (Ed.), *International Antitrust Law & Policy: Fordham Competition Law 2008* (pp. 611–634). Juris Publishing, Inc.

Prasad, R., Sridhar, V., & Bunel, A. (2016). An Institutional Analysis of Spectrum Management in India. *Journal of Information Policy, 6*, 252–293. doi:10.5325/jinfopoli.6.2016.0252

Raitt, G. (2019). *The Metaphysics of Market Power: The Zero-sum Competition and Market Manipulation Approach*. Bloomsbury Publishing. doi:10.5040/9781509928101

Ritter, L., & Braun, W. D. (2005). *European Competition Law: A Practitioner's Guide*. Kluwer Law International B.V.

Robb, G., Paelo, A., & UNU-WIDER. (2020). *Competitive dynamics of telecommunications markets in South Africa, Tanzania, Zambia, and Zimbabw*. UNU-WIDER. doi:10.35188/UNU-WIDER/2020/840-5

Rwanda Utilities Regulatory Authorities. (2022). *Annual Report 2021-2022*. RURA. https://rura.rw/fileadmin/Documents/docs/report/Annual_Report_for_2021-2022.pdf

Schütze, R. (2018). *European Union Law*. Cambridge University Press. doi:10.1017/9781108555913

Schweitzer, H. (2022). A European Market Investigation: Institutional Setup and Procedural Design. In M. Motta, M. Peitz, & H. Schweitzer (Eds.), *Market investigations: A new competition tool for Europe?* (pp. 90–163). Cambridge University Press. doi:10.1017/9781009072007.003

Sims, M., Youell, T., & Womersley, R. (2016). *Understanding Spectrum Liberalisation*. CRC Press.

Smith, A. (1971). *History of the East African Posts and Telecommunications Administration 1837 to 1967* [Doctor of Philosophy, University of Nairobi]. http://erepository.uonbi.ac.ke/handle/11295/26809

Stigler, G. J. (1972). Economic competition and political competition. *Public Choice*, *13*(1), 91–106. doi:10.1007/BF01718854

Tanga Fresh v FCC, Appeal No 5 of 2014, Fair Competition Tribunal.

Tanzania Telecoms Market Report. (2023). Tanzania Telecoms. https://www.budde.com.au/Research/Tanzania-Telecoms-Mobile-and-Broadband-Statistics-and Analyses#:~:text=Tanzania%27s%20mobile%20market%20enjoys%20effective,has%20struggled%20to%20gain%20subscribers

TCRA. (2010a). *Telecommunications Statistics from 2000 to 2010*. TCRA.

TCRA. (2010b). *Quarterly Telecom Statistics*. TCRA.

TCRA. (2011). 50 Years of Communications in Tanzania. *The Regulator*, 5–10.

TCRA. (2023). *Communications Statistics: Quarter Ending 30th June 2023*. TCRA. https://www.tcra.go.tz/uploads/text-editor/files/Communication%20Statistics%20for%20Q4%202023_1689602781.pdf

Temu, G. (2021). *Regulation and Enforcement of Competition Law in Tanzania's Telecommunications Sector: Law, Institutional Design and Practice* [PhD Thesis, Bayreuth; Application/pdf]. https://epub.uni-bayreuth.de/id/eprint/5921

The Editor. (2012, December 30). *Why the first EA Community collapsed*. Daily Monitor. https://www.monitor.co.ug/OpEd/Letters/Why-the-first-EA-Community-collapsed-/806314-1653726-arwsdy/index.html

The United Nations General Assembly. (2015). *Resolution adopted by the General Assembly on 25 September 2015, A/RES/70/1*. The United Nations. https://documents-dds-ny.un.org/doc/UNDOC/GEN/N15/291/89/PDF/N1529189.pdf?OpenElement

The United Republic of Tanzania (URT), Ministry of Finance and Planning, Tanzania National Bureau of Statistics and President's Office - Finance and Planning, Office of the Chief Government Statistician, Zanzibar. (2022). *The 2022 Population and Housing Census: Administrative Units Population Distribution Report*. National Bureau of Statistics.

The World Bank in Tanzania. (2023). *Overview*. World Bank. https://www.worldbank.org/en/country/tanzania/overview

Train, K. (1991). *Optimal regulation: The economic theory of natural monopoly*. MIT Press.

Turner, D. F. (1965). Conglomerate Mergers and Section 7 of the Clayton Act. *Harvard Law Review*, *78*(7), 1313–1395. doi:10.2307/1338906

Uganda Communications Commission. (2022). *Market Performance Report 4Q22*. Uganda Communications Commission. https://www.ucc.co.ug/wp-content/uploads/2023/06/UCC-4Q22-Market-Performance-Report-compressed.pdf

United Nations Department of Social and Economic Affairs. (2023). SDGs. https://sdgs.un.org/goals/goal9

Vickers, J. (1995). Concepts of Competition. [JSTOR.]. *Oxford Economic Papers*, *47*(1), 1–23. doi:10.1093/oxfordjournals.oep.a042155

Vodacom Tanzania Limited v Tanzania Communications Regulatory Authority & Six Telecommunications Company Limited, Fair Competition Tribunal, Appeal No 2/2007.

Vodacom Tanzania PLC v Tanzania Communications Regulatory Authority, Fair Competition Tribunal, Appeal No 8/2018.

Walden, I. (2018). Access and Interconnection. In I. Walden (Ed.), *Telecommunications Law and Regulation* (5th ed., pp. 435–490). Oxford University Press. doi:10.1093/oso/9780198807414.003.0011

Whish, R., & Bailey, D. (2012). *Competition law* (7th ed.). Oxford University Press.

White, L. (2015). Monopoly and Dominant Firms: Antitrust Economics and Policy Approaches. In R. D. Blair & D. D. Sokol (Eds.), *The Oxford Handbook of International Antitrust Economics* (Vol. 1, pp. 313–344). Oxford University Press.

Winkler, K., & Baumgarten, G. (2009). The Framework for Network Access and Interconnection. In C. Koenig (Ed.), *EC competition and telecommunications law* (2nd ed., pp. 421–469). Wolters Kluwer Law & Business.

Winn, J. K., & de Koker, L. (2013). Introduction to Mobile Money in Developing Countries: Financial Inclusion and Financial Integrity Conference Special Issue. *Washington Journal of Law. Technology & Arts*, *8*(3), 155–163.

World Bank. (2023). *World Bank Data*. World Bank. https://data.worldbank.org/indicator/IT.CEL.SETS.P2?locations=BI

Wurmnest, W. (2011). Predatory Pricing: From Price/Cost Comparisons to Post-Chicago Thinking. In J. Basedow & W. Wurmnest (Eds.), Structure and effects in EU competition law: Studies on exclusionary conduct and state aid. Kluwer Law International; Sold and distributed in North, Central, and South America by Aspen Publishers.

Yi, C., & Cai, J. (2016). *Market-Driven Spectrum Sharing in Cognitive Radio*. Springer. doi:10.1007/978-3-319-29691-3

KEY TERMS AND DEFINITIONS

Abuse of Dominance: deliberate practices of a dominant firm in a market that exploit or misuse its market power to the detriment of competition, consumers, and other market participants. Acts of abuse of dominance seek to drive competitors out of the market and may include practices such as price discrimination, margin squeezing, cross subsidization, predatory prices, exploitative prices and tying and bundling, among others.

Access to Telecommunications: the availability and affordability of communication services that allow individuals and other entities to communicate with one another. On a broader scale, access would imply the availability of communication infrastructure, the affordability of communications services, and a supportive legislative framework. services to allow individuals and other entities to communicate with each other.

Competition Law: set of rules and regulations that promote fair competition and prevent anticompetitive practices in the marketplace. Key aspects of competition law include regulation of anticompetition practices, abuse of dominance and mergers and acquisitions.

Mergers and Acquisitions: types of corporate reorganization in which two or more entities merge to form one entity. Mergers occur when two or more entities agree to combine their assets and liabilities in order to form a new entity. Acquisitions, on the other hand, entail one entity acquiring the assets and liabilities of another.

Restrictive Trade Practices: practices by firms at the marketplace which seeks to restrict or distort competition. Price fixing, market allocation, collusive tendering, exclusive dealing, refusal to deal and misleading advertisements are some of restrictive trade practices.

Sustainable Development: a development concept that tries to achieve balanced economic development by ensuring that current generations' social and economic needs are addressed without jeopardizing those of the future generations. Sustainable development includes, among other things, elements such as responsible business conduct, economic inclusiveness, resource efficiency, strategic investment in technology, quality and improved social services, and environmental conservation.

Telecommunication Law: a set of rules and regulations that govern the provision of telecommunications. This would include, among other aspects, licensing, frequency spectrum, access, competition, quality of service, and consumer protection.

Telecommunications: a term used to describe the transmission of information over long distances using various methods. In the context of this study, telecommunications include voice and data transmission over various information and communications technology channels.

Chapter 3
Promoting Sustainable Development in Malaysia:
Exploring the Interplay Between Competition Law and Sustainable Development Goals

Adlan Abdul Razak
Universiti Teknologi MARA, Malaysia

ABSTRACT

This chapter delves into the intricate interplay between competition law and sustainable development goals (SDGs), uncovering their interplay by unravelling how competition law's principles of fair play, economic efficiency, consumer protection, and prevention of market power abuse align seamlessly with multiple SDGs in Malaysia. It investigates the similarities between the objectives of competition law in Malaysia and the UN SDGs. It dissects how competition law fosters economic growth, innovation, and access to essential goods and services, aligning with SDGs that seek to eradicate poverty, enhance industry, promote inclusive societies, and ensure responsible consumption. The chapter will show the symbiotic relationship between competition law and SDGs, where principles of fair competition align harmoniously with broader development goals. Thus, the enforcement of competition law just like the pursuit of the SDGs should be seen as a dynamic force for societal progress, economic equity, and global betterment.

INTRODUCTION

The underlying principle of competition is to encourage enterprises to be more competitive, thus resulting in businesses becoming more efficient, innovative, and responsive to consumer needs and demands. A competition policy addresses the concern that an enterprise or enterprises with market power can harm consumer welfare by, for example, reducing output, raising prices arbitrarily, producing low-quality products and services in the market, discouraging innovations and limiting choices available to the consumers

DOI: 10.4018/979-8-3693-0390-0.ch003

Copyright © 2024, IGI Global. Copying or distributing in print or electronic forms without written permission of IGI Global is prohibited.

(Whish & Bailey, 2021). An uncompetitive market leads to wastage of resources while a competitive market utilises resources efficiently. A market that is fully utilised is beneficial to the economy. (Whish & Bailey, 2021). The preamble of the Competition Act 2010 in Malaysia acknowledges that "the process of competition encourages efficiency, innovation and entrepreneurship, which promotes competitive prices, improvement in the quality of products and services and wider choices for consumers.

Economists generally consider the welfare of consumers and producers through the benefits they receive from consuming or producing goods and services (Van den Berg & Camesasca, 2001). It also indicates that consumers can switch to other enterprises if they are not happy with the products or services being sold by one enterprise with relative ease (Cooter & Ulen, 2008). The abundance of choices for consumers pushed enterprises to be better and to improve themselves by becoming more efficient. Further, these enterprises are subject to competitive restraints, denying them the market power to profitably raise prices at the expense of consumers, restrict their outputs or limit the choices available to consumers (Cooter & Ulen, 2008). These efficiencies are important in the improvement and growth of the economy (Cooter & Ulen, 2008). As scarce resources will be allocated efficiently, the country will prosper through better management of its economic resources (Cooter & Ulen, 2008). It is the aim of competition policy and law, therefore, to ensure that competition in the marketplace has a beneficial impact on economic efficiency, growth, development and promotes and protects consumer welfare (Whish & Bailey, 2021).

Whereas, the United Nations Sustainable Development Goals (SDGs) stand as a visionary roadmap, conceived in 2015 through the 2030 Agenda for Sustainable Development, to confront the intricate challenges confronting humanity and the planet. Comprising 17 interlinked goals, these objectives encapsulate the collective dedication of nations to construct a realm that is more impartial, just, and sustainable (SDG Knowledge Platform, 2023). Every SDG addresses a distinct facet of global advancement, enshrining economic, social, and environmental dimensions. The main aim of SDGs is to meet the needs of the present without compromising the ability of future generations to meet their own needs (Report of the World Commission on Environment and Development: Our Common Future, 1987).

The SDGs were born from a recognition that issues such as poverty, inequality, climate change, and environmental degradation transcend borders and necessitate a collaborative global response (SDG Knowledge Platform, 2023). The goals span a spectrum of imperatives: from eradicating poverty and hunger (SDG 1 and 2), ensuring quality education and gender equality (SDG 4 and 5), to promoting decent work and responsible consumption (SDG 8 and 12), and combating climate change and preserving ecosystems (SDG 13, 14, and 15). Moreover, they embody a commitment to strong institutions and global partnerships (SDG 16 and 17) that can galvanize concerted action (SDG Knowledge Platform, 2023).

The 2030 Agenda, underpinned by the SDGs, underscores the imperative of an integrated approach to development that respects the interdependence of economic, social, and environmental dimensions (SDG Knowledge Platform, 2023). Through this holistic lens, the SDGs not only address the immediate challenges but also acknowledge their systemic roots. By fostering cross-sectoral collaboration and envisioning a world where no one is left behind, the SDGs epitomize a harmonized endeavour to build a sustainable and inclusive global society (SDG Knowledge Platform, 2023). The SDGs symbolise a comprehensive response to the complexities that shape our world. By delineating a transformative trajectory encompassing all dimensions of development, they underline the mutual responsibility of nations and individuals (SDG Knowledge Platform, 2023). As we strive toward 2030, the SDGs stand as a testament to the capacity for collective action and a beacon guiding us toward a future that is not only more equitable but also sustainable for generations to come.

In this chapter, the focus of the discussion will be on the interplay between competition law objectives and the objectives advocated by the United Nations Sustainable Development Goals (SDGs). We will begin by looking at the impetus of competition law in Malaysia and the objectives that push for the implementation of competition law in Malaysia. Readers will find that the introduction of competition law in Malaysia was guided by the desire of Malaysia to be competitive and attractive as investments destination. Unlike in other countries such as Indonesia or Singapore, which has to introduce competition law either by the demand of the International Monetary Fund (IMF) or as part of their commitment under a bilateral trade agreement, Malaysia was cautious and embraced the ideal of competition law voluntarily. It understands the need for competitive boost for the development of Malaysia's economy to attract foreign direct investment and to ensure efficiency in the use of economic resources in Malaysia. Malaysia wants its economic development to be sustainable and efficient. Thus, when UN SDGs were later introduced, Malaysia finds that there are many similarities in the aim of SDGs and the aim of competition law, hence, it was able to ensure seamless application of UN SDGs in the application of its competition law. Throughout the chapter, readers will find that there are a lot of similarities in the pursuit of competition law objectives and the objectives of SDGs. Both put the interest of consumer welfare as their central objectives to achieve sustainable development. Nonetheless, there is a strong interplay between the SDGs objectives and the objectives of competition law in Malaysia that allows the adoption of UN SDGs objectives much easier in Malaysia. However, due to space constraint, only specific SDGs objectives will be discussed in this chapter.

THE IMPETUS FOR THE INTRODUCTION OF A COMPREHENSIVE COMPETITION LAW IN MALAYSIA

As a member of the World Trade Organisation (WTO), Malaysia becomes aware of the competition issues when it was brought up in the 1996 Singapore Ministerial Conference. Working groups compromising of WTO members were established to look into the relationship between trade and competition policies (UNDERSTANDING THE WTO: CROSS-CUTTING AND NEW ISSUES, n.d.). The Ministerial Conference also recognised the work underway in the UN Conference on Trade and Development (UNCTAD) and other international organisations in promoting competition laws and policies to WTO members (Singapore Ministerial Declaration, 1996). The working groups established, were to cooperate with these organisations to make best use of available resources and to ensure that development issues are fully taken into account (Singapore Ministerial Declaration, 1996). A Working Group on the Interaction between Trade and Competition Policy (WGTCP) was established under the Doha Ministerial Declaration (2001) (Interaction between Trade and Competition Policy, n.d.), the study work within the Working Group was focusing on the clarification of:

- core principles, including transparency, non-discrimination and procedural fairness
- provisions on hardcore cartels;
- modalities for voluntary cooperation; and
- support for progressive reinforcement of competition institutions in developing countries through capacity building.

Unfortunately, in 2004, it was decided that the interaction between trade and competition policy would no longer form part of the Work Programme set out in the Doha Ministerial Declaration and therefore, no work towards negotiations on this issue will take place within the WTO during the Doha Round (Interaction between Trade and Competition Policy, n.d.).Nonetheless, the experience and the exposure that Malaysia gained from the working group have helped shape the direction of competition policies in Malaysia (Ahmad, 2013).

Malaysia also realised, from the many encounters that it has had with Free Trade Agreements (FTA) negotiations, competition policies and laws continue to become a subject of negotiations (Ahmad, 2013). Concerns were often raised on the status of Government Link Companies (GLCs) and Small and Medium Enterprises (SMEs) in trade negotiations (Researcher's observation of negotiations of ASEAN Australia New Zealand Free Trade Agreement (FTA), Malaysia-Australia FTA, Malaysia-EU FTA and Malaysia -US FTA, 2007-2009). In the negotiations for the US- Malaysia FTA, for example, the American Chambers of Commerce in Malaysia (AMCHAM), urged the government to introduce a competition law that provides the same treatment for local and international companies and an end to providing an alleged unfair advantage to GLCs (Commerce., 2006). AMCHAM also mooted the idea that good competition laws and policies would be welcome by international businesses and would attract more Foreign Direct Investments into Malaysia (Commerce., 2006).

At the same time, Malaysia was also worried that local businesses could be exposed to abuses of market powers by larger multinationals to the detriment of local businesses including GLCs. In 2003, Malaysia signed the Declaration of the ASEAN (Bali) Concord II, which aimed to integrate the ASEAN market economy through the establishment of the ASEAN Economic Community (AEC) (Rahman & Ahamat, 2021). An AEC Blueprint was adopted, and one of the key characteristics of the AEC is the establishment of a "highly competitive" ASEAN economic regime. Under the Blueprints, all ASEAN Member States (AMS) are required to have their own competition laws and policies by 2015 (DECLARATION ON THE ASEAN ECONOMIC COMMUNITY BLUEPRINT, 2003).

Thus, it is not a surprise to note that Malaysia has been toying with the idea of competition law since the 8th Malaysia Plan (Malaysia country profile, n.d.). Nevertheless, the economic crisis of 1997 delayed the introduction of the law and policies to a much later date. However, the Government realised that to maintain Malaysia's competitiveness and attractiveness as an investment destination, competition laws and policies are something that cannot be ignored (Fair Trade Practices Policy, n.d.). Under the 8th Malaysia Plan, the Ministry of Domestic Trade and Consumer Affairs is tasked with the formulation of competition policy in Malaysia (Malaysia country profile, n.d.).

Malaysia believes that competition policy is necessary to promote growth and efficiency by eliminating or minimising distortion in competition and by preventing and deterring anti-competitive practices through effective enforcement of competition law. On 13 January 2004, at a New Economic Action Council Forum, then Prime Minister Abdullah advised the policymakers to be careful in drafting competition law and policies so as not to place ourselves in danger by adopting foreign competition law and policies wholly, without taking into account local conditions (Malaysia country profile, n.d.).

When Malaysia was contemplating the introduction of its competition law and policy, the ASEAN Member States (AMS) came out with an ambitious plan to strengthen the regional integration known as the ASEAN Economic Community (AEC) (DECLARATION ON THE ASEAN ECONOMIC COMMUNITY BLUEPRINT, 2003). The regional economic integration agenda would offer opportunities in the form of a huge market of US$2.6 trillion and over 622 million people. In 2014, AEC was collectively the third-largest economy in Asia and the seventh largest in the world (ASEAN Economic Community,

2015). For ASEAN leaders, they believe that competition laws and policies are important tools to attract investment into ASEAN and make the region more competitive. Thus, ASEAN, together with its trading partners, actively promotes the adoption of competition laws and policies among its members (ASEAN Experts Group on Competition (AEGC), n.d.).

Among the key objectives of the AEC 2008 Blueprint is to promote a competitive economic region (ASEAN Economic Community, 2015). This is to be achieved by a variety of indicators, among which is the promotion of competition policy. The main objective of the competition policy under the AEC 2008 Blueprint is to foster a culture of fair competition. (ASEAN Economic Community, 2015) At the time of the introduction of the Blueprint, only four AMS had their competition laws and competition regulatory agencies (ASEAN Economic Community, 2015). Malaysia, at that time, did not have a central competition law nor a central competition agency.

While the AEC may be the impetus for the introduction of competition law in Malaysia, according to Mrs. Dhaniah Ahmad (Ahmad, 2013), Malaysia's Competition Act has its roots in one of the model laws that was being promoted by the United Nations Conference on Trade and Development (UNCTAD). The model law provides the guidelines for a good and working competition law. It covers the area of anti-competitive agreements, abuse of dominant positions and merger control (Ahmad, 2013). It gives an idea of the types of laws that Malaysia should have.

According to UNCTAD, developing economies are vulnerable to anti-competitive practices (Why competition and consumer protection matter, n.d.). It is difficult for companies in developing economies to enter the markets due to poor business infrastructure, as well as complex regulatory and licensing regimes (Qaqaya & Lipimile, 2008). As such, price increases in markets involving output-restricting or price-fixing cartels and dominant firms abusing their power are prevalent in such economies. In this situation, consumers suffer directly from the anti-competitive market. Competition policy aims to overcome this anti-competitive environment by applying a set of market rules that guarantees a level playing field for all businesses (Qaqaya & Lipimile, 2008). UNCTAD further acknowledges that the successful implementation of competition policy results in the elimination of anti-competitive regulation and unnecessary barriers to competition imposed by government policies. Anti-competitive business practices are also discouraged by effective enforcement of competition rules (Qaqaya & Lipimile, 2008). Competition, on the other hand, creates incentives for innovation, increases efficiencies and improves the quality of goods and services provided. Competition enhances consumer welfare through wider choices for consumers and at competitive prices (Why competition and consumer protection matter, n.d.).

To achieve this, UNCTAD promotes its agenda through THREE key functions (Why competition and consumer protection matter, n.d.). The first one is through forums for intergovernmental deliberations, second, by undertaking research, policy analysis and data collection to inform these forums, and finally via technical assistance provided for developing countries. According to Mrs Dhaniah, it was through these forums that Malaysia was influenced to formulate a Fair Trade Policy and Law to promote growth and encourage competition in its economies. Since Malaysia has been following UNCTAD's proposal rigorously, it became easier to adopt when the UNSDGs were introduced later.

Malaysia is also mindful that a perfectly competitive market requires many players in the market, with each seller having only a small market share selling homogeneous products. There should be no barriers to enter or exit the market and the sellers and buyers are aware of the actions of one another (Cooter & Ulen, 2008). A perfectly competitive market would enable both allocative and productive efficiency and thus, maximise social welfare (Cooter & Ulen, 2008). However, in the real world in Malaysia, this would be far from the truth especially since there are not many players in the market and the government is heavily involved in the market via government-linked companies (GLCs) (Menon, 2017).

The word "competition" is not defined in the Malaysian Competition Act. The Oxford online dictionary defines competition as, "*The action of endeavouring to gain what another endeavours to gain at the same time*" (Competition, n.d.). Competition in the commercial world means striving to gain the business of people in the marketplace. Competition is essential because it leads to innovation. Companies that innovate win customers and grow financially. And consumers benefit from a wider and more innovative range of products, leading to more choices for all (MyCC, 2011). Since firms are competing for the customs of people, customers will be provided with greater choices of products and services and at a higher quality. The competition will result in firms becoming more efficient and innovative. They will make use of resources more efficiently. People will benefit from greater choices of products and at lower prices. Competitive markets are, therefore, desirable for the benefits that they bring. Markets that are not competitive lead to wastages of resources and are not being efficient (MyCC, 2011). Consumers pay a higher price for inferior products because they do not have choices. Businesses have no incentives to be efficient as they are aware that customers have no choice apart from getting the products from them. This can result in the productivity of nations being affected. The nation becomes less competitive to compete in the global arena and will eventually lose out to more competitive nations. Wealth will not grow and in the end, the people's standard of living will be affected (MyCC, 2011).

Competition policy seeks to create and maintain a market environment that enhances competitive processes. According to Viscusi (Viscusi & Vernon, 2005), the purpose of competition law is to make the market work better by preserving competition and competition increases the welfare of consumers. The market works better in perfect competition where there is a large number of sellers and buyers selling the same homogenous product (Viscusi & Vernon, 2005). Nonetheless, in the real world, it is not possible to achieve perfect competition all the time. There are many other types of market, including perfect competition; monopoly, where there are a single or very few sellers and many buyers and oligopoly; a state of limited competition, in which a market is shared by a small number of producers or sellers (Oxford Languages and Google, n.d.). The types of markets explain the structure of an enterprise in the market. Competition law does not limit the types of structure in the market, it only seeks to regulate the conduct of the enterprise in the market (Razak, 2019). Since the aim of competition law is to preserve competition, the conduct of an enterprise that affect competition will be punished (Viscusi & Vernon, 2005).

Competitions bring about lower prices, a variety of choices, better quality products and greater efficiency than would be obtained by a monopolistic market. In perfect competition, the market can allocate societal resources towards those markets where they can best provide value to consumers (Elhauge & Geradin, 2011). Perfect competition should be the benchmark that should help identify the sort of measures necessary to ensure the efficient allocation of resources (Elhauge & Geradin, 2011). Social welfare is also maximised in conditions of perfect competition (Bishop & Walker, 2010). It is argued that competitive markets lead to a higher level of consumer welfare in both the short run and in the long run than markets that are not competitive, and where markets are competitive, regulatory intervention is not required and could even be detrimental (Bishop & Walker, 2010). Nevertheless, in a monopolistic market, regulatory interventions become necessary to protect the interests of the consumers. It is the loss to efficiency and welfare that justifies state intervention through competition law. While both perfectly competitive markets and true monopolies are rarely observed in reality, the general hypothesis based on the stylised model is that competition tends to increase economic welfare and that striving towards a goal of "workable competition" can enhance economic welfare (Khoo & Sng, 2019). The development of competition law in Malaysia seems to enhance the demand for sustainable development goals.

OBJECTIVES OF COMPETITION LAW IN MALAYSIA

In Malaysia, the objective of the Competition Act is laid down in the preamble of the Act. It clearly states that the objective of the Act is to promote economic development by promoting and protecting the process of competition, thereby protecting the interests of consumers and providing for matters connected therewith. The Act recognises that competition brings out the best uses of resources and benefits the consumers. By promoting and protecting the process of competition, efficiency can be attained, productivity will increase, and this will result in greater economic development (APEC Competition Policy and Law Group, 2023). This will, in the end, improve consumer welfare through better and cheaper products and improved standard of living. A market economy that functions optimally can result in greater economic development in Malaysia (MyCC, 2011). This indicates that consumer welfare is the ultimate aim of its competition law. If businesses were engaged in anti-competitive behaviour, by, for example, engaging in cartel activities, they are effectively stealing from the consumers and harming the economy. In 2009, European Union (EU) Commissioner Kroes in her speech stated that an estimated 60 billion euros worth of consumer harms were successfully deterred by the endless pursuit of cartel activities in the European Union (Kroes, 2009).

However, if we took the experience of the EU as our guide, protecting the process of competition is akin to the concept of economic freedom in the EU (Vanberg, 2011). Competitive prices, improvement in the quality of the products and services and wider choices of goods and services for the consumers are factors that would increase consumer welfare but protecting the process of competition is the cornerstone of the ordoliberal school in the EU. It is the hallmark of the concept of economic freedom which seeks to prevent unreasonable restraint on competition (Khemani). This is also similar to the objectives of the United Nations Sustainable Development Goals (UN SDGs) number eight which is to promote sustained, inclusive and sustainable economic growth (United Nations Department of Economics and Social Affairs, n.d.).

Nonetheless, in Persatuan Insurans Am Malaysia (PIAM)'s case, the Malaysian Competition Commission (MyCC) took the view that the process of competition encourages efficiency, innovation and entrepreneurship, which promotes competitive prices, improvement in the quality of products and services and wider choices for consumers (MyCC v General Insurance Association of Malaysia (PIAM) and 22 others, 2020). There was no mention of protecting the process of competition as part of protecting the economic freedom of competitors to compete. In Labuan Ferry, the Malaysian Court of Appeal held that the object of the Competition Act is to protect the interests of consumers by prohibiting anti-competitive conduct and to regulate conduct among competitors (Labuan Ferry Corp Sdn Bhd v Chin Mui Kien (trading under the name and style of Econ Focus Enterprise) & Ors, 2018). The High Court in its judicial review of the *MAS and AirAsia's* case stated that one of the main purposes of enacting the Competition Act is to protect the interest of consumers by having competitive prices and a wider choice of products or services for consumers (MyCC v CAT, AirAsia and MAS, 2016). Again, there was no mention of economic freedom as one of the objectives pursued by Malaysia. The interpretation by the competition authorities and courts in Malaysia focussed more on consumer welfare and efficiency as the main objective of the Act in Malaysia as this will result in the greater economic development of Malaysia.

The preamble of the Act also indicates that by promoting and protecting the process of competition, efficiency can be attained, productivity will increase, and this resulted in greater economic development for Malaysia. In the end, this will improve consumer welfare through better and cheaper products and improved standard of living. It seems that the Malaysian competition law objectives are similar to the UN SDGs especially on promoting economic growth.

When tabling the Malaysian Competition Act in Parliament, the then Minister of Domestic Trade and Consumer Affairs, YB Dato Seri Ismail Sabri states that Malaysia believes that the process of competition leads to innovation as entrepreneurs compete for the customs of their customers with better and more innovative products (Malaysian Parliament Hansard, 2010). Such innovations and competition will ensure resources are fully utilised leading to greater efficiency in the economy (Malaysian Parliament Hansard, 2010). The competition will also encourage the emergence of new entrants into the market offering more choices to consumers with better quality products and services (Malaysian Parliament Hansard, 2010). As consumer welfare improves, so too will the economic development of Malaysia. Hence, the process of competition must be protected and promoted, while any anti-competitive behaviour must be penalised. The Minister also revealed that the Act was also introduced to attract foreign investment and as part of Malaysia's commitment to the ASEAN Economic Blueprint (Malaysian Parliament Hansard, 2010). Again, this shows that the Malaysian competition law objectives, despite being introduced much earlier, are in tandem with the objectives of UN SDGs.

At the time that Malaysia was about to introduce its Competition Act, multiple engagements with various parties were made to study the effect of anti-competitive behaviours on the economy. Malaysia also participated in the Intergovernmental Group of Experts on Competition Law and Policy organised by the United Nations Conference on Trade and Development (UNCTAD) in Geneva, regularly. Through such participation and literature received, Malaysia becomes more aware of the adverse effects of anti-competitive practices on the economy as well as on her population as it affects their purchasing power through increased prices (Qaqaya & Lipimile, 2008).

Thus, it is not surprising to see Malaysia embrace this idea and have it as its objective to promote and protect the process of competition. It can also be seen that Malaysia believes that the process of competition leads to innovation as entrepreneurs compete for the customs of their customers with better and more innovative products. Such innovations and competition will ensure resources are fully utilised leading to greater efficiency in the economy. The High Court in its judicial review of the *MAS and AirAsia's* case (MyCC v CAT, AirAsia and MAS, 2016) stated that one of the main purposes of enacting the Competition Act is to protect the interest of consumers by having competitive prices and a wider choice of products or services for consumers. The competition will also encourage the emergence of new entrants into the market offering more choices to consumers with better quality products and services. As consumer welfare improves, so too will the economic development of Malaysia. Hence, the process of competition must be protected and promoted, while any behaviour which is anti-competitive must be penalised (Qaqaya & Lipimile, 2008)

Competition law also stands as a cornerstone of economic development, serving as a catalyst for fostering innovation, efficiency, and fair business practices. In the context of Malaysia, a nation with a robust economy and a commitment to progress, competition law plays a pivotal role in accelerating economic growth (Rahman & Ahamat, 2021). By creating an environment that encourages healthy competition, prevents anti-competitive behaviour, and ensures a level playing field, Malaysia's implementation of effective competition law contributes significantly to its economic development objectives (MyCC, 2011).

At its core, competition law is instrumental in nurturing an environment that stimulates innovation and entrepreneurship, both of which are integral to economic growth. By preventing monopolistic practices and promoting fair competition, businesses are incentivised to continually innovate and differentiate their products and services (Tisdell, 2013). This culture of innovation, driven by the imperative of staying competitive, not only enhances the quality of offerings but also contributes to the overall technological advancement of the nation (Tisdell, 2013).

Moreover, competition law directly contributes to improving efficiency and productivity within industries (Bakhoum, 2012). Businesses operating in competitive markets are compelled to optimize their operations, reduce costs, and enhance productivity to maintain their competitiveness. This drive for efficiency has a cascading effect, leading to improved resource allocation, increased production, and heightened economic output (Bakhoum, 2012). In Malaysia, where sustainable economic growth is a paramount goal, the efficiency gains derived from competition law are pivotal for achieving long-term prosperity (Ministry of Economy, n.d.).

Malaysia's commitment to fostering a business-friendly environment that attracts both domestic and foreign investment is reinforced by the principles of competition law (MyCC, 2011). Effective competition regulations signal to investors that the nation values transparency, fairness, and the rule of law in business dealings (Malaysian Parliament Hansard, 2010). This confidence in the integrity of the market fosters increased investment inflows, which in turn catalyse economic growth and contribute to job creation (Malaysian Parliament Hansard, 2010). Moreover, the benefits of competition law extend beyond established businesses to encourage market entry and expansion, particularly among Small and Medium Enterprises (SMEs) (Deyo, 2013). These enterprises play a pivotal role in economic growth through job creation and the infusion of innovation (Deyo, 2013). It is submitted that, by preventing anti-competitive behaviour and ensuring a level playing field, competition law paves the way for SMEs to flourish, enhancing economic diversification and resilience.

A significant facet of competition law's impact on economic growth lies in its ability to stimulate consumer welfare. By preventing practices such as price-fixing and market manipulation, competition law safeguards consumers' interests, ensuring that they have access to quality products at competitive prices (Whish & Bailey, 2021). This, in turn, stimulates consumer spending, driving demand for goods and services and boosting economic activity. Furthermore, competition law's influence on trade and exports cannot be overstated. A competitive marketplace encourages businesses to produce high-quality goods and services that can compete on a global stage. Businesses have no choice but to improve themselves if they want to stay relevant. As local businesses thrive and excel, they become attractive players in international markets, boosting exports and contributing to foreign exchange earnings—a critical factor for sustainable economic growth (Tisdell, 2013).

Technological advancement is a direct outcome of competitive pressures. Competition law drives businesses to adopt new technologies and best practices to maintain their competitive edge. This progressive adoption of technology enhances business efficiency, streamlines operations, and, on a macro level, contributes to Malaysia's journey toward becoming a digitally driven economy (Ramaiah, 2019).. Equally significant is the boost to consumer confidence that effective competition law provides. When consumers trust that they are getting value for their money and that businesses are competing fairly, they are more inclined to spend, thereby contributing to economic growth through increased consumption. This can also be seen in the preamble of Competition Act 2010 in Malaysia, where it clearly states that effective competition will lead to competitive pricing to the benefit of the consumers (Preamble, Competition Act 2010). Competitive markets are characterized by the efficient allocation of resources, where supply and demand interact naturally to determine prices. This economic equilibrium ensures that goods and services are priced in accordance with their actual value and the costs of production. As a result, businesses are compelled to optimize their operations to remain competitive, which often translates to reduced production costs. These lower costs, driven by the dynamics of competition, directly influence the affordability of goods and services (Whish & Bailey, 2021). From essential commodities to healthcare and education, the availability of competitively priced offerings widens the horizon of accessibility for individuals who previously faced barriers due to financial constraints.

Artificial barriers, whether in the form of monopolistic practices or anti-competitive behaviour, hinder fair market competition and perpetuate inequality (Whish & Bailey, 2021). Competition law serves as a potent tool to dismantle these barriers, ensuring that businesses compete not by wielding undue influence but by offering value and quality. This principle is particularly impactful for marginalized communities and individuals with limited resources. By preventing entities from exploiting their dominance or stifling competition, competition law empowers new entrants and smaller players to enter the market and provide viable alternatives. In doing so, it fosters a diverse marketplace that offers consumers choices aligned with their needs and preferences (Bishop & Walker, 2010). This is evidence when the Malaysian government decided recently that Touch n Go should not be the only payment mechanism for use of tolled highways. Touch n Go payment system has been the only payment mechanism allowed for use on the Malaysian tolled highways, thus, resulting in the company becoming a dominant player in the payment mechanism for tolled highways, especially. Thus, the use of other payment mechanism including via credit and debit cards provide alternatives for Malaysian consumers and they do not have to purchase Touch n Go to use cashless toll booth (MyCC stands firm with the public on Touch n Go, 2023).

The ripple effects of accessible and affordable goods and services extend far beyond economic equations—they reach into the heart of poverty reduction (Fox, 2008). When necessities become affordable, individuals and families with limited means can allocate their resources more effectively, enhancing their overall quality of life (Fox, 2008). Access to nutritious food, education, healthcare, and other essential services becomes less of a burden, empowering individuals to break free from the cycle of poverty. This empowerment reverberates across generations, as improved access to education and healthcare equips future generations with the tools to create a better future. The alignment between competition law and poverty reduction is not a solo performance; it is a collaborative symphony where businesses, regulatory bodies, and civil society play their parts. Competition law sets the stage by creating the framework for fair competition, and businesses perform by competing ethically and innovatively. Regulatory bodies conduct the orchestration by ensuring compliance, and civil society becomes the audience whose choices and demands influence the direction of the melody. In the end, it is the consumers welfare that will be enhanced through competitive pricing in the market (Whish & Bailey, 2021).

It is submitted that competition law in Malaysia is an important agenda in the nation's pursuit of economic growth and prosperity. By promoting the process of competition, innovation, efficiency, and fair practices, it creates an environment where businesses flourish, consumers benefit, and investment thrives. Malaysia's commitment to implementing and enforcing competition law underscores its dedication to fostering an economic ecosystem that nurtures progress, attracts investment, and ensures the equitable distribution of benefits across society. This is evidence in the special mentioned and the higher allocation made in the recent budget that was announced by the Minister of Finance who is also the Prime Minister of Malaysia (Hansard Parliament Malaysia, 2023). As the nation strides forward, it is hope that competition law stands as a driving force in realizing Malaysia's vision of sustainable and inclusive economic growth.

THE INTERCONNECTION OF ANTI-COMPETITIVE PRACTICES WITH SUSTAINABLE DEVELOPMENT GOALS

The SDGs' 17 interconnected goals encompass a diverse range of economic, social, and environmental objectives aimed at creating a more equitable and sustainable world. Malaysia, as a nation committed to progress and inclusivity, has strategically integrated the SDGs into its development plan, aligning its priorities with the global vision for a better future (Ministry of Economy, n.d.). In this section we will focus on Malaysia's competition law and policy in achieving its SDGs' objectives. The discussion will centre around the uses of Malaysia's competition law to achieve SDGs objectives. It will look at the use of competition law as a sword and shield to achieve sustainability. Competition law can be used as a sword when measures that are harmful from a sustainability perspective are prevented/prohibited (Nowag, 2020). It can also be used as a shield which allow measures that are otherwise anti-competitive but was directed at achieving sustainability to escape liability from the Competition Act 2010 (Holmes, 2020).

The Malaysian Competition Act 2010 does allow for certain exceptions and exclusions to be made. Section 5 of the CA 2010 allows for a relief of liability if enterprises engaged in anti-competitive behaviour to achieve significant social benefits which would otherwise not be possible under the CA2010 (Nowag, 2022). In Section 3 of the CA2010, any activity conducted based on the principle of solidarity will also be excluded from the application of the Act. Section 13 of the Competition Act 2010 do provide for an exclusion of services provided for the general economic interest of the country. For example, it is possible for telecommunication company be allowed to engage in anti-competitive behaviour if they provided services of general economic to specific segment of the society which would otherwise be left out if we were to leave it to the operation of market to determine the provision of such services. Thus, the competition law in Malaysia allows and do take into considerations some of the specific factor faced by marginalised communities or any policies adopted by the government to pursue affirmative actions in Malaysia. This sword and shield approach in the application of competition law to pursue the SDGs objectives are also being used widely in the European Union, thus, it is not unique to Malaysia (Holmes, 2020, July). Nonetheless, there must be uniformity in the application of this approach to ensure consistency and certainty for the business community (Malinauskaite, 2022).

Malaysia's journey towards sustainable development begins with its commitment to eradicate poverty and achieve inclusive economic growth (SDG 1 and 8). The country's development plan centres around poverty reduction initiatives, such as cash assistance programs and skills training, ensuring that economic growth is inclusive and benefits all segments of society (Economic Planning Unit, Malaysia, 2021). The government's emphasis on decent work conditions and entrepreneurship further resonates with SDG 8, promoting not only economic growth but also equitable opportunities. Activities that were conducted to promote equitable opportunities are most likely to be shielded from the application of Competition Act 2010 under section 5 of the Act. It is submitted that helps from UNCTAD in the early development of Malaysia's competition law and policy enable it to incorporate SDGs objectives with relative ease.

In the pursuit of sustainable development, Malaysia has embraced the essence of Sustainable Development Goal 16 (SDG 16) by acknowledging the paramount importance of robust institutions (Economic Planning Unit, Malaysia, 2021). With a clear understanding of the pivotal role that strong institutions play in fostering an environment conducive to progress, Malaysia has initiated governance and institutional reforms aimed at enhancing accountability, access to justice, and effective governance. These endeavours align seamlessly with the objectives of SDG 16, which underscores the foundational role of institutions in promoting peace, justice, and inclusivity.

Recognising that institutions serve as the bedrock of a just and equitable society, Malaysia's commitment to governance and institutional reforms reflects its dedication to sustainable development. By bolstering transparency, accountability, and the rule of law, Malaysia seeks to build institutions that not only support economic growth but also safeguard the rights and well-being of its citizens (Economic Planning Unit). The establishment of the Malaysian Competition Commission (MyCC) and the Competition Appeal Tribunal (CAT) shows Malaysia's commitment to establish specific and separate institutions that deal primarily with issues of competition law. These are quasi-judicial bodies that operates independently of each other, that have specific powers to enforce the application of competition law in Malaysia (Rahman & Ahamat, 2021). These efforts are intrinsically intertwined with the goals of SDG 16, which emphasize the pivotal role of institutions in creating an environment of trust, security, and respect for human rights.

The emphasis on enhancing access to justice is a poignant example of Malaysia's alignment with SDG 16. The nation recognizes that equal access to legal remedies and a fair judicial system are integral components of a just society. By working to eliminate barriers to justice and ensuring that all individuals, regardless of their background, can access legal recourse, Malaysia epitomizes the aspirations of SDG 16, which seeks to foster institutions that provide avenues for resolving disputes and upholding human rights. The creation for an independent such as the Malaysian Competition Commission (MyCC) allows for affected parties an avenue for them to file a complaint. The complaint can even be filed via an online platform (section 15, Competition Act 2010). This allows for easy access to legal remedies and allow for the affected parties an avenue to present their case.

Efforts to establish effective governance mechanisms further underscore Malaysia's commitment to SDG 16. The nation's dedication to good governance, transparency, and citizen participation serves as a catalyst for inclusive development. In its recent exercise to amend the Competition Act 2010, the MyCC has engaged with various stakeholders to inform and solicit feedback on the changes to the Competition Act 2010 especially on the introduction of merger controls regulations (MyCC). By creating a framework that encourages public engagement and holds decision-makers accountable, Malaysia aligns with SDG 16's call for institutions that prioritize the interests of all stakeholders and promote sustainable and inclusive development.

Furthermore, Malaysia's focus on the role of institutions in promoting peace resonates with SDG 16's objectives. The nation acknowledges that institutions that uphold the principles of justice, inclusivity, and human rights contribute significantly to creating a peaceful and harmonious society. Malaysia's efforts to address societal challenges through dialogue, mediation, and conflict resolution mechanisms underscore its commitment to building institutions that facilitate peaceful coexistence and social stability. Thus, it can be said that the establishment of the MyCC and its commitment in fighting cartels and anti-competitive behaviour in the market allows for a fair competition in the market. As an agency that regulates on anti-competitive behaviour, the existence of the MyCC promotes good governance and transparency and is aligned with SDG 15's objectives.

The spirit of partnerships, embodied within Sustainable Development Goal 17 (SDG 17), serves as a guiding principle in Malaysia's approach to development. The nation recognizes that the interconnected challenges facing the world today demand collaborative efforts that transcend boundaries and sectors. By actively fostering partnerships that encompass governments, businesses, civil society, and international organizations, Malaysia contributes significantly to the realisation of all SDGs and paves the way for a more sustainable and inclusive future (Economic Planning Unit, Malaysia, 2021).Malaysia's commitment to partnerships reflects its understanding that no single entity can address the multifaceted challenges of our time in isolation. The nation acknowledges that by forging alliances, pooling resources, and sharing knowledge, it can achieve outcomes that are more impactful and far-reaching. This resonates with the essence of SDG 17, which emphasizes the significance of global cooperation and collaboration.

Governments play a pivotal role in driving sustainable development, and Malaysia's approach is no exception. The nation actively engages in partnerships with other governments, leveraging international platforms to exchange best practices, knowledge, and expertise. By participating in forums, summits, and diplomatic channels, Malaysia contributes to a collective effort to find solutions to shared challenges, such as climate change, poverty, and inequality. Malaysia's active participation in ASEAN Experts Group on Competition (AEGC), International Competition Network (ICN) and other competition authorities allows it to gain meaningful cooperation and transplantation of the enforcement of competition law, thus, ensuring that basic principles of competition law in Malaysia is in uniformity with competition laws in other countries. These similarities ensure certainties and helps businesses make their investment decisions, better.

These international organisations provide platforms for knowledge exchange, capacity building, and resource mobilization (Deyo, 2013). Malaysia's engagement with these organizations amplifies its efforts to achieve the SDGs. By participating in international dialogues and leveraging the expertise of global institutions, Malaysia enhances its ability to tackle complex challenges that transcend national borders. Furthermore, Malaysia's commitment to achieving the SDGs is reflected in its interactions with global initiatives, such as the United Nations' various agencies and programs (Rahman & Ahamat, 2021). By aligning its strategies with international frameworks, Malaysia ensures coherence in its development efforts and contributes to a harmonized global response to pressing challenges.

One prominent example of Malaysia's commitment to partnerships is its engagement in the ASEAN region. Through ASEAN collaborations, Malaysia contributes to regional stability, economic growth, and sustainable development (Economic Planning Unit, 2021). The ASEAN community embodies the spirit of partnership, where member states collectively work towards shared goals, demonstrating the power of collaborative action in addressing common challenges. Malaysia's active participation in AEGC and in the ASEAN Economic Community (AEC) ensures that its understanding of the demand for competition law and SDGs can be enhanced through such participation.

Malaysia's approach to development is firmly rooted in the spirit of partnerships, as envisaged by SDG 17 (UN Department of Economics and Social Welfare, n.d.). By acknowledging the necessity of collaboration among governments, businesses, civil society, and international organizations, Malaysia demonstrates its dedication to addressing complex global challenges. Through alliances and joint efforts, Malaysia not only advances its own development but also contributes to the realization of all SDGs, leaving an indelible mark on the journey toward a more sustainable, equitable, and prosperous world (Economic Planning Unit, 2021).

Thus, Malaysia's alignment with the SDGs underscores its commitment to sustainable and inclusive development. The integration of SDGs into its national development plan reflects the nation's dedication to addressing economic, social, and environmental challenges holistically (Economic Planning Unit, Malaysia, 2021). By pursuing poverty eradication, quality education, gender equality, environmental sustainability, and more, Malaysia paves the way for a future that is not only prosperous but also just and sustainable. As Malaysia strides towards its development goals, it embodies the essence of global collaboration for a better world.

Additionally, Malaysia's focus on developing industry clusters, protecting the process of competition, promoting innovation, and encouraging small and medium-sized enterprises (SMEs) contributes significantly to poverty eradication (Economic Planning Unit, 2021). These initiatives stimulate economic activity, enhance competitiveness, and create diverse employment avenues. By nurturing a dynamic business ecosystem, Malaysia not only generates income opportunities but also fosters social mobility, enabling individuals to break free from the grip of poverty (Economic Planning Unit, 2021). This is also the aim of the Malaysian Competition Act 2010 as stated in its preamble.

A robust competitive environment stimulates economic growth by incentivizing businesses to innovate, differentiate, and optimize their processes (Tisdell, 2013). The pursuit of competitive advantage compels companies to enhance their efficiency, lower costs, and improve the quality of their products and services (Tisdell, 2013). As businesses strive to outperform one another, economic activity intensifies, contributing to higher Gross Domestic Product (GDP) growth rates. This growth, in turn, generates income opportunities and expands the overall economic pie, lifting people out of poverty.

Innovation is a cornerstone of sustainable development. Competitive markets propel businesses to innovate, whether through technological advancements, process optimizations, or product differentiation (Tisdell, 2013). These innovations create value-added goods and services, attracting consumer demand and driving economic growth. Moreover, innovation can lead to the creation of entirely new industries, generating fresh employment opportunities and fostering the emergence of entrepreneurial ventures that empower communities to escape poverty cycles. Thus, the introduction of a comprehensive competition law in Malaysia is seen as a catalyst to achieve these aims.

Competition law ensures that businesses compete based on factors like quality, price, and innovation rather than artificial barriers. Competitive markets lead to efficient allocation of resources, resulting in lower production costs and competitive pricing (Tisdell, 2013). This translates to accessible and affordable goods and services for consumers. As necessities become more affordable, individuals with limited means can meet their essential needs, enhancing their quality of life and contributing to poverty reduction.

Competition law's focus on levelling the playing field encourages the participation of smaller businesses and new entrants in the market. By preventing dominant players from engaging in anti-competitive behaviour, competition law allows these smaller entities to flourish (Whish & Bailey, 2021). This diversification of the business landscape creates decentralized opportunities for economic participation, a crucial aspect of poverty eradication and inclusive growth.

When competition law is effectively enforced, it becomes a catalyst for unlocking economic potential, fostering innovation, and creating opportunities for individuals and communities to lift themselves out of poverty. By ensuring that markets remain competitive, open, and fair, competition law emerges as a driving force in realizing the ambitious goal of eradicating poverty through sustained economic development. In this symphony of progress, competition law stands as a conductor, orchestrating the harmonious melodies of economic growth and social upliftment that resonate with the aspirations of SDG 1.

SELECTED SDG'S OBJECTIVES AND THEIR INTERPLAY WITH COMPETITION LAW IN MALAYSIA

The pursuit of sustainable development stands as a defining challenge of our era, and the United Nations' Sustainable Development Goals (SDGs) provide a compass to navigate this complex landscape. As nations strive to realize these global aspirations, the role of competition law emerges as a dynamic force that intersects with and influences the journey towards achieving specific SDG objectives. This section delves into the interplay between selected SDG objectives and competition law within the context of Malaysia (APEC Competition Policy and Law Group, 2023).

In Malaysia, a nation with a burgeoning economy and a commitment to sustainable growth, the alignment between competition law and select SDGs takes on profound significance. This analysis focuses on the interrelationships between competition law and specific SDGs, investigating how the principles of fair competition, economic efficiency, consumer protection, and prevention of market power abuse harmonize with the objectives of eradicating poverty, fostering innovation, ensuring responsible consumption, and promoting inclusive economic growth.

Through contextual insights, this exploration unravels the intricate connections that underscore the importance of competition law in shaping the realisation of select SDG objectives in Malaysia. The analysis sheds light on how competition law, when aligned with these goals, becomes not only a regulatory framework but also a catalyst for equitable and sustainable progress in a nation brimming with potential. As there is no real-life case law that examines the interplay between the objectives of competition law and SDGs, this section examines the interplay between selected SDG objectives and the aim of competition law in Malaysia.

Innovation as a Catalyst for Progress: Sustainable Development Goal Eight

The intricate interplay between competition law and Sustainable Development Goals (SDGs) shapes a trajectory towards a more equitable and prosperous world. At the forefront of this dynamic relationship is the pivotal role of promoting competition—an endeavour intricately linked to SDG 8. With its focus on fostering sustained, inclusive, and sustainable economic growth, promoting full and productive employment, and ensuring decent work for all, SDG 8 serves as an indicator for global progress. In this section, we delve into the profound connection between promoting competition and SDG 8, highlighting how competition law becomes a powerful instrument for enhancing economic efficiency, spurring innovation, and creating abundant job opportunities—key ingredients for achieving the aims of SDG 8 (UN Department of Economics and Social Welfare, n.d.).

SDG 8 emerges as a beacon, illuminating a path towards economic prosperity and dignified employment. Aspiring for economies that thrive without leaving anyone behind, SDG 8 mirrors the aspirations of competition law. By promoting competition, competition law becomes a bridge that connects the legal and regulatory realm with the realm of economic advancement, enhancing the realization of SDG 8's multifaceted goals.

The engine of economic growth is fuelled by the efficient allocation of resources, and competition law is the catalyst that ensures this allocation is optimal and unbiased. By preventing anti-competitive practices and market manipulation, competition law fosters an environment where businesses compete on the merits of their offerings. This competition compels companies to enhance their efficiency, minimize wastage, and optimize their operations. As a result, resources are utilized more judiciously, leading to increased economic efficiency—a cornerstone of SDG 8.

Promoting competition is synonymous with fostering innovation—an inherent driver of economic advancement and societal transformation. Competitive markets compel businesses to continuously innovate, whether through technological advancements, novel business models, or creative solutions to consumer needs. Competition law, through its mandate to prevent monopolistic behaviour, ensures that innovation is not stifled by dominance. Section 10 of the Competition Act 2010 makes it illegal for dominant companies to limit or control technical or technological development. The MyCC Guidelines on Intellectual Property Rights and Competition Law further regulates on the use of technological advancements and innovation to prevent anti-competitive behaviour (HM Government Gazette). This innovation ecosystem aligns perfectly with SDG 8's vision of sustainable economic growth that thrives on the back of innovation and novel approaches.

The correlation between promoting competition and job creation is unequivocal. Competitive markets lead to a flourishing business landscape, where enterprises strive to meet consumer demands, create differentiation, and seize new opportunities. As businesses expand their operations to remain competitive, they generate a plethora of job opportunities across sectors, from manufacturing to services. These opportunities align seamlessly with SDG 8's aspiration for full and productive employment, creating a workforce that contributes to the prosperity of their economies.

Competition law serves as a counterforce against monopolies and concentrated market power, ensuring that no single entity dominates the economic landscape (Whish & Bailey, 2021). This principle not only promotes economic inclusivity but also enhances equal opportunity for businesses of all sizes to thrive. Smaller enterprises, startups, and new entrants can compete fairly, leading to diversification in industries and a broader range of offerings. It prevents the concentration of market to a dominant player and ensure economic freedom through the prevention of barriers to entry in the market. This diversification resonates with the essence of SDG 8, where economic growth is envisioned as a collective endeavour that marginalises no one.

The harmonious convergence of promoting competition and SDG 8 encapsulates the essence of sustainable development—a journey towards a more just, equitable, and prosperous world. As competition law shapes the contours of competitive markets, it simultaneously shapes the landscape of opportunity, innovation, and decent work that SDG 8 envisions. The interplay between these two forces is not a mere alignment of objectives; it's a symphony of progress where the chords of economic growth resonate with the aspirations of inclusive development. As we navigate the complex terrain of global advancement, recognizing the instrumental role of promoting competition within the framework of SDG 8 becomes a testament to the power of collaborative approaches that unite legal frameworks with the pursuit of consumer welfare.

Protecting Consumers: A Nexus of Competition Law and Sustainable Development Goal Three

In the symphony of global development, where the aspirations of nations harmonise to create a better world, the essence of protecting consumers emerges as a profound interplay between law and well-being. This dynamic alignment reverberates with the spirit of Sustainable Development Goal 3 (SDG 3), which echoes the universal desire for healthy lives and overall well-being. At the core of this harmonious relationship is competition law—a sentinel that safeguards consumers from the detrimental effects of anti-competitive practices. In this essay, we explore the intricate web that links the protection of consumers through competition law with the realization of SDG 3's noble objectives.

SDG 3 encapsulates the collective yearning for well-being—a state where health is safeguarded, diseases are prevented, and access to essential healthcare services is equitable (UN Department of Economics and Social Welfare, n.d.). Fresh from the experience that we had with the Covid-19 pandemic, the vision of SDG 3 resonates with the principles that underpin competition law, where fairness and transparency in markets ensure the well-being of consumers by curbing exploitative practices and promoting quality.

At the heart of protecting consumers lies the commitment to ensure access to products and services that do not compromise health or safety. Competition law, by preventing businesses from engaging in anti-competitive practices, acts as a bulwark against the proliferation of substandard or unsafe goods. This safeguarding ensures that consumers have access to products that meet stringent quality standards, resonating deeply with SDG 3's aspiration for healthier lives. From pharmaceuticals to consumer goods, competition law's vigilance translates into a market where safety and quality are paramount. Freer competition enables consumers to choose the best product for themselves (Whish & Bailey, 2021). It also ensures that pharmaceuticals companies are given exclusions and protections from competition law so that they can find cure for a global disease faster. Temporary exclusions from the enforcement of competition law during the time of pandemic also ensures that the national and global economy can recover faster (OECD).

Fair competition drives businesses to compete based on factors like quality and innovation rather than through price manipulation. When prices are determined by market dynamics rather than by anti-competitive behaviour, consumers benefit from competitive pricing that reflects actual value. This protection against price manipulation aligns with SDG 3's vision of affordable healthcare, where the financial burden of access to medical services is mitigated.

Consumer protection is not just about shielding consumers from harm—it's also about empowering them to make informed choices. Competition law's emphasis on transparency and fair practices ensures that consumers receive accurate information about products and services, enabling them to make decisions that align with their well-being. This empowerment resonates with SDG 3's goal of informed health choices that lead to improved health outcomes.

The tapestry of consumer protection, woven by competition law, seamlessly merges with the intricate threads of SDG 3's vision. As competition law prevents anti-competitive practices and upholds fair market dynamics, it fortifies the foundation of healthier lives and well-being. By ensuring access to safe, high-quality products and services, preventing monopolies, and empowering informed choices, competition law propels the fulfilment of SDG 3's aspirations. The harmony between these two realms is not a mere coincidence; it's a reflection of the potential that emerges when legal frameworks and sustainable development objectives converge. As we move forward in our pursuit of collective well-being, recognizing the pivotal role of consumer protection through competition law becomes an ode to the symphony of progress—an embodiment of the shared vision for healthier, more prosperous lives for all.

Preventing Market Power Abuse: Bridging Competition Law with Sustainable Development Goal Ten

In the intricate tapestry of global development, where the threads of equity and opportunity interweave, the role of preventing the abuse of market power emerges as a vital link between legal frameworks and the aspirations of Sustainable Development Goal 10 (SDG 10) (UN Department of Economics and Social Welfare, n.d.). This dynamic connection echoes the universal call for reduced inequality within and among countries—a call that resonates profoundly with the principles upheld by competition law. In this essay, we navigate the intricate path that binds the prevention of market power abuse through competition law with the pursuit of SDG 10's noble vision.

Monopolistic practices often lead to the concentration of power in the hands of a few, enabling them to dictate terms and pricing to the detriment of consumers. Competition law's mandate to prevent abuses of dominant position ensures that markets remain open and diverse, fostering competition that benefits consumers through fair pricing and better choices Whish & Bailey, 2021). Section 10 of the Competition Act 2010 lists down these potential abuses of dominant position and the consequences of engaging in such abusive behaviour. This preventive measure aligns seamlessly with SDG 3's pursuit of affordable and accessible healthcare services that cater to the needs of all, irrespective of economic standing.

SDG 10 stands as a beacon of inclusivity—an embodiment of the shared human aspiration for a world where inequality is minimized and opportunities are accessible to all, regardless of background or circumstances. This aspiration aligns closely with the principles that competition law seeks to uphold—ensuring that dominant market players do not manipulate their position to the detriment of others and that opportunities remain accessible to a diverse range of businesses. This can be seen in the Guidelines on Abuse of Dominant Position published by the MyCC which seeks to explain the definition of dominant position and the various behaviour that it deems as abusive (MyCC Guidelines).

At the heart of preventing market power abuse lies the principle of a level playing field—a cornerstone of both competition law and SDG 10. When businesses abuse their dominant position, they create barriers that hinder fair competition and elevate inequality (Whish & Bailey, 2021). Competition law's mandate to prevent such abuse ensures that the market remains open and competitive, allowing businesses of varying sizes and backgrounds to compete on a fair basis. For example, in the case of Dagang Net, the MyCC found that Dagang Net was involved in exclusive dealings arrangement, thus, preventing others from participating in the market (MyCC v Dagang Net Technologies Sdn Bhd, 2021). This levelling of the playing field resonates deeply with SDG 10's mission to bridge the gaps that perpetuate inequality.

Competition law's focus on preventing the abuse of market power directly contributes to creating an environment where equal opportunities flourish. When dominant players are restricted from using their position to exclude or harm competitors, new entrants and smaller businesses have the chance to thrive (Whish & Bailey, 2021). This diversification of the business landscape aligns seamlessly with SDG 10's goal of reducing inequality by ensuring that opportunities for economic growth are not concentrated within a select few.

Market power abuse often leads to the concentration of economic influence in the hands of a few entities (Whish & Bailey, 2021). This concentration perpetuates economic imbalances, hindering social mobility and contributing to inequality. By preventing market power abuse, competition law safeguards against this undue concentration, fostering a marketplace where economic power is distributed among a multitude of players. This decentralization directly echoes SDG 10's vision of reducing inequalities by distributing economic benefits more equitably.

SDG 10 places a special emphasis on empowering vulnerable and marginalized communities. Competition law becomes a vital instrument in this endeavour by ensuring that businesses do not exploit their dominance to the detriment of these communities. When market power abuse is prevented, vulnerable communities are shielded from exclusionary practices and have a fair chance to participate in economic activities. This empowerment aligns seamlessly with SDG 10's mission of leaving no one behind.

The convergence of preventing market power abuse and SDG 10's vision is not a coincidence—it's a testament to the intricate interplay between legal frameworks and human aspirations. As competition law safeguards against the undue concentration of power and ensures fair competition, it becomes a guardian of equitable opportunity. By promoting a diverse business landscape and preventing exclusionary practices, competition law weaves a narrative that resonates with SDG 10's pursuit of reduced inequality. This confluence of equity and regulation paints a portrait of a world where fairness and opportunity prevail, transcending boundaries and ideologies. As we navigate the complex terrain of global development, recognizing the vital role of preventing market power abuse through competition law becomes a declaration of commitment to creating a world where the promise of SDG 10 is fulfilled—a world that honours the principles of inclusivity and shared prosperity.

Promoting Economic Efficiency: A Nexus of Competition Law and Multiple SDGs

In the grand tapestry of global development, the resonance between promoting economic efficiency and Sustainable Development Goals (SDGs) forms a symphony of progress that resonates across multiple dimensions. The principles upheld by competition law are inherently intertwined with the objectives set forth by SDGs, encompassing not just economic growth but also innovation, responsible consumption, and sustainable infrastructure. This section navigates the intricate harmony that unites the promotion of economic efficiency through competition law with the aspirations of SDG 8, SDG 9, and SDG 12, underscoring how this synergy becomes a potent force for positive transformation.

Promoting economic efficiency encapsulates the notion of optimizing resource allocation, enhancing productivity, and fostering an environment where innovation thrives. This principle echoes the ideals of several SDGs, transcending individual goals to form a holistic framework for sustainable development.

SDG 9, which centres on industry, innovation, and infrastructure, resonates profoundly with the mandate of promoting economic efficiency (Whish & Bailey, 2021). Competition law, by ensuring a level playing field and preventing monopolistic practices, nurtures an environment where businesses compete based on innovation and value. It also ensures that economic resources are allocated efficiently in a competitive market (Whish & Bailey, 2021). This fosters a culture of continuous improvement and technological advancement, aligning seamlessly with SDG 9's aspiration to build resilient infrastructure, promote inclusive and sustainable industrialization, and foster innovation (UN Department of Economics and Social Welfare, n.d.).

The connection between competition law's objective of promoting economic efficiency and SDG 12, which emphasizes responsible consumption and production, is undeniable. Efficient resource allocation and production processes driven by competition law led to reduced waste and improved sustainability. When businesses are compelled to optimize their operations to remain competitive, they inherently reduce inefficiencies that lead to waste. This alignment resonates with SDG 12's vision of promoting sustainable consumption patterns and ensuring that resources are used efficiently, thereby contributing to environmental preservation.

SDG 9 envisions the creation of sustainable and resilient infrastructure, which is intrinsically linked to promoting economic efficiency. Competition law, by curbing anti-competitive practices and enabling fair market dynamics, fosters an environment conducive to the development of sustainable infrastructure. As businesses compete to provide innovative solutions, resources are allocated more efficiently, enhancing the quality and longevity of infrastructure projects. This convergence with SDG 9's objectives extends beyond growth—it embraces responsible and forward-thinking development.

The resonance between promoting economic efficiency and multiple SDGs is not a fragmented alignment—it's a holistic approach to sustainable development. The principles that competition law upholds—the pursuit of innovation, waste reduction, and sustainable consumption—form a common thread that weaves through the fabric of SDGs 8, 9, and 12. This approach underscores the interconnectedness of goals and the need for collaborative efforts to achieve them.

The confluence of promoting economic efficiency and multiple SDGs is a testament to the power of holistic development frameworks. Competition law, as a catalyst for fair competition, innovation, and efficient resource allocation, stands as a linchpin that bridges legal principles with aspirations for a better world. From fostering innovation under SDG 9 to reducing waste under SDG 12, the alignment underscores the intricate relationship between economic efficiency and progress. As we navigate the complex journey of global development, recognizing this interplay becomes an affirmation of commitment to a world where innovation flourishes, resources are optimized, and infrastructure is sustainable—a world that resonates with the essence of SDGs 8, 9, and 12, where progress is woven into the very fabric of economic advancement.

CONCLUSION

It is safe, therefore, to say that competition is a good thing. It improves the economic performance of a nation. Economic resources are fully utilised and consumer welfare would be maximized (Whish & Bailey, 2021). Thus, we need to promote effective competition to achieve these desirable outcomes. It is also argued that competition law was introduced to achieve economic progress and improve the economic welfare of the people and firms that make up society (Goyder & Albors-Lloren, 2009). There are other aims of introducing competition law as well. These include the protection of small businesses, promoting economic freedom and ensuring fairness in the economy (Whish & Bailey, 2021). Social-economic development and the industrial objectives of a particular nation, too, influence their rationales for the introduction of competition law.

The objectives of competition law give the competition authorities the direction in which to apply the law. It reflects the desire of the state to address market imperfections and the allocation of economic resources in their respective countries. The economy of the state would perform better if its market were competitive and efficient.

Understanding the key concepts of competition law and SDGs lays the foundation for their convergence. It is a recognition of their shared mission to create a better world, one where vibrant market coexists with responsible consumption, innovation harmonizes with equitable access, and economic progress intertwines with inclusive growth.

However, acknowledging the challenges is imperative. Balancing competition with broader policy goals and the intricacies of SDG implementation demand careful navigation. As competition law seeks to drive growth, it must be approached in ways that respect diverse sectors and societal needs. The collaboration of policymakers, regulatory bodies, businesses, and civil society becomes the catalyst to harmonize these pursuits.

The journey towards promoting fair competition and achieving Sustainable Development Goals (SDGs) is not without its challenges—challenges that demand recognition, analysis, and strategic solutions. As we delve into this intricate landscape, we encounter limitations inherent in competition law, potential conflicts between competition law and broader policy objectives, and the complexities tied to implementing SDGs. Acknowledging these challenges is essential for crafting holistic strategies that foster both competition and sustainable development.

Competition law, while a formidable tool, is not a panacea. It faces inherent limitations that can impede its efficacy in promoting competition. The thresholds for intervention may vary across jurisdictions, with some markets remaining outside the purview of enforcement due to their size or characteristics.

Additionally, with only very few enforcement officers, the MyCC may lack the resources needed to effectively monitor and regulate all sectors, resulting in under-enforcement. This is compounded by the fact that there are not many people who are well versed in competition law which may have contributed to the lack of understanding of competition law among the judges and lawyers. In fact, the judgement that were written rarely discussed the objective of competition law in the cases that have been decided, thus preventing the public and also the legal fraternity on the importance of competition law in promoting economic growth in Malaysia. These limitations can hinder the promotion of competition in certain industries, preventing them from contributing optimally to sustainable development.

The dynamic between competition law and other policy objectives can be intricate. While competition is essential for innovation, efficiency, and consumer welfare, there are instances where it may seem to conflict with other priorities (Whish & Bailey, 2021). For example, competition enforcement might hinder the consolidation of certain industries for strategic reasons, potentially colliding with national security considerations or achieving certain national social developmental objectives. Balancing these concerns while preserving the core principles of competition law requires careful deliberation and nuanced approaches.

The complexities tied to implementing SDGs span multifaceted domains. As these goals intersect with various sectors, challenges arise. Limited resources, institutional capacity, and regulatory frameworks can impede the comprehensive execution of SDGs (Economic Planning Unit, 2021). Moreover, the interconnected nature of the goals demands collaboration across borders and sectors, adding a layer of complexity. Local contexts, cultural nuances, and varying economic conditions further complicate the implementation process. This web of challenges underscores the need for innovative solutions that combine policy, governance, and partnerships. As a young agency in Malaysia enforcing a law that is intertwined with economic objectives, the MyCC is faced with the public who did not understand the application of economics principles in its decision making.

Addressing the challenges of promoting competition and achieving SDGs requires a comprehensive approach that considers both the nuances of competition law and the broader sustainable development context. Collaboration between the MyCC, policymakers, and stakeholders becomes imperative. Capacity-building initiatives that equip competition authorities with resources and expertise are vital. Regulatory frameworks must be adaptive, fostering competition without stifling innovation or broader policy goals.

Balancing competition with other policy objectives is a delicate art. While competition is a driver of economic efficiency, innovation, and consumer welfare, it should be pursued in harmony with broader societal needs. Regulatory frameworks can be designed to accommodate both competition and overarching policy goals. Anti-competitive conduct assessments can include evaluations of potential impacts on national security or public welfare. This balance ensures that competition law's pursuit of fair play aligns with the comprehensive objectives of sustainable development.

To overcome the challenges of SDG implementation, integrated strategies are essential. This involves coordination between governments, international organizations, civil society, and private sectors. Collaborative partnerships foster knowledge-sharing, resource mobilization, and the pooling of expertise. National and regional strategies that contextualize SDGs based on local conditions amplify the impact of implementation efforts. A pragmatic understanding of local contexts helps tailor policies that prioritise specific goals while considering overarching objectives.

The journey towards promoting competition and achieving SDGs is multifaceted—a tapestry woven with complexities, conflicts, and opportunities. Recognizing and addressing challenges holistically is a testament to the commitment to balance economic advancement with societal welfare. In this pursuit, acknowledging the limitations of competition law, navigating conflicts, and crafting resilient implementation strategies become pivotal. Ultimately, this holistic approach transforms challenges into catalysts, forging a pathway where competition and sustainable development converge in harmony, contributing to a more just, equitable, and prosperous global landscape.

Recommendations for Unifying Competition Law and Sustainable Development Goals

The seamless integration of competition law and Sustainable Development Goals (SDGs) holds the potential for transformative change, fostering economic growth, innovation, and equitable development. As policymakers and stakeholders navigate this intricate terrain, strategic measures are imperative to ensure that the linkages between these two spheres are robust, synergistic, and impactful. Here, we offer a comprehensive set of recommendations to fortify the nexus between competition law and SDGs, promoting fair competition while advancing sustainable development objectives.

Policymakers and stakeholders should establish platforms for collaboration between competition authorities, regulatory bodies, and sustainable development agencies. Encouraging regular dialogues, joint workshops, and knowledge-sharing sessions can illuminate the interconnections between competition dynamics and development goals. This collaborative approach fosters the formulation of policies that balance competitive markets with broader socio-economic priorities. The MyCC can work together with the agencies responsible in ensuring the implementation of SGDs objectives in Malaysia. By working together, they will be able to avoid any policy overlaps while ensuring that the development agenda in Malaysia is in tandem with its competition law objectives.

Investing in the expertise of competition authorities and stakeholders is crucial. Capacity-building programs can equip officials with the knowledge and skills to recognize and address the nuanced intersections between competition law and sustainable development. Workshops, training, and educational resources should be designed to illustrate the ways in which competition can support various SDGs. Existing cooperations with other competition authorities can be further enhanced via internship programmes for staff of the MyCC to be placed at other competition authorities to learn the way of doing things. The competencies of members of the Competition Appeal Tribunal should also be developed. The appointment of members of the Commission and the Appeal Tribunal should be chosen based on merits and not through political appointments. Ideally, they should be chosen from those who have knowledge of competition law. Otherwise, their knowledge and exposure to competition laws should be enhanced. Understanding of SDGs will also help them perform better as the custodians of competition laws in Malaysia. The judgement that they wrote should contain elements of SDGs to further the cause of sustainable development via the enforcement of competition law.

Collaboration with research institutions and data-driven analysis is pivotal. Data insights can illuminate how competition dynamics influence economic growth, innovation, and consumer welfare. Policymakers and stakeholders should harness data to understand the linkages between competition outcomes and SDG progress, enabling evidence-based decision-making. This will enable better decision making and policy consideration in ensuring the success of pursuing both objectives. Regulatory frameworks should strike a balance between promoting competition and achieving sustainable development goals. This involves crafting competition policies that accommodate sectors critical to SDGs, such as healthcare, education, and infrastructure. Tailored regulations can incentivise competition while addressing unique challenges posed by these sectors. Regularly assessing the impact of competition policies on SDGs is vital. Policymakers should establish mechanisms to track progress, evaluate successes, and identify areas for improvement. Monitoring the impact enables adjustments and refinements that ensure the effective realization of both competition and development objectives.

Forums that bring together government officials, businesses, civil society, and international organizations can facilitate discussions on aligning competition policy with sustainable development. These platforms enable the sharing of best practices, case studies, and collaborative solutions that enhance both competitive markets and development outcomes.

Engaging the public and raising awareness about the connections between competition law and sustainable development is crucial. Educational campaigns can help citizens understand how fair competition contributes to economic growth, job creation, and improved living standards. Public support can bolster the implementation of policies that prioritize both competition and sustainable development.

The harmonization of competition law and Sustainable Development Goals requires proactive, collaborative efforts that bridge the realms of policy, regulation, and societal progress. By embracing cross-sectoral engagement, data-driven decision-making, and inclusive frameworks, policymakers and stakeholders can navigate the challenges and seize the opportunities at the confluence of competition and sustainable development. This convergence is not just a theoretical alignment; it's a transformative force that propels economic growth, equity, and innovation—a symphony where competition law and SDGs create harmonious progress for all.

In the intricate dance between competition law and Sustainable Development Goals (SDGs), a profound symphony of progress emerges—a harmony where legal principles interweave with global aspirations for a more equitable and prosperous future. This comprehensive exploration delves into the multifaceted connections, unravelling how competition law's tenets resonate with the essence of SDGs across various dimensions.

From fostering competition and economic efficiency to preventing market power abuse, competition law becomes a linchpin that fortifies the pursuit of SDGs. This alignment underscores the interconnectedness of economic growth, social welfare, and environmental sustainability. Recommendations, borne from a synthesis of insights, are the guideposts to this harmonization. Collaboration, integration of sustainable development in assessments, capacity-building, data-driven approaches, and incentives for responsible practices form a robust framework. Multistakeholder platforms and public awareness campaigns foster engagement and support for this unified agenda.

In conclusion, the symphony of competition law and SDGs is not merely theoretical—it's a narrative of possibility, a story of how legal frameworks and global aspirations can intertwine to create a more just, prosperous, and sustainable world. It's a recognition that the pursuit of competition and the pursuit of development are not disparate endeavours; they are harmonious pursuits that, when interwoven, amplify each other's impact. This convergence offers a roadmap, not just for legal frameworks and policies, but for a shared human journey towards progress—a journey where fairness, innovation, sustainability, and equitable growth flourish in concert, inspiring a future that resonates with the ideals of competition law and the aspirations of SDGs.

REFERENCES

ASEAN Economic Community. (2015, December 7). ASEAN. https://asean.org/asean-economic-community/

ASEAN Experts Group on Competition (AEGC). (n.d.). ASEAN. https://www.asean-competition.org/aegc

Bakhoum, M. (2012). Reflections on the concepts of 'economic freedom', 'free competition' and 'efficiency' from the perspectives of developing countries. In D. Zimmer (Ed.), *The Goals of Competition Law* (pp. 408–440). Edward Elgar. doi:10.4337/9780857936615.00029

Bishop, S., & Walker, M. (2010). *The Economics of Competition Law: Concepts, Application and Measurement* (3rd ed.). Sweet & Maxwell.

Commerce, A. M. (2006). *Public Submission for the Proposed U.S.-Malaysia Free Trade Agreement (USMFTA)*. Bilaterals. https://www.bilaterals.org/IMG/pdf/003eb926-8a8a-49e8-9901-700353a31e93.pdf

A. P. E. C., & the Law Group. (2023). *Competition Policy and Sustainable Development*. Bangkok: Trade Competition Commission of Thailand. https://www.apec.org/docs/default-source/publications/2023/7/223_ec_competition-policy-and-sustainable-development.pdf?sfvrsn=cfd2c2f9_2

Cooter, R., & Ulen, T. (2008). *Law and Economics*. Pearson.

Declaration On The Asean Economic Community Blueprint. (2003, October 7). ASEAN. https://www.asean.org/wp-content/uploads/images/archive/5187-10.pdf

Deyo, F. C. (2013). Addressing the development deficit of competition policy: the role of economic networks. In J. G. Michael W. Dowdle, & I. Maher (Eds.), Asian Capitalism and the regulation of Competition: Towards a Regulatory Geography of Global Competition Law (pp. 283-300). Cambridge: Cambridge University Press. doi:10.1017/CBO9781139226349.018

Economic Planning Unit. (2021). *Malaysia Voluntary National Review Report*. Sustainable Development United Nations. https://sustainabledevelopment.un.org/content/documents/285982021_VNR_Report_Malaysia.pdf

Economic Planning Unit. (n.d.). *SDG Roadmap Phase 1 2016-2020*. Economic Planning Unit. www.ekonomi.gov.my: https://www.ekonomi.gov.my/sites/default/files/2021-05/SDG_Roadmap_Phase_I_2016-2020.pdf

Elhauge, E., & Geradin, D. (2011). *Global Competition Law and Economics* (2nd ed.). Hart Publishing.

Fox, E. M. (2008). Antitrust, Economic Development and Poverty: The Other Path. In G. L. Hassan Qaqaya (Ed.), The Effects of Anti-competitive Business Practices on Developing Countries and Their Development Prospects (p. 179). Geneva: United Nations.

Goyder, J., & Albors-Lloren, A. (2009). *Goyder's EC Competition Law* (5th ed.). Oxford University Press.

Hansard Parliament Malaysia. (2023, October 13). *DEWAN RAKYAT PARLIMEN KELIMA BELAS PENGGAL KEDUA MESYUARAT KETIGA*. Portal Rasmi Parlimen Malaysia. https://www.parlimen.gov.my/files/hindex/pdf/DR-13102023.pdf

HM Government Gazette. (n.d.). *COMPETITION ACT 2010 THE MyCC GUIDELINES ON INTELLECTUAL PROPERTY RIGHTS AND COMPETITION LAW*. MyCC Guidelines. https://www.mycc.gov.my/sites/default/files/pdf/newsroom/WJW013224%20Teks%20%282%29.pdf

Holmes, S. (2020, July). Climate change, sustainability, and competition law. *Journal of Antitrust Enforcement*, *8*(2), 354–405. doi:10.1093/jaenfo/jnaa006

Interaction between Trade and Competition Policy. (n.d.). World Trade Organisation. https://www.wto.org/english/tratop_e/comp_e/comp_e.htm

Khemani, R. S. (n.d.). *Objectives of Competition Law.* OECD. https://www.oecd.org/regreform/sectors/aframeworkforthedesignandimplementationofcompetitionlawandpolicy.htm

Khoo, K., & Sng, A. (2019). Singapore's competition regime and its objective: The case against formalism. *Singapore Journal of Legal Studies*, *1*, 67–107. https://law1.nus.edu.sg/sjls/articles/SJLS-Mar-19-67.pdf

Kroes, N. (2009, October 8). Tackling cartels – a never-ending task. *Speech*. Brasilia. https://ec.europa.eu/commission/presscorner/detail/en/SPEECH_09_454

Malaysia country profile. (n.d.). Malaysia Competition Commission. https://www.mycc.gov.my/files/advocacy/Malaysia-UNCTADPaper.pdf

Malaysian Parliament Hansard. (2010). *Official Parliament Hansard Third Session First Meeting on 20.4.2010.* Parliament Malaysia. https://www.parlimen.gov.my/files/hindex/pdf/DR-20042010.pdf

Malinauskaite, J. (2022, July). Competition Law and Sustainability: EU and National Perspectives. *Journal of European Competition Law & Practice*, *13*(5), 336–348. doi:10.1093/jeclap/lpac003

Menon, J. (2017, December). Government-Linked Companies: Impact on the Malaysian Economy. *Policy IDEAS*(No 45). https://www.ideas.org.my/wp-content/uploads/2017/12/PI45-Government-Linked-companies-and-its-Impacts-on-the-Malaysian-Economy-V4.pdf

Ministry of Economy. (n.d.). *SDG Roadmap Phase 1 2016-2020*. Ministry of Economy. https://www.ekonomi.gov.my/sites/default/files/2021-05/SDG_Roadmap_Phase_I_2016-2020.pdf

Ministry of Economy. (n.d.). *Sustainable Development Goals*. Ekonomi. https://www.ekonomi.gov.my/en/sustainable-development-goals

MyCC. (2011). *MyCC Annual Report.* Kuala Lumpur: MyCC. https://www.mycc.gov.my/sites/default/files/pdf/newsroom/MyCC-AR-2011-English.pdf

MyCC. (n.d.). *MyCC Advocacy Programmes.* MyCC. www.mycc.gov.my: https://www.mycc.gov.my/programmes-events?page=1

MyCC Guidelines. (n.d.). *MyCC Guidelines on Abuse of Dominant Position.* MyCC. www.mycc.gov.my: https://www.mycc.gov.my/guidelines

MyCC. (2023, March 22). MyCC stands firm with the public on Touch n Go. *The Star*. https://www.thestar.com.my/news/nation/2023/03/22/mycc-stands-firm-with-the-public-on-touch-n-go

MyCC v CAT, AirAsia and MAS, WA-25-82-05/2016 (High Court 2016). https://www.mycc.gov.my/sites/default/files/pdf/decision/wa-25-82-05%282016%29%20competition%20commission%20v%20competition%20appeal%20tribunal%20and%20mas%20berhad%20and%20airasia%20berhad.pdf

MyCC v Dagang Net Technologies Sdn Bhd, 700–2/2/003/2015 (MyCC February 16, 2021). https://www.mycc.gov.my/case

MyCC v General Insurance Association of Malaysia (PIAM) and 22 others, 700-2.1.3.2015 (MyCC September 14, 2020). https://www.mycc.gov.my/sites/default/files/pdf/decision/Public%20Version%20Decision%20PIAM%20%26%2022%20Members_28.2.2021_2.pdf

Nowag, J. (2020, December 1). *Sustainability & Competition Law and Policy – Background Note.* OECD. https://one.oecd.org/document/DAF/COMP(2020)3/En/pdf

Nowag, J. (2022). Competition Law's Sustainability Gap? Tools for an Examination and a Brief Overview. Nordic Journal of European Law Issue 2022(1) 149-165. doi:https://dx.doi.org/10.2139/ssrn.3484964.

OECD. (n.d.). *OECD COVID-19 Competition policy actions for governments and competition authorities.* OECD. https://www.oecd.org/competition/competition-policy-responses-to-covid-19.htm

Qaqaya, H., & Lipimile, G. (2008). *The effects of Anti-competitive Business Practices on Developing Countries and their Development Prospects.* United Nations.

Rahman, N. A., & Ahamat, H. (2021). *Competition Law in Malaysia* (2nd ed.). Sweet & Maxwell.

Ramaiah, A. K. (2019). Competition in Digital Economy: Fate of Consumer Welfare in Malaysia. Malaysian Journal of Consumer and Family Economics, 22, 223-245.

Razak, A. A. (2019). Competition Act 2010 (Act 712). In *The Annotated Statutes of Malaysia.* Lexis Nexis.

Report of the World Commission on Environment and Development: Our Common Future. (1987). United Nations Digital Library. https://digitallibrary.un.org/record/139811

SDG Knowledge Platform. (2023, August 15). Retrieved from Sustainable Development Goals: https://sdgs.un.org/goals

Singapore Ministerial Declaration. (1996, December 18). Word Trade Organisation. https://www.wto.org/english/thewto_e/minist_e/min96_e/wtodec_e.htm#investment_competition

Tisdell, C. A. (2013). *Competition, Diversity and Economic Performance: Processes, Complexities and Ecological Similarities.* Edward Elgar Publishing, Inc. doi:10.4337/9781781002391

UN Department of Economics and Social Welfare. (n.d.). *17th Goals of Sustainable Development.* UN Department of Economics and Social Welfare Sustainable Development. https://sdgs.un.org/goals

Understanding The WTO: Cross-Cutting And New Issues. (n.d.). WTO. https://www.wto.org/english/thewto_e/whatis_e/tif_e/bey3_e.htm

United Nations Department of Economics and Social Affairs. (n.d.). *Promote sustained, inclusive and sustainable economic growth, full and productive employment and decent work for all.* United Nations Departments of Economics and Social Affairs, Sustainable Development. https://sdgs.un.org/goals/goal8

Van den Berg, R., & Camesasca, P. (2001). *European Competition Law and Economics: A Comparative Perspective.* Intersentia NV.

Vanberg, V. J. (2011). Consumer Welfare, Total Welfare and Economic Freedom – On the Normative Foundations of Competition Policy. In W. K. Josef Drexl (Ed.), *Competition Policy and the Economic Approach.* Edward Elgar Publishing. https://econpapers.repec.org/bookchap/elgeechap/13786_5f2.htm

Viscusi, W., & Vernon, J. (2005). *Economics of regulation and antitrust* (4th ed.). MIT Press.

Whish, R., & Bailey, D. (2021). *Competition Law* (10th ed.). Oxford University Press. doi:10.1093/he/9780198836322.001.0001

Why competition and consumer protection matter. (n.d.). UNCTAD. https://unctad.org/Topic/Competition-and-Consumer-Protection

Chapter 4
Energy Transition Toward a Low-Carbon Economy in Malaysia:
Do We Need a Liberalizing Electricity Market?

Farahdilah Ghazali
https://orcid.org/0000-0002-1966-9690
University of Putra Malaysia, Malaysia

Siti Fazilah Abdul Shukor
https://orcid.org/0000-0003-3504-4102
Universiti Tunku Abdul Rahman, Malaysia

Nur Yuhanis Ismon
Universiti Tun Hussien Onn, Malaysia

ABSTRACT

Some studies have found that liberalized electricity market led to acceleration of the development of renewable energy sector, particularly with community-based financing for local renewable projects in place. The idea of liberalization of electricity market focuses on the fair competition especially among the key players which subsequently entice more investment on infrastructures and reduce electricity tariff. Energy liberalization has dramatically enhanced monopoly utility governance, competition, innovation prospects, and the policy for environmental emissions management by creating trading mechanisms. This chapter discusses the practices of power liberalization, especially in Europe, regarding the benefits and challenges. Moreover, the chapter examines Malaysian practices in pursuing renewable energy programs to attain sustainability and energy security goals, which is also vital to support a more competitive energy sector.

DOI: 10.4018/979-8-3693-0390-0.ch004

Copyright © 2024, IGI Global. Copying or distributing in print or electronic forms without written permission of IGI Global is prohibited.

INTRODUCTION

Climate change has become a global issue with profound implications for the economies and societies simultaneously directed countries to enforce policies to minimize carbon dioxide emissions to secure long-term economic growth and development (Ponce et al., 2020). However, high reliance on natural gas might impede the transition to an economy with minimal carbon emissions. Natural gas is not only known as a part of a climate change mitigation strategy but rather a transitional resource (Najm & Matsumoto, 2020). The development of affordable and sustainable energy solutions and measures requires technological advancements, increased energy efficiency, competitive economies, enhanced energy security, and a focus on addressing climate change (Kabeyi & Olanrewaju, 2022). Employment, poverty, pollution, and ecosystem concerns, directly and indirectly, connect to the energy sector. The nation is still underdeveloped and suffers from widespread hunger due to its limited access to energy (Büyüközkan et al., 2018). On the other hand, self-electrification in rural areas has significantly increased this access to electricity due to the remarkable expansions of renewable energy in the power sector (Kitchen & O'Reilly, 2016).

To maximize the potential of these renewable resources and ultimately get towards Target 7 of the Sustainable Development Goals (SDG 7), comprehensive and effective renewable energy legislation and regulations are essential. By ensuring that everyone has access to affordable and clean energy, especially concerning electricity, the world can address issues like poverty, climate change, health, and unsustainable urban development (Mustafa et al., 2022). In Southeast Asia, in particular, the region's energy mix can be significantly improved by utilizing renewable energy sources (Mustafa et al., 2022). Nevertheless, it will need more effort, especially for a developing country. Therefore, a country must find ways to expand its generation capacity while maintaining and maybe even increasing its share of renewable energy in order to meet the difficulties posed by the consequences of climate change (Santos et al., 2021).

Electricity is a primary driver of economic growth for all countries worldwide, and Malaysian economic progress will be significantly reliant on providing excellent infrastructural services, particularly in the power sector (Nerini et al., 2018). Electricity infrastructure is not only critical for development but also has a significant impact on global competitiveness and economic growth (Paryono et al., 2020). To promote the growth of physical and social infrastructures and to eradicate poverty, existing energy infrastructures should be enhanced. Centralized and decentralized energy infrastructures are preferred to meet Target 7 of the Sustainable Development Goals (SDG 7), as more than a billion people have insufficient access to energy (Nerini et al., 2018). Issues related to access to energy can only be resolved through meticulous infrastructure planning that is transparent and focused, as well as long-term project implementation (Paryono et al., 2020).

With the increasing movements towards private ownership and competition through power liberalization, many countries can rationalize the sector's development by treating electricity as a commodity that needs optimal allocation (Bryne & Mun, 2003). Although energy and power infrastructure are critical for economic development, thus, the legal framework is required to construct and implement nationally and internationally. Nevertheless, various challenges concern using renewable energy sources and the execution of laws and policies (Schwartz, 2009). He et al. (2016) argued that policies must be revised to promote renewable energy development. For example, profits on liberalized electricity markets must be increased to stimulate private investment in renewable energy production. Thus, diverse economic instruments are required in order to make renewables a profitable investment (Zipp, 2017). Moreover, variable renewable energy needs direct reliance on natural resources, which may cause an interruption in generation as they cannot supply demand at any moment (Pietzcker et al., 2014; Zipp, 2017).

Figure 1. Conventional electricity sector structure

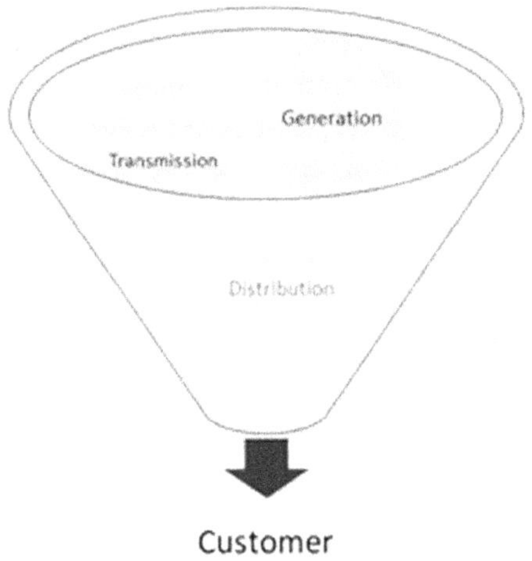

Figure 1 shows the conventional electricity structure in which a vertically integrated utility in the power sector owns and operates all aspects of the electricity supply chain, including generation, transmission, and distribution. This model has been used for all countries; as a company engages in more activities along a single supply chain, it may result in a market monopoly. One significant drawback of monopoly is the absence of regulation and enforcement; there will be limited electricity production, and the electricity rates will increase as they have no competitor supply to the customer in the territory (Belyaev, 2010). Energy market liberalization promotes fair competition among companies to encourage more infrastructure investment and lower electricity tariffs. This chapter discusses the practices of power liberalization, especially in Europe, regarding the benefits and challenges.

Moreover, the chapter examines Malaysian practices in pursuing renewable energy programs to attain sustainability and energy security goals, which is also vital to support a more competitive energy sector. The chapter is divided into seven parts. Following this introduction, the landscape of the Malaysian electricity sector in the second part of the chapter. The third part explained the concept of Liberalization in the Electricity Sector by referring to Europe. Within the fourth part, the authors discuss the benefits and drawbacks of the liberalized electricity market. In Part 5, the chapter further elaborates on the impacts of renewable energy in the liberalized power sector. In the next section, the author discussed the Malaysian position in developing renewable energy as well as moving towards the liberalized electricity market.

ELECTRICITY SECTOR IN MALAYSIA

Generally, vertically integrated utilities in the power sector consist of three stages of electricity services: generation, transmission, and distribution, which these utility companies were frequently state-owned monopolies. Even when private ownership was present, corporations operated as monopolies supervised by governments that set rates and investments (Byrne & Mun, 2003). Moreover, in the traditional power sector, they have primarily relied on large-scale power plants and substantial transmission and distribution networks to deliver electricity, which has led to environmental, social, and economic issues (Byrne

& Mun, 2003). Nevertheless, in the early 1990s, a set of institutional reforms, including unbundling, privatization of ownership, and the introduction of competition into the generation sector, were presented to solve the problems in the power sector (Zhang et al., 2008). Privatization in the generation sector might lead to competition in the wholesale supply through transmission access, but the distribution network could remain a natural monopoly, with consumers having access to retail options (Panda & Patel, 2011).

In a regulated power market, a utility company may control the whole process, from generation through distribution to end buyers. But in Malaysia, utilities needed complete control over the generation industry. Every energy stakeholder in Malaysia has a critical responsibility to play in ensuring uninterrupted electricity supply. Historically, the Central Electricity Board was established in Malaysia and began operating on 1 September 1949. The Board of Directors, through the Electricity Supply Department, considered establishing three more major projects in April 1946, including Connaught Bridge Power Station, Cameron Highlands Hydroelectric Project, and National Grid Development (Kumar et al., 2021). In 1965, the Central Electricity Board was renamed the National Electricity Board, and the national grid was established as the main electricity transmission network that connects the generation, transmission, distribution, and consumption of electricity in Malaysia (Kumar et al., 2021). In 1988, the Prime Minister announced the government's decision on privatization policy. Two laws were passed to replace the existing Electricity Act and provide for the establishment of a new corporation. Tenaga Nasional Berhad (TNB) was established on 1 February 1990 under the Companies Electricity Supply Act 1990 to replace the National Electricity Board (Kumar et al., 2021).

The new privatization policy through the New Economic Policy (NEP) focused on reducing the government's financial burden, improving the effectiveness and quality of public services, and encouraging the spread of private entrepreneurship in the public sector (Kumar et al., 2021). The current Malaysian power market is segmented by power generation source, transmission and distribution, and end-user (residential, commercial, industrial, transport, and agriculture). The Malaysian power market is moderately fragmented. Some of the key players in the market include Tenaga Nasional Berhad, Korea Electric Power Corporation, Sunway Construction Group Bhd, LYS Energy Group, and Cutech Green Ventures (Mordor Intelligence, n.d.).

Tenaga Nasional Berhad has been registered under the Companies Act 1965 and is the sole service provider (generate, transmit, distribute, and sell energy) in Peninsular Malaysia, as in Figure 2. The operation and maintenance of electricity installation for generating, transmitting, and distributing electricity are governed by the Electricity Supply Act, the Licensee Supply Regulation 1990, and the Electricity Regulations 1994. A similar application in Sabah whereby Sabah Electricity Sdn. Bhd., a subsidiary of Tenaga Nasional Berhad and is 20 percent owned by the State of Sabah. It provides reliable generation, transmission, and distribution services in Sabah and Labuan. However, Sarawak Energy Berhad was incorporated under the Sarawak Electricity Supply Corporation (Successor Company) Ordinance, 2004. As a Sarawak's wholly owned company, SEB is responsible for generating, transmitting, and distributing electricity for Sarawak.

Figure 1 shows the electricity structure in Malaysia, where the Energy Commission (EC) has a vital role in implementing and monitoring the energy sector's activities in Malaysia. As a statutory body incorporated under the Energy Commission Act 2001 and which became operational in 2002, the EC has replaced the Department of Electricity and Gas Supply. The EC plays a significant role with respect to economic regulation, technical regulation, and safety regulation. The EC's roles and functions are to promote the economy by generating, transmitting, distributing, supplying, and using electricity. Its functions also include the reticulation and use of gas, promoting competition, enabling fair and efficient market conduct, and preventing the misuse of monopoly or market power in the electricity and piped-gas industries. Section 3 (3) of the Competition Act 2010 (Act 712) excludes the jurisdiction of this Act on any commercial activity regulated under the Energy Commission Act 2011 (Act 610). Moreover, the EC has jurisdiction over matters stipulated under the Energy Commission Act 2001, the Electricity Supply Act 1990, and the Gas Supply Act 1993.

Figure 2. Electricity sector structure in Malaysia

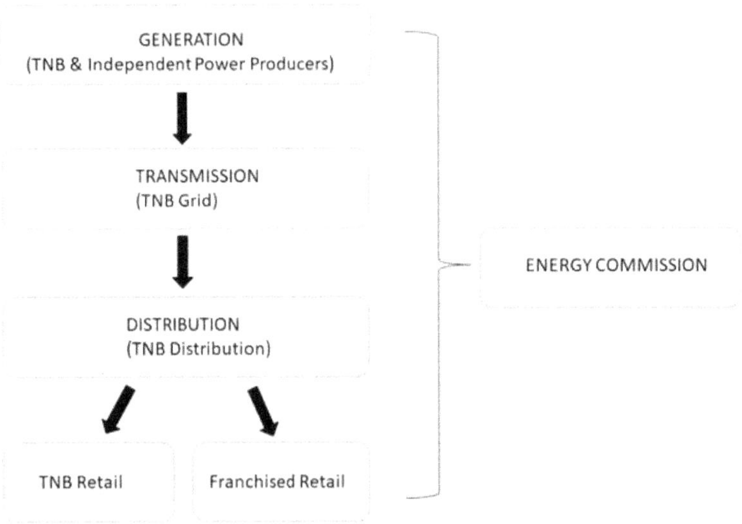

LIBERALIZATION IN THE ELECTRICITY SECTOR: EXAMPLE FROM EUROPE

The Single European Act (1987) was the first major revision to the Treaty of Rome (1957), which sought to facilitate the free movement of products, people, services, and capital across European borders. The liberalization stream aims to gradually remove borders in order to build internal markets for electricity and natural gas, resulting in a competitive energy market (Diaz-Rainey et al., 2017). The early 1990s witnessed the global liberalization of power sectors, which altered the organizational and operational situation. Liberalization in the United Kingdom, in particular, has resulted in significant structural changes, the introduction of competition in the wholesale generating and retail supply sectors, regulatory reform, and the establishment of an autonomous regulatory body. These movements have increased technological efficiency (Jamasb & Pollitt, 2011).

Furthermore, energy liberalization has culminated in many advantages, although studies in many countries have shown a need for more direct household benefits. It has dramatically enhanced monopoly utility governance, competition, innovation prospects, and the policy for environmental emissions management by creating trading mechanisms (Pollit, 2012). Siksnelyte and Zavadskas (2019) listed four factors that led to European electricity market liberalization: cost efficiency, renewable energy development, increased investment, and social welfare. Similarly, Ponce et al. (2020) stipulated that the energy market's liberalization will be crucial for renewable energy generation.

The European Union (EU) has initiated European Commission Directives 96/92/EC and 2003/54/EC, advising all European countries to switch to market-based prices or to amend and improve proposed regulations due to flaws in market design (Guerci et al., 2010). While Directive 944/2019 demands that member states take appropriate actions to guarantee effective competition between suppliers and eliminate the remaining non-transitional forms of price control (Amenta et al., 2022). Apart from the three energy packages, the EU has introduced other policy instruments for more innovative and more sustainable EU electricity, such as Energy 2020, Energy Roadmap 2050, 2015 Energy Union Package, and 2016 Clean Energy for All Europeans (Siksnelyte & Zavadskas, 2019). Although the development of a common EU electricity market has been almost 30 years, the EU is still in progress. The reasoning behind this transition is that the liberalization of monopolistic energy structures should lead to the creation of sustainable and flexible energy ecosystems via an energy policy that supports sustainable development, energy security, and the promotion of renewable energy sources (Amenta et al., 2022; Vlados et al., 2021). The EU Commission advocates for the total liberalization of retail electricity markets to achieve more profound national market integration and a strategy of enabling all customers to take an active role in the energy transition (Stagnaro et al., 2020). The EU's internal energy market is being liberalized to create a competitive and sustainable market (Ponce et al., 2020).

Despite some unique aspects related to their socioeconomic environments, European countries found the liberalization of the domestic energy market to be an effective policy. As shown, the program was successful at the EU level and in high-income nations, considering other social and economic factors in addition to the economy's dynamization (Ponce et al., 2020). Since 2007, EU Member States have been required to allow all customers to change energy providers. As the European Union moves towards full liberalization, the United Kingdom has partially re-regulated its retail electricity market by instituting a transitional price-cap mechanism covering around 15 million users under a Standard Variable Tariff (Amenta et al., 2022). The government no longer governs the electricity markets in the EU member states. Instead, electricity is traded as a unique commodity under supply and demand market conditions and according to various laws and contracts (Bojnec & Križaj, 2021). Realizing that electricity is the most important energy resource for homes, the EU is committed to ensuring that its citizens have affordable and unrestricted access to this essential social benefit through a more decentralized electricity system (Halkos & Tsirivis, 2023). Following the UN's sustainable development goals, particularly SDG 7 for producing clean, affordable energy, the study by Halkos & Tsirivis (2023) examines the effects of renewable energy, economic factors, and the liberalization of electricity generation and supply market on household electricity prices.

The single-buyer model, competitive wholesale, and competitive retailing are the three fundamental models that may be used to regulate competitive markets, thereby raising the pace of liberalization. (Santos et al., 2021). The single-buyer models are a rapid method of luring money to the generation without significantly altering the status quo. A facility, typically state-owned, is given exclusive authority to purchase energy from producers and resell it to distributors (Santos et al., 2021). Nevertheless, in developing countries, the single-buyer model has significant loopholes as it encourages corruption, impairs payment discipline, and puts substantial contingent obligations on the government (Lovei, 2000). In comparison, the 2001 California crisis prompted the US Federal Energy Regulatory Commission to propose a common wholesale power market for adoption by all (Guerci et al., 2010). In this model, large customers can purchase energy directly from non-vertical generating companies in competitive wholesale models using one of two fundamental contractual methods, typically incorporating auction techniques.

According to this model, traders or distributors themselves continue to provide services to small businesses and households, who then purchase goods from the wholesale market (Santos et al., 2021).

The competitive energy retail market (retail wheeling), which is the most advanced stage of the liberalization process, is where the monopoly of energy commercialization for small business and residential users ends, and they may ultimately freely pick their providers. The United Kingdom opened its retail market to competition with the most significant industrial customers in 1990 and residential customers in 1998 (Littlechild, 2021). The most significant advances in the industry have been the liberalization of retail and wholesale markets, the segregation of production and transmission operations, and the formation of distinguished national regulatory instruments (Siksnelyte & Zavadskas, 2019). The drawback of this model is that the expenses of maintaining a retail market are higher and small customers must have access to all the information required to choose the goods and vendors that best meet their requirements. Many experts wonder if this model's veracity is due to the energy industry's complexity and all the disparities between major providers and small users (Santos et al., 2021).

Based on a study by Siksnelyte and Zavadskas (2019) on the assessment of the sustainability of EU countries' electricity sector in 2017 following the assessment using the TOPSIS method, the electricity market of Slovenia was the most sustainable, followed by Luxembourg and Austria was in third. Lithuania ranked last (no. 28) due to its dependency on electricity imports from Russia and Belarus. The liberalization of European electricity markets resulted in lowering wholesale energy costs, providing more choices for customers as suppliers compete to lower prices and deliver better services (Siksnelyte & Zavadskas, 2019). However, there are still several challenges facing the EU, including import dependency, old infrastructure, limited investment, a lack of a properly functioning retail market, the need to combat climate change, and a shift towards a low-carbon economy (Siksnelyte & Zavadskas, 2019).

LIBERALIZED ELECTRICITY MARKET: DEBUNKING THE ADVANTAGES AND CHALLENGES

Generally, the goal of liberalization is to encourage competition among service providers in order to improve market efficiency and lower retail costs, as well as to drive technical innovation (Shin & Managi, 2017). Nevertheless, electricity market liberalization has sparked restructuring and competition, resulting in minor efficiency gains in production and distribution (Pollitt, 2012). Liberalization does not necessarily provide consumer advantages; for instance, the historic Californian power crisis of 2001, in which an insufficient supply of electricity severely impacted customers, sparked questions about failing regulatory architecture and the legal basis for the liberalization process (Shin & Managi, 2017). Electricity liberalization was contentious and challenging in the United States, Europe, and other nations (Joskow, 2022). While according to Itaoka et al. (2022), other drawbacks of this system include an inflexible energy system and downward price rigidity. The government's erroneous policy of power reform, and low standard transmission and distribution infrastructure, are part of the electricity problem. The role of the state will still be crucial, even though the privatization of plants raises questions about the motives for privatization, the impact of misguided liberalization has led to a transfer of ownership from the state to the private (foreign) party, which will amputate the state's power in controlling (Paryono et al., 2020). Apart from the existing challenges in the liberalized sector, governments face the challenge of implementing intense decarbonization commitments; policymakers are focused on meeting these goals and the associated decarbonization trajectories from here to these endpoints on time and as economically as possible given the commitments that have been made (Joskow, 2022).

Liberalizing the energy market is an intricate process that must first consider several factors. The econometric research demonstrated that increasing household electricity prices might result from a decline in the market share of the biggest producer (Halkos & Tsirivis, 2023). Contrary to Stagnaro et al. (2020), consumers may gain significantly from retail competition in the power market, and these advantages may increase as technology advances. Effective supplier competition and strong demand-side participation are essential for customers to profit. A study by Bojnec and Križaj (2021) demonstrated that more significant industrial power usage led to higher industrial electricity costs and that deregulation of the electricity market and price liberalization did not cut electricity prices as anticipated. In Japan, market liberalization depicts the demand for a more decentralized energy system to mitigate energy insecurity issues and the possibility of catastrophic mishaps like the Fukushima nuclear plant tragedy 2011. It also reflects growing market competition with the recent growth of renewable energy, which coincides with the liberalization timeline, and further promotes decentralization (Itaoka et al., 2022).

Sector deregulation was primarily motivated by a desire to boost the energy system's efficiency and achieve the anticipated supply-side consequences, particularly to lower electricity rates. Energy sector entrepreneurship was made possible by the deregulation and liberalization of the power market, whereby the production of renewable electricity was positively impacted, which encouraged the completion of the market for energy derivatives (Bojnec & Križaj, 2021). Verbong and Geels (2010) elaborated that energy market liberalization and installing high-voltage transmission lines have enhanced international electricity flows. Furthermore, through liberalization, consumers can choose low-emission power producers inside the liberalized market, helping to reduce pollution (Itaoka et al., 2022). Additionally, this liberalization allows players to select the cheapest price generation source to balance electricity supply and demand in the short term (Limura & Cross, 2018).

Although the European electricity market liberalization process started more than 20 years ago, with most Member States of the EU having liberalized their electricity market, several remaining problems still need to be addressed (Pepermans, 2019). removed. Improved governance quality and power market privatization as appropriate accelerators toward power market sustainability in the short and long run, whereas any increase in electricity price may slow the pace of achieving power market sustainability in both the short and long run. Therefore, governments must issue strategy plans and roadmaps with defined visions and missions for power market sustainability (Taghizadeh-Hesary et al., 2022)

Enhancing the reliability and security of the electricity supply is one of the critical goals of electrical energy deregulation. Thus, a regulation must pay attention to the people's interest in affordable access to electricity rather than being co-opted by capitalism (Paryono et al., 2020). In a tandem progression of privatization, the competition aims to rationalize the development of the electricity sector by treating electricity as a commodity and bringing electricity problems into the realm of power politics. The capitalist system in the existing power sector operates internationally by multinational or transnational firms by carrying out activities in all emerging nations by influencing the country's electrical goods, which then invests in the country's electricity infrastructure (Paryono et al., 2020). With comprehensive regulation and an influential interventive role by the government, the philosophical idea of embracing liberalization that allows the market to compete while incentivizing operators to perform well and subsequently creating a market that is more efficient, affordable, and sustainable.

RENEWABLE ENERGY IN THE LIBERALIZED POWER SECTOR

Europe has progressively switched to renewable energy sources for electricity generation and achieved significant progress over the last decade. In 2001, Directive 2001/77/EC set an indicative target of 22.1% of gross electricity consumption from renewables by 2010 (Diaz-Rainey et al., 2017). In 2007, the EU endorsed a mandatory target of a 20% share of final energy consumption from RES by 2020, ultimately becoming Directive 2009/28/EC. Emission reductions were expected to be achieved through increased use of renewable energy sources in electricity generation and transport (Diaz-Rainey et al., 2017). The EU's spirit of reducing carbon emissions is consistent with many international conventions on environment and climate change, notably the Kyoto Protocol and the Paris Agreement. In order to meet the goals of increasing the average global temperature to below 2 °C, the Paris Agreement calls for a significant reduction in greenhouse gas emissions through the Nationally Determined Contributions (NDC) made by signatories to the Paris Agreement. The Intergovernmental Panel on Climate Change (IPCC) noted that in order to meet the Long-Term Temperature Goal of the Paris Agreement, it is imperative to decarbonize energy systems, phase out coal for power generation by 2050, and increase the share of renewable energy (Shem et al., 2019). Likewise, Kabeyi and Olanrewaju (2022) pointed out that the three main breakthroughs in technology creating sustainable transition initiatives are energy savings and efficiency and substituting fossil fuels with nuclear and renewable energy sources. According to Abdmouleh et al. (2015), numerous important factors influencing RE implementation and aiding in creating a favorable environment for RE exploitation are financial, fiscal, legislative, political, technological, and environmental. They also emphasized the importance of clear regulations and legal frameworks to promote investor interest in the RE market (Abdmouleh et al., 2015). Other regions' experience, especially the Nordic, reveals that liberalized ESI aligns quite well in accommodating renewables and achieving efficiency, whereby depleting fossil fuels and energy demand are predicted to exceed traditional energy resource generation. Thus, increased penetration of renewables into the grid and more efficient energy use would be the silver bullet in mitigating the impact of depleting natural indigenous energy resources for the benefit of future generations (Aris et al., 2020).

With the advance of policy and the maturity of the renewable energy market, much research has been embarked on assessing the links between renewable energy, low-carbon development, energy supply security, and climate change. At the same time, there are studies on renewable energy's effects in a liberalized market. A study by Murshed (2020) examines the compatibility of national trade liberalization policies in promoting the widespread use of renewable energy resources in 71 countries from South Asia, East Asia, the Pacific, Central Asia, Latin America, Caribbean islands, and Sub-Saharan Africa. Panel data cointegration and regression studies are performed using annual time series data from 2000 to 2017. While a study by Blazquez et al. (2018) highlights the incompatibility between power liberalization and renewable policies, independent of nation, geography, or renewable technology. They further contend that Renewable deployment has plateaued in liberalized markets whereby the decentralized market's capacity has limited transparency which may hinder the complete decarbonization of the power sector. Ironically, electricity prices depend on conventional technologies and support renewable deployment and, as a result, indirectly towards decarbonization (Blazquez et al., 2018). Nicolli and Vona (2019) examined the impact of energy liberalization on renewable energy policy across a large panel of OECD countries. They found that energy liberalization improves public sentiment for renewable energy. Their study concluded that reducing the monopolistic dominance of state-owned utilities has influenced renewable energy policy when access to the grid is granted to a diverse range of players (Nicolli & Vona, 2019).

Research by Chapman and Itaoka (2018) explores the precedents, regulations, and elements crucial to a successful energy regime change that could be used in the Japanese liberalized electricity market by referring to Germany, Italy, and Spain. Newbery et al. (2018) propose a set of policy ideas for the market design of a future European electricity system with a high proportion of renewable energy sources. They addressed the market flaws that must be addressed to incorporate renewable energy in liberalized electricity markets, evaluated the progress of the EU's renewable energy regulatory instruments, and proposed policy suggestions based on economic concepts for wholesale market design (Newbery et al., 2018). In a study by Agyeman and Lin (2023), they applied the staggered difference-in-difference (SDID) design to 25 OECD member states from 1985 to 2015 to investigate the impact of deregulation on innovation in the electricity sector, with a focus on low-emission technology. Their empirical data suggest that only extensive market deregulation may encourage innovation in carbon capture and storage (CCS). Wang et al. (2021) empirically assessed how Germany, Denmark, and the United Kingdom successfully implemented free-market-oriented policies to attain their renewable energy policy. Since the Hayekian-Thatcherism free-market reform of 1979, the UK has maintained a comparatively low energy tax rate and opted for more pro-market measures. The research also discovered that Fredrich Hayek's theories have significantly impacted its energy liberalization reform agenda. Moreover, they found that energy companies are critical in providing better and more economical RE to home and industrial consumers (Wang et al., 2021).

With much research focused on Europe and the OECD, Ali et al. (2022), on the other hand, examined the effects of Singapore's and the Philippines' energy market liberalization processes on adopting renewable energy electricity generation from 2015 to 2020. They found that Singapore's energy market liberalization resulted in lower household and industrial electricity rates and increased RE share over the stipulated period. The liberalization process has yet to have a discernible influence on carbon emissions. Meanwhile, their results indicate that as the Philippines' energy market liberalization progressed, household electricity prices and carbon emissions increased (Ali et al., 2022). In the same vein, Aris et al. (2020) have also studied the progress of the Philippines and Singapore in liberalizing their electricity sector. Their study aims to identify best practices and problems in respect of legislative framework, implementation phases, market components, and impact on renewable energy penetration for Malaysia to learn.

Pollit (2012) stated that liberalization has significantly improved regulation, competition, innovation, and emissions control. Nonetheless, liberalization per se is not significant in supporting the energy transition. Promoting renewables in liberalized electricity markets poses a paradox, as renewable energy deployment will inevitably be more expensive and less flexible. Furthermore, transitioning to a 100% renewable power industry is unachievable. Thus, they must coexist with fossil fuel technologies (Blazquez et al., 2018). Policy interventions and regulations can help to ameliorate a lack of competitiveness, although many possibilities remain niche uses due to perceived high costs (Verbong & Geels, 2010). Policy measures are required to direct the global electrical transition towards a sustainable energy and electricity system to remain technically possible and economically advantageous. Measures to increase the effectiveness of current non-renewable sources, which still play a significant role in cost reduction and stabilization, should be included in implementing renewable energy (Kabeyi & Olanrewaju, 2022). Many countries implement public funding options such as public investments, loans, grants, and subsidies, which are seen to be especially ideal for encouraging renewable energy at the early stages of technological development (Guliyev, 2023). For example, many countries have financially supported the deployment of renewable energy through policy mechanisms such as Feed-in-Tariffs (FITs) and Renewable Portfolio Standards (RPS) to cover high installation costs and reduce investment risks (Limura & Cross, 2018).

Murshed (2020) found that increased trade openness is most successful in accelerating the transition to renewable energy in low-income economies, with the percentage of renewable energy in total energy consumption predicted to increase by 0.24%. Trade liberalization also contributes to higher renewable energy development regardless of the country's economic status (Murshed, 2020). Private investments, both domestic and international, are essential to advancing the present reform. The government will still play a crucial part in market planning and regulation. Through a stable and consistent system of regulations that favor meritocracy, significant private investments will be appropriately directed to the general societal benefit (Santos et al., 2021).

Aris et al. (2020) discovered that liberalization boosts public enthusiasm for renewable energy, but the same study indicated no significant association between RE uptake and energy market deregulation (Aris et al., 2020). Nevertheless, in several countries, an increase in electricity prices has been recorded in conjunction with an increase in renewable energy, even though the primary goal of electricity market reform was to deliver lower-cost electricity (Limura & Cross, 2018). Although liberalization in Singapore did not reduce carbon emissions from energy generation, it was an effective policy in lowering household and industrial electricity prices and increasing the RE share (Ali et al., 2022). On the other hand, the Philippines' energy market has yet to be fully liberalized, and energy market liberalization in the Philippines has contributed to carbon emissions from electricity generation. While liberalization did not stop the increase in carbon emissions, it did enhance the percentage of fossil fuel-generated power during the stipulated period. Rising carbon emissions are caused by the Philippines' over-reliance on fossil-fuel-generated energy and the government's failure to prioritize sustainability goals (Ali et al., 2022).

Regardless of whether liberalization supports renewable energy development, any measure taken toward decreasing reliance on traditional energy sources could be counted as progress toward a sustainable and accessible energy system. Such a move might make electricity more accessible to more people, more evenly divide the benefits and expenses of electricity generation, and reduce the power sector's ecological footprint (Bryne & Mun, 2003). The primary impediments to energy transition consist of the scant natural resources, insufficient expertise, and inadequate infrastructures required to support the use of renewable energy. Thus, it is frequently recommended that partnerships through international trade engagements and foreign financial flows play a crucial role in expediting the development of renewable energy (Murshed, 2020). Given that the regulation was implemented gradually, its advantages take time to become apparent. In order to increase the production and consumption of renewable energy sources, financial and operating facilities should be made available to renewable energy providers. Trade barriers that restrict effective resource usage should also be moderated as part of policies aiming at reducing emissions (Ponce et al., 2020). By virtue of liberalization, the government should ideally establish and enforce the regulation without meddling in the game itself or attempting to sway the result. A successful decentralized renewable energy system model depends on small private producers working in different market sectors (Guliyev, 2023).

ELECTRICITY LIBERALIZATION AND RENEWABLE ENERGY POLICY IN MALAYSIA

Taghizadeh-Hesary et al. (2022) suggested that countries in Southeast Asia accelerate privatization in the power sector through various measures, including financial assistance as well as interim tax exemptions. They also stressed the importance of the government's actions in providing private investors greater autonomy and incentives to participate in power markets (Taghizadeh-Hesary et al., 2022). The Philippines and Singapore are two ASEAN countries that have fully liberalized their electricity sector and have their energy markets. Since both have disparities in geographical location, economic development status, and overall population, these countries have undergone different experiences with electricity market liberalization. Singapore has a more seamless transition compared to the Philippines. At the same time, Malaysia is projected to be the next ASEAN member to join this liberalization (Aris et al., 2020). Singapore's electricity market is the region's first liberalized electricity market. The energy market in the country is distinguished by free access to its transmission and distribution networks, a distinction between contestable and non-contestable market segments, a wholesale bidding market, and full retail competition (Ali et al., 2022). The energy market authority (EMA) was established in 2001 to monitor the power business and advance energy market liberalization activities. The EMA's principal purpose as an independent regulator of the electricity business was to assure a dependable and secure electricity supply to its users at cost-effective rates (Ali et al., 2022).

While an increase in the electricity price undermines achieving a sustainable power market in Southeast Asia, governments should introduce an electricity tariff classification (ETC) to assist vulnerable, low-income electricity customers (Taghizadeh-Hesary et al., 2022). Providing the most favorable electricity price lists to individuals, businesses, and industries would be a smart idea. Malaysia has effectively implemented such an approach, with the Malaysian multinational electrical utility, Tenaga Nasional Berhad, employing the ETC strategy, particularly during the COVID-19 pandemic (Taghizadeh-Hesary et al., 2022). Generally, the power sector structure mainly consists of generation, where the power is generated either from thermal power plants or innovative technologies, as well as transmission and distribution networks, which is the process of transporting electricity from the point of generation to the point of consumption. In Malaysia's context, only in the generation sector, where generators sell electricity to the Single Buyer (SB), does competition exist. There is no wholesale market; energy trading is commenced through bilateral agreements that are negotiated between generators and the SB. TNB, Malaysia's largest electricity supplier, is still a major player in the generation sector, with more than 50% of the generation capacity in Peninsular Malaysia (Aris et al., 2020). It continues monopolizing the transmission and distribution sectors and ultimately controls the retail sector. Since 2001, the Energy Commission (EC) has regulated the electricity sector. The EC is projected to continue acting as the regulator until the open electricity market is functioning, with the requisite definitions of the scope and maybe renaming or rebranding. Rebranding and redefining the regulator's scope are required to underline the regulator's independence from the government, modify public opinion, and clarify the updated scope of the EC (Aris et al., 2020).

Besides, Malaysia's Competition Act (Act 712) was enacted in 2010 and is regulated by the Malaysian Competition Commission (MyCC). According to this Act, anti-competitive agreements, including price-fixing, bid-rigging, market-sharing, and the misuse of a dominating position in any market for goods or services, are all prohibited. This is done to encourage healthy competition and ethical business practices and, in the end, to safeguard customers' interests. This Act applies to all economic activities in Malaysia, except sectors listed in the First Schedule of Section 3 of the Act; communication, aviation, and energy, including the petroleum industry. The government has not made a decision on the steps to break the electricity supply service monopoly. In the current situation, there is no measure taken by the government toward liberalization of the power sector in Malaysia despite the calls for the government to break the monopoly of the national electricity supply service sector and to provide healthy competition among electricity suppliers, in addition to being able to offer tariff rate differences (Mutalib & Karim, 2022). the government's intention is to guarantee control of the electricity supply service sector, thereby ensuring that consumer demand can be met at all times. With the liberalization in place, the key players in the industry will increase and cause difficulties in the management of the whole energy service (Mutalib & Karim, 2022).

Energy demand is expected to rise as the nation develops. By expanding the share of RE in many industries, it will be possible to successfully meet the goals in climate plans. Effective management of natural resources, especially renewable and non-renewable energies, is indispensable (Pettitpierre,2015). With respect to the development of renewable energy in Malaysia, the government has made efforts to promote and develop RE as part of their agenda in accordance with the international accords to combat climate change and ensure sustainable development for energy as Malaysia is one of the signatories to the Paris Agreement and the Kyoto Protocol. The Ninth, Tenth, and Eleventh Malaysia Plans demonstrate this. The Small Renewable Energy Power Programme (SREP) was launched as part of the Ninth Malaysia Plan to encourage the use of RE resources (Ghazali, 2018). Following Malaysia's ratification of IRENA's statute in 2010, the RE Act 2011 was gazetted in June 2011 and served as the country's primary regulatory framework for boosting the production of renewable energy supported by a feed-in tariff mechanism. Present eligible sources for incentives under the FiT scheme run by the Malaysian Sustainable Energy Development Authority (SEDA) include solar PV, biomass, biogas, small hydro, and geothermal (Mustafa et al., 2022). While the New Energy Policy (2011-2015) and the Renewable Energy Act 2011 were the main emphases of the Tenth and Eleventh Malaysia Plans, they both aimed to increase energy security and speed the integration of renewable sources into Malaysia's electricity generation mix. In the Eleventh Malaysia Plan, introducing new renewable energy sources, improving technical expertise, and adopting net energy metering have been given priority (Ghazali, 2018).

The tariff system for renewable energy (RE) generation in Malaysia was introduced with the implementation of the Small Renewable Energy Project (SREP), which was to support small-scale renewable electricity, from 2001 to 2010. SREP focused on the development of solar photovoltaics, biomass and biogas, mini-hydro, and municipal solid waste. However, Malaysia has remained behind the target, although the tariff rate was revised in 2006 (Sovacool & Drupady, 2011). In 2019, the National Renewable Energy Policy and Action Plan in order to increase renewables share in the energy. The enactment of the first legislation on Feed-in tariff in 2011 in virtue of the Renewable Energy Act 2011 (Act 725) has enlightened this industry. In the same year, the Sustainable Energy Development Authority (SEDA) was established under the SEDA Malaysia Act 2011. SEDA is the crucial player in promoting RE development in Malaysia as in Section 15 (b) of the Sustainable Energy Development Authority Act 2011 (Act 726) and implementing and monitoring the FiT Program in Malaysia as per Section 15 (d) of the same Act. The renewable energy generator plants for feed-in approval holders will be linked directly to the national grid to provide clean electricity. The RE (in kWh) generated by feed-in approval holders will be sold at a fixed premium price (FiT Rate) to the "distribution licensee" or the holder of the license to distribute the electricity (Johari et al., 2013). FiT has been deployed by over 75 jurisdictions worldwide, including Germany, Denmark, Spain, and China (Yang et al., 2021).

Figure 3. Feed in tariff in Malaysia

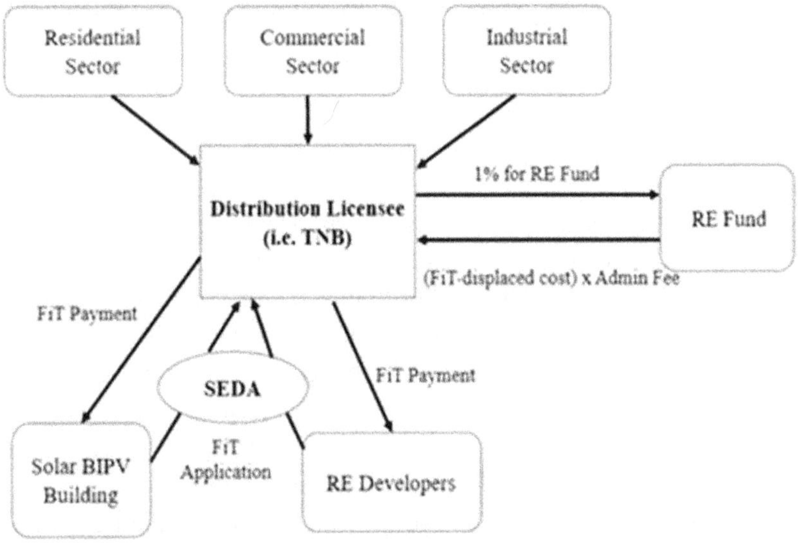

Figure 3 shows how the FiT mechanism works in Malaysia. SEDA will regulate FiT implementation, including FiT application. Under this mechanism, qualifying individuals or non-individuals can sell electricity (up to 30MW) generated from RE resources to power utility firms at a fixed premium price. Although FiT has been implemented in various jurisdictions, this mechanism is appropriate for the early stages of the renewable energy industry's development. Once the industry matures, the integration of FiT and renewable energy portfolio standard (RPS) are needed to ensure a competitive and sustainable renewable energy sector (Yang et al., 2021). Apart from FiT, the government also introduce renewable energy auctions for Large Scale Solar (LSS) Photovoltaic Plant. Section 50C of the Electricity Supply Act 1990 (Act 447) empowers the Energy Commission (EC) to issue guidelines on a Large Scale Solar Photovoltaic Plant for Connection to Electricity Networks. In auctions, the government will offer contracts that guarantee subsidized remuneration for renewable energy producers. Through this mechanism also, price discovery and competition have resulted in generation prices that are far lower than expected (Matthäus, 2020). Although competition in auctions provides an incentive to innovate and provide low-profit margins, this mechanism may only support mature technology such as solar photovoltaic and wind energy (Del Río & Kiefer, 2022).

Moreover, the Malaysian Investment Development Authority (MIDA) has played an active role in promoting green technology development by instituting the Green Investment Tax Allowance (GITA) and Green Income Tax Exemption (GITE). These incentives will allow small and medium-sized businesses (SMEs) to expand the renewable energy industry and encourage potential investors and industry participants to engage in renewable energy, energy efficiency, green building, green data center, and integrated waste management. In the absence of liberalization in the Malaysian power sector, the renewable energy sector is still progressing. However, renewable energy expansion may be impeded due to a lack of appropriate technology and infrastructure. However, by encouraging technological advancement and innovation, economic complexity can help overcome technical barriers to renewable energy development, resulting in new industries and technologies that facilitate the transition to a more sustainable energy system (Wang et al., 2023). Furthermore, financial globalization allows the transfer of technology and best practices between countries in order to overcome technical limitations in the development of renewable energy (Wang et al., 2023).

CONCLUSION

Liberating and breaking the national electricity supply monopoly will lead to various problems, affecting the continuity of services to consumers. This transition incurred high indirect costs and thus can affect the tariff rate of electricity supply to consumers. Additionally, this liberalization may not necessarily be capable of reducing the electricity supply price to consumers. Malaysia is likewise making good progress in terms of greater renewable penetration even in the monopolistic power sector. There is no apparent indication that the liberalized electricity market has impacted growing renewable energy adoption. In most circumstances, most governments rely on more than electricity liberalization to boost renewable energy development. Other initiatives are also supporting renewable energy development. Nevertheless, government intervention is also required to fulfill the goals of the liberalized power sector. Power producers or generators should have a large market for the products they create to earn the best possible price, and the government may assist in enacting the required legislation to support this.

Power utilities in regulated markets that restrict competition may have limited capacity to develop renewable energy technologies, so the liberalization of the electricity market theoretically affects the search space for these technologies. By allowing new competitors to enter the market who are not reliant on the incumbents' core competencies and generation paradigm, the liberalization of the energy market can aid in breaking this route dependency. Nevertheless, the government has a crucial role in promoting renewable energy technology in order to emphasize the necessity of a competitive electricity market for clean energy innovation. Moreover, environmental policies that highlight low-carbon initiatives have greater significance. Through these low carbon policies, the government's roles do not diminish despite the fact that the power sector shifts from a monopoly to a competitive one. As completely new technologies emerge, certain market participants may be unable or unwilling to change their core generation paradigm since the energy market depends on capital-intensive infrastructures. Continuous investments in electricity supply are required, and this cannot be accomplished without a regulator to monitor market activity and guarantee that the market operates efficiently.

REFERENCES

Aguirre, M., & Ibikunle, G. (2014). *Determinants of renewable energy growth: A global sample analysis*. Energy Policy. doi:10.1016/j.enpol.2014.02.036

Agyeman, S. D., & Lin, B. (2023). Electricity industry (de) regulation and innovation in negative-emission technologies: How do market liberalization influences climate change mitigation? *Energy*, *270*, 126863. doi:10.1016/j.energy.2023.126863

Ali, H., Phoumin, H., Suryadi, B., Farooque, A. A., & Yaqub, R. (2022). Assessing ASEAN's Liberalized Electricity Markets: The Case of Singapore and the Philippines. *Sustainability (Basel)*, *14*(18), 11307. doi:10.3390u141811307

Amenta, C., Aronica, M., & Stagnaro, C. (2022). Is more competition better? Retail electricity prices and switching rates in the European Union. *Utilities Policy*, *78*, 101405. doi:10.1016/j.jup.2022.101405

Aris, H., Mohd Zawawi, I. S., & Jørgensen, B. N. (2020). The Philippines' and Singapore's Journeys towards Liberalised Electricity Supply Industries—Takeaways for Malaysia. *Energies*, *13*(14), 3514. doi:10.3390/en13143514

Baris, K., & Kucukali, S. (2012). Availability of renewable energy sources in Turkey: Current situation, potential, government policies, and the EU perspective. *Energy Policy*, *42*, 377–391. doi:10.1016/j.enpol.2011.12.002

Belyaev, L. S. (2010). *Electricity market reforms: Economics and policy challenges*. Springer Science & Business Media.

Blazquez, J., Fuentes-Bracamontes, R., Bollino, C. A., & Nezamuddin, N. (2018). The renewable energy policy Paradox. *Renewable & Sustainable Energy Reviews*, *82*, 1–5. doi:10.1016/j.rser.2017.09.002

Bojnec, Š., & Križaj, A. (2021). Electricity markets during the liberalization: The case of a European Union country. *Energies*, *14*(14), 4317. doi:10.3390/en14144317

Büyüközkan, G., Karabulut, Y., & Mukul, E. (2018). A novel renewable energy selection model for United Nations' sustainable development goals. *Energy*, *165*, 290–302. doi:10.1016/j.energy.2018.08.215

Byrne, J., & Mun, Y. M. (2003). Rethinking reform in the electricity sector: Power liberalization or energy transformation. Electricity reform: Social and environmental challenges, pp. 48–76.

Chapman, A. J., & Itaoka, K. (2018). Energy transition to a future low-carbon energy society in Japan's liberalizing electricity market: Precedents, policies, and factors of a successful transition. *Renewable & Sustainable Energy Reviews*, *81*, 2019–2027. doi:10.1016/j.rser.2017.06.011

Del Río, P., & Kiefer, C. P. (2022). Which policy instruments promote innovation in renewable electricity technologies? A critical review of the literature with a focus on auctions. *Energy Research & Social Science*, *89*, 102501. doi:10.1016/j.erss.2022.102501

Diaz-Rainey, I., Tulloch, D. J., Ahmed, I., McCarten, M., & Taghizadeh-Hesary, F. (2021). *An energy policy for ASEAN? Lessons from the EU experience on energy integration, security, and decarbonization*.

Guerci, E., Rastegar, M. A., & Cincotti, S. (2010). Agent-based modeling and simulation of competitive wholesale electricity markets. Handbook of power systems II, 241-286.

Guliyev, F. (2023). Renewable Energy Targets and Policies in Traditional Oil-Producing Countries: A Comparison of Azerbaijan and Kazakhstan. *Journal of Eurasian Studies*.

Haidar, A. M., John, P. N., & Shawal, M. (2011). Optimal configuration assessment of renewable energy in Malaysia. *Renewable Energy*, *36*(2), 881–888. doi:10.1016/j.renene.2010.07.024

Halkos, G. E., & Tsirivis, A. S. (2023). Electricity Prices in the European Union Region: The Role of Renewable Energy Sources, Key Economic Factors and Market Liberalization. *Energies*, *16*(6), 2540. doi:10.3390/en16062540

He, Y., Xu, Y., Pang, Y., Tian, H., & Wu, R. (2016). A regulatory policy to promote renewable energy consumption in China: Review and future evolutionary path. *Renewable Energy*, *89*, 695–705. https://www.mordorintelligence.com/industry-reports/malaysia-power-market. doi:10.1016/j.renene.2015.12.047

Iimura, A., & Cross, J. S. (2018). The impact of renewable energy on household electricity prices in liberalized electricity markets: A cross-national panel data analysis. *Utilities Policy*, *54*, 96–106. doi:10.1016/j.jup.2018.08.003

Itaoka, K., Chapman, A., & Farabi-Asl, H. (2022). Underpinnings of consumer preferences and participation in Japan's liberalized energy market. *Utilities Policy*, *76*, 101379. doi:10.1016/j.jup.2022.101379

Jamasb, T., & Pollitt, M. G. (2011). Electricity sector liberalization and innovation: An analysis of the UK's patenting activities. *Research Policy*, *40*(2), 309–324. doi:10.1016/j.respol.2010.10.010

Johari, A., SitiHafshar, S., Hashim, H., & Ramli, M. (2013). Feed-in-Tariff (FiT) concept to promote the usage of renewable energy in Malaysia. *International Journal of Energy and Power*, *2*(2), 33–37.

Joskow, P. L. (2022). From hierarchies to markets and partially back again in electricity: Responding to decarbonization and security of supply goals. *Journal of Institutional Economics*, *18*(2), 313–329. doi:10.1017/S1744137421000400

Kabeyi, M. J. B., & Olanrewaju, O. A. (2022). Sustainable energy transition for renewable and low carbon grid electricity generation and supply. *Frontiers in Energy Research*, *9*, 1032. doi:10.3389/fenrg.2021.743114

Kitchen, T., & Oreilly, P. (2016). Energy poverty amidst abundance in Malaysia: Placing energy in multidimensional poverty. *Development in Practice*, *26*(2), 203–213. doi:10.1080/09614524.2016.1133562

Kumar, M., Poudineh, R., & Shamsuddin, A. (2021). *Electricity supply industry reform and design of competitive electricity market in Malaysia* (No. 44). OIES Paper: EL.

Littlechild, S. (2021). *The evolution of competitive retail electricity markets. Handbook on Electricity Markets*. Edward Elgar Publishing Limited.

Love, L. (2000). *The single-buyer model: A dangerous path toward competitive electricity markets.* OpenKnowledge. https://openknowledge.worldbank.org/server/api/core/bitstreams/b13421df-1bf3-5207-9d99-001284177404/content

Matthäus, D. (2020). Designing effective auctions for renewable energy support. *Energy Policy*, *142*, 111462. doi:10.1016/j.enpol.2020.111462

Murshed, M. (2020). Are Trade Liberalization policies aligned with Renewable Energy Transition in low and middle-income countries? An Instrumental Variable Approach. *Renewable Energy*, *151*, 1110–1123. doi:10.1016/j.renene.2019.11.106

Mustafa, M., Ghazali, F., & Yuniza, M. E. (2022). Governance interventions in providing affordable, reliable, sustainable, and modern energy in the ASEAN region (Goal 7). In Good Governance and the Sustainable Development Goals in Southeast Asia (pp. 84-97). Routledge.

Najm, S., & Matsumoto, K. I. (2020). Does renewable energy substitute LNG international trade in the energy transition? *Energy Economics*, *92*, 104964. doi:10.1016/j.eneco.2020.104964

Nerini, F. F., Tomei, J., To, L. S., Bisaga, I., Parikh, P., Black, M., & Milligan, B. (2018). Mapping synergies and trade-offs between energy and the Sustainable Development Goals. *Nature Energy*, *3*(1), 10–15. doi:10.103841560-017-0036-5

Newbery, D., Pollitt, M. G., Ritz, R. A., & Strielkowski, W. (2018). Market design for a high-renewables European electricity system. *Renewable & Sustainable Energy Reviews*, *91*, 695–707. doi:10.1016/j.rser.2018.04.025

Nicolli, F., & Vona, F. (2019). Energy market liberalization and renewable energy policies in OECD countries. *Energy Policy*, *128*, 853–867. doi:10.1016/j.enpol.2019.01.018

Panda, A., & Patel, A. (2011). Competition law and competition issues affecting the energy sector in India. *Journal of Infrastructure Development*, *3*(2), 107–115. doi:10.1177/097493061100300201

Paryono, P., Absori, A., Dimyati, K., Basri, M., & Rismawati, S. D. (2020). Liberalization and electricity policy changes: Problems and challenges in the electricity sector in Indonesia. *International Journal of Energy Economics and Policy*, *10*(1), 170–177. doi:10.32479/ijeep.8636

Pepermans, G. (2019). European energy market liberalization: Experiences and challenges. *International Journal of Economic Policy Studies*, *13*(1), 3–26. doi:10.100742495-018-0009-0

Petinrin, J., & Shaaban, M. (2015). Renewable energy for continuous energy sustainability in Malaysia. *Renewable & Sustainable Energy Reviews*, *50*, 967–981. doi:10.1016/j.rser.2015.04.146

Pettitpierre, A. (2015). *Environmental Law in Switzerland*. Kluwer Law International.

Pietzcker, R. C., Stetter, D., Manger, S., & Luderer, G. (2014). Using the sun to decarbonize the power sector: The economic potential of photovoltaics and concentrating solar power. *Applied Energy*, *135*, 704–720. doi:10.1016/j.apenergy.2014.08.011

Politt, M. G. (2012). The role of policy in energy transitions: Lessons from the energy liberalization era. *Energy Policy*, *50*, 128–137. doi:10.1016/j.enpol.2012.03.004

Ponce, P., Oliveira, C., Álvarez, V., & del Río-Rama, M. D. L. C. (2020). The liberalization of the internal energy market in the European Union: Evidence of its influence on reducing environmental pollution. *Energies*, *13*(22), 6116. doi:10.3390/en13226116

Santos, A. Q. O., da Silva, A. R., Ledesma, J. J. G., de Almeida, A. B., Cavallari, M. R., & Junior, O. H. A. (2021). Electricity Market in Brazil: A Critical Review on the Ongoing Reform. *Energies*, *14*(10), 2873. doi:10.3390/en14102873

Shem, C., Simsek, Y., Hutfilter, U. F., & Urmee, T. (2019). Potentials and opportunities for low carbon energy transition in Vietnam: A policy analysis. *Energy Policy*, *134*, 110818. doi:10.1016/j.enpol.2019.06.026

Shin, K. J., & Managi, S. (2017). Liberalization of a retail electricity market: Consumer satisfaction and household switching behavior in Japan. *Energy Policy*, *110*, 675–685. doi:10.1016/j.enpol.2017.07.048

Siksnelyte, I., & Zavadskas, E. K. (2019). Achievements of the European Union countries in seeking a sustainable electricity sector. *Energies*, *12*(12), 2254. doi:10.3390/en12122254

Sovacool, B., & Drupady, I. (2011). Examining the Small Renewable Energy Power (SREP) Program in Malaysia. *Energy Policy*, *39*(11), 7244–7255. doi:10.1016/j.enpol.2011.08.045

Stagnaro, C., Amenta, C., Di Croce, G., & Lavecchia, L. (2020). Managing the liberalization of Italy's retail electricity market: A policy proposal. *Energy Policy*, *137*, 111150. doi:10.1016/j.enpol.2019.111150

Taghizadeh-Hesary, F., Rasoulinezhad, E., & Phoumin, H. (2022). Ways to achieve universal access to sustainable electricity in Southeast Asia. *Economic Change and Restructuring*, *55*(4), 2031–2050. doi:10.100710644-022-09386-4

Verbong, G. P., & Geels, F. W. (2010). Exploring sustainability transitions in the electricity sector with socio-technical pathways. *Technological Forecasting and Social Change*, *77*(8), 1214–1221. doi:10.1016/j.techfore.2010.04.008

Vlados, C., Chatzinikolaou, D., & Kapaltzoglou, F. F. (2021). Energy market liberalization in Greece: Structures, policy, and prospects. *International Journal of Energy Economics and Policy*, *11*(2), 115–126. doi:10.32479/ijeep.10804

Wang, W. H., Moreno-Casas, V., & Huerta de Soto, J. (2021). A free-market environmentalist transition toward renewable energy: The cases of Germany, Denmark, and the United Kingdom. *Energies*, *14*(15), 4659. doi:10.3390/en14154659

Wang, X., Chen, G., Afshan, S., Awosusi, A. A., & Abbas, S. (2023). Transition towards sustainable energy: The role of economic complexity, financial liberalization and natural resources management in China. *Resources Policy*, *83*, 103631. doi:10.1016/j.resourpol.2023.103631

Yang, D. X., Jing, Y. Q., Wang, C., Nie, P. Y., & Sun, P. (2021). Analysis of renewable energy subsidy in China under uncertainty: Feed-in tariff vs. renewable portfolio standard. *Energy Strategy Reviews*, *34*, 100628. doi:10.1016/j.esr.2021.100628

Zhang, Y. F., Parker, D., & Kirkpatrick, C. (2008). Electricity sector reform in developing countries: An econometric assessment of the effects of privatization, competition, and regulation. *Journal of Regulatory Economics*, *33*(2), 159–178. doi:10.100711149-007-9039-7

Zipp, A. (2017). The marketability of variable renewable energy in liberalized electricity markets–an empirical analysis. *Renewable Energy*, *113*, 1111–1121. doi:10.1016/j.renene.2017.06.072

KEY TERMS AND DEFINITIONS

Carbon Footprint: The total amount of greenhouse gases (including carbon dioxide and methane) that are generated by our activities.

Distribution: Provides the necessary link between producers and consumers, within, and across borders.

Generation Sector: An industry in which the process of generating electric power from sources of primary energy or is an industrial facility for the generation of electric power.

Liberalization: The process or means of the elimination of control of the state over economic activities. It provides greater autonomy to business enterprises in decision-making and eliminates government interference.

Low Carbon Economy: Also known as a decarbonized economy; is an economy that has a minimal output of greenhouse gas (GHG) emissions into the environment's biosphere. In this context, it usually refers to the emission of carbon dioxide and methane.

Renewable Energy: Energy produced from sources like the sun and wind that are naturally replenished and do not run out. Renewable energy can be used for electricity generation, space and water heating and cooling, and transportation.

TOPSIS Method: The Technique for Order of Preference by Similarity to the Ideal Solution is a multi-criteria decision analysis method based on the fundamental premise that the best solution has the shortest distance from the positive-ideal solution and the longest distance from the negative-ideal one.

Transmission: Means a facility for transmitting electricity and includes any structures, equipment, or other facilities used for that purpose.

Chapter 5
Competition Law and the Transition to Low-Carbon in Indonesia

Cenuk Widiyastrisna Sayekti
Airlangga University, Indonesia

Suparto Wijoyo
Airlangga University, Indonesia

ABSTRACT

This chapter investigates the possibility of policy in support of low carbon transition under the competition law. It is true that competition law and environmental policies are key drivers of innovation, but their interplay is need to be explored more. The main question in this chapter is: does the competition law can help to achieve the Indonesia's Net Zero and sustainability goals? This study uses a qualitative approach that analysis the success of competition law in fighting climate change and boosting the transition to low carbon. Qualitative techniques are carried out through literature studies or references that describe analysing of implementing a competition law on the environment and mitigating climate change caused by carbon emissions.

INTRODUCTION

Competition law can play an important role in facilitating low-carbon transitions and be part of the solution to climate change and sustainability is relevant in the context of the analysis of mergers and dominance cases (Holmes, 2020). Competition law can take into account environmental and social priorities through substantive competition rules, exceptions, exemptions and exclusions, and enhanced the enforcement of competition law (Gehring, 2006). Competition law should not prohibit competitors from agreeing to produce more energy-efficient goods, as this could lead to higher prices for consumers. Dominant undertakings should not be allowed to abuse their dominant position by switching to pricier recyclable packaging (Kingston, 2021).

DOI: 10.4018/979-8-3693-0390-0.ch005

Copyright © 2024, IGI Global. Copying or distributing in print or electronic forms without written permission of IGI Global is prohibited.

This paper investigates the possibility of policy in support of low carbon transition under Indonesia's competition law. Our contribution is motivated by the fact that both competition and environmental policies are key drivers of innovation and their interplay need to be explored. The main question in this paper is: Can the competition law help to achieve Indonesia's Net Zero and sustainability goals? Indonesia has set a goal of achieving net zero emissions by 2060, which requires large funds and competition between business actors and the government (Munadiya, 2022). In its Nationally Determined Contribution (hereinafter referred as "NDC"), Indonesia committed to reducing the emissions by 29% against a 2030 business-as-usual (hereinafter referred as "BAU") scenario and reducing emissions by up to 41% below the 2030 BAU level, subject to international assistance for finance, technology transfer, and capacity building (Wijaya et al., 2017).

As an implementing rule to reduce national carbon emissions, the Government of Indonesia has issued Presidential Regulation no. 98 of 2021 as a specific climate financing instrument to achieve Indonesia's NDC, gives the Government of Indonesia effective control over carbon rights by introducing several carbon pricing mechanisms, including carbon trading. Despite efforts by the Indonesian government to transition to net zero by enacting climate law regarding carbon tax, there is not enough consideration for current policies, particularly policies to focus more on deforestation. This is mainly through the palm oil industry (Putri, 2023) as well as the significant expansion of coal mining (CNBC, 2023).

Previous research have agreed that the competition law has a crucial role in transitioning low-carbon energy, and presents recommendations for how competition policy can promote a successful transition (Moss & Kwoka, 2010). Luo (2016) finds that co-opetition can lead to more profit and less total carbon emissions in low carbon manufacturing (Luo et al., 2016). Chen also examines the impact of competition on low carbon manufacturing, and finds that market power structure can affect the achievement of low carbon manufacturing (Chen et al., 2017). Overall, the papers suggest that competition law can help incentivize low carbon practices and promote a successful transition to a low carbon economy.

Even there is no immediate response in the specialized literature regarding the interface between environmental requirements and competition law, scholars have argued that a certain dialogue between the environment and competition is possible (Nogueira & de Araujo, 2020). On the other side, others have argued that they are elements not compatible or even conflicting (Nogueira & de Araujo, 2020). In the end, environmental protection should be integrated into competition policy-making and how this goal might be achieved (De Stefano, 2020).

INDONESIA CARBON EMISSIONS

Carbon emissions are troublesome. To date, CO2 is blamed for the climate change and accounts for about 76% of total greenhouse gas emissions (EPA, 2022). Carbon dioxide emissions, primarily from the combustion of fossil fuels, have risen dramatically since the start of the industrial revolution. Most of the world's greenhouse gas emissions come from a relatively small number of countries (C2ES, 2020). China, the United States, and the nations that make up the European Union are the three largest emitters on an absolute basis (Crippa et al., 2020). Per capita greenhouse gas emissions are highest in the United States and Russia (C2ES, 2020). Globally, the main sources of greenhouse gas emissions are electricity and heat (30.4%), land use change (6.5%), agriculture (11.8%), and transportation (15.9%) (C2ES, 2020).

In 2016, total global greenhouse gas (GHG) emissions, not including those from land use, continued to increase slowly by around 0.5% (±1%), to around 49.3 gigatons of CO2 equivalent (Gt CO2 eq). However, 2015 and 2016 emissions increases were the slowest compared to the early 1990s, but not during the years of global recession (Olivier et al., 2017). This is mainly due to lower coal consumption, a shift in fuel to natural gas, and an increase in renewable power generation; especially wind and solar power (Olivier et al., 2017). Most of the emissions (about 72%) consist of carbon dioxide (CO2), but methane (CH4), nitrous oxide (N2O) and fluorinated gases (so-called F-gases) also make up substantial shares (19%, 6% and 3%, respectively) (Olivier et al., 2017).

Indonesia, as an archipelagic country with extensive coastal areas and small islands, is very vulnerable to the impacts of climate change (Measey, 2010). Indonesia has experienced extremes climate change such as floods and droughts (Jensen, 2020), as well as the long-term impacts of sea level rise (Triana & Wahyudi, 2020). The use of fossil CO2 emissions in Indonesia were 530,035,650 tons in 2016. CO2 emissions in that year increased by 6.41% compared to the previous year in 2015, which was an increase of 31,937,870 tons, when CO2 emissions were 498,097,780 tons (Worldmeters, 2016).

CO2 emissions per capita in Indonesia are equivalent to 2.03 tons per person (based on a population of 261,556.381 in 2016), an increase of 0.10 from 1.93 tons CO2 per person in 2015; this represents a 5.1% change in CO2 emissions per capita. In 2020, the impact of climate change worsening due to the CO2 emissions increasing by 1.6% between 2018 and 2019, with average annual change is 6.2% since 2015 (Crippa et al., 2020). In line with the increase in population, natural disasters that are affected by carbon emissions have a wider impact on the community and their assets.

Currently, carbon emission is one of the most infuriated issues of that is directly responsible for climate changes at out of ordinary rates. However, climate change is not the main concern of Indonesian community (Nugroho, 2020), despite Indonesia is the world's fourth largest emitter of greenhouse gases emissions (Azmi et al., 2022), which are mostly the result of forest fires and environmental degradation due to human activities (Alisjahbana & Busch, 2017; Butt et al., 2015).

The ignorance also stated by the Indonesian government who confirmed that Indonesia will not set targets on the increasingly dire climate change projections and focus instead on its economic growth (Jong, 2020). This reminds us of a story of the Lorax of Dr. Seuss where the green grass, the wet pond, and the clean clouds is destroyed by the Once-ler's insatiable appetite to sell more thneeds (Glass, 2014). With the worsening climatic conditions (Case et al., 2007; Irwansyah, 2016), Indonesia along with other countries around the world have agreed to fight against climate change through various carbon reduction efforts (Handayani et al., 2020; Pauw et al., 2021).

One of the causes of carbon emissions is the use of electrical energy (Azmi et al., 2022). In Indonesia, the electricity consumption increases each year by an average of about 3.60% (from 2015-2020) which contributes to these carbon emissions. According to Indonesia State Electricity Company (PLN), the electricity sector accountable for 14% of carbon emissions from total national emissions (Azmi et al., 2022). In 2019, the Indonesia Ministry of Energy and Mineral Resources (MEMR) through Electric Directorate General Performance Report (LAKIN DJK), published a report announced that the country consumption of electricity as much as 1,084 kWh/capita (Sukarso, 2021), which around 87.99% of total power plant was generated from fossil fuel base energy: 62.71% from coal, 21.24% from natural gas, 4.00% from oil and diesel (Sukarso, 2021). Meanwhile, the International Energy Agency (IEA) reported that the total emission of carbon dioxide (CO2) in Indonesia reached 33.9 gigatons throughout 2020. A total of 13.5 gigatons of which came from electricity and heating, being the most compared to other sources (Azmi et al., 2022).

CHARACTERISTICS OF COMPETITION LAW

Competition law is a set of regulation necessary to create an efficient economy to prevent and deal with various forms of abuse of market power (de Araujo & Nogueira, 2020). Competition has the following functions: economic optimization, technological progress, implementation of economic phenomena and flexibility of adaptation. These functions are achieved effectively through competitive actions undertaken by rational agents operating rationally in a free market (de Araujo & Nogueira, 2020). The main task of competition law is to protect competition itself (Kloosterhuis & Mulder, 2015), regardless of whether corporate behaviour protects the environment or not. Therefore, competition law does not differentiate between the two as long as corporate behaviour does not eliminate competition.

Competition law is an important part of greater part of the economic sectors, with a special place belongs to the field of environmental protection. Currently, competition law is used as a weapon to prevent environmental damages made through business agreements among the competitors, which is one of the impactful agreements is cartel. There is no company that does not know a cartel is violation towards competition law (Forgioni, 2013). Companies even recognize the importance of pre-notifications to competition authorities when there is certain market concentration ongoing (Forgioni, 2013). However, different respond does not occur in the environmental case (de Araujo & Nogueira, 2020). Forgioni (2013) argues that the principle of environmental defence in structuring the economic order often clearly refers to different methods and treatments based on the environmental impact of products and services and the process of providing them.

Competition law does not mean to replace environmental law to prevent more damage, but it can be an instrument to prevent behaviour or agreements between business actors that can cause environmental damage. On the other hand, competition law actually becomes the main obstacle to implementing policies to protect the environment from damage. In this context, the interaction between environmental issues and competition presents a complex conflict (de Araujo & Nogueira, 2020).

ENVIRONMENTAL LAW

Environmental law as a vast area of law that addresses environmental problems and explores its complex nature and role in society (Fisher, 2017), it regulates the quantity and nature of impacts of human activities (Lesirma, 2016). Competition law serves to preserve competition, with a focus on the maximization of consumer welfare (Inderst & Thomas, 2023), while environmental law main task is to protect and preserve the environment to prevent further environmental degradation, and promote sustainable development. Another study emphasizes that environmental law's primary task is to define terms and offer legal solutions to address environmental degradation (Ilić-Petković & Ilić-Krstić, 2016).

Environmental problems began to receive serious attention in almost all countries after the UN Conference on the Human Environment was held in 1972 in Stockholm, Sweden. The negative impact of economic development activities is recognized as one of the causes of various environmental problems (Akib & Sumarja, 2019). Environmental pollution and damage due to the impact of the use of technology in industrial activities and the low quality of behaviour of communities is believed to be a source of obstacles to the realization of sustainable development to improve human welfare (Abalansa et al., 2021). Competition law can play its role by requiring economic entities to promote human welfare and implement environmental policy without affecting the competitiveness in the market (Domazet, 2013).

Given the increasing role of competition law to protect environment, it is important to consider the relationship between environmental policy and competition. Ignoring these considerations only gives rise to negative externalities to the environment (Hurić-Larsen & Münch, 2016). This means that environmental considerations must have an important position in competition policy. Implicitly, Indonesian law and policy reflect this important position in Article 33(3) and (4) of the 1945 Constitution, as stated: "The land and the water and the natural resources contained therein are controlled by the State and shall be used for the greatest benefit of the people".

The position even clearer after the amendment to the 1945 Constitution, which the consideration of environment is reflected in the Article 33(4) of the 1945 Constitution, which states that: "The national economy is organized on the basis of economic democracy which upholds the principles of [inter alia] ... environmental sustainability, ..., and maintaining the balance of progress and unity of the national economy". This article provides the basis for the official implementation of state economic activities in a manner that does not cause environmental damage. This also firmly strengthens the link between economic and environmental policies (Akib & Sumarja, 2019).

COMPETITION LAW AND ENVIRONMENTAL ISSUES

PLN Market Power Structure

Indonesia State Electricity Company (PLN) is the key player in carbon trade, but also its monopolized power market is the key obstacle to fossil fuel phase out. The electricity market in Indonesia is fully managed by the PLN, a company which has various business units that carry out multiple functions including generation, transmission and distribution. Fossil-fuel-centered PLN has substantial dominance and exerts profound influence in the power market structure with 11 subholding and subsidiaries own more than 75% of the generation capacity in Indonesia (Heffron et al., 2022; Maulidia et al., 2019).

The 1985 electricity law marked the beginning of structural reforms that contributed to the opening of the electricity market to private investors and allowing the participation of the private sector in electricity generation for its own use and to sell to PT PLN (Setyawan, 2013), but had little impact on the administrative governance structure. The restructuring of electricity in Indonesia began in early 1992 when the Government opened the electricity generation market to competition. Then the government issued Presidential Decree Number 37 of 1992 which provided a road to enter the generation market. A number of permits were issued to Independent Power Producers (IPPs) to build, install and operate power plants, as well as sell the electricity produced to PT PLN for distribution to the public (Setyawan, 2013). The Indonesian Electricity Law of 2002 considered competition and private participation in both electricity generation and retail. However, this reform step was hampered in December 2004 because the Indonesian Constitutional Court annulled the 2002 Electricity Law on the grounds that the law violated Article 33 of the Indonesian Constitution. According to the Constitutional Court, electricity is a public good and its distribution must remain under the exclusive control of the central government.

As a result of the repeal of the 2002 Electricity Law, the 1985 law was reauthorized which limited private participation in the electricity sector. Although IPPs participate in electricity generation, this does not occur under competitive wholesale market conditions, but rather as an 'outsourced' element in PLN's monopoly supply chain (Setyawan, 2013). In other words, electricity generation in Indonesia operates within uncompetitive market structure.

In 2009, the legislature passed a new Electricity Law to strengthen the previous regulatory framework and give local governments a greater role in licensing and determining basic electricity tariffs. The Law No. 30 of 2009 firmly confirms the state as the regulator of electricity supply and PLN as the provider in accordance with the mandate of Article 33 of the Constitution (Articles 3 and 4 of the Electricity Law No. 30/2009). The fundamental change that occurred was that the law gave the provincial government the authority to issue regulations regarding electricity. This also allows local governments (province level) to adjust electricity tariffs (Article 5 of the Electricity Law No. 30/2009). Although this is a positive step to improve electricity sector operations, PLN's monopoly position remains intact. In 2010, the government gave a mandate to PLN to accelerate the development of electricity generation projects using renewable energy, coal and gas, in particular inviting private investors to participate in the construction of power plants, including related transmission lines, and for PLN to purchase them made it as the only buyer creating monopsony power in the relevant market (Minister of Energy and Mineral Resources Regulation No. 15/2010, 2010).

PLN's electricity monopoly practice is contrary to the Law No.5 of 1999 concerning Prohibition of Monopoly Practices and Unfair Competition. The electricity monopoly has actually made PLN unable to operate efficiently. In this context, what needs to be considered in the future is the involvement of more participation of private sectors so that PLN will be operate efficiently, as shown by experience in countries that are considered successful in reforming their electricity sector (Maulidia et al., 2019).

Coal-Fired Power Plants

The Indonesian government has submitted its pledge to decrease carbon emissions to 29% by 2030 and 41% in 2050 by preparing a progressive emissions reduction program to control the carbon trade, including incentives based on success in lowering greenhouse gas emissions and imposing various policies (Suroyo & Munthe, 2021). Indonesia's NDC climate pledge targets a 29%-41% emission reduction by 2030 and 2050. This pledge was submitted to the United Nations Framework Convention on Climate Change (UNFCCC) ahead of the Paris Climate Conference. Indonesia aimed to decarbonize its economy through a phased approach – that is, through policies for improved land use and spatial planning, energy conservation and promotion of clean and renewable energy sources, and better waste management (Simon, 2015).

However, the pledge is highly insufficient due to the emissions have increased at a faster rate compare to expected in recent years (Tracker, 2021). The rating indicates that Indonesia's climate policies and commitments are not at all consistent with the Paris Agreement's 1.5°C temperature limit (Tracker, 2021). Recent developments confirm that Indonesia plans to reduce its long-term dependence on coal. Since 2010 Indonesia has established around 23 GW of coal-fired power generation capacity and by the end of 2020 has 11 GW under construction (Shearer et al., 2017).

The new plan for the electricity sector (RUPTL) does not indicate a transition away from coal-fired power generation, which accounts for about 14 GW of additional capacity planned between 2021 and 2030 and is set to meet 64% of demand by 2030. In addition, the ambitious low-carbon scenario (LCCP) still takes advantage of the important. The role of coal – accounting for about 58% of the energy mix by 2030 and 38% by 2050. This plan does not match the content of the Paris Agreement's objective in which Indonesia needs to reduce share of coal-fired power plants up to 10% by 2030 and phase out coal by 2040 (Tracker, 2020).

Indonesia has no strong strategy as well as to ensure a transition to clean renewable energy. For example, Indonesia cannot afford to switch from fossil fuel production to clean renewable energy. This is because stakeholders at risk from the transition, such as the coal and palm oil industries, manage to influence regulatory frameworks that are more favourable to them. More recently, the stakeholders who benefited from the transition were able to slightly influence climate policy, as reflected by the government's announcement to enforce the PR 98/2021 which should be effective on April 1, 2022 but delayed to July 2022 (Shofa, 2023). It also reflected by the government's action to halt construction of new coal-fired power plants by 2023 and PLN's announcement that coal-fired power plants would be phased out towards emissions net zero by 2060 (Tracker, 2021).

Unfortunately, during 2022 to date there is an excess supply of electricity supplied by the Indonesian state electricity company (PT PLN) as the results of coal-fired power plants (Muhammad, 2022). PLN's electricity surplus will still occur in large numbers in line with the ongoing mega project to increase domestic electricity capacity. Based on data from the Directorate General of Electricity of the Ministry of Energy and Mineral Resources as of April 2021, the completion of coal-fired power plants has reached 10,069 megawatts (MW) or has increased 107 MW compared to the end of 2022 of 9,931 MW (Muhammad, 2022).

There are 418 units of power plant (PLTU) have been contracted or have signed a power purchase agreement (PPA). A total of 218 PLTU units with a capacity of 10,069 MW or the equivalent of 28% have been operating, 91 units with a capacity of 17,964 MW or the equivalent of 50% have been contracted and are entering the construction phase, while 43 units with a capacity of 6,228 MW or the equivalent of 18% have been contracted but not yet construction (Muhammad, 2022).

The effect of the excess supply made PLN creating entry barriers for new players in the energy market. PLN's market power has prevented privately owned New and Renewable Energy (EBT)-based power plants from being able to sell their power directly to the public (Wahyudi, 2022). The lack of investment gain in the domestic EBT sector is due to the monopoly of PLN to distribute electricity to the community. As a consequence, the selling price of EBT electricity developed by a number of private power plants is not competitive to attract prospective investors (Wahyudi, 2022).

PLN also monopolizes the issuance of Renewable Energy Certificates (REC) under the Letter No. 43803/KEU.01.02/D01020300/2022 dated 2 August 2022, which confirms that the issuance of RECs and renewable generating sources in the PLN electricity system (both PLN or IPP generators) is only carried out by PLN. It is also emphasized that IPP parties were not allowed to sell Green Energy attributes directly to the consumers. The competitors consider that the private sector should be able to issue a certificate as long as it is not agreed upon in a Power Purchase Agreement (PPA) and has registered it in the REC market instrument. (Riyandanu, 2022). PLN clearly makes unsubstantiated claims that their products are environmentally friendly and provide some green benefit for consumers.

Electric Vehicles Policy

The Indonesian government, especially the Ministry of Energy and Mineral Resources, continues to develop battery-based electric motorized vehicles (KBLBB) with the aim of reducing emissions in order to achieve net-zero emission (Suprobowati et al., 2021). This is also supported by the creation of the KBLBB ecosystem starting from making policies that contain incentives for industry and potential consumers, 0% tax for electric vehicles, and to the construction of Public Electric Vehicle Charging Stations (SPKLU) across the country (Hudzaifi, 2023).

However, the charging station is still sourced from coal-fired power plants, and the mass production of the electric vehicles is dominated by fossil energy. It means that the electric vehicles policy is inconsistent with Indonesia's NDC which is committed to reducing fossil energy consumption in Indonesia in order to achieve net-zero emissions in 2060 (Hudzaifi, 2023). The development of KBLBB was monumental for involved parties to facilitate the ecosystem to build infrastructure, providing incentives, and others. In the end, the development of KBLBB will perpetuate the monopoly on electricity management and dependency on coal in Indonesia (Hudzaifi, 2023). The issuance of Presidential Instruction 7/2022 confirmed this by allowing the mining companies and automotive corporations considering that the beneficiaries of electric vehicles and the policy makers that support the ecosystem are on the same side (Hudzaifi, 2023).

Palm Oil Policy

Utilization of renewable energy potential is currently very low, ranging from only 0.03% for solar power to 5% for hydropower. However, in order to realize the full potential of renewable energy, the Indonesian government faces various obstacles it faces for the development of renewable energy (IESR, 2021). This of course goes against Indonesia's biofuel mandate as one of the most ambitious in the world. Indonesia has plans to increase its national energy consumption mandate to 40% by 2022 and produce biodiesel only from palm oil (Arinaldo et al., 2021). However, although Indonesia's biofuel targets are ambitious, they are quite controversial and problematic as they create environmental problems with increased palm oil production and deforestation (Tracker, 2021).

The appetite for palm oil has transformed the Indonesia's landscape. From 2000 to 2015, Indonesia lost about 498,000 hectares of forest every year. Most of the deforestation that occurred in the past was due to the slash and burn method of land clearing. This has played a huge role in driving massive haze pollution across Indonesia and some ASEAN countries (Alam & Nurhidayah, 2017). When fires occur on peatlands, most of their carbon stores are released into the atmosphere (Brief, 2021).

In 2014, Indonesian palm oil industry players and the Indonesian Chamber of Commerce and Industry (Kadin) was jointly signed in an agreement or Indonesia Palm Oil Pledge (IPOP) at the Climate Conference in New York (Pramudya et al., 2018). The cores of the agreement stated that business actors in the Indonesian palm oil industry adopted a sustainability policy which included no deforestation, no peat, and no exploitation in their respective companies and applied to the entire supply chain. through traceability.

IPOP's goal is to seek sustainable palm oil that is free of deforestation, respects human and community rights, and provides shareholder value (Dermawan & Hospes, 2018). IPOP has four components. These components do not offer specific rules, measurable goals or concrete criteria, but rather a sort of agenda with general aims and steps to be taken. The first component is improving environmental management. Within this component, the companies will adopt and promote sustainable palm oil production practices. The second component is collaborating with other stakeholders and engaging with the Government of Indonesia to promote the development of policies, legal and regulatory frameworks that support the implementation of these promises (Dermawan & Hospes, 2018). The third component is extending social benefits. This includes increasing the productivity of smallholders by providing technical assistance and improving extension services to smallholders. The fourth component is increasing the competitiveness of the palm oil business. Its main activities include encouraging other palm oil companies to comply with the pledges (Dermawan & Hospes, 2018).

Despite of the pledge, the components of the IPOP gained attention and resistance from state actors in Indonesia. The existence of the pledge would bring danger to smallholders development; as not acknowledging government rules and priorities; and would be ended up as an illegal cartel (Dermawan & Hospes, 2018). In October 2015, Indonesia Competition Commission (KPPU) received a request for opinion on the business actor's agreement on IPOP. Under the IPOP, a commitment and/or agreement between palm oil industry players is to carry out sustainable oil palm plantation practices throughout their supply chain while increasing the competitiveness of Indonesian palm oil in the global market. However, in the Indonesian palm oil industry, the Government of Indonesia has made Indonesia Sustainable Palm Oil (ISPO) a certification policy that must be met by every oil palm company or plantation which has become a standard in carrying out sustainable oil palm plantation practices, namely economically viable, socio-culturally feasible and friendly. environment in accordance with the provisions of the law (Munadiya, 2022).

There is a significant difference between the IPOP agreement and Government policy (ISPO) regarding the setting of good environmental criteria for oil palm plantations. ISPO uses the standard High Conservation Value Forest (HCVF) criteria, while IPOP members agreed to add High Carbon Stock (HCS) criteria. This opens up the potential for barriers to market entry for IPOP member partners who comply with Government policies, but do not meet the HCS criteria standards (Munadiya, 2022). Business actors who are members of IPOP control a fairly large share of the CPO market, so that IPOP members have considerable market power.

KPPU's analysis results show that IPOP agreement is essentially an agreement between certain business actors, which contains rules that bind business actors to implement them. IPOP implementation will have an impact on other business actors outside of IPOP, in the form of barriers to entry, to supply to companies that are members of IPOP. This condition is experienced by business actors who have complied with implementing Government regulations (ISPO), which are regulations for the Indonesian palm oil industry. In this case, there is a potential that IPOP agreements have a higher position than government regulations, even though IPOP is only an agreement of business actors.

Considering that the values in IPOP are only agreements between business actors, IPOP has the potential to become a vehicle for cartels to become an entry barrier for business actors partnering IPOP members. On the basis of this analysis, KPPU stated that the IPOP agreement has the potential to become a vehicle for a cartel that will lead to monopolistic practices and or unfair business competition. Therefore, KPPU firmly stated that the IPOP agreement could not be implemented and the business actor shall cancel the IPOP agreement.

Observing the latest developments, where it turns out that IPOP as an agreement of business actors has been effective and has had a negative impact on business competition so that it is suspected of violating Law No. 5 of 1999, in which KPPU will conduct an investigation into the alleged violation (Munadiya, 2022).

COMPETITION LAW: WILL IT WORK TO HELP THE TRANSITION?

Indonesia's policy to low carbon explicitly exists in the 2020-2024 National Medium-Term Development Plan (RPJMN) with three priority programs, namely improving environmental quality, increasing disaster resilience and climate change, and low-carbon development. Indonesia has also ratified the SDG document "Transforming Our World: The 2030 Agenda for Sustainable Development" through Presidential

Regulation No 59 of 2017. KPPU, as the competition authority, accommodates this goal in its mission, one of which is achieving a sustainable living environment. However, so far, there is still no clear and legally binding guideline for business players how to align sustainable business decisions with competition policies in Indonesia unlike in UK and EU towards its Green Deal (Kamiński, 2021). Yet, this is an important factor for business players to obtain legal certainty regarding the scope and limitations of continuous agreements and cooperation based on the Competition Law.

Competition law can help to address low carbon transition in various ways. Competition law can assist the transition by improving quality of sustainable products, more sustainable product options, and promoting green innovation while addressing market failures (OECD, 2021). Indonesia with its Law No. 5 of 1999 on the Prohibition of Monopoly Practices and Unfair Competition can be used as a legal basis to exempt restrictive sustainability agreements among competitors from cartel prohibition in order to protect the environment from damage. The Law is applicable as long as the behaviour or agreements among the business actors eliminate competition.

The government should encourage efficient and competitive business climate so as to create equal opportunities for every party to participate in the production and marketing processes of goods and services. However, the actual facts that the Indonesian government encourages inefficient and uncompetitive business climate through making policies that only benefit certain people and groups, which results in monopolistic practices and unfair competition. The Government has deliberately created an entry barrier for new players in the electricity supply industry by issuing regulations to give more power to PLN.

The above conditions occur because the orientation of Indonesia's policy prioritizes economic growth, causing all economic policies to be made to support all activities that are expected to stimulate the level of growth. In the end, this approach requires the government to reorganize business activities in Indonesia in order to create a competitive business climate.

In this case, the position of competition authority is clear: to protect the competitiveness from anti-competitive behaviours—which often involve agreements or coordinated actions among competitors—that contribute to more sustainable methods of production or distribution and thus achieve sustainability goals. In addition, there needs to be guidance for businesses on how to overcome legal barriers to competition related to cooperation with the aim of achieving sustainability goals. This is done so that the Competition Law does not become a barrier to sustainability policy initiatives among business players.

In this way, competition law has a significant position in sustainability issues to encourage energy transition. Competition authorities also have a big role to play by overcoming climate change issues such as anti-competitive cartel agreements (Kahn, 2023). By synergizing with environmental policies, both can strengthen each other by combining efficient resource allocation and innovation to encourage sustainable business practices and still protect competition.

Competition can play its role in three conditions. First, competition supports environmental protection goals whereby consumer preferences are oriented toward green products or services, meaning that companies are likely to adjust their supply of green products and direct their investments to meet that demand. When there is a willingness of consumers to pay for more sustainable products, competition will produce the most efficient results and encourage companies to invest in product differentiation towards being environmentally friendly (OECD, 2021).

Second, the objectives of competition and environmental protection are organically interdependent when adverse anti-competitive behaviour and environmental damage are aligned. An example is a greenwashing cartel, where companies may collectively charge consumers too high a price on grounds of environmental protection, or cases where companies jointly unite or eliminate competition on the parameter of product differentiation i.e. quality or sustainable innovation (OECD, 2021).

Third, competition law supports environmental protection when the law recognizes the benefits of public policy, exemption, or efficiency in relation to positive behaviour towards the environment which is also pro-competitive. Pro-competitive measures would include an analysis of the overall economic impact, including non-price impacts on quality, choice and innovation, such as increased environmental quality, or more sustainable and cleaner process and product innovations as a form of greater efficiency (OECD, 2021).

The fact that large companies are better able to gain incentives from the marketing of sustainable products will overlap with competition law oversight measures. This is because the competition authority will carry out tighter supervision of large business actors (Munadiya, 2022). On the one hand, this of course can hamper the intention of business actors to achieve these sustainability goals. However, on the other hand, the business competition authority is forced to look more closely at the greenwashing cartel agendas of business actors behind environmentally friendly sustainable products (Dolmans, 2021).

Competition can only help if companies know that enough consumers have ability to pay to eliminate all greenhouse gas emissions. In the markets, companies have an incentive to compete not only to be the most efficient and best supplier, but also to be the cleanest and greenest supplier. Unfortunately, the company's ability to be environmentally friendly is not accompanied by the willingness and ability of consumers to pay (Dolmans, 2021).

CONCLUSION

The main function of competition law is to protect competition itself. Regardless of whether the competition is environmentally friendly or not. However, competition law can consider environmental and social priorities through substantive competition regulations, exceptions, and enhance competition law enforcement. Competition law can provide exemptions or relaxation for certain sectors in order to encourage the achievement of sustainable development. Not infrequently various countries provide sectoral exceptions in several sectors. Therefore, companies in this sector that promote sustainability are generally exempted from competition laws. However, further clarification and guidance is needed on how competition law can address issues related to carbon emissions.

DECLARATION OF INTERESTS

The authors declare no competing interests.

REFERENCES

Abalansa, S., El Mahrad, B., Icely, J., & Newton, A. (2021). Electronic waste, an environmental problem exported to developing countries: The GOOD, the BAD and the UGLY. *Sustainability (Basel)*, *13*(9), 5302. doi:10.3390u13095302

Akib, M., Sumarja, F., & Heryandi. (2019). Environmental Law Policy as an Approach to Achieve Sustainable Development and Prosperity in an Era of Regional Autonomy. *Environmental Policy and Law, 49*(1), 83–87. doi:10.3233/EPL-190130

Alam, S., & Nurhidayah, L. (2017). The international law on transboundary haze pollution: What can we learn from the Southeast Asia region? *Review of European, Comparative & International Environmental Law, 26*(3), 243–254. doi:10.1111/reel.12221

Alisjahbana, A. S., & Busch, J. M. (2017). Forestry, forest fires, and climate change in Indonesia. *Bulletin of Indonesian Economic Studies, 53*(2), 111–136. doi:10.1080/00074918.2017.1365404

Arinaldo, D., Prasojo, H., Tampubolon, A. P., Simamora, P., Kurniawan, D., Marciano, I., & Adiatma, J. C. (2021). *Indonesia Energy Transition Outlook 2021*. IESR. file:///C:/Users/hp/Downloads/IETO%20-%202021_IESR.pdf

Azmi, R., Maslahat, P., & Wahono, J. W. (2022). *The carbon footprint from the power plant in Indonesia and renewable energy supply for reduce the carbon emission.* NASA.

Butt, S., Lyster, R., & Stephens, T. (2015). *Climate change and forest governance: Lessons from Indonesia*. Routledge. doi:10.4324/9781315735351

C2ES. (2020). *Global Emissions*. C2ES. https://www.c2es.org/content/international-emissions/

Case, M., Ardiansyah, F., & Spector, E. (2007). Climate change in Indonesia: Implications for humans and nature. In Climate change in Indonesia: Implications for humans and nature. (p. 13). World Wide Fund for Nature, UK (WWF).

Chen, X., Luo, Z., & Wang, X. (2017). Impact of efficiency, investment, and competition on low carbon manufacturing. *Journal of Cleaner Production, 143*, 388–400. doi:10.1016/j.jclepro.2016.12.095

CNBC. (2023, January 2). Perppu Jokowi! Angin Segar Perusahaan Batu Bara: Setoran 0%. *CNBC Indonesia*. https://www.cnbcindonesia.com/news/20230102012111-4-401887/perppu-jokowi-angin-segar-perusahaan-batu-bara-setoran-0

Crippa, M., Guizzardi, D., Muntean, M., Schaaf, E., Solazzo, E., Monforti-Ferrario, F., Olivier, J., & Vignati, E. (2020). *Fossil CO2 emissions of all world countries*. European Commission.

de Araujo, R. C., & Nogueira, J. M. (2020). Environmental law & competition law: Conflicts & complementarities from an environmental economics perspective. *Direito e Desenvolvimento, 11*(1), 92–105. doi:10.26843/direitoedesenvolvimento.v11i1.1220

De StefanoG. (2020). Measurable environmental protection as a necessity for competition law. SSRN 3533499. doi:10.2139/ssrn.3533499

Dermawan, A., & Hospes, O. (2018). When the state brings itself back into GVC: The case of the Indonesian Palm Oil Pledge. *Global Policy, 9*(S2), 21–28. doi:10.1111/1758-5899.12619

DolmansM. (2021). Sustainability Agreements and Antitrust–Three Criteria to Distinguish Beneficial Cooperation from Greenwashing. *Available at* SSRN 3920369. doi:10.2139/ssrn.3920369

Domazet, S. (2013). Environmental Protection and Competition Law of the European Union: Complementary or Conflicting Goals? *Agriculture in Serbia and Portugal: Recent*, 208.

EPA. E. (2022). *Inventory of U.S. Greenhouse Gas Emissions and Sinks: 1990-2020. U.S. Environmental Protection Agency* (EPA 430-R-22-003). Environmental Protection Agency. https://www.epa.gov/system/files/documents/2022-04/us-ghg-inventory-2022-main-text.pdf

Fisher, E. (2017). *Environmental law: A very short introduction*. Oxford University Press. doi:10.1093/actrade/9780198794189.001.0001

Forgioni, P. A. (2013). *Os fundamentos do antitruste*. Editora Revista dos Tribunais.

Gehring, M. W. (2006). Competition for sustainability: Sustainable development concerns in national and EC competition law. *Review of European Community & International Environmental Law*, *15*(2), 172–184. doi:10.1111/j.1467-9388.2006.00519.x

Glass, K. E. (2014). *I speak for the trees": An exploration of environmental advocacy and speaker credibility in Dr. Seuss'" The Lorax*. San José State University. doi:10.31979/etd.3r4c-qhxm

Handayani, K., Filatova, T., Krozer, Y., & Anugrah, P. (2020). Seeking for a climate change mitigation and adaptation nexus: Analysis of a long-term power system expansion. *Applied Energy*, *262*, 114485. doi:10.1016/j.apenergy.2019.114485

Heffron, R. J., Körner, M.-F., Sumarno, T., Wagner, J., Weibelzahl, M., & Fridgen, G. (2022). How different electricity pricing systems affect the energy trilemma: Assessing Indonesia's electricity market transition. *Energy Economics*, *107*, 105663. doi:10.1016/j.eneco.2021.105663

Holmes, S. (2020). Climate change, sustainability, and competition law. *Journal of Antitrust Enforcement*, *8*(2), 354–405. doi:10.1093/jaenfo/jnaa006

Hudzaifi, N. N. (2023, March 29). Membedah Skenario Praktik Monopoli Kendaraan Listrik di RI. *CNBC*. https://www.cnbcindonesia.com/opini/20230329173428-14-425586/membedah-skenario-praktik-monopoli-kendaraan-listrik-di-ri

Hurić-Larsen, J. F., & Münch, A. (2016). Competition and Environmental Policy in the EU: Old Foes, New Friends? *Journal of Industry, Competition and Trade*, *16*(2), 137–153. doi:10.100710842-015-0201-0

IESR, I. (2021). *Hitting Record-Low Solar Electricity Prices in Indonesia*. Institute for Essential Service Reform. file:///C:/Users/hp/Downloads/IESR-Solar%20Final%20-%20Digital.pdf

Ilić-Petković, A., & Ilić-Krstić, I. (2016). The role of environmental law in the implementation of sustainable development. *Safety Engineering*, *6*(2), 99–105. doi:10.7562/SE2016.6.02.07

Inderst, R., & Thomas, S. (2023). Competition Policy and the Environment. *Annual Review of Resource Economics*, 15.

Irwansyah, I. (2016). What do scientists say on climate change? A study of Indonesian newspapers. *Pacific Science Review B. Humanities and Social Sciences*, *2*(2), 58–65.

Jensen, K. (2020, March 23). Water at Heart of Climate Action. *The Jakarta Post*. https://www.thejakartapost.com/academia/2020/03/23/water-at-heart-of-climate-action.html

Jong, H. N. (2020). Indonesia Won't Sacrifice Economy for More Ambitious Emissions Cuts. *Mongabay Series: Jokowi Commitments.* Https://News. Mongabay. Com/2020/04/Indonesia-Emissionsreduction-Climate-Carbon-Economy-Growth/Philips-Meltzer

Kahn, A. (2023). *Distinguishing Genuine Sustainability Agreements from Disguised Cartels under Article 101 (3) TFEU.*

Kamiński, M. (2021). Energy Transition Enhanced by the European Green Deal-How National Competition Authorities Should Tackle This Challenge in Central and Eastern Europe? [YARS]. *Yearbook of Antitrust and Regulatory Studies*, *14*(23), 101–121.

Kingston, S. (2021). Introduction to Competition Law, Climate Change and Environmental Sustainability. UCD Working Papers in Law, Criminology & Socio-Legal Studies Research Paper.

Kloosterhuis, E., & Mulder, M. (2015). Competition law and environmental protection: The Dutch agreement on coal-fired power plants. *Journal of Competition Law & Economics*, *11*(4), 855–880. doi:10.1093/joclec/nhv017

Lesirma, S. (2016). Effect of Environmental Laws on Protection of Ecosystem. *International Journal of Environmental Sciences*, *1*(1), 29–40.

Luo, Z., Chen, X., & Wang, X. (2016). The role of co-opetition in low carbon manufacturing. *European Journal of Operational Research*, *253*(2), 392–403. doi:10.1016/j.ejor.2016.02.030

Maulidia, M., Dargusch, P., Ashworth, P., & Ardiansyah, F. (2019). Rethinking renewable energy targets and electricity sector reform in Indonesia: A private sector perspective. *Renewable & Sustainable Energy Reviews*, *101*, 231–247. doi:10.1016/j.rser.2018.11.005

Measey, M. (2010). Indonesia: A vulnerable country in the face of climate change. *Global Majority E-Journal*, *1*(1), 31–45.

Minister of Energy and Mineral Resources Regulation No. 15/2010, 15 (2010). https://gunungbale.co.id/v2/wp-content/uploads/2015/04/1201-RMEMRRI-Amendments-to-the-regulations-Minister-of-Energy-and-Mineral-Resources.pdf

Moss, D. L., & Kwoka, J. E. Jr. (2010). Competition policy and the transition to a low-carbon, efficient electricity industry. *The Electricity Journal*, *23*(7), 6–15. doi:10.1016/j.tej.2010.06.018

Muhammad, R. (2022, September 22). Menteri ESDM Ungkap Penyebab Surplus Listrik PLN. *Bisnis Indonesia*. https://ekonomi.bisnis.com/read/20220922/44/1580299/menteri-esdm-ungkap-penyebab-surplus-listrik-pln

Munadiya, R. (2022). Isu Keberlanjutan dan Persaingan Usaha: Kapan Otoritas Harus Campur Tangan? *Jurnal Persaingan Usaha*, *2*(2), 127–137. doi:10.55869/kppu.v2i2.66

Nogueira, J. M., & de Araujo, R. C. (2020). Environmental Law & Competition Law: Conflicts & Complementarities from an Environmental Economics Perspective. *Direito e Desenvolvimento*, *11*, 93.

Nugroho, A. W. (2020). What students know about climate change? A case study of high school students in Samboja. *Indonesia*, *487*(1), 012001.

OECD. O. (2021). *Environmental Considerations in Competition Enforcement* [OECD Competition Committee Discussion Paper]. OECD. https://www.oecd.org/daf/competition/environmental-considerations-in-competition-enforcement-2021.pdf

Olivier, J. G., Schure, K., & Peters, J. (2017). Trends in global CO2 and total greenhouse gas emissions. *PBL Netherlands Environmental Assessment Agency*, *5*, 1–11.

Pauw, W. P., König, M., Sadikhova, K., & Stutzmann, T. (2021). *Financing Low-Carbon and Climate Resilient Development: Do countries integrate Article 2.1 (c) of the Paris Agreement in their long-term strategies?* Frankfurt School- UNEP Centre. https://dspace.library.uu.nl/bitstream/handle/1874/417005/Pauw_et_al_2022_Financing_Low_carbon_and_Climate.resilient_development_final.pdf?sequence=1&isAllowed=y

Pramudya, E. P., Hospes, O., & Termeer, C. (2018). Friend or foe? The various responses of the Indonesian state to sustainable non-state palm oil initiatives. *Asian Journal of Sustainability and Social Responsibility*, *3*(1), 1–22. doi:10.118641180-018-0018-y

Putri, A. M. H. (2023, June 23). Deforestasi dan Hasrat Eropa "Membunuh" Sawit Indonesia. *CNBC Indonesia*. https://www.cnbcindonesia.com/research/20230620072029-128-447429/deforestasi-dan-hasrat-eropa-membunuh-sawit-indonesia

Riyandanu, M. F. (2022, August 16). PLN Diminta Tak Monopoli Hak Serifikat Energi Baru dan Terbarukan. *Katadata*. https://katadata.co.id/agustiyanti/ekonomi-hijau/62fae83983b4f/pln-diminta-tak-monopoli-hak-serifikat-energi-baru-dan-terbarukan

Setyawan, D. (2013). Assessing the current Indonesia's electricity market arrangements and the opportunities to reform. *Int. Journal of Renewable Energy Development*, *3*(1), 2014.

Shearer, C., Ghio, N., Myllyvirta, L., Yu, A., & Nace, T. (2017). *Boom and bust 2017: Tracking the global coal plant pipeline*. CoalSwarm, Sierra Club, Greenpeace International. https://apo.org.au/node/75523

Shofa, J. N. (2023, September 21). Carbon Tax to Put Indonesia on Track Toward 2030 Climate Goal. *Jakarta Globe*. https://jakartaglobe.id/business/carbon-tax-to-put-indonesia-on-track-toward-2030-climate-goal

Simon, E. (2015). *Indonesian Pledge Suggests No Increase in Emissions to 2030*. Carbon Brief. https://www.carbonbrief.org/indonesian-pledge-suggests-no-increase-in-emissions-to-2030/

Sukarso, P. (2021). Decarbonizing Electricity in Indonesia. *Opportunity in the Implementation of Rooftop Solar PV.*, *1096*(1), 012098.

Suprobowati, G. D., Apriliana, G. M. C., & Hutami, W. P. (2021). *Indonesian Electric Vehicle Policy, Realization and Development*. 99–102.

Suroyo, G., & Munthe, B. C. (2021, November 15). *Indonesia introduces carbon trading policy to reduce emission.* Reuters. https://www.reuters.com/business/cop/indonesia-introduces-carbon-trading-policy-reduce-emission-2021-11-15/

Tracker, C. A. (2020). *Paris Agreement Compatible Sectoral Benchmarks: Elaborating the decarbonisation roadmap*. Climate Action Tracker. https://climateactiontracker.org/documents/753/CAT_2020-07-10_ParisAgreementBenchmarks_FullReport.pdf

Tracker, C. A. (2021). *Indonesia Policy Action*. Climate Action Tracker. https://climateactiontracker.org/countries/indonesia/

Triana, K., & Wahyudi, A. (2020). Sea level rise in Indonesia: The drivers and the combined impacts from land subsidence. *ASEAN J. Sci. Technol. Dev*, *37*(3), 115–121. doi:10.29037/ajstd.627

Wahyudi, N. A. (2022, June 28). Monopoli Listrik PLN Dinilai Hambat Investasi EBT. *Bisnis.Com*. https://ekonomi.bisnis.com/read/20220628/44/1549029/monopoli-listrik-pln-dinilai-hambat-investasi-ebt

Wijaya, A., Chrysolite, H., Ge, M., Wibowo, C. K., Pradana, A., Utami, A. F., & Austin, K. (2017). How can Indonesia achieve its climate change mitigation goal? An analysis of potential emissions reductions from energy and land-use policies. *World Resources Institute. World Resour Inst Work Pap*, 1–36.

Worldmeters, W. (2016). *Indonesia CO2 Emissions*. Worldmeters. https://www.worldometers.info/co2-emissions/indonesia-co2-emissions/

KEYTERMS/DEFINITIONS

Business-as-Usual (BAU): An expression that refers to normal behaviour regardless of current circumstances, especially in circumstances that are out of the ordinary or when a difficult event occurs that has the potential to cause negative impacts. This expression can also mean maintaining the status quo with no policy changes or government intervention.

Carbon Emissions: Gases released as a result of the combustion of compounds resulting from burning oil, gas and coal, continue to increase on a global scale.

Climate Change: Long-term changes in temperature and weather patterns. Human activity has been the main driver of climate change, especially with the burning of fossil fuels (such as coal, oil, and gas) which produces heat-trapping gases.

Electricity Supply Business Plan (RUPTL): A guideline for implementing the provision of electricity for electricity supply business license holders and operating license holders.

Market Power: Market power is the ability that a company has so that it can influence the price of its product in the market. All consumers and producers can be considered as someone who influences. In the market itself, manipulated prices can be in the form of goods or services. So that directly or indirectly the level of demand and supply will be affected. In general, this is done to obtain profits that can exceed long-term costs and marginal costs.

Monopoly Supply Chain: Monopoly occurs where a company/organisation controls the entire supply chain, from production to sales through vertical integration, or buying competing companies in the market through horizontal integration, becoming the sole producer.

Nationally Determined Contribution (NDC): A non-binding national plan highlighting climate change mitigation, including climate-related targets for greenhouse gas emission reductions.

Chapter 6
Understanding the Impacts of the Non-Compete Clause in Employment Contracts From the Perspective of the Sustainable Development Goals

Siti Fazilah Abdul Shukor
https://orcid.org/0000-0003-3504-4102
University Tunku Abdul Rahman, Malaysia

Farahdilah Ghazali
https://orcid.org/0000-0002-1966-9690
University of Putra Malaysia, Malaysia

ABSTRACT

With the effect of the Covid pandemic, people lost their jobs, and it magnified the rate of workforce turnover in the labour market. It has caused difficulty for employees to find new jobs because the non-compete clause has been incorporated into the employment agreement. The purpose of inserting the clause is to protect the employer's business interest, however, it also gives some difficulties to employees to proceed with new employment. The validity of the non-compete clause in the employment agreement seems reasonable for the employer, however it seems to be a restrictive measure for the employees. The chapter intends to review the impact of non-compete clauses in employment contracts in Malaysia. Besides, the chapter also intends to review the cases related to a non-compete clause in Malaysia and provide legal protections to protect the best interest of both employers and employees. Lastly, this study focuses on promoting decent work opportunities as well as productive employment for all.

DOI: 10.4018/979-8-3693-0390-0.ch006

Copyright © 2024, IGI Global. Copying or distributing in print or electronic forms without written permission of IGI Global is prohibited.

INTRODUCTION

In today's economy, employment has become crucial for an individual to provide support for themselves and their families. Today's workforce is impatient to achieve their goal of being successful people, thus they grab the opportunities that exist in front of them. Besides, the advancement of technology and growth in living standards as well as in the education sector, enable individuals to be kept updated and attentive in the present environment. Under Sustainable Development Goal 8 (SDG 8), the world calls for inclusive and sustainable economic growth, full and productive employment, and decent work for all that include measures to promote policies to support job creation, improve resource efficiency in consumption and production, to provide full employment and decent work with equal pay and to promote youth employment, education, and training. Sustainability is known as durability or the ability to maintain at a certain level. In employment, sustainability means meeting the needs of the employee in the long term as well as the short-term advantages in economic, environmental, and social development factors (Novitz, T., 2021). Moreover, sustainability aims to protect the present and future generations' needs without compromising the ability and ensure the balance between economic growth, environmental care, and social well-being (Novitz, T., 2021). Businesses are important for economic growth which is known as good opportunities for society in assessing decent work that can provide employment security. In current practice, it has become a social norm to leave a job and pursue a better opportunity and career progression because employees are concerned about their long-term career paths. On the contrary, employers are eager to protect the relationship built with their employees during the employment period. Employers spend their time, money, and effort in providing career development to their employees. Still, employees opt to switch their jobs for career growth. In this situation, there is no breach of employment on the part of employees if they leave the company, according to law.

According to Marx (2011), some employers practice non-compete agreements to retain their employees or to limit technical professionals' mobility, leading to involuntary career detours. Nevertheless, Lestari et al. (2017) contended that the implementation of the non-competition clause in employment agreements must be conducted based on the Indonesia's Trade Secret Law. Hieu et al. (2020) further explained the enforcement of such a clause must be transparent and reasonable in order to balance the interests of both employers and employees. Kuzminac (2022) revealed that employees decided to accept the non-compete agreement as they needed the position although there is no justified basis for such a clause. Posner (2019) discovered that the disclosure of the non-compete agreement caused public turmoil as it did not protect trade secrets or customer benevolence but prevented low-income employees from in the hunt for better compensation. However, Starr and Robert (2019) believed that the employees are aware of the effects of non-compete agreements and they would not agree to such restrictions unless they obtained a justified return from the employers. Through the enforcement of this clause, employers can invest in their employees and share confidential information with less fear of information leakage. While employees are obligated not to use the training and information to assist competitors (Kang & Fleming, 2020).

This non-compete clause restricts employees' ability to participate in competitive work. Such a clause causes economic harm to the employees as well as harm the society as it is a restraint of trade (Arnow-Richman, 2019). Marx et al. (2014) exhibited that non-compete agreements are responsible for a "brain drain" of skilled employees who enforce such contracts in states where they are not enforceable. A study by Wilkergren (2017) analyzes the use of non-compete clauses to prevent an employee from utilizing the knowledge that he gained to start a new business. He also suggested legal restrictions on the length of the non-compete clause can increase the joint welfare of the employee and the employer (Wilkergren, 2017). Arnow-Richman (2019) stressed the law to protect employers' investments in information and human capital, and simultaneously promote fair competition.

Although there are limited studies discussing the link between SDGs and the non-compete clause, the principles, and impacts of the social economy with Sustainable Development Goals (SDGs) have favored a paradigm shift toward an economic system that resolves growth and sustainability. In this context, governments could implement policies to promote and drive the social economy. Fair competition in employment and business could have an impact on the achievement of the Sustainable Development Goals (SDGs), especially the promotion of equal opportunities (SDG 5), the promotion of decent work and economic growth (SDG 8), and the reduction of inequalities (SDG 10). This chapter discusses the context of the non-compete clause in employment. The authors further review the application of non-compete clauses in employment contracts in Malaysia with references to legal cases and provisions that provide legal protections to protect the best interests of both employers and employees. Lastly, this study focuses to emphasize promoting decent work opportunities as well as productive employment for all.

NON-COMPETE CLAUSE IN EMPLOYMENT CONTRACT

In Malaysia, we are governed by the Employment Act 1955, the Industrial Relations Act 1967, and some other regulations. Generally, the employment contract would be drafted by the employer or the company with references to the Employment Act, 1955, which binds parties to the contract. Besides, the contract would also be drafted by taking into consideration certain provisions from the Contracts Act 1950, the Companies Act 2016, and the Federal Constitution of Malaysia. The references to these legislations are required to ensure the contractual relationship as well as the statutory duties and fundamental liberties were considered in the facet of the agreement (Husnina & Kevin, 2023). The term of employment contracts varies depending on the job purpose and work arrangement in the company. Employment contracts provide legal protection to both employers and employees during the employment period.

In an employment relationship, employer and employee protection is one of the most important principles expressed in the statutes. The legitimate rights and interests of the employer and employee are major concerns in creating harmony and stability in labor relations. A non-compete agreement is a type of agreement that restricts employees from working with competitors or the ability of employees to use the resources obtained from the current employer to the benefit of future employers (Nicholas, 2022). These clauses prohibit employees from working for a rival or starting a competing venture after they leave their job. Such a provision can be included in the initial employment contract or added afterward, and it often specifies the time and geographic limitations within which it applies (Boeri et al., 2023).

According to Blake (1960), the agreement which includes a non-compete clause is considered not a competition and is understood as an employee's commitment to their current or future employer to not compete with the employer after the labor relationship is completed. Whereas Gilson (1999), mentioned that a non-compete clause in the agreement was stipulated for termination of employment for any reason, the employee will not compete with employers in existing enterprises available or expected by the employer over a period of time certain period - usually one to two years in one geographical area corresponding to the market in which the employer join. Besides Marx and Fleming (2012) said that a non-compete clause is an employee's commitment not to work for a competitor in a period after resignation or termination of an employment contract. Black's Law Dictionary defines a *"non-competition covenant"* as *"a promise usually in a sale-of-business, partnership or employment contract, not to engage in the same type of business for a stated time in the same market as the buyer, partner or employer".*

In general, the non-compete clause is an agreement between employees and the employer, whereby the employee commits not to become a competitor or work for a competitor of the employer over a period and certain geographical location after the end of the employment contract. This clause was included by employers as an effort to protect their company trade secrets from competitors so that the company secrets are protected, and the employees cannot work in a competitor company (Nadiyya, 2021). Although the non-compete clause is to protect the interests of the employer, it could also infringe upon the rights of the employer and employee. Besides, countries around the world have recognized and have strict regulations on the agreement of non-competitiveness in the employment relationship, especially the provisions on the conditions for an agreement of non-compete clauses are considered legal and enforceable (Hang & Huy, 2022). A non-compete clause in employment agreements is about restricting employees from working for competitors, and employers use it to protect the legitimate interests of employers (Hang & Huy, 2022). However, the applicability of the non-compete clause may create confusion and difficulty in distinguishing the scope and conditions of validity of an agreement as well as the law governing this type of agreement (Hang & Huy, 2022). Non-compete clauses have traditionally been viewed as "restraints of trade," therefore presumably unenforceable under common law. Non-compete clauses are subject to a "reasonableness" test and enforceable only if the limits imposed on the employee are no more severe than necessary to protect the employer's legitimate business interests. However, the common law approach is insufficient since employers suffer no major penalties if a court invalidates a noncompete, and the common law does not provide the appropriate approach for reviewing this clause (Posner, 2019).

NON-COMPETE CLAUSE: PRACTICES IN OTHER JURISDICTIONS

In the United Kingdom, there are no statutory limitations on non-compete provisions. Non-compete clauses are only enforceable under case law if they are no broader than reasonably necessary to protect a legitimate interest and are not averse to the public interest. In *Tillman v Egon Zehnder Ltd [2019] UKSC 32 (UKSC 2017/0182),* Ms Tillman left her position at Egon Zehnder Ltd, to work for a competitor. Her contract prohibited her from engaging or being concerned or interested in any business carried on in competition with the firm's operations. The Supreme Court granted the injunction sought by Egon Zehnder, banning her from working for the competition for six months, overturning the decision of the Court of Appeal. In the case of *Harcus Sinclair LLP v Your Lawyers Ltd [2021] UKSC 32,* Mr Parker is a former HSLLP member and a solicitor. In April 2016, HSLLP and YLL engaged in a non-disclosure agreement addressing the sharing of proprietary information. That agreement included a non-compete clause, as well as a solicitor's undertaking, requiring HSLLP to "not accept instructions for or act on behalf of any other group of Claimants in the contemplated Group Action without the express permission of YLL. Mr Parker shared confidential information with another firm, in breach of the agreement of April 2016. The Supreme Court ruled that a six-year non-competition clause in a business non-disclosure agreement between these two law firms was not an illegal trade restraint and was enforceable as a contractual term.

However, a recent policy paper "Smarter Regulation to Grow the Economy" has proposed to limit the duration of non-compete clauses in employment contracts to three months. The three-month limit will apply solely to non-compete clauses in employment contracts and contracts of certain other workers who are entitled to certain protections under UK employment law. The UK government does not intend to extend the limit to other types of employment contracts, such as partnership or shareholder agreements. Nevertheless, this proposal excludes non-solicitation clauses, paid notice periods or gardening leave, or confidentiality agreements. According to the proposal, such clauses are a burden and serve no definite purpose. These non-compete provisions can discourage employees from seeking better-paying jobs and limit businesses' ability to compete and innovate. Hence, this reform is expected to empower employees with greater freedom to switch jobs, apply their skills elsewhere, and even earn a pay rise as well to support the UK economy by assisting employers in growing their businesses and increasing productivity.

While in the United States, in the case of *Central Monitoring Service, Inc v. Stanley Zakinski*, Zakinski appealed from a trial court decision granting an injunction prohibiting him from working for any competitor of Central Monitoring Service, Inc. (Central) in South Dakota for two years or disclosing certain information about Central at any time. Non-competition (non-compete) and secrecy (non-disclosure) agreements are both contracts in restraint of commerce, which are normally unenforceable. Zakinski's deal was a "Non-Compete and Confidentiality Agreement." A non-compete agreement is different from a confidentiality or non-disclosure agreement. The United States Federal Trade Commission released a Notice of Proposed Rulemaking (NOPR) on January 5, 2023, that would prohibit non-compete clauses in employer-employee contracts. California, Oklahoma and North Dakota have banned non-compete agreements while some other states have passed laws limiting their use although many business groups claimed that non-compete clauses are a crucial way for companies to protect trade secrets. The proposal would prohibit employers from imposing non-compete clauses on employees including independent contractors and unpaid workers and it would apply to all contract provisions that create "de facto" non-compete clauses. The rule would apply retroactively, not only would pre-existing non-compete agreements be rendered invalid, but employers would also be required to proactively withdraw the non-compete.

Non-competition in the relationship between employers and employees is not explicitly governed by European Union legislation. Article 15 of the Charter of the European Union's Fundamental Rights 2009 provides that "Everyone has the right to engage in work and to pursue freely chosen or accepted occupation". In Italy, non-compete clauses are regulated by the Civil Code whereby they are employed to preserve legitimate business interests. The application of these non-compete agreements is more common among managers and professionals, as well as more educated and higher-earning employees. They are also more common in mid-sized businesses than in small businesses, and in international corporations (Boeri et al., 2023). According to Civil Code Article 2125, the period of the non-compete agreement must not exceed five years for executives and three years for other employees and there are no constraints of geographical scope or subject content. Moreover, the duty of loyalty is provided by Article 2105 which also prohibits the employee from competing against their employer during the term of employment.

THE EFFECT OF THE NON-COMPETE CLAUSE IN MALAYSIA

In Malaysia, it has become a norm to include a non-compete clause in employment contracts to protect the interest of employers. The non-compete clause was included to prevent an employee from working for a competitor after they leave the organization for a fixed period. The construction of a non-compete clause in employment contracts is also known as a restraint of trade. Types of contracts where the restraint of trade may exist are contracts of employment between employer and employee; contracts between vendor and purchaser for the sale of the goodwill of a business; contracts between partners such as prior to the dissolution of a partnership, and during the continuance of the partnership; and other commercial contracts.

Section 28 of the Contracts Act 1950, clearly stipulates that every agreement by which anyone is restrained from exercising a lawful profession, trade, or business of any kind, is to that extent void. However, Section 28 provides certain exceptions to the general rule which are an agreement not to carry on the business of which goodwill is sold; an agreement between partners prior to dissolution; and an agreement between partners during the continuance of the partnership. As a result, any of the above exceptions that are not included in the non-compete clauses in employment contracts will be null and void. A strict interpretation of Section 28 would render all covenants in restraint of trade void even if the covenants in question were reasonable. In *Wrigglesworth v. Wilson Anthony [1964] 1 LNS 1 222,* the judge views that exception 2 of Section 28 is not applied in this case, and at the time of employment the defendant is not the partner of the plaintiff. Besides, the clause in the agreement stated, "that the plaintiff discharges the defendant from the terms and obligations of the service agreement." Therefore, it strengthens the view that the plaintiff had no desire to place any restraint on the defendant.

It is worth noting to refer to cases that applied a non-compete clause in their employment agreement. In the case of *Polygram Records Sdn Bhd v The Search [1994] 3 CLJ 806,* it is noted that there are two separate non-compete clauses, one about during employment and another is a post-contract non-compete clause. For the first non-compete clause, Visu Sinnadura J held that section 28 is only applicable in cases where a person is restrained from carrying on his trade or profession in the post-contract period and not during the currency of the contract. It appears to the judge that the covenant whereby the defendants undertook to provide exclusive recording rights to the plaintiffs during the currency of their recording contract is not a covenant in restraint of trade and is therefore not rendered void under section 28 of the Contracts Act. For the second non-compete clause, it was held that the validity of the non-compete clause stands on a different basis that Defendants were prohibited from making any recordings without the written consent of Plaintiff within two (2) years after the contract ends. The Court had also remarked that this clause is most inelegantly drafted. Therefore, the effect of the post-contract restraint clause in any covenant and/or agreement is *void ab initio* and unenforceable.

Besides, in the case of *Nagadevan a/l Mahalingam v Millenium Medicare Services* [2011] 4 MLJ 739, the non-compete clause more on the restraining Plaintiff from setting up any medical practice within three (3) years after ceasing to be a partner within a radius of 15KM from any partnership clinic as medical practitioner either by himself or as a partner or employee of any person or company without the Defendant consent or permission. The Court of Appeal held that restricting the liberty of the employee to carry on the practice of a medical practitioner for a period, was an agreement which has no legal effect under Section 28 of the Contract Act 1950. Subsequently, in *Vision Cast Sdn Bhd & Anor v Dynacast (Melaka) Sdn Bhd & Ors [2015] 1 MLJ 424,* the Court determined whether the execution of a confidentiality agreement and deed of restrictive covenant during employment was valid under Exception 1 of Section 28. The Court held that no restraint was allowed against the Appellant's involvement in any competing business or in dealing with Dynacast's customers after the end of the contractual period and any restraint against the Appellant from pursuing lawful trade/business was unsustainable and should be struck down by Section 28.

In *Lim Yoke Lin v Roy Hong Ping Wei [2019] 1 LNS 1439,* the High Court had significantly emphasized the principle laid down in Section 28 of the CA by ruling that the plaintiff was not able to demonstrate how Clause 3.8 which prohibits the defendant from operating a similar business to that of the plaintiff worldwide and not allowing the defendant to compete with the plaintiff for a period of ten years, could escape from being caught under section 28 of the Contracts Act 1950. Training in budgeting, financing and marketing carries no trade secrets. No confidential information was alleged to have been taken away by the defendant. Hence, Clause 3.8 is void and the Plaintiff cannot seek to enforce it.

Exclusion to General Rule

Notably, the general rule in Section 28 does apply to a non-compete clause for post-employment contracts, however, the rule does not apply to employees during the course of employment. To be clear, employees are prohibited from having a direct or indirect interest in any competitor company, and employers may impose certain restrictions. It is important to understand that the is no section stating the employer may restrict the course of employment, however in the common law, employees owe a duty of care towards their employers to act in good faith for the benefit of the employer. As an employee, they have certain standards to act in good faith, show loyalty, and avoid any conflict of interest. The standards depend on the position of the employee, the nature of the corporate opportunity, and the nature of employment. The important factor to be noted is whether the action causes any substantial harm to their employer or not. For example, an engineer who provides a drawing plan design for a competitor company on his off day is likely to breach his duty to his employer, whereas a construction worker who works on a construction site after working hours for a competitor is not considered as breaching his duties.

On the other hand, the employee may use the knowledge and skills acquired during employment because the information once learned, becomes part of the skill and knowledge applied in the course of business or employment. Therefore, it is crucial to understand that employers cannot restrain their employees from using the skills or knowledge learned in practicing competing businesses or in the competitor business. There is no breach of confidentiality as it's a skill acquired during the course of employment, and an employee's livelihood depends on the skill, knowledge and experience acquired while in employment. In most occupations, we teach and learn from one another, knowing full well that our students will become our competitors. Yet, we share our knowledge, gifting our experience without fees, patents, non-disclosure contracts, and non-compete clauses. This is what defines us as a specialty; the importance of detail, our desire for excellence and our ability to evolve (Chong, D. K., 2021).

Moreover, the employees may work in competitor companies or start up any business to compete after leaving the organization, as the rule states that void to imposed non-compete clause after leaving the employment. However, the employers may impose restrictions or restrain the employees from disclosing any confidential information obtained during employment to third parties or use for their personal gain. The purpose of using the restrictive covenant or clause in the employment contract should be clear to protect the employer's trade secret, business confidential information such as the company's operations, results, earnings projections, strategies, clients or client relationships, proprietary products, or employee records. In determining what interests an employer may legitimately protect, the courts have limited them to two; trade secrets and preventing an employee from soliciting the customers and employees of the business.

Reference to a few cases on this matter could enlighten the usage of specific trade secrets. In the case of *Schmidt Scientific Sdn Bhd v Ong Han Suan & Ors [1998] 1 CLJ 685*, court held that it is a breach of duty of fidelity and good faith on the part of the employee to remove a customer list or to deliberately set out to memorize the said list to use it later, even though any use or disclosure is confined to the post-employment period, with the intention of using it to solicit orders from them after he had left his employer's service and set up a similar business on his own account. In the case of *Worldwide Rota Dies*

Sdn Bhd v Ronald Ong Cheow Joon [2010] 8 MLJ 297, the court held that restraint is permissible if it is fashioned in such a way as to prevent a misuse of trade secrets or business connection. In determining reasonableness, the Court will take into account the nature of the business, the extent of restrictions, as well as the commercial reality of the matter.

In *Svenson Hair Care Centre Sdn Bhd v. Irene Chin Zee Ling [2008] 8 CLJ 386*, the court held that customers' names, lists, and details have also been judicially recognized as being confidential, and wrongful utilization of such particulars warrants injunctive protection. In the case of *Medien Sdn Bhd v. Dominic Chai Le Seng [2019] 1 LNS 2017*, the Court recognized the clause restraining the disclosure of confidential information. The decision referred to the definition submitted by the judge in *Saltman Engineering Co. Ltd v. Campbell Engineering Co. Ltd [1963] 3 All ER* which reads:

"the information, to be confidential, must, I apprehend, apart from contract, have the necessary quality of confidence about it, namely, it must not be something which is public property and public knowledge. On the other hand, it is perfectly possible to have a confidential document, be it a formula, a plan, a sketch, or something of that kind, which is the result of work done by the maker on materials that may be available for the use of anybody; but what makes it confidential is the fact that the maker of the document has used his brain and this produced a result which can only be produced by somebody who goes through the same process."

In *Karen Yap Chew Ling v. Binary Group Services Bhd & Another Appeal (2023) 7 CLJ 534, CA*, the court has stated that the Appellant has committed a breach of duty of fidelity and good faith. The appellant has pre-planned to utilize the confidential information of the Respondent, based on the action performed by the appellant as below:

"A spike in the activities of copying Confidential Information especially in the months, days and hours before Karen Yap left the Plaintiff and some in the middle of the night, can only speak of a clandestine and carefully concealed conduct designed to escape detection if possible. She underestimated the fact that technology has been developed to trace one's digital footprints and that nothing is ever lost forever in cyberspace. Companies run a real risk of and are vulnerable to theft of confidential information that can have damaging consequences for their business ultimately someone senior in the companies would have to be entrusted with such confidential information to protect its integrity and to prevent unlawful access and copying of it to the detriment of the companies. The tough question has always been who would guard the guardians and watch the watchmen and gatekeepers".

The decision of the judge in the Karen Yap case seems to be a boon for employers and serves as a strong deterrence to employees who attempt to abscond with confidential and proprietary information, as well as to uphold good and honest conduct. Besides, it is important to ensure that the employment agreement is conclusive and contains the necessary clauses for the protection of confidential information. To conclude, confidential information in nature is known as trade secrets, and the wrongful utilization of information subject to injunction protection from the court, as well as it, is judicially recognized in Malaysia.

Non-Solicitation Clause

In general, a non-solicitation clause that prohibits solicitation and/or hiring of employees and customers in the employment contract is not valid owing to Section 28 of the Contracts Act 1950 (Vijayan, V. 2019). To be precise, it will be difficult to prove that the employee or customer was solicited or enticed by the ex-employee to leave the employer (Vijayan, V. 2019). A non-solicitation clause such as a customer clause, supplier clause, or employee clause may be included in the employment contracts. These non-solicitation clauses should be made expressly in the agreement, whereas implied non-solicitation clauses will not give effect to the employment contract. Non-solicitation clauses are sometimes called "non-poaching" clauses, and it is provided that these clauses are reasonable and protect the legitimate interest of employers and employees. Therefore, the employer may bring an action against their employee for breaching any confidential or trade secret or non-solicitation clauses. The action brought by the employer should be in the best interest of the company and reasonable manner.

Moreover, a non-solicitation clause is recognized in Malaysian courts. In *Agensi Pekerjaan Talent2 International Sdn Bhd v Kenneth Yong Fu Loong & Anor [2012] 10 CLJ 217 [HC]*, the court recognizing the significance of a non-solicitation clause, allowed the injunction application. The non-solicitation clause in the said case reads:

"directly or indirectly approach, induce, solicit or persuade or attempt to approach, induce, solicit or persuade any person or entity who or which was or is a client of Talent2 within the last 12 months of your employment with Talent2 to undertake or perform work or services for that person or entity or to cease doing business with Talent2 or reduce the amount of business which the person or entity would normally do with Talent2."

Another case where the court recognized the non-solicitation clause is *Ace Capital Growth Sdn Bhd v Kua Kee Koon & Ors [2021] 1 LNS 1846*. In this case, the clause reads: "the employee must not canvas, or solicit the business of, or maintain any personal records of any client of Ace Global Metal Sdn Bhd and Ace Capital Growth Sdn Bhd.". With that, the court held a non-solicitation clause has been expressly prohibited in a contract it survives even after the employment ceases and decided this suit in the plaintiff's favor. A non-solicitation clause in an employment contract would bind the parties in the contracts during and post-employment. To be precise, a reasonable non-solicitation clause should be set out clearly and properly as well as drafted perfectly. If the clause were drafted poorly, improperly, or vague, it would render the clause ineffective and void.

In common law, the validity of a trade restraint is measured by the reasonableness test whereby the courts will to a certain degree permit a trade restraint based on the time and space that it considers reasonable (Vijayan, 2019). In Malaysia, a non-compete clause is only enforceable during the existence of the employment relationship, and any restraint, post-cessation of the employment relationship, is unenforceable (Vijayan, 2019). It should be noted that the non-compete clause is applicable in employment agreements to protect businesses' intellectual property, trade secrets, proprietary information, and client information, and maintain competitive advantages. Moreover, the clauses should not be used to prohibit employees from seeking a new job or better opportunity. To be noted, the clauses included in the agreement should be reasonable, and the covenant not to compete with the employer in the future.

NON-COMPETE CLAUSE AS A THREAT TO SUSTAINABLE DEVELOPMENT GOALS: A PERSPECTIVE

There is limited literature that directly discusses the link between the non-compete clause in the employment contract and the Sustainable Development Goals (SDGs). Several studies specifically addressed the role of competition law in achieving SDGs. Marquis (2017) stated that whilst competition law does not of itself guarantee sustainable and inclusive growth and development, it is still an important policy that can help to achieve such goals. Furthermore, Gal and Fox (2014) argued that competition law is required in developing countries to support economic development, yet "one competition law and policy size does not fit all socio-economic contexts." On the other hand, with respect to trade law, members of the WTO are required to re-align their trade policies accordingly as the WTO itself emphasizes the need for trade regulation in achieving the SDGs through a robust regulatory framework and protection of market access as well as commitments in trade liberalization (Sieber-Gasser et al., 2021).

Kafker (1993) regarded the non-compete clause as "golden handcuffs" that restrict the professional development of accountants, physicians, and attorneys. Wilcox (1999) acknowledged that the claimed public interest is insufficient to justify a blanket rejection of all non-competition agreements. The degree and extent of any public harm caused by enforcement of such provision, as well as the nature of the interest that the business may allege to justify the restraint, vary depending on the type of restraint at issue and the circumstances surrounding the attempted enforcement (Wilcox, 1999). McMahon and Eustace (2022) reinstated that law enforcement has long struggled with weighing a trio of principles in the context of employment: the interests of businesses in competition, an individual's right to use his skills and knowledge and the public interest in economic development. Besides, non-compete agreements benefit companies disproportionately at the expense of employees. The method through which these parties agree to such contracts is hardly an appropriate negotiation (Marx, 2018). Thus, it was suggested that employers are required to implement procedures to make non-disclosure agreements (NDAs) easier to enforce, enabling them to serve as an excellent alternative to non-compete agreements (Marx, 2018).

With the United States and the United Kingdom signals in amending non-compete clauses in employment contracts appear as a motivation to address allegedly anti-competitive labor market activity. With progressive economic development that needs to be in line with SDGs, the current practice that prohibits an employee from joining their competitor may be abused by the employers which reinforces dominant employers' dominance by blocking off others' progression. This clause hinders labor market mobility and wage growth, and it contributes to racial and gender wage disparities, which is an actual threat in achieving the SDGs, especially the promotion of equal opportunities (SDG 5), the promotion of decent work and economic growth (SDG 8), and the reduction of inequalities (SDG 10).

CONCLUSION

It is important to highlight that the Malaysian law on trade restraint differs from the common law position. The exceptions to Section 28, namely: agreements involving sales of goodwill of a business; partners prior to dissolution; and continuance of the partnership. The rationale of Section 28 and the court's decisions to provide fair and equity protection to both employers and employees in the employment sector. To be added, Section 28 was designed in such a way as to ensure that everyone was given equal opportunities in pursuing legitimate work or business. Although employers cannot succeed in the civil claim for a post-termination non-compete clause, it becomes common for employers to include non-compete clauses in their employment contracts. The inclusion of the non-compete clauses with the aim to protect the legitimate business interest. In other words, to prevent employees from disclosing confidential information as well as poaching the employees, customers, or suppliers. With the growth of employment at present, it is crucial to be aware of the obligations owed by both employer and employee during employment and post-employment. Notably, the legitimate interests of the employer and employee should be balanced between their rights and obligations. Competition is needed to ensure the harmony of rights and interests and the legitimacy of employees and employers. In addition, many countries prioritize sustainable and equitable economic growth to curb low unemployment and promote decent work. At the same time, exploitation and breaches of labor rights continue to be widespread all over the world. As many countries limit the application of non-compete clauses in the employment contract, the promotion of fair competition might influence employment market dynamics, in order to sustain economic growth and social stability.

REFERENCES

AdamsJ. M. Non-Compete Agreements: A Review of the Literature. December 31, 2019; Available from: https://ssrn.com/abstract=3513639orhttp://dx.doi.org/10.2139/ssrn.3513639

Arnow-Richman, R. (2019). The new enforcement regime: Revisiting the law of employee competition (and the scholarship of Professor Charles Sullivan) with 2020 vision. *Seton Hall L. Rev., 50*, 1223. doi:10.2139/ssrn.4396108

Blake, H. M. (1960). Employee Agreements Not to Compete. *Harvard Law Review*, *73*(4), 625–691. doi:10.2307/1338051

Chong, D. K. (2021). The times they are a-changin'. *AJOPS*, *4*(1), 6–8. doi:10.34239/ajops.v4n1.298

Gal, M., & Fox, E. (2014). Drafting Competition Law for Developing Jurisdictions: Learning from Experience. *Contracts & Commercial Law eJournal*.

Garner, B. A. (2004). *Black's Law Dictionary* (8th ed.). West Publishing Co.

Hang, T. T., & Huy, N. D. (2022). Non-compete agreement in labor relations according to the regulations of some countries and recommendations for Vietnam. Journal of Science and Technology Development – Economics. *Law and Management*, *6*(3), 3118–3127.

Hieu, T. (2020). Restraint of business clauses in employment contracts: experience from some countries. *VNUHCM Journal, 4.* . doi:10.32508/stdjelm.v4i2.619

Husnina, N., & Kevin, W. (26 May 2023). *The Extent and The Applicability of Non-Compete Clause in Employment Agreement.* Kevin Wu & Associates. https://www.mondaq.com/contract-of-employment/1320820/the-extent-and-the-applicability-of-non-compete-clause-in-employment-agreement-

Kafker, S. L. (1993). Golden handcuffs: Enforceability of non-competition clauses in professional partnership agreements of accountants, physicians, and attorneys. *American Business Law Journal*, *31*(1), 31–58. doi:10.1111/j.1744-1714.1993.tb00674.x

Kang, H., & Fleming, L. (2020). Non-competes, business dynamism, and concentration: Evidence from a Florida case study. *Journal of Economics & Management Strategy*, *29*(3), 663–685. doi:10.1111/jems.12349

Kuzminac, M. (2022). *Non-competes in employment contracts: (Un)justified restrictions on the freedom to work.* Glasnik Advokatske komore Vojvodine. . doi:10.5937/gakv94-36244

Lestari, S., Sova, S., & Njatrijani, R. (2017). Implementation of non-competition clause as the basis of trade secret protection in indonesia. *Implementation Of Non-Competition Clause As The Basis Of Trade Secret Protection In Indonesia.*, *17*(3), 320–327. doi:10.20884/1.jdh.2017.17.3.1278

Marquis, M. (2017). Competition law in the Philippines: Economic, legal, and institutional context. *Journal of Antitrust Enforcement*, *6*, 79–122. doi:10.1093/jaenfo/jnx014

Marx, M. (2011). The Firm Strikes Back. *American Sociological Review*, *76*(5), 695–712. doi:10.1177/0003122411414822

Marx, M. (2018). Reforming non-competes to support workers. *Policy Proposal, 4.*

Marx, M., & Fleming, L. (2012). Non-compete Agreements: Barriers to Entry...and Exit? *Innovation Policy and the Economy*, *12*, 40–64. doi:10.1086/663155

Marx, M., Singh, J., & Fleming, L. (2014). Regional disadvantage? Employee non-compete agreements and brain drain. *Research Policy*, *44*(2), 394–404. doi:10.1016/j.respol.2014.10.006

Mcmahon, C., & Eustace, A. (2023). Nothing to Lose but Their Restraints of Trade: Lessons for Employment Non-Compete Clauses from EU Competition Law. *Industrial Law Journal*, *52*(2), 409–450. doi:10.1093/indlaw/dwac025

Nadiyya, A. (2021). Analisis Pengaturan Klausul Non-Kompetisi dalam Perjanjian Kerja: Studi Perbandingan Indonesia, Malaysia, dan Singapura. *Hukum dan Masyarakat Madani, 11*(2).

Nicholas, K. (May 12, 2022). *Can You Work for Competitors in Malaysia After Leaving Your Company?* Althr. https://althr.my/resources/can-you-work-for-competitors-in-malaysia

Novitz, T. (2021). Gig work as a manifestation of short-termism: Crafting a sustainable regulatory agenda. *Industrial Law Journal*, *50*(4), 636–661. doi:10.1093/indlaw/dwab027

PosnerE. (2019). The Antitrust Challenge to Covenants Not to Compete in Employment Contracts. [S.l.]: SSRN. https://ssrn.com/abstract=3453433. . doi:10.2139/ssrn.3453433

Ronald, J. G. (1999). The Legal Infrastructure of High Technology Industrial Districts: Silicon Valley, Route 128, and Covenants not to Compete. *New York University Law Review*, *74*(3), 575–629.

Sieber-Gasser, C., Kalra, S., & Sheth, A. V. (2021). Sustainable Development Goals vs Non-Discrimination in WTO Law: Does the End Justify the Means? *Indian J. Int'l Econ. L.*, *13*, 82.

Starr, E., & Robert, H. (2019). The use, abuse, and enforceability of non-compete and no-poach agreements. *Washington, DC: Economic Innovation Group*. United Nations. https://sdgs.un.org/topics/employment-decent-work-all-and-social-protection

Vijayan, V. (2019). Employment. Chamber Global Practice Guide. http://www.shearndelamore.com/pdfs/Chambers-Global-Practice-Guide-Employment-2019.pdf

Wai, C. K., & Derek, C. T. Q. (2021). *Contracts in Restraint of Trade in Malaysia.* Low Partners. https://www.lowpartners.com/contracts-restraint-trade-malaysia/

Wickelgren, A. (2017). A novel justification for legal restrictions on non-compete clauses. *International Review of Law and Economics.*

Wilcox, R. M. (1999). Enforcing lawyer non-competition agreements while maintaining the profession: The role of conflict of interest principles. *Minnesota Law Review*, *84*, 915.

KEY TERMS AND DEFINITIONS

Agreement: The condition of having the same opinion, or a decision or arrangement between two or more people or groups to do something or to obey the same rules.

Confidential: Containing information whose unauthorized disclosure could be prejudicial to the national interest.

Contract: A contract is an agreement, either written or spoken, between two or more parties that creates a legal obligation.

Covenant: A formal agreement or promise between two or more people.

Employee: One employed by another usually for wages or salary and in a position below the executive level.

Employer: A person or company that provides a job paying wages or a salary to one or more people.

Employment: Work for which one has been engaged and is being paid by an employer.

Non-Compete Clause: A promise usually in a sale-of-business, partnership or employment contract, not to engage in the same type of business for a stated time in the same market as the buyer, partner or employer.

Non-Solicitation Clause: This serves as a form of protection of the company's trade secrets and information of their clients that is essential to their trade and ensuring loyalty of their existing clientele.

Restraint: Something that limits the freedom of someone or something, or that prevents something from growing or increasing.

APPENDIX

Cases

Ace Capital Growth Sdn Bhd v Kua Kee Koon & Ors [2021] 1 LNS 1846

Agensi Pekerjaan Talent2 International Sdn Bhd v Kenneth Yong Fu Loong & Anor [2012] 10 CLJ 217 [HC]

Karen Yap Chew Ling v. Binary Group Services Bhd & Another Appeal (2023) 7 CLJ 534, CA

Lim Yoke Lin v Roy Hong Ping Wei [2019] 1 LNS 1439

Medien Sdn Bhd v. Dominic Chai Le Seng [2019] 1 LNS 2017

Nagadevan a/l Mahalingam v Millenium Medicare Services [2011] 4 MLJ 739

Polygram Records Sdn Bhd v The Search [1994] 3 CLJ 806

Saltman Engineering Co. Ltd v. Campbell Engineering Co. Ltd [1963] 3 All ER

Schmidt Scientific Sdn Bhd v Ong Han Suan & Ors [1998] 1 CLJ 685

Svenson Hair Care Centre Sdn Bhd v. Irene Chin Zee Ling [2008] 8 CLJ 386,

Vision Cast Sdn Bhd & Anor v Dynacast (Melaka) Sdn Bhd & Ors [2015] 1 MLJ 424

Wrigglesworth v. Wilson Anthony [1964] 1 LNS 1 222

Worldwide Rota Dies Sdn Bhd v Ronald Ong Cheow Joon [2010] 8 MLJ 297

Statutes

Contracts Act 1950

Chapter 7
On Consumer Protection in the Digital Age and the Intersection Between EU Competition Law and Data Privacy Law

Arletta Gorecka
https://orcid.org/0000-0001-6555-4264
University of Strathclyde, UK

ABSTRACT

The intersection of competition law and data privacy presents a significant challenge in the current legal framework. The connection between data privacy law and competition law lacks clarity and definition, requiring further exploration. The immense scale of data collection poses challenges and gives companies a market advantage, sometimes at the expense of individuals' control over their personal data. The shift from price-focused to data-focused markets complicates the integration of privacy concerns within competition law. This chapter aims to enrich discussions on the intersection of competition law and data protection, highlighting the potential for a mutually beneficial connection between these frameworks. It examines the relationship between competition law and sustainable development goals, with a focus on digital and green market development. This chapter contributes to the understanding of consumer protection in the digital age and the need for a comprehensive approach to address the challenges posed by the data-driven economy.

1. INTRODUCTION

The discussion surrounding how competition law and privacy intersect presents a significant hurdle for the current competition law structure (Douglas, 2021), as immense data collection introduced incentives for large digital undertakings to abuse their market power. In turn, this potential ripple effect could ultimately result in novel theories of harm having a negative and cascading impact on the overall competitive process, hampering economic growth and consumer welfare.

DOI: 10.4018/979-8-3693-0390-0.ch007

Copyright © 2024, IGI Global. Copying or distributing in print or electronic forms without written permission of IGI Global is prohibited.

Numerous digital services, such as online advertising, search engines, social media platforms, and location-based services, heavily rely on the utilisation of personal data (BKA, Facebook case 2019). The immense scale of data collection poses challenges for society and laws, giving companies an advantage in the market (Kira, 2021). In some cases, competition drives businesses to gather user information, reducing individuals' control over their personal data. This occurs when companies introduce innovative features to attract new users and extract more data (Saura, 2021). Ultimately, the increasing collection and analysis of personal data provide valuable insights for digital companies (Schäfer, 2023). Processing personal data allows digital platforms to predict personality traits and develop advanced sociometrics by transforming raw data into meaningful information and knowledge. Relying on this knowledge can enhance product quality, services, innovation, and predictions. The dynamic nature of the data market chain, along with its reciprocal dimension, creates feedback loops (Douglas 2021). As a result, the acquisition, collection, and analysis of personal data can reduce costs and improve services in the digital market.

Competition in the online market has created a conflict between consumers' privacy and the motivations of businesses (Kira, 2021). The discussion about the intersection of competition law and data privacy primarily revolves around the practices of dominant players like Google, Apple, Facebook, Amazon, and Microsoft (GAFAM) who act as gatekeepers in the digital economy (DMA, 2022). The shift from price-focused to data-focused markets has presented significant challenges in addressing privacy concerns within the framework of competition law. The central issue at hand is whether the existing tools for enforcing competition law are appropriate and how competition law should interact with privacy concerns.

This chapter focuses on consumer protection in the age of digital revolution, with a focus on uncovering opportunities for a harmonious and mutually beneficial integration of these legal frameworks. The focus especially on EU competition law and privacy-related harms. Additionally, it highlights the critical importance of safeguarding consumers' rights and interests within the ever-evolving and data-centric digital environment, where competition is fierce. Consumer rights are of paramount importance in addressing potential privacy infringements. In an era where personal data is increasingly collected and utilised, safeguarding these rights ensures that individuals have control over their information, protection from abuse, and the ability to make informed choices. Upholding consumer rights not only preserves privacy but also fosters trust in digital services and promotes fair competition, ultimately benefiting both individuals and society as a whole. Competition law and consumer protection are instrumental in promoting economic growth, reducing inequality, and ensuring access to essential goods and services—all of which contribute to the achievement of the Sustainable Development Goals (SDGs).

The crux of this research is to analyse the relationship between competition law and privacy-related harms and its possible impact on consumer protection and SDGs. The chapter begins with the theoretical background between competition law and data privacy, highlighting the EU competition law approach to privacy-related harms. The discussion considers the legal background and an attempt to define privacy through the lens of competition law. Then, the chapter moves to discuss the relationship between EU competition law and SDG. In particular, the consideration will be placed on the digital economy and its impact on consumer protection. The concluding section of this article examines whether the competition law framework can effectively recognise and address privacy-related harms, in addition to safeguarding consumer protection.

2. EU COMPETITION LAW AND PRIVACY: THEORETICAL BACKGROUND

2.1 Defying Privacy

Privacy protection lacks a universally recognised definition, but it encompasses the importance of personal privacy in relation to political affiliation, social life, and dignity. This importance may be considered a distinct goal that goes beyond the scope of competition policy. The dangers posed by privacy invasions and data breaches are widely acknowledged. While some competition enforcement could potentially account for the increased consequences of commercial data processing or collection, neither competition law nor economic analysis currently supports this argument (Kimmelman et al., 2015; Kimmelman et al., 2017). The global recognition of privacy varies in terms of the level of data protection and the role of competition law. Different cultures, social systems, and consumer preferences contribute to varying conceptions of privacy, with some valuing it less and others valuing it more (Tsai et al., 2011).

Privacy can be understood in both a broad and narrow sense, and breaches of privacy have far-reaching implications that can potentially undermine democratic processes (Cadwallard et al., 2018). However, the specific boundaries and effects of privacy are extensively debated in academic circles. The European Union (EU) legal order is often regarded as providing robust personal data protection. Article 16 of the Treaty on the Functioning of the European Union (TFEU, 2008) forms the basis for data protection in the EU. The Charter of Fundamental Rights of the European Union (2010) further safeguards personal data by recognising it as a fundamental right under Article 8, protecting individuals from state intervention. According to Article 8 of the Charter, personal information can be processed by anyone, including the State. However, this broad right is subject to the requirements of fairness, transparency, and lawfulness outlined in Article 8(2) and (3) to ensure adequate protection for individuals. More recently, the implementation of the General Data Protection Regulation (hereinafter referred as "GDPR 2016") has further enhanced data protection measures.

The primary principle of the GDPR (2016) is to require a valid legal basis for the processing of personal data, which necessitates explicit consent from the individual whose data is being processed (article 4(2)). According to the GDPR, processing includes any action carried out with personal data, which encompasses any information obtained concerning individuals that could potentially identify them. The GDPR also brought about clarity by addressing crucial concepts such as the definition of a 'data subject' as any person from whom data is collected, and a 'data controller' as any person who processes the collected data (GDPR, 2016, article 4(1)). Notably, the key aspect of the GDPR's framework is consent, which must be clear, specific, informed, and given voluntarily. The GDPR significantly enhanced the safeguarding of personal data and, at the same time, bolstered users' privacy.

The GDPR (2016) establishes a fundamental requirement for ensuring the validity of consent in data processing. This requirement states that consent must be specific, unambiguous, freely given, and informed (GDPR, 2016, article 7, recitals 32, 33, 42, 43). It can be granted by individuals through explicit affirmative action or a statement indicating their consent to the processing of their personal data. The GDPR embodies a dual nature in this regard: individuals are required to provide consent for any data processing, making it clear that digital platforms or services rely on their data and therefore have a right to be informed about how their data will be processed. Simultaneously, the data controller is obligated to fulfill their data processing responsibilities, ensuring that the processing aligns with the agreed-upon extent, which is both well-founded and capable of being demonstrated to individuals.

The Breyer case (2016) suggests that the concept of personal data has a wide range of applicability, leading some to claim that personal data protection has become a comprehensive legal framework. It can be argued that the GDPR covers any utilisation of personal data, including its use by algorithms. This is because Article 4(2) of the GDPR (2016) provides a broad definition of personal data processing:

"... any operation or set of operations which is performed on personal data or on sets of personal data, whether or not by automated means, such as collection, recording, organisation, structuring, storage, adaptation or alteration or otherwise making available, alignment or combination, restriction, erasure or destruction"

2.2. EU Competition Law and its Approach to Privacy-Related Harms

EU competition law is driven by a diverse set of objectives, encompassing the safeguarding of market structures, economic freedom, efficiency, and the well-being of consumers (Guidelines on the Commission's Enforcement 2009). These regulations are codified within articles 101-106 of the Treaty on the Functioning of the European Union (TFEU), with a focus on preventing anti-competitive practices, countering distortions of competition, and prohibiting the abuse of dominant market positions. As stipulated in the EU Guidelines, the scope of EU competition law extends to encompass any "economic activity" that has the potential to impact trade among Member States (Guidelines on the effect on trade concept contained in Articles 81 and 82 of the Treaty 2004).

The expanding presence of data-driven platforms has made it increasingly relevant to apply Article 102 TFEU within the digital economy. This is because privacy infringements, particularly instances of unfair data acquisition on an unprecedented scale, can create opportunities for abuse of dominance (Facebook, case summary, 2019). Additionally, Article 102 TFEU can be invoked to address anticompetitive actions by data-driven digital platforms, which encompass both exploitative and exclusionary forms of abuse as defined by the article (Commission Guidance 2009). This section offers an overview of the EU competition law approach to privacy-related harms.

The competition law approach to privacy involves examining how privacy-related concerns intersect with antitrust or competition regulations. This approach recognises that certain behaviours by dominant firms, particularly those involving the use of consumer data, can have anticompetitive effects and harm consumers. The Bundeskartellamt's (hereinafter referred as „BKA 2019") Facebook case reflects an attempt to define privacy within the context of competition law. The evaluation of privacy protection rights, in this case, is based on a fundamental principle: personal data processing can only occur if the data subjects have provided their consent or if the law permits such processing. The BKA (2019) approached the case as a data protection authority and concluded that Facebook's terms and conditions were in compliance with the GDPR, but highlighted certain aspects from a privacy protection perspective. Firstly, the BKA observed that Facebook users were unaware of the extent to which their personal data was being collected and processed, which indicated that their consent was not fully informed and well-founded. Additionally, users did not anticipate that Facebook would analyse data obtained from different websites.

Moreover, the BKA (2019) determined that Facebook's terms and conditions were intricate, employing language that was challenging for users to comprehend. The true intentions of the platform, particularly regarding data processing purposes, were difficult to fully grasp. As a result, the consent obtained from users was deemed insufficiently specific, informed, and freely given, thus failing to meet the requirements outlined in the GDPR. This was primarily due to Facebook's practice of collecting data from multiple sources and subsequently merging the acquired data from both Facebook and third-party sources. The BKA (2019) concluded that this data combination process was in violation of the law because:

"[p]rocessing data from third-party sources to the extent determined by Facebook in its terms and conditions is neither required for offering the social network as such nor for monetising the network through personalised advertising, as a personalised network could also be based to a large extent on the user data processed in the context of operating the social network."

Nonetheless, the BKA emphasised that users' consent could be considered coerced in this case. According to the BKA, if consent is a mandatory requirement for utilizing the Facebook.com service, it cannot be regarded as voluntary. Additionally, the BKA stated that the practice of combining data from different sources was not essential for the proper functioning of the social network. Consequently, this data combination was not dependent on users' consent and constituted a violation of privacy.

However, it is important to note that the BKA's judgment did not indicate that the GDPR's consent requirement was based on the market power of the data controller. The GDPR does not explicitly address the theory of competitive harm or distinguish based on market power, nor does it impose specific privacy responsibilities on dominant firms. Therefore, determining privacy violations based on anticompetitive behavior becomes challenging. In the context of the BKA's case against Facebook, the conduct of acquiring and processing data without clearly defined and understandable purposes was considered a privacy harm. The BKA concluded that these privacy harms could constitute a recognizable competition law injury, primarily targeting Facebook's data accumulation strategy. Additionally, the BKA identified the violation of the right to informational self-determination, which safeguards individuals' freedom to make decisions about the processing of their personal data, particularly in relation to dominant market positions. Moreover, the BKA relied on German case law to establish that market power could be further evidenced by abusive business terms. This notion of unbalanced negotiations was applicable not only in competition law but also in data protection law, which also aims to protect the right to informational self-determination. In this case, the BKA applied German competition law to address the issue and used data protection law as a benchmark to determine the abusive nature of Facebook's conditions.

Indeed, the intersection between competition law and privacy protection is intricate and extends beyond the realm of competition law enforcement alone. Privacy is a multifaceted concept that is deeply rooted in social practices, making it challenging to define precisely (Leese, 2022). When it comes to users contracting with platform providers regarding privacy, there is limited scope for negotiation, often resulting in mere assurances provided by the platforms (Kerber & Zolna, 2022). The digital society is continuously evolving, introducing new risks and vulnerabilities. This complexity further complicates the relationship between data protection and competition law, as it is influenced by asymmetric information, where one party possesses more knowledge or resources than the other. The evolving nature of the digital landscape necessitates ongoing considerations of how competition law and privacy protection can effectively intersect and address the challenges posed by the digital age.

The BKA's case does not exclusively define the aspects related to privacy protectionism. Additionally, at the European level, the relationship between competition law and privacy protection has been addressed in different ways in various cases. In the Asnef-Equifax case (2006), the Court of Justice of the European Union (CJEU) indicated that issues regarding the sensitivity of personal data are not inherently a matter for competition law but can be resolved based on relevant data protection provisions.

Similarly, the vertical merger of TeleAtlas/TomTom (2008) did not raise data issues explicitly and did not incorporate data protection arguments in its assessment.

However, in the Microsoft/LinkedIn (2017) case, the European Commission adopted a more comprehensive approach to data within EU competition law. The Commission considered the impact of combining the databases of the two companies on users' privacy protection. Notably, the decision referred to the GDPR, even though it was not yet applicable at the time of the assessment, and highlighted how the GDPR would empower individuals to have control over their data and limit Microsoft's access and processing of personal data.

Nevertheless, the Commission did not entirely prevent Microsoft from accessing LinkedIn's data after the merger. Instead, the Commission focused on addressing two horizontal issues resulting from the merger: the absence of distortion to competition as the companies were competitors in a hypothetical market, and the combination of their databases leading to market power and increased barriers to entry (Microsoft/LinkedIn, 2017). The Commission prioritized ensuring a competitive process but did not provide explicit guidance on data protection within the sphere of competition law. The intersection between competition law and data protection in the EU remains an evolving area without clear-cut rules or precedents, as recently AG Rantos (2022) proved in the EU Facebook case that incidental acceptance of privacy within competition law assessment might be available in certain instances. In that reasoning, competition law authorities might consider privacy-related harms only if the privacy-related harm directly results in hindering competition.

Indeed, there is currently no consensus on the optimal method of evaluating data within EU competition law. In fact, it is beyond the scope of competition law to incorporate any possible privacy-related harms into its framework. Phelps (2000) suggests that privacy can have a twofold economic value. Firstly, privacy can be viewed as a positive attribute or an intermediate good when non-disclosure of data benefits the data subject or when users willingly disclose their personal data in exchange for monetary compensation (Kerber 2016). This implies that privacy can have a certain monetary value. On the other hand, privacy can also be considered a final good, representing a normative dimension as noted in Article 8 of the Charter of Fundamental Rights, as argued by Botta (2019). However, privacy itself is a complex and diverse concept, and the nature of its sensitivity can vary across different societies. The interpretation and understanding of privacy may differ, making it challenging to establish a universally agreed-upon definition or valuation.

The current approach of EU competition law indicates a focus on protecting competitive balance in hypothetical markets when evaluating decisions related to personal data (Berghamp, 2002). However, the concept of privacy is complex and multifaceted, requiring a comprehensive consideration of all dimensions and the interests of parties involved in relevant markets (Thibodeau, 2014). Both data protection and competition legal frameworks aim to promote market integration and prioritize the welfare of individuals, as consumers benefit from the collection of their data in the form of free services, products, or content. This suggests that data protection and competition law can intersect and maintain a balanced approach when assessing anticompetitive behaviors (Kemp, 2020).

2.3. Regulatory Failures of Consumer Protection Law to Privacy-Related Harms

This chapter discusses consumer protection law as supplementing the discussion on the relationship between competition law and privacy, assessing the impact of privacy-related harms on consumers which envisages the assessment of harms associated with personal data exploitation, and any privacy infringement. Consumer protection law may emphasise that privacy-related harms are oriented toward the exploitation of digital users.

By virtue of Article 38 of the Charter and Article 12 TFEU, EU policies are required to ensure a high level of consumer protection, requiring other EU policies to acknowledge consumer protection requirements. The consumer protection rules are designed to ensure that consumers could effectively choose from the various options offered in a particular market. In other words, a particular market should comprise a diversity of standards and consumer confidence, which allows for the smooth functioning of the internal market and competition, while choice and fairness are beneficial (Ferrari, 2022). Essentially, the consumer policies implementation at the EU level could allow the consumer to reach informed decisions and choices that positively impact competition and support resource-efficient growth while safeguarding consumers' needs (Papadopoulu et al., 2022).

To achieve these objectives, consumer protection law intends to target any inefficiencies resulting from market failures that correspond to asymmetric information between consumers and producers (Cifuentes-Faura, 2022). Additionally, consumer protection law aims to address market failures, arising from consumer rationality such as framing effects, or over-optimising (Kerber & Zolna, 2022).

For the purposes of the digital economy, the following Directives are particularly relevant:

2.3.1 Directive on Unfair Terms in Consumer Contracts

This directive affects consumer contracts, which consumers cannot negotiate (Unfair Terms in Consumer Contracts, 1993). It applies to contracts where suppliers enjoy an advantage in defining terms and provisions. Under the directive, a non-negotiated term might be deemed as unfair if a term could cause a significant imbalance in parties' obligations arising under the contract, which are detrimental to consumers (Article 3(1) Directive on Unfair Terms in Consumer Contracts, 1993). Consequently, the directive calls for the contract to be provided in intelligible language, with consumers having a right to examine the contract and apply a most favourable presumption in understanding if doubt arises.

2.3.2 Unfair Commercial Practices Directive

This directive defines unfair commercial practices that are likely to distort economic behaviour about a particular product (Unfair Commercial Practices Directive, 2005). The most common examples of misleading commercial practices are: (i) deliberately omitting material information that a consumer needs to make a reasonable choice (Unfair Commercial Practices Directive, 2005, article 7(1)); and (ii) including false information which is decisive for an average consumer (Unfair Commercial Practices Directive, 2005, article 6(1)). Within the meaning of the Directive, a misleading practice takes place when an undertaking's practice is misleading in the overall presentation. Hence, a misleading practice is manifested through the presentation of deceptive information, even if the provided information is correct. For instance, a misleading commercial practice could take the form of a trader providing unclear, ambiguous or intelligible information, or where a trader hides to identify the real commercial intent ((Unfair Commercial Practices Directive, 2005, article 7(2)).

2.3.3 Directive on Better Enforcement of Consumer Protection Rules

This Directive aims at introducing effective power to strengthen consumers' rights online, and transparency about goods and services online (Directive 2019/2161/EU). The Directive introduces an obligation on digital traders to provide clear information about the criteria used to rank their products online, as well as disclose the paid advertising methods. In line with the recent CMA (2019) work, the Directive introduces new rules aiming to target fake reviews that could adversely affect consumer decision-making. The Directive also discusses personalised pricing, obliging the transparency requirements on traders who use personalised pricing algorithms. Here, traders are obliged to inform their consumers that the presented price has been calculated through the use of a pricing algorithm. Finally, the Directive introduces a highly significant aspect concerning digital services — the Directive extends the definition of price to include payments with personal data. In other words, the Directive recognises that consumers pay with their data to access 'free' digital services. Correspondingly, traders are obliged to inform consumers about the characterises of their offered services.

3. EU COMPETITION LAW AND SUSTAINABLE DEVELOPMENT GOALS

Consumer protections, competition law, and privacy are interconnected aspects of the legal framework that govern how businesses and individuals interact in the modern economy. This is essential for maintaining a fair and balanced marketplace while safeguarding the rights and interests of consumers. Many studies suggest that competition laws and competition authorities can effectively contribute to the achievement of the SDGs (Holmes, 2020; Malinauskaite, 2022; Snoep, 2023). It is imperative to conduct a thorough evaluation to determine the extent to which the SDGs and the principles of competition are in harmony or at odds with one another. This assessment is a crucial prerequisite for devising the most effective strategies to address sustainability challenges within the framework of competition laws and policies.

Nowadays, the competition policy is very much tied to the wider objectives of the EU, which aim at promoting and protecting competitiveness, job creation and sustainable growth. Hence, the competition law needs to be analysed in terms of the common goals of the community, taking into account the unique enforcement mechanism and institutional arrangements. The 2030 Agenda for Sustainable Development goal provided a shared idea to guide all countries towards sustainable development for people, the planet and prosperity. In response to such international commitment, the EU launched its European Green Deal, covering all sectors of the economy. This agenda focuses on transforming the EU into a competitive economy. In fact, the key intention of this initiative indicated the EU's intention to move towards more sustainable competition law.

In the above message, the key indication remained that competition law has had an important role to play in achieving sustainable development of the market, including tackling the issues such as climate change and corresponding to the creation of green policy (Malinauskaite, 2022). Importantly, the EU Commission (2019) ran several public consultations reflecting on the goals of sustainable development of the EU. Although such consultations were aimed to ensure better future regulations on horizontal block exemptions, and evaluation of competition rules on horizontal agreements, the most important development concentrated on climate change and challenges concentrating on sustainability goals. Hence, it was a piece of evidence for increased demand from consumers and businesses for ethical, sustainable and environmentally friendly business practices (European Commission, 2019).

In relation to the current approach towards sustainability, the European Green Deal has introduced impetus to businesses to pursue sustainability. As far as practically seen, there have not been any cases that are purely related to sustainability in the EU. Sustainability was rather considered as being a by-product of the assessment. For example, the German carmakers' case requires attention, where the EU Commission imposed a fine on key car manufacturers for breaching competition law rules by colluding on technical development in the area of car emissions. The Commission concluded that by the nature of the German car manufacturers behaviour, competition in the relevant market was significantly reduced. Notably, competition on product characteristics in terms of sustainable development was reduced.

The green development of the EU presents certain challenges that need to be considered (Hafner, 2020). In today's context, competition policy is closely linked to the broader goals of the EU, which aim to promote and safeguard competitiveness, job creation, and sustainable growth (Ezrachi, 2016). Therefore, the analysis of competition law should take into account the common objectives of the EU, while considering the unique enforcement mechanisms and institutional arrangements in place. A major issue arises when the sole criterion for assessing agreements between companies is the consumer-welfare goal, which focuses on the efficiencies brought about by market mechanisms (Marty, 2021). This approach makes it difficult to account for non-market interests that these companies claim to protect. These non-market interests could include sustainability-focused agreements, initiatives to improve animal welfare, prevent deforestation, provide fair wages, or protect the ecological balance in the long term (Gerbrandy, 2019). However, pursuing such interests may lead to higher consumer prices. Competition lawyers refer to these interests as "non-economic" or "public" interests, but in the context of discussing the social market economy, they could also be labeled as "societal" or "non-market" interests, as opposed to "market" interests (Gerbrandy, 2019). Nevertheless, assessing the impact of these non-market interests is challenging. It is difficult to quantify the benefits that accrue to society at large (rather than individual consumers), benefits that may be realized by different groups than those experiencing the consumer-welfare loss, or benefits that manifest in the long term (Cseres, 2006).

Additionally, the pursuit of the Green Deal in the EU raises concerns regarding privacy issues. As the EU places a strong emphasis on achieving environmental sustainability, various measures and technologies are being implemented to monitor and regulate activities that impact the environment. These measures often involve the collection and analysis of large amounts of data, including personal and sensitive information (Malinauskaite, 2022).

The integration of advanced monitoring systems, such as smart meters, IoT devices, and data-driven analytics, enables the efficient management of resources and the identification of areas for improvement in terms of sustainability. However, this increased data collection and processing raise privacy concerns for individuals (Douglas, 2021). The data gathered through these systems may contain personally identifiable information, consumption patterns, or even location data, potentially infringing upon individuals' privacy rights. Moreover, the EU's General Data Protection Regulation (GDPR) serves as a crucial framework for addressing privacy concerns within the Green Deal context. Compliance with GDPR principles, such as transparency, purpose limitation, data minimization, and individual rights, can help mitigate potential privacy risks while pursuing sustainable objectives.

Balancing the objectives of the Green Deal with privacy protection requires careful consideration. Striking the right balance involves implementing robust data protection mechanisms, such as anonymization and encryption techniques, and establishing clear guidelines for data handling, storage, and sharing. It is essential to ensure that individuals' privacy is adequately safeguarded throughout the entire process, from data collection to its utilization for sustainability purposes.

By recognizing the intersection of the Green Deal and privacy issues, policymakers and stakeholders can work together to develop comprehensive frameworks that uphold both environmental goals and individuals' right to privacy. This entails implementing privacy-enhancing technologies, fostering public awareness and education regarding data collection practices, and establishing effective oversight mechanisms to ensure compliance with privacy regulations in the pursuit of green and sustainable development (Malinauskaite, 2022).

4. COMPETITION LAW AND PRIVACY: WHAT DO WE KNOW SO FAR ABOUT THE INTERSECTION?

Both data protection and competition laws aim to promote market integration and prioritise the well-being of individuals, leading to various benefits for consumers in terms of free services, products, or content (Douglas, 2021). Acquiring Big Data does not immediately lead to anti-competitive behaviour. However, a small number of technology companies have significant control over vast amounts of personal data and its processing, primarily focused on individual practices. The extensive collection of data poses a threat to the privacy of end-users (BKA, Facebook, 2019). Consequently, the evolving economic landscape creates uncertainty regarding competitive pressures, particularly concerning the scope of enforcing competition laws and whether EU competition law can be seen as a societal norm that also promotes wealth advancement.

Data markets consist of three main components: data acquisition, processing, and the utilisation of information and knowledge derived from that data (Kerber & Zolna, 2022). Processing personal data allows digital platforms to make predictions about individuals and enables the development of advanced analytics. The raw data is transformed into valuable information and knowledge, which can enhance the quality of products, services, innovation, and predictions (Economides & Lianos, 2021). The dynamic nature of the data market and its reciprocal relationships can establish feedback loops.

Competition law takes a market failure approach and is concerned with consumer welfare and overall societal well-being, which can be influenced by the lack of data protection in personal data acquisition markets (Economides & Lianos, 2021). An approach based on market failure recognises the potential harms associated with the exploitation of personal data, even if specific rules may not explicitly acknowledge the right to privacy (Surden, 2014). The following analysis is based on three assumptions regarding the current state of data markets in the digital economy (Gal & Aviv, 2020). Firstly, there is a significant emphasis on the importance of data, often referred to as the fuel of global economy (Packin, 2021). However, the value of data can vary among participants in the data value chain. For instance, the right to data portability may be viewed as a potential facilitator of market dominance abuse (Douglas, 2021). This is because the value of data downloaded from a digital service or platform is considered negligible for end-users in the social media platform market (Michon, 2018).

The second assumption pertains to the varying concerns and impact of data analysis practices among digital platforms, particularly regarding their influence on innovation. The quality of knowledge derived from data analysis is dependent on the variety, velocity, and veracity of the data (Stucke & Grunes, 2016). This contributes to the ongoing debate on the economies of scale and scope associated with data, suggesting that the availability of more data in the market leads to better knowledge, resulting in improved product quality and innovation (Douglas, 2021; (Kerber & Zolna, 2022). Moreover, the lack of a precise definition of Big Data adds complexity, as its interpretation varies depending on the research perspective, whether it be technological, industrial, business, or public policy-oriented. However, a common thread acknowledges the rapid generation, acquisition, processing, and storage of Big Data by digital platforms, which is used to enhance services or generate revenue. This leads to an observation regarding a flaw in the data portability rule: while an individual set of data becomes significantly more valuable when combined with other data sources, it holds minimal value for users of digital platforms on its own (Gal & Aviv, 2020). Therefore, data can be seen as a puzzle piece where individual data has little value, but a collection of data becomes highly valuable. Consequently, better data leads to improved predictions, establishing positive externalities such as reduced search costs, information access, or service delivery compared to offline alternatives, as technology and platform design enable unique efficiencies. The role of data in the value chain is thus exceptionally high and may exceed previous expectations. The collection of personal data is often essential for introducing innovation and new services (Goldfarb & Tucker, 2017).

The third assumption highlights the dual nature of data collection and its potential implications for privacy. On one hand, the General Data Protection Regulation (GDPR) aims to provide a framework of rules to protect data subjects against potential privacy breaches. However, some argue that the limited scope of its protection actually strengthens the market dominance of data controllers. This raises concerns about the role of data sharing in the context of data-driven market models (Mayer-Schonberger & Range 2018). The analysis suggests that as more data is collected, the knowledge derived from its analysis becomes more widely distributed (Gal & Aviv, 2020). For instance, Google's model relies on data to provide real-time information on traffic within its Google Maps service. However, the degree of reliance on data may vary among different digital platforms, implying that the competitive advantage will differ across various businesses and activities.

While data itself is non-rivalrous and non-exclusive, there are still barriers to entry within data collection markets that can create data synergies, impede innovation, and limit the improvement of analytical tools by reducing spillover effects (Rubinfeld, Gal 2017). As a result, data sharing can potentially provide a competitive advantage to firms. Furthermore, the phenomenon of multihoming, where internet users spread their data across multiple digital platforms and services, adds to the importance of data as an asset for firms (Gal & Aviv, 2020). Digital platforms are not prevented from collecting the same personal data from their users, which further underscores the value of data (Lambrecht & Tucker 2017). Theoretically, there are identifiable negative effects related to price discrimination or potential psychological discomfort, leading to a reduction in overall welfare. Therefore, any potential plans for personal data sharing must consider these complex trade-offs and require a balancing mechanism (Gorecka, 2020). Competing considerations need to be carefully analysed, as they can introduce scenarios that both increase and decrease welfare.

When evaluating the market assumptions, it becomes apparent that there can be variations in the business models employed to acquire relevant data. Nonetheless, the fundamental requirement for all models is data collection. Platforms obtain data either by acquiring it themselves or by purchasing it from external suppliers. This data is subsequently processed to extract the necessary knowledge. Digital undertakings have the flexibility to choose an approach based on cost-effectiveness and feasibility, which can be influenced by technological, strategic, or legal barriers (Gal & Aviv, 2020).

Data protection aspects often fall outside the purview of competition law intervention. In merger decisions such as Facebook/WhatsApp (2014) and Microsoft/LinkedIn (2016), the EU Commission acknowledged the privacy dimension but primarily focused their assessment on economic considerations, particularly price-related factors. The prevailing approach in competition law investigations revolves around economic considerations. However, the recent Facebook case (2019) handled by the Federal Cartel

Office introduced a potential perspective on a new theory of harm, suggesting that privacy breaches could amount to the abuse of a dominant position. Nonetheless, privacy degradation is generally considered beyond the scope of interpretation under EU competition law, as it may present challenges in establishing a direct link between privacy terms and harm to consumer welfare. Nevertheless, the ongoing debate regarding incorporating privacy concerns into competition law may lead to the development of regulatory tools that address the evident political and industrial policy dimensions at hand (Douglas, 2021). The current personal data protection legislation is criticized for its myopic nature, creating loopholes in data subject protection and enabling the rise of powerful digital gatekeepers with significant market power. Recently, AG Rantos (2022) and the CJEU (2023) assessed the intersection between competition law demonstrating that the incidental analysis of data privacy law in competition law assessment might as a proxy for findings an exploitative abuse in a broader economic manner.

The assumptions put forth in the discussion highlight the evaluation of normative objectives within competition law when dealing with cases involving potential privacy breaches. The absence of a clearly defined theory of harm in the context of GDPR assessment raises the question of whether competition law should be scrutinized in such situations. The crux of the issue lies in comprehending these claims and determining whether intervention within the competition law framework is desirable (CJEU, 2023).

4.1. Social Welfare Objectives in the Assessment of Privacy Concerns

An effective competition process is essential for ensuring economic freedom and promoting market integration. These objectives also play a crucial role in safeguarding competition equilibrium within investigations conducted in the digital economy. However, the application and scope of these objectives can be limited due to inherent ambiguities (CJEU, 2023).

The narrow focus of the GDPR implies that the problem extends beyond consumer protection alone, and competition law may have limitations when addressing potential privacy breaches in cases involving apparent competition abuse. However, the problem should not be solely centered on expanding the role of competition law to include privacy concerns. Instead, it suggests that the problem is structural, and solely assessing the protection of competition processes may not provide a comprehensive solution. Considering this, it is reasonable to explore other economic frameworks that, in conjunction with competition, can bring about societal benefits and are protected due to their potential to increase overall societal welfare (Hajighasemi et al., 2022). Addressing the issue may require a broader perspective and the consideration of alternative arrangements that can effectively protect both competition and societal well-being.

Competition law primarily focuses on economic processes within society, emphasizing the benefits that competition can bring to society as a whole. While concepts of fairness and freedom are relevant, they generally play a secondary role in competition law. These concepts are important for providing a broader understanding of the goals of competition law. However, on their own, they are not sufficient for determining whether specific behaviors should be allowed or prohibited under the competition law framework. In competition law, the assessment of anticompetitive behavior is typically based on more concrete criteria, such as market power, market dominance, and the impact on consumer welfare. While fairness and freedom are important considerations, they are often secondary to the core economic principles and objectives of competition law.

To move beyond the abstract notion of protecting competition structures solely based on the concepts of freedom and fairness, competition law assessments should take into account more practical considerations. Similarly, the concept of privacy is abstract and primarily associated with the individual's right to protection. This nature of privacy makes its assessment primarily fall outside the scope of competition law, which focuses on economic considerations. The General Data Protection Regulation, which aims to safeguard the personal data of private end-users, lacks a clear definition of the theory of harm associated with privacy breaches. Moreover, the rights granted to data controllers can potentially strengthen their position as private gatekeepers. In this context, it becomes important to place emphasis on the concept of consumer welfare and its value in privacy assessments. The assessment should consider the impact on consumers in terms of their well-being, control over their personal data, and potential harm arising from privacy breaches. By focusing on consumer welfare, competition law can incorporate privacy concerns and ensure that the protection of personal data aligns with the broader goals of competition law.

Advocate General Kokott (2022) has emphasized that the protection of market structures indirectly safeguards consumers, as any harm to competition also affects consumers. The European Union courts have established that competition law aims to address practices that are damaging to both consumers and effective competition structures. In the T-Mobile case, it was recognized that competition law is concerned with practices that have an anticompetitive objective, even in the absence of a direct link between the practice and consumer prices. Similarly, in the TeliaSonera case (2011), the significance of preserving competition and preventing distortions that negatively impact public interests, individual undertakings, and consumers was acknowledged. This ensures the overall well-being of the European Union. In the Intel v Commission case (2017), the same reasoning was reiterated, emphasizing that the Commission was not required to establish a causal link between the data and consumers in question. This is because Article 102 TFEU aims to address practices that are detrimental to both consumer welfare and competition structures. In summary, competition law seeks to address practices that harm both consumers and effective competition structures, and it does not necessarily require a direct causal link between the practice and consumer prices. The focus is on remedying practices that are detrimental to both consumer welfare and the competitive landscape.

4.2. Consumer Protection, Privacy, and Competition Law: The Case for Consumer Welfare

Daskalova's (2015) observation highlights that the precise definition of "consumer" has not been adequately explored in the context of competition law. Additionally, the measurement of consumer welfare has also been a topic that lacks detailed discussion. In her analysis, Daskalova (2015) raises several unanswered questions regarding competition law. Firstly, the question arises as to who exactly qualifies as a consumer—is it limited to final consumers or does it also include intermediate consumers within the supply chain? This distinction is relevant in understanding the scope of consumer protection under competition law. Secondly, Daskalova (2015) challenges whether price alone should be considered the sole measure of consumer welfare in competition law assessments. Price is a crucial factor, but there may be other important considerations such as choice, quality, innovation, and domestic preferences that should be considered in evaluating the impact on consumer welfare (Douglas, 2021). These questions highlight the need for a more comprehensive and nuanced understanding of consumer welfare within the competition law framework, considering various dimensions beyond price. A broader examination is necessary to capture the full range of factors that impact consumers' well-being and preferences.

Linking privacy protection to consumer welfare within the antitrust regime can indeed present challenges. Privacy protection is primarily considered a public right and falls under specific regulations that may not necessarily involve a direct analysis of consumer welfare. Regulators would need to anticipate how new data or data sets would be utilized by undertakings and how privacy, as a quality parameter, would be affected. Moreover, regulators would be tasked with assessing the impact, if any, of such changes on consumer welfare. In this context, potential changes to the "privacy parameter" could be approximated by examining variations in the amount of data acquired or changes in its use, or both. However, accurately measuring the impact on consumer welfare resulting from alterations to privacy-related factors can be complex and uncertain (Douglas, 2021). Regulators would need to assess not only the potential benefits in terms of consumer welfare but also any potential harms or negative effects on privacy. Therefore, linking privacy protection and consumer welfare within the antitrust regime requires careful consideration and analysis, taking into account the specific regulatory framework and the potential impact on both privacy and consumer interests.

Indeed, the notion of consumer welfare can serve as a practical benchmark for intervention in digital markets, enabling the addressing of exploitative and/or exclusionary practices that aim to restrict competition. Within the digital economy, the concept of consumer welfare can be used to assess the impact on various groups of consumers. It proves particularly effective in addressing multi-sided markets, which are prevalent in digital markets (Douglas, 2021). The European Commission (2019) has acknowledged that the notion of "consumers" encompasses not only the final consumers but also all the direct and indirect users covered by an agreement. This includes producers, retailers, wholesalers, and other entities involved in the market ecosystem. Recognizing this broader scope of consumers allows for a comprehensive evaluation of the impact on various market participants in the digital economy. By using the concept of consumer welfare, competition authorities and regulators can take into account the effects on different market participants and assess whether practices in digital markets are in line with promoting consumer welfare and maintaining competitive market conditions.

In this context, it is important to note that EU competition enforcement should indeed be oriented towards contributing to a fairer society (Lamadrid, 2017). The objective of market integration, which is a fundamental element of the EU's foundation, takes into account not only competition but also consumer welfare (Lamadrid, 2017). Competition among undertakings is related to various factors such as price, a wider choice of products, and better quality. In the digital market, user behavior plays a significant role in driving consumption (Gorecka, 2020). Consumers often remain on a platform used by their family and friends, which can limit their awareness of competitive pricing due to their increased consumption habits. Moreover, relying solely on a price-centric approach to consumer welfare might provide a distorted picture. In the digital market, many services are ostensibly provided for free to consumers, and in such cases, quality becomes an important parameter of competition (Kerber & Zolna, 2022). For example, in the Facebook (2019) case, the distortion of privacy was recognized as harming consumer welfare, despite the absence of direct price effects. Privacy concerns can encompass a range of variables that impact consumer welfare, and these variables may not be easily quantifiable (Kerber & Zolna, 2022). Therefore, it can be inferred that privacy concerns do not revolutionize competition law itself, as the established framework of competition law is adaptable and can provide appropriate remedies to establish competitive equilibrium in relevant markets. The existing competition law can be applied to address privacy-related issues and ensure that consumer welfare is protected effectively in the digital market.

Indeed, competition is a normative concept that is influenced by legal incentives and constraints, as well as social, ethical, and moral norms. The assessment of legislative approaches that aim to provide individuals with greater control over their personal data can enhance the accountability of powerful entities in negotiating data privacy (Kerber & Zolna, 2022). However, it is important to acknowledge that such approaches may not always provide sufficient protection. There are potential alternatives to consider in this context. One example is behavioral discrimination, where digital users often encounter information while using digital services and products and simply select "accept all" without fully understanding the implications (Kerber & Zolna, 2022). Another example is default privacy notices, such as those seen in the case of Microsoft, which offer an all-encompassing privacy policy. While privacy by design and other incentives may sound promising, users may still opt for minimal data disclosure as privacy notices can be disruptive and akin to advertisements (Douglas 2021; Kerber & Zolna, 2022). At the EU level, the GDPR (2016) provides protection for personal data, aiming to foster innovation and create opportunities within the European Digital Single Market. However, the GDPR may inadvertently strengthen the power of private regulators, as certain features like the right to data portability might only offer a short-term solution. The data has already been processed and used to fuel the growth of specific digital platforms. Additionally, individual pieces of data may hold little value to end-users who rely on the right to data portability (Kerber & Zolna, 2022). To address the informational asymmetry that exists, it is crucial to protect the interests of under-active consumers and mitigate the negative externalities that can arise from their lack of engagement. Failing to protect consumer discourse in this context can have adverse effects on competition (Ezratchi & Stucke 2016).

Indeed, the welfare of individuals is a central objective of consumer law, data protection, and competition law (Lynskey et al, 2017). Consumer law aims to protect the rights and well-being of individuals as consumers, while data protection laws seek to safeguard users' fundamental rights and freedoms in relation to their personal data. Competition law, on the other hand, is focused on ensuring undistorted competition within the internal market. The application of EU competition law has a horizontal scope, meaning it applies to both public entities operating in the market and private, state-owned undertakings (Ritcher, 2023). Similarly, data protection laws are part of the primary law of the EU legal regime. However, it is worth noting that while competition law enforcement is conducted by an EU-wide authority (the European Commission), there is no equivalent EU-wide data protection authority. Data protection enforcement is primarily decentralized, with national supervisory bodies serving as the main enforcers. Overall, these legal regimes have distinct objectives but overlap in certain areas, particularly when it comes to safeguarding individual welfare, ensuring fair competition, and protecting fundamental rights in the digital era.

The concept of notice-and-consent scenarios can provide insights into consumer welfare. Pasquale has highlighted the problematic relationship between privacy and competition law, suggesting that it can lead to a structural production of ignorance. This is exemplified by the opt-in/opt-out scenarios that consumers face, which can be perceived as monopolistic (Pasquale, 2013). On the other hand, other commentators argue for a more holistic approach that connects competition law and privacy (Kerber & Zolna, 2022). They advocate for a comprehensive vision that takes into account the different perspectives of privacy and competition law. By adopting such an approach, state authorities and competition law regulators can develop nuanced orientations to address the challenges arising from the intersection of data and competition law (CJEU, 2023). This includes deterring and punishing unfair and harmful behavior and improving market processes. Overall, considering the complexities of privacy and competition law and their impact on consumer welfare, it is important to adopt a comprehensive and nuanced approach that takes into account the evolving nature of data-driven markets. This approach can help address the challenges and promote fair competition while safeguarding individual privacy rights.

It is true that the majority of consumers do not read privacy policies due to their length, legal complexity, and lack of clarity (Akman, 2022). As a result, consumers have a limited understanding of the terms and conditions, which leads to the creation of a digital self-based on their behaviors (Kerber & Specht-Riemenschneider, 2020; Kerber & Zolna, 2022). However, this impaired understanding also means that consumers have little confidence in their ability to detect unfair or discriminatory conduct by digital platforms. In today's age, where users are expected to safeguard their data, there is a lack of understanding among consumers about how platforms use their data. Many argue that there are normative justifications for giving users control over their data, and privacy advocates seek to address potential conflicts (Kerber & Specht-Riemenschneider, 2020; Douglas, 2021). Notice-and-consent policies, often recommended by privacy advocates, follow a neoliberal model. However, there may be limited empirical evidence to support the current notice-and-consent framework as the ideal model for privacy protection. This highlights the need to reassess and potentially improve the notice-and-consent approach (Kerber & Specht-Riemenschneider, 2020). It is important to explore alternative models and regulatory frameworks that can enhance privacy protection and empower consumers without burdening them with complex policies. The goal should be to establish more transparent and user-friendly mechanisms for data control, ensuring that privacy protection is effective and aligned with the evolving challenges posed by digital platforms (CJEU, 2023).

The concept of the privacy paradox highlights market failures in the digital economy. It refers to the phenomenon where users express a desire for privacy and broad data protection but do not exhibit corresponding preferences in their actual behavior (Pasquale, 2013). Two caveats within this concept contribute to market failures. Firstly, users may want to protect their data but fail to take measures to do so. They may be too lazy to read terms and conditions or not carefully review privacy protections. This lack of action can result in their personal data being exposed to risks. Secondly, users may lack understanding of what happens to their data due to a lack of transparency and intelligibility (Kerber & Specht-Riemenschneider, 2020). This can hinder their ability to make informed choices about data privacy. Both of these caveats are indicative of a lack of ability on the part of users. They may face challenges in understanding complex privacy policies or have limited knowledge about how their data is used and shared (Douglas, 2021; Kerber & Specht-Riemenschneider, 2020). As a result, they may unintentionally expose their personal information and contribute to market failures in data protection. Addressing these market failures requires efforts to simplify privacy policies and enhance transparency (Kerber & Specht-Riemenschneider, 2020). It is crucial to ensure that users have the ability to make informed decisions about their data privacy and that the privacy protections offered are easily understandable. By empowering users with the necessary information and tools, market failures can be mitigated, and data protection can be strengthened in the digital economy.

The debate surrounding the need for privacy reform in the digital economy is ongoing (Cremer, 2019). Some proponents of libertarian privacy argue that consumers' preferences indicate a willingness to engage with privacy-invasive services (Douglas, 2021). However, further analysis of this proposition reveals potential flaws in the rationale (Kerber & Zolna, 2022). It is challenging to ascertain that consumers actively choose privacy-invasive services like Facebook based on conscious preferences for their privacy policies. Rather, users are often drawn to these platforms due to the personalized search and social networking services they offer, which benefit from the collection and use of user data to achieve near-or monopoly status (Kerber & Specht-Riemenschneider, 2020; Douglas, 2021). The operations of these platforms are complex, and consumers may not fully understand the true value of their privacy within these business models (Cremer, 2019). This highlights the need for a more comprehensive understanding of users' motivations and preferences when it comes to privacy. It is important to consider the context in which users engage with privacy-invasive services and whether they have a genuine choice or are simply accepting the trade-offs for the convenience or functionality provided. Reforms should focus on promoting transparency, empowering users with meaningful control over their data, and fostering competition in the digital market. By enhancing users' understanding and providing them with viable alternatives, privacy protections can be strengthened, and consumers can make more informed choices about the services they use and the handling of their personal information.

4.3. Can Privacy-Related Harms Be Considered During Competition Law Assessments?

Indeed, competition law traditionally focuses on economic parameters to assess consumer harm, such as monitoring prices or evaluating potential reductions in input, quality, and innovation. Privacy considerations have generally been excluded from competition assessments, mainly due to the challenges in determining their anticompetitive impact (Cremer, 2019; CJEU, 2023). However, there are ongoing discussions about incorporating data privacy into competition assessments, with two approaches being widely debated.

(1) Expanding the concept of consumer harm: One approach suggests broadening the concept of consumer harm in competition law to include privacy-related concerns. It argues that privacy violations can harm consumers by undermining their control over personal data, potentially leading to negative social, economic, and psychological consequences (Kerber & Specht-Riemenschneider, 2020; Douglas, 2021). By including privacy as a dimension of consumer harm, competition authorities could evaluate the impact of privacy infringements on competition and take appropriate actions. There is a growing consensus that privacy is a fundamental right that should be protected. Accordingly, there is a viewpoint suggesting that competition law should be able to address certain behaviors that negatively impact privacy rights. Esayas (2019) argues that competition authorities should block mergers or acquisitions if they pose a threat to individuals' privacy, unless the merging companies can demonstrate that they have implemented privacy safeguards. This approach would go beyond the traditional competition concerns of price increase, output, or quality, and instead focus on the protection of privacy as a paramount consideration. By incorporating privacy as a criterion for evaluating mergers, competition authorities would be tasked with ensuring that privacy rights are not compromised in the long run (Esayas, 2019). Implementing this approach would pose challenges as it would require competition authorities to navigate complex legal and technical aspects related to privacy. It would also necessitate cooperation and coordination between competition authorities and data protection regulators to effectively address the intersection between competition and privacy (Kerber & Specht-Riemenschneider, 2020; Douglas, 2021; Kerber & Zolna, 2022). Overall, this perspective advocates for a broader understanding of the role of competition law in protecting individuals' privacy rights, recognizing that the impact of mergers and acquisitions on privacy should be considered alongside traditional competition concerns.

(2) Privacy as a competition parameter: Another approach suggests that privacy can be considered as a relevant parameter in competition assessments. It argues that privacy can be seen as a factor that influences consumer preferences and choices in the digital market. Privacy-friendly practices and platforms may attract consumers who value their privacy, leading to competition based on privacy-related features. Therefore, competition authorities could take into account privacy as a competitive parameter, promoting competition based on privacy protection. It is indeed recognized

> by the EU Commission and the US Federal Trade Commission that privacy protection can be considered as a dimension of competition. This perspective acknowledges that while competition law primarily focuses on traditional competitive issues, privacy concerns can play a role in shaping competition dynamics. The consideration of privacy as a competition dimension is particularly relevant in cases where services are provided at no monetary cost in exchange for personal data (Microsoft/LinkedIn, 2007). This raises questions about the value exchange between consumers and platforms, and the potential impact on competition and consumer welfare. However, there are methodological concerns associated with incorporating privacy as a competition dimension. One concern is the complex nature of data processing by companies, where privacy breaches can be seen as a by-product of the analysis of Big Data. Determining the exact harm caused by privacy breaches and establishing a clear causal link between privacy violations and competition can be challenging (Kerber & Specht-Riemenschneider, 2020; Douglas, 2021; CJEU, 2023). To address these methodological concerns, further research and analysis are needed to develop frameworks that effectively assess the intersection between privacy and competition. This would involve considering not only the immediate privacy harms but also the broader implications for competition, consumer choice, and innovation. Overall, while there is recognition that privacy can be considered as a competition dimension, it remains an evolving area of discussion that requires careful analysis and consideration of methodological challenges.

These approaches seek to address the potential interplay between privacy and competition, recognizing the importance of privacy as a dimension of consumer welfare. Incorporating privacy into competition assessments would require careful consideration and the development of appropriate frameworks to analyze the complex dynamics between privacy, competition, and consumer interests (Kerber & Specht-Riemenschneider, 2020; Douglas, 2021; Kerber & Zolna, 2022).

In conclusion, prioritizing long-term social welfare can serve as a guarantee for promoting free competition, the efficient functioning of common markets, and the freedom of consumers and competitors. This aligns with the core objectives of competition law. Long-term welfare can be considered theoretically superior to other objectives, as it takes into account the broader societal impacts and benefits of competition (Kerber & Specht-Riemenschneider, 2020).

The evolving digital economy has highlighted the need to address the growing power of digital gatekeepers and their potential effects on competition and consumer welfare (Kerber & Specht-Riemenschneider, 2020). The extensive consumer perspective in the digital market emphasizes the importance of instrumentalizing competition law to protect and enhance competition, ensuring efficient resource allocation and promoting consumer welfare (Kerber & Specht-Riemenschneider, 2020.

By considering competition in the market as a means to enhance consumer welfare and achieve an efficient allocation of resources, competition law can play a crucial role in balancing the interests of consumers, competitors, and the overall social welfare. It requires ongoing analysis and adaptation to address the unique challenges posed by digital markets and the increasing importance of privacy considerations.

In this context, the goal is to create a regulatory framework that ensures fair competition, safeguards consumer welfare, and fosters innovation and choice in the digital economy. Societal goals, as exemplified by the United Nations' Sustainable Development Goals (SDGs), play a significant role in shaping policies and regulations, including EU competition law. However, the intersection of societal goals, such as environmental sustainability and social justice, with privacy concerns poses a challenge. While competition law primarily focuses on promoting consumer welfare and market efficiencies, it must also adapt to consider broader societal objectives. Balancing these objectives requires careful attention to privacy rights, as the collection and use of data to achieve SDGs may infringe upon individuals' privacy. The EU competition law framework might incorporate privacy safeguards and principles, ensuring that the pursuit of societal goals under the SDGs aligns with the protection of individuals' privacy rights. By striking this balance, the EU can promote sustainable development while upholding privacy standards and maintaining a competitive market environment.

5. CONCLUSION

This article presents a proposed approach to reevaluate how competition law and data privacy law intersect. In order to effectively address concerns arising from the digital economy and acknowledge privacy-related risks, it is necessary to adopt an integrated approach that combines competition law and data protection law. While competition law can play a role in protecting user privacy, it is important not to view data privacy law as an expansion of competition law or as a one-size-fits-all solution to address all potential issues related to data collection. The specific impact of competition law on privacy-related risks is often unclear in practice. To establish the boundaries of competition law in relation to privacy matters, it would be necessary to establish a formal cooperation agreement. Furthermore, practical steps could involve the introduction of relevant legislation and guidelines to ensure that data privacy regulations are appropriately taken into account when enforcing competition law.

The problem between competition law and privacy might be amounting to the structural production of ignorance, which is only focused on the notice-and-consent privacy models, based on the opt-in/opt-out scenarios, which are used for a coercive monopolistic scenarios. The myopic focus on privacy as an efficiency gain might be just seen as a temporary, and for the long-term pathologies of corporate concentration, there are no sufficient means to protect the process of competition. Hence, the identified elements such as a notice-and-consent privacy regime in its first analysing might create only temporary efficiencies, which are further emphasised on the consumers' judgement to enter into a one-sided contract, over the reflections to optimise the data flow for the long terms interests of consumers.

On the other side, the debate aims at the development of an interlinking relationship between competition law, which aims at developing holistic proximity between these fields. With several differentiating approaches to the privacy and competition law, it is important to focus on a more comprehensive vision, which develops a regulatory regime which develops a new orientation toward the process of competition law and privacy concerns and aims at detecting harmful behaviour and aims at market process improvement. Hence, it is evident that the further discussion would consider how the dominant digital undertakings, with the data orientated models, might be regulated, as the current regulatory regime is in itself limited in the digital gatekeepers: this would aim at analysing possible angles of regulatory intervention protection the processes of competition law, consumers, and the internal market.

REFERENCES

Akman, P. (2022). A Web of Paradoxes: Empirical Evidence on Online Platform Users and Implications for Competition and Regulation in Digital Markets. *Virginia Law and Business Review*, *16*(2), 217.

Bergkamp, L. (2002). The Privacy Fallacy: Adverse Effects of Europe's Data Protection Policy in an Information-Driven Economy. *Computer Law & Security Review*, 31. doi:10.1016/S0267-3649(02)00106-1

BKA. (2019). *Case B6-22/16 Facebook, Exploitative business terms pursuant to Section 19(1) GWB for inadequate data processing*. BKA. <https://www.bundeskartellamt.de/SharedDocs/ Entscheidung/EN/Fallberichte/Missbrauchsaufsicht/2019/B6-22-16.html?nn=3600108>

Botta, M., & Wiedemann, K. (2019). The Interaction of EU Competition, Consumer and Data Protection Law in the Digital Economy: The Regulatory Dilemma in the Facebook Odyssey. *Antitrust Bulletin, 64*(3), 428–446. doi:10.1177/0003603X19863590

Cadwalladr, C., & Graham-Harrison, E. (2018, March 17). Revealed: 50 million Facebook profiles harvested for Cambridge Analytica in major data breach. *The Guardian*. https://www.theguardian.com/news/2018/mar/17/cambridge-analytica-facebook-influence-us-election

Charter of Fundamental Rights of the European Union. (2010). *Official Journal of the European Union, C, 83*(02).

Cifuentes-Faura, J. (2022). European Union policies and their role in combating climate change over the years. *Air Quality, Atmosphere & Health, 15*(8), 1333–1340. doi:10.100711869-022-01156-5 PMID:35035604

CMA. (2019). *Expects Facebook and eBay to tackle sale of fake reviews*. UK Gov. https://www.gov.uk/government/news/cma-expects-facebook-and-ebay-to-tackle-sale-of-fake-reviews

(2008). Consolidated Version of the Treaty on the Functioning of the European Union. *Official Journal of the European Union, C, 115*(47).

Council Directive 93/13/EC of 5 April 1993 on Unfair Terms in Consumer Contracts [1993] OJ L 95/29.

Cremer, J., de Montjoye, Y., & Schweitzer, H. (2019). Competition policy for the digital era *(European Commission Report No. 30)*. https://ec.europa.eu/competition/publications/reports/kd0419345enn.pdf

Cseres, K. (2006). The controversies of the consumer welfare standard. *Competition Law Review, 3*(2), 121–173.

Daskalova, V. (2015). Consumer welfare in EU competition law: what is it (not) about? *The Competition Law Review, 133.*

Directive 2005/29/EC of the European Parliament and of the Council concerning unfair business-to-consumer commercial practices in the internal market, (Unfair Commercial Practices Directive) [2005] OJ L 149/22.

Directive 2019/2161/EU amending Council Directive 93/13/EEC (unfair contract terms) and Directives 98/6/EC (price indications), 2005/29/EC (unfair commercial practices) and 2011/83/EU (consumer rights) as regards the better enforcement and modernisation of EU consumer protection rules.

Douglas, E. (2021). Digital Crossroads: The Intersection of Competition Law and Data Privacy. *Temple University Legal Studies Research Paper No. 2021-40.*

Economides, N., & Lianos, I. (2021). Restrictions On Privacy and Exploitation In The Digital Economy: A Market Failure Perspective. *Journal of Competition Law & Economics*, *17*(4), 765–847. doi:10.1093/joclec/nhab007

Esayas, S. (2019). Data Privacy in European Merger Control: Critical Analysis of Commission Decisions Regarding Privacy as a Non-Price Competition. *European Competition Law Review, 40*(4).

European Commission. (2009). Guidance on the Commission's Enforcement Priorities in Applying Article 82 of the EC Treaty to Abusive Exclusionary Conduct by Dominant Undertakings. *Official Journal of the European Union, C*, *45*(7).

European Commission. (2015, December 15). *Agreement on Commission's EU data protection reform will boost Digital Single Market [Press release].* EC. https://ec.europa.eu/commission/presscorner/detail/en/IP_15_6321

European Commission. (2019). *Factual Summary of the Contributions Received during the Public Consultation on the Evaluation of the Two Block Exemption Regulations and the Guidelines on Horizontal Cooperation Agreements*. EC. https://ec.europa.eu/competition/publications/reports/kd0419345enn.pdf

European Commission. (2021, July 8). *Antitrust: Commission fines car manufacturers €875 million for restricting competition in emission cleaning for new diesel passenger cars [Press Release].* EC. https://ec.europa.eu/commission/presscorner/detail/en/ip_21_3341

Ezrachi, A. (2016). *Sponge. Journal of Antitrust Enforcement, 1, Ezrachi, A., & Stucke, M. (2016). Virtual Competition*. Harvard University Press.

Ferrari, V. (2022). The platformisation of digital payments: The fabrication of consumer interest in the EU FinTech agenda. *Computer Law & Security Report*, *45*, 45. doi:10.1016/j.clsr.2022.105687

Gal, M. S., & Aviv, O. (2020). The Competitive Effects of the GDPR. *Journal of Competition Law & Economics*, 1.

Gerbrandy, A. (2019). Rethinking competition law within the European economic constitution. *Journal of Common Market Studies*, *57*(1), 127–142. doi:10.1111/jcms.12814

Goldfarb, A., & Tucker, C. (2017). *Digital Economics*. NBER Working Paper No. 23684.

Gorecka, A. (2020). A confusing relationship between privacy and competition law — a way forward for EU competition law and algorithms pricing. Indi*an Journal of AI and Law, 7.*

Gorecka, A. (2020). Is "Privacy" a Means to Protect the Competition or Advance Objectives of Innovation and Consumer Welfare? In M. Tzanou (Ed.), *Personal Data Protection and Legal Developments in the European Union*. IGI Global. doi:10.4018/978-1-5225-9489-5.ch006

Hafner, M., & Raimondi, P. P. (2020). Priorities and challenges of the EU energy transition: From the European Green Package to the new Green Deal. *Russian Journal of Economics*, *6*(4), 374–389. doi:10.32609/j.ruje.6.55375

Hajighasemi, A., Oghazi, P., Aliyari, S., & Pashkevich, N. (2022). The impact of welfare state systems on innovation performance and competitiveness: European country clusters. *Journal of Innovation & Knowledge*, *7*(4), 100236. doi:10.1016/j.jik.2022.100236

Holmes, S. (2020). Climate change, sustainability, and competition law. *Journal of Antitrust Enforcement*, *8*(2), 354–405. doi:10.1093/jaenfo/jnaa006

Kemp, K. (2020). Concealed data practices and competition law: Why privacy matters. *European Competition Journal*, *16*(2-3), 628–672. doi:10.1080/17441056.2020.1839228

Kerber, W. (2016). Digital Markets, Data and Privacy: Competition Law, Consumer Law and Data Protection. *MAGKS Joint Discussion Paper Series in Economics, No. 14-2016.* https://www.econstor.eu/bitstream/10419/144679/1/850599016.pdf

Kerber, W., & Specht-Riemenschneider, L. (2020). *Synergies Between Data Protection Law and Competition Law.* Bundesverband. https://papers.ssrn.com/sol3/papers.cfm?abstract_id=3977039

Kerber, W., & Zolna, K. K. (2022). The German Facebook case: The law and economics of the relationship between competition and data protection law. *European Journal of Law and Economics*, *54*(2), 217–250. doi:10.100710657-022-09727-8

Kimmelman, G., & Cooper, M. (2015). Antitrust and Economic Regulation: Essential and Complementary Tools to Maximize Consumer Welfare and Freedom of Expression in the Digital Age. *Harvard Law & Policy Review*, *9*(2), 403–436.

Kimmelman, G., & Cooper, M. (2017). *A Communications Oligopoly on Steroids—Why Antitrust Enforcement and Regulatory Oversight in Digital Communications Matter*. Equitable Growth. https://equitablegrowth.org/research-paper/communications-oligopoly-steroids/

Kira, B., Sinha, V., & Srinivasan, S. (2021). Regulating digital ecosystems: Bridging the gap between competition policy and data protection. *Industrial and Corporate Change*, *30*(5), 1337–1360. doi:10.1093/icc/dtab053

Lamadrid, A. (2017). Competition law as Fairness. *JIPLP, 147.*

Lambrecht, A., & Tucker, C. E. (2017). Can Big Data Protect a Firm from Competition? *CPI, 3*. https://www.competitionpolicyinternational.com/can-big-data-protect-a-firm-from-competition/

Leese, M. (2022). Privacy, data protection, and security studies. *Research Handbook on Privacy and Data Protection Law: Values, Norms and Global Politics*, 214.

Lynskey, O., & Da Costa Cabral, F. A. (2017). Family Ties: The Intersection between Data Protection and Competition in EU Law. *Common Mkt L Rev, 11.*

Malinauskaite, J. (2022). Competition law and sustainability: EU and national perspectives. *Journal of European Competition Law & Practice*, *13*(5), 1–13. doi:10.1093/jeclap/lpac003

Marty, F. (2021). Is Consumer Welfare Obsolete? A European Union Competition Perspective. *Prolegómenos*, *24*(47), 55–78. doi:10.18359/prole.4722

Mayer-Schönberger, V., & Ramge, T. (2018). *Reinventing Capitalism in the Age of Big Data*. Basic Books.

Michon, A., & Hyppolite, P.-A. (2018, December 13). Data Portability: An Antitrust Weapon for the Digital Economy? *Le Monde*. https://www.fondapol.org/en/the-foundation/medias-en-en/data-portability-an-antitrust-weapon-for-the-digital-economy/

Ohm, P. (2013). Branding Privacy. *Minn. L. Rev., 907.*

PackinN. G. (2021). Show Me the (Data About the) Money! *University of Chicago Law Review*, 1277. / doi:10.26054/0D1VS8WMM3

Papadopoulou, M., Papasolomou, I., & Thrassou, A. (2022). Exploring the level of sustainability awareness among consumers within the fast-fashion clothing industry: A dual business and consumer perspective. *Competitiveness Review*, *32*(3), 350–375. doi:10.1108/CR-04-2021-0061

Pasquale, F. (2013). Privacy, Antitrust, and Power. *Geo. Mason L. Rev., 1009.*

Phelps, J., Nowag, G., & Ferrell, E. (2000). Privacy Concerns and Consumer Willingness to Provide Personal Information. *Journal of Public Policy & Marketing*, *19*(1), 27–41. doi:10.1509/jppm.19.1.27.16941

Regulation (EU) 2016/679 of the European Parliament and of the Council of 27 April 2016 on the protection of natural persons with regard to the processing of personal data and on the free movement of such data, and repealing Directive 95/46/EC (General Data Protection Regulation).

Regulation (EU) 2022/1925 of the European Parliament and of the Council of 14 September 2022 on contestable and fair markets in the digital sector and amending Directives (EU) 2019/1937 and (EU) 2020/1828 (Digital Markets Act) (Text with EEA relevance). Official Journal of the European Union, L 265, 12.10.2022.

Richter, H. (2023). The public interest dimension of the single market for data: Public undertakings as a model for regulating private data sharing. *European Law Journal*, eulj.12476. doi:10.1111/eulj.12476

Saura, J. R., Ribeiro-Soriano, D., & Palacios-Marqués, D. (2021). From user-generated data to data-driven innovation: A research agenda to understand user privacy in digital markets. *International Journal of Information Management*, *60*, 60. doi:10.1016/j.ijinfomgt.2021.102331

Schäfer, F., Gebauer, H., Gröger, C., Gassmann, O., & Wortmann, F. (2023). Data-driven business and data privacy: Challenges and measures for product-based companies. *Business Horizons*, *66*(4), 493–504. doi:10.1016/j.bushor.2022.10.002

Snoep, M. (2023). What is fair and efficient in the face of climate change? *Journal of Antitrust Enforcement*, *11*(1), 1–4. doi:10.1093/jaenfo/jnad001

Stucke, M. E., & Grunes, A. P. (2016). *Big Data and Competition Policy*. Oxford University Press.

Surden, H. (2014). Machine Learning and Law. *Wash. L. Rev., 8.*

TeliaSonera Sverige, Case C-52/09, [2011] ECR I-527

Thibodeau, P. (2014). The Internet of Things Could Encroach on Personal Privacy. *Computerworld*. https://www.computerworld.com/article/2488949/emerging-technology/the-internet-of-things-could-encroach-on-personal-privacy.htm

Tsai, J., Egelman, S., Cranor, L., & Acquisti, A. (2011). The Effect of Online Privacy Information on Purchasing Behavior: An Experimental Study. *Information Systems Research*, *22*(2), 234–248. doi:10.1287/isre.1090.0260

Vestager, M. (2021, September 10). *Competition policy in support of the Green Deal. Speech presented at the 25th IBA Competition Conference*. Europa. https://ec.europa.eu/commission/commissioners/2019-2024/vestager/announcements/competition-policy-support-green-deal_en

KEY TERMS AND DEFINITIONS

Big Data: Under the GDPR, personal data is defined as any information relating to an identified or identifiable natural person. This definition includes a wide range of data types that can be collected and processed, including those that fall under the umbrella of big data. Big data generally refers to extremely large and complex datasets that are often collected, analyzed, and processed using advanced technology and algorithms. While there is no specific legal definition of big data, the GDPR applies to the processing of personal data regardless of whether it is part of a big data set or not. The GDPR imposes obligations on organizations that process personal data, such as obtaining consent, ensuring transparency, providing data subject rights, implementing appropriate security measures, and complying with the principles of data protection. In summary, while there is no explicit definition of big data in EU law, the GDPR and other data protection regulations apply to the processing of personal data, including when it is part of big data sets.

Consent: In the context of European Union (EU) law, consent is defined under the General Data Protection Regulation (GDPR), which is the primary data protection legislation in the EU. According to Article 4(11) of the GDPR, consent is defined as: "Any freely given, specific, informed, and unambiguous indication of the data subject's wishes by which he or she, by a statement or by a clear affirmative action, signifies agreement to the processing of personal data relating to him or her." This definition highlights the key elements of consent under the GDPR, including its voluntary nature, the need for specific information, clarity, and an affirmative action or statement indicating agreement. Consent serves as one of the legal grounds for the lawful processing of personal data within the EU.

Digital Consumer: Digital consumer refers to an individual who engages in various online activities, transactions, and interactions as part of their consumption behavior in the digital realm. Digital consumers utilize digital technologies and platforms to access goods, services, information, and entertainment. Digital consumers engage in a wide range of activities, including online shopping, using digital payment methods, streaming content, accessing online services, participating in social media, and interacting with digital advertising. They may also create and share content, communicate with others, and seek information through digital channels.Digital consumers are characterized by their reliance on digital technologies, such as computers, smartphones, tablets, and the internet, to access and consume products and services. They may be geographically dispersed, allowing them to access and engage with businesses and services globally.

Digital Economy: The digital economy refers to the economic activities that are driven by digital technologies, the internet, and the use of data. It encompasses a wide range of sectors and activities that rely heavily on digital technologies and connectivity. In the digital economy, businesses and individuals engage in various online activities, such as e-commerce, digital services, digital media, online advertising, cloud computing, and data analytics. It involves the production, distribution, and consumption of goods and services that are facilitated or conducted through digital platforms, networks, and devices. The digital economy has transformed traditional business models, enabling new forms of entrepreneurship, innovation, and economic growth. It has also facilitated global connectivity and expanded market opportunities beyond geographical boundaries. The digital economy has a significant impact on various aspects of society, including commerce, employment, communication, education, and governance. It presents opportunities for economic growth, productivity gains, and efficiency improvements, but also raises challenges related to data privacy, cybersecurity, digital divide, and ethical considerations.

European Green Deal: A comprehensive strategy and policy initiative introduced by the European Commission to transform Europe into a climate-neutral continent by 2050. It sets out ambitious goals and measures to combat climate change, promote sustainable economic growth, enhance energy efficiency, increase the use of renewable energy sources, protect biodiversity, and transition to a circular economy. The European Green Deal aims to address environmental challenges while fostering sustainable development and creating new opportunities for businesses and citizens across Europe.

Innovation: Innovation is a process of creating and implementing new ideas, concepts, products, or services that result in a significant improvement or advancement in various fields. It involves introducing novel solutions, methods, or approaches that bring about positive change or offer added value. In general, innovation plays a crucial role in driving economic growth, fostering competitiveness, and improving the overall quality of life. It encompasses activities such as research and development, technological advancements, process improvements, and the introduction of new business models or practices.

Sustainability: Sustainability refers to the practice of meeting the needs of the present generation without compromising the ability of future generations to meet their own needs. It involves the responsible and balanced use of resources, consideration of social and environmental impacts, and the pursuit of long-term economic prosperity.

Chapter 8
Scrutinizing the Malaysian Competitive Law From the Perspective of the Decided Cases

Hatijah Mohamed Salleh
Universiti Tunku Abdul Rahman, Malaysia

Khairunnisa Ishak
Universiti Tunku Abdul Rahman, Malaysia

ABSTRACT

Competition law plays a significant role in ensuring fair practices in economy market and in protecting consumers' interests. Malaysia has been moving forward in recognizing the essential of competition law in parallel with the growing economy and a dynamic business environment. This chapter provides a comprehensive review and discussion on the development and application of competition law through tribunal/court cases in Malaysia. The judgments from each case enable us to gain further insight, identify the pattern, and suggest for better improvement in protecting the consumers' interest and welfare. The existence and application of the CA 2010 is therefore ensuring the sustainability of good competition between enterprises and corporations so that the end users, namely the consumers, would be better helped and receive much better quality products and services in each market.

INTRODUCTION

Competition law plays a significant role in ensuring fair practices in economy market and in protecting of consumers' interests. Malaysia has moving forward in recognizing the essential of competition law in parallel with the growing economy and a dynamic business environment. Malaysian competition law aims at preventing the creation of agreements that deter competition. This includes agreement involving setting prices collectively, manipulating bids, dividing markets, and exploiting dominant positions

DOI: 10.4018/979-8-3693-0390-0.ch008

Copyright © 2024, IGI Global. Copying or distributing in print or electronic forms without written permission of IGI Global is prohibited.

in product or service markets. It also aims at fostering fair trade and encourages robust competition, ultimately safeguarding consumer interests. The law of competition in Malaysia is regulated by the Competition Act 2010 (Act 712) (CA 2010) which comes into effect on 1 January 2012.

The Competition Law and Policy (CLP) gained significant advocacy in ASEAN nations as a result of the ASEAN Economic Community (AEC, 2015) agreement, outlined in the AEC Blueprint 2025. Adopted by ASEAN Leaders during the 27th ASEAN Summit on November 22, 2015, in Kuala Lumpur, Malaysia, this initiative has spurred the active development of CLP, particularly under the Competition Act 2010 (CA 2010) in Malaysia and the Competition Act 2004 (CA 2004) in Singapore. Notably, Singapore introduced the CA 2004 even before the establishment of the AEC. Both nations regulate market competition by strictly prohibiting anti-competitive agreements and the abuse of dominant positions, which encompasses all forms of cartel activities. It's worth noting that while Singapore's CA 2004 covers mergers, Malaysia's CA 2010 does not address this aspect (Ramaiah & Hussein 2021).

The process of competition nurtures efficiency, innovation and entrepreneurship. It leads to competitive prices, product enhancement and service quality, and a broader range of choices for consumers. To promote economic development and safeguard consumer interests, the CA 2010 is enacted with the aim of encouraging and safeguarding the competition process, which in turn encourages economic growth and protects consumer interests. It is understood therefore that the main objective of the CA 2010 is to prevent anti-competitive conduct towards protecting consumers' interests by avoiding the so-called anti-competition agreement or the use of a dominant position (Ramaiah, 2017). The Act aims at achieving the fair process of competition. Entering into such arrangements would be against the Act and render enterprises to be liable for infringement of the Act.

This chapter provides a comprehensive overview and discussion on the development and application of competition law through tribunal/court cases in Malaysia from the Malaysian contextual and demographic, taking into account the different cultures, multi racial, and its unique legal system. It further provides the authority's interpretation (the Commission, Tribunal and Courts) on the statutory provisions of the Act and the derived new legal principles on the subject of competition law. The judgments from each case enable us to gain further insight, identify the pattern and suggest for better improvement in protecting the consumers' interest and welfare. The existence and application of the CA 2010 is therefore ensuring the sustainability of good competition between enterprises and corporations so that the end users namely the consumers would be better helped and received much quality products and services in each market. Specifically, this chapter aims to:

i. Provide some insights on any legal principles needed before invoking the provisions under the Act;
ii. Explore the ambits of anti-competitions conducts – from the MCC and judiciary's perspective. It further discusses the nature of agreements that fall under horizontal, vertical and abuse of power and intend to harmonise those interpretation within the context of Malaysian law.
iii. Discover the available defences via block exemptions provided therein and reviewing the jurisdiction of Competition Commission and Commission Appeal Tribunal as well as the judicial review jurisdiction of the Malaysian Civil Courts. The study also tends to harmonize the interpretations within the context of Malaysian Competitive law.

Addressing anti-competitive behaviors contributes to creating a fair and competitive business environment, fostering economic growth and promoting decent work opportunities. It also ensures fair competition aligns with the goal of promoting inclusive and sustainable industrialization, fostering innovation, and upgrading infrastructure. Besides, it promotes justice, strengthens institutions, and ensures fair and transparent legal processes, promoting collaboration and partnerships between regulatory bodies, businesses, and the judiciary to achieve common goals, including fair competition. Understanding the legal principles will provide insights in preventing anti-competitive practices. It helps to reduce economic inequalities by ensuring fair opportunities for businesses of all sizes, promoting a level playing field.

This paper falls under 'doctrinal research' which originates from the Latin term *'doctrina,'* signifying instruction, knowledge, or learning. The encompassed doctrine involves diverse legal concepts and principles, spanning cases, statutes, and rules. 'Doctrine' is defined as a synthesis of various rules, principles, norms, interpretive guidelines, and values. It serves to elucidate, create coherence, or justify a specific aspect of the law within a broader legal system. Doctrines may vary in abstraction and binding nature (Hutchinson & Duncan 2012). Doctrinal research is employed to analyze and evaluate laws, allowing for a thorough examination of legal principles across two jurisdictions. Any legal matter can undergo a comprehensive assessment through a scrutiny of published works and cases. This process aims to identify and define an academic niche, paving the way for the contribution of original knowledge on the subject (Fayaz, 2023). This methodology is chosen since the paper deals with intricate legal scenarios pertaining to the new adoption and implementation of Competition Act 2010 that require a comprehensive understanding and interpretation of various legal elements, rules, principles, and norms based on the statutory provisions of the Act and the decided cases within Malaysian context.

LITERATURE REVIEW

Invoking The Statutory Provision With Good Faith

Invoking a fair competition process and seeking assistance under the Act would be applicable only if enterprises are acting in good faith and are not in breach of law. The existence and application of the CA 2010 is therefore ensuring the sustainability of good competition between enterprises and corporations so that the end users namely the consumers would be better helped and received much quality products and services in each market.

For example, one is prohibited to rely on legitimate competition underlined by the Act if he is in the first place infringing and breaching the law. As in *Honda Giken Kogyo Kabushiki Kaisha (Also Known As "Honda Motor Co, Ltd") v. Dnc Asiatic Holdings Sdn Bhd & Ors and Another Suit* [2018] 9 CLJ 229. In an action by a Japanese corporation (plaintiff), who was a manufacturer of automobiles, motorcycles, internal combustion engines and parts for automobiles and motorcycles against a Malaysian company amongst others on the infringement of the ownerships of their rights subsisting artistic works of motorcycle model 'Honda EX-5', it was contended by the defendant that the copy was a legitimate competition under the CA 2010. Nonetheless, the High Court Judge, Azizah Nawawi J was of a different view and held that since the defendants infringed the plaintiff's copyright, there could not be said to be a legitimate competition, or it could not be said as a 'legitimate competing product'. The plaintiff would suffer unjust and unfair competition if its competitors were free to copy its EX-5 works protected by copyright, under the semblance of the operation of the 2010 Act. However, regardless of this judgment, the facts here did not fall under the purview of the 2010 Act.

Application

The Ambits of Anti Competition Conducts

The main objectives as mentioned in the Act must specifically address its specific context. Agreements or conducts which are outside the scope of the Act are excluded from the prohibition. The provisions are meant to regulate conducts among competitors. To illustrate, the common law doctrine of prime necessity, dealing the obligation by monopoly suppliers of essential products and services to supply the products and services in consideration for fair and reasonable payment, is different with what the Act intend to protect namely anti competition agreements, hence is outside the purview of the Act.

In the case of *Labuan Ferry Corporation Sdn Bhd v. Chin Mui Kien (Trading under the Name and Style of Econ Focus Enterprise) & Ors and Other Appeals* [2018] 2 CLJ 142, by virtue of a licence granted by the Sabah Government, the appellant, Labuan Ferry Corporation Sdn Bhd became the only operator and has monopolized the ferry services between Sabah and Labuan until 2012. The respondents alleged that the appellant had increased the charges for ferry services between Sabah and Labuan unilaterally and illegally. These complaints were publicized by the media resulting the respondents could not deliver goods and services to their clients. Respondents' vehicles were also stranded in Labuan for months. Hence, there was total lost of the usage of these vehicles in these period. The respondents contended by reason of such monopoly and under the common law doctrine of prime necessity, Labuan Ferry was under a duty to act in the public interest to serve all without discrimination, without unreasonable exclusion and at reasonable prices. In their defence it was contended by the appellant that such doctrine could not be applied in Malaysia due to the existence of the Competition Act 2010. The judges of the Court of Appeal, ruled the Competition Act is silent on the provisions that regulate monopoly of essential services including the ferry service as provided by the appellant. The application of the common law doctrine of prime necessity is not excluded by the Competition Act as the aims of the same are promoting and protecting the competition process, protecting the interests of consumers by prohibiting anti-competitive conduct and regulating conduct among competitors. Whereas the doctrine of prime necessity has nothing to do with the process of competition. Hence, the reliance to the provisions of the Act as to escape liability under such doctrine of prime of necessity failed.

Anti-competition practices are addressed in Part II of the Competition Act 2010. Chapter 1 provides prohibition on anti-competitive agreements (horizontal or vertical agreements) that have the object or effect of significantly preventing, restricting, or distorting competition in any market for goods or services in Malaysia. Whereas Chapter 2 lays down the prohibition, on any conduct by enterprises that amount to an abuse of a dominant position in any market for goods or services in Malaysia (Ramaiah, 2017).

Any agreement, horizontally or vertically, which is entered between enterprises for the purposes of significantly preventing, restricting or distorting competition in any market for goods or services is prohibited and will be subject to penalties under the Act. Horizontal agreements ***are deemed*** to have such purposes if they are entered with the objects of (a) fixing, directly or indirectly, a purchase or selling price or any other trading conditions; (b) sharing market or sourcing of supply; (c) limiting or controlling production; market outlets or market access; technical or technological development; or investment; or perform an act of bid rigging.

Ramaiah and Hussein (2021) added, the provisions on Malaysian anti competitions do cover cartel prohibitions specifically under subsection (2) to Section 4. Cartelization entails strategic cooperation and techniques aimed at enhancing firms' profitability by limiting output, manipulating prices, or allocating market shares. During this collaboration, members maintain distinct identities and financial independence. Consequently, cartel conduct eradicates competition, jeopardizing consumer welfare and undermining the principles of consumerism. While the CA 2010 does not explicitly define the term "cartel", Section 4(2) of the Act specifies that certain horizontal agreements, with the "object" of participating in cartel practices, are "deemed to have the object of significantly preventing, restricting, or distorting competition." This provision underscores the legislative intent to regard cartels as a particularly serious prohibition, emphasizing the importance of preventing actions that could substantially impede, limit, or distort competition.

The criteria for cartel prohibition (Ramaiah, 2017), enforcement, and infringement assessment vary based on the legally defined classification of cartel conduct, taking into account its types and position within the market competition chain. This classification encompasses private and public cartels, crisis or depression cartels, and their orientation on either a horizontal or vertical level of business. Therefore, the challenge for national competition authorities lies in the task of determining how to assess these agreements, aiming to strike the right balance between the pro-competitive effects and the potential anti-competitive effects that could distort the market. The common types of private cartel agreements among sellers encompass include price fixing and market sharing, involving an agreement among competitors to divide a market, providing participants with protection from competition. On the other hand, prevalent cartel agreements among buyers include price-fixing agreements and allocating agreements (Ramaiah & Hussein, 2021).

Section 4(1)(2) Competition Act 2010

The important provisions of Section 4 (1) (2) of CA 2010 are summarised as follows:-

(i) Agreements, horizontally or vertically, that has the **object or effect** that significantly preventing, restricting or distorting competition in any market for goods or services.
(ii) **Horizontal agreements** that has the **object** of significantly fixing a purchase or selling price, sharing the market or sources of supply by limiting or controlling production, market outlets or market access, technical or technological development; investment; or performance of bid rigging activities will fall within the deemed provision namely is anti competitive – the deemed provisions.

The object and effect. The meaning of 'effect' was touched by the Court of Appeal in *Malaysian Airline System Bhd v. Competition Commission & another* [2022] 1 CLJ 856 where it was ruled, as provided by Parliament, when the very nature of an agreement that sought to share market would have negative effects on the market such as the price, quality or quantity of goods and services and such agreement is prohibited under Section 4 of the CA 2010. "Effect" or "object" holds alternative and not cumulative requirements which means to be read disjunctively. It is important to consider the precise purpose of the agreement, in the economic context in which it is to be applied. On the disjunctive application of the deemed provisions, the court added, (i) Once it is established that the agreement has an anti-competitive object, it would be unnecessary to show or prove the agreement would have a considerable effect on competition. (ii) When the object of the agreement is not clear in respect of its anti-competitive intent, then this would require an examination of whether the agreement has an anti-competitive effect or not. This case involved horizontal agreement pertaining to flying routes of Malaysian civil aircrafts.

The disjunctive application of the benefits consumers in many ways. It provides infringement from two angles, namely anti-competition objects or effects. Hence, offers boundless protection and benefits consumers. This is indeed important as the underlying policy of competition law aims to ensure that consumers have adequate and affordable choices. In addition, consumers can exercise their choices effectively. Besides, it may provide and venture resource efficiency both in consumption and production towards the betterment of Malaysia's economy.

The deemed provision. This provision is considered a deeming provision and MyCC is under no duty to carry out detailed economic analysis to determine whether conduct that is listed under deemed provision (Section 4(2)) is anti-competitive (Rahman, Ahamat, & Abdul Ghadas, 2017). Despite this, it was argued that the theory of competitive harm, as per the 'object' rule, is conspicuously apparent. The legal framework established within this provision rests on the assumption that the intentions behind cartel agreements, such as fixing prices and allocating markets, unequivocally aim at impeding competitors from engaging in fair competition (Rahman, Ahamat, & Abdul Ghadas, 2017).

The classification of specific behavior under the 'object' rule enables MyCC to bypass a comprehensive analysis of competitive harm when determining the anti-competitive nature of a particular conduct. The key concern lies not in the correct application of the harm theory but rather in determining the extent to which the competition authority must demonstrate actual harm suffered by consumers. Consequently, the focus shifts from the application of the theory of harm to the burden of proof. Under the object rule, MyCC can pursue cases against anti-competitive conduct based on speculation or abstract notions of competitive harm, without the necessity of substantiating the allegations with concrete evidence. This approach is presumably aimed at easing the competition authority's burden in proving each serious cartel case (Rahman, Ahamat, & Abdul Ghadas, 2017). The MAS-Air case illustrated that MyCC considered actual consumer harm. Nevertheless, it remains unclear whether MyCC is obligated to consistently consider such harm in all cases falling under the 'object' category. This ambiguity arises from the regulatory framework of Section 4(2), which operates on the presumption that hardcore cartel activities inherently harm consumers (Rahman, Ahamat, & Abdul Ghadas, 2017).

The COA in the MAS Air Asia case also ruled on the deemed provisions under Section 4(2)(b) that the intention of Parliament, the very nature of an agreement that sought to share market would have negative effects on the market, and the effects may be on the price, quality or quantity of goods and services.

Ramaiah and Hussein (2021), if an agreement is deemed to have an anticompetitive object then no need for further examination of its anticompetitive effects. MyCC is primarily concerned with agreements that have a substantial impact (i.e., more than a trivial impact) and combined market shares exceeding 20 percent of the relevant market, provided that such agreements do not fall under the category of hard-core cartels.

In *SAL Agencies Sdn Bhd & 4 Ors v Competition Commission* (2021) Appeal No.: TRP 2-2021, an investigation had been done by the Commission in 2018 regarding the possible anti-competition practices conducted by the Appellant and two other parties involving price fixing on the services of long-length handling and heavy lift handling for import and export cargo. The appellant's core business is providing warehousing storage services for import and export cargoes which also involves the loading and unloading of cargoes from containers in and out of their warehouses. A surcharge is imposed on the customers for the loading and unloading of their cargo. As the investigation and the representation by the appellants were completed, the Commission found that the Appellant has infringed Part II of the CA 2010.

The Commission has invoked and applied the 'deemed' provision in Section 4(2), where it would be conclusive as to the deemed meaning and consequence. In order to trigger this 'deemed' provision, there are conditions that must be strictly complied namely: (i) there must be a horizontal agreement; (ii) the horizontal agreement is made between enterprises; (iii) the agreement has the object to fix, directly or indirectly a purchase or selling price or any other trading conditions. All these were found in affirmative. On appeal, the Tribunal has unanimously confirmed the Competition Commission's decision that the Appellant had infringed the CA 2010 on the price fixing.

Significant effect. The keyword to determine infringement of Section 4(1) pertaining to vertical and horizontal agreements, as well as the deeming provisions of Section 4 (2) is "significant". In other words, the agreements must have the effect of ***significantly*** preventing, restricting or distorting competition. In *Fantasy Ruby Sdn Bhd v. Padiberas Nasional Bhd* (2018) 10 CLJ 385 the High Court ruled that the 2010 Act does not prohibit all agreements but it only confers the prohibitions to horizontal and vertical agreements (Section 4(1)). By virtue of the section, only horizontal or vertical agreements between enterprises which "has the object or effect of significantly preventing, restricting or distorting competition in any market for goods or services" are prohibited. However, the word "significantly" is not defined in the CA 2010, hence the MyCC Guidelines defines it as having more than a trivial impact. It should be noted that impact would be assessed in relation to the identified relevant market. A good guide to the trivial impact of an anti-competitive agreement might be the combined market share of those participating in such an agreement. In general, anti-competitive agreements will not be classified as "significant" if:

(i) The involved parties in the agreement are competitors operating within the same market, and their combined market share in the relevant market does not exceed 20%.
(ii) The parties to the agreement are not competitors and all of the parties individually hold less than 25% in any relevant market.

The plaintiff and the defendant do not operate in the same market. The plaintiff's market is the manufacture of bee hoon. The defendant's market is the importation of rice. On this basis, to determine the significant impact, it is to be assessed through the identified market. As the High Court ruled - where the parties are not competitors in the same market, their market share individually in the relevant market shall be more than 25%. However, there was no evidence adduced as to what the plaintiff's and defendant's market shares are in their respective relevant markets. On these grounds, the High Court decided that the 2011 contract is not an anti-competitive agreement. Thus, it did not in breach the Act.

Hence, based on the above guidelines, the first thing to be determined is whether the parties' agreement, either vertical or horizontal has significant effect of reventing competition and this must be looked at from the angles of market sharing percentage.

In *Competition Commission v. Competition Appeal Tribunal & Ors* [2019] 6 CLJ 623 the word market itself receives due consideration and it was held by the High Court that the imposition to identify the relevant market was not the prerequisite in invoking the deeming provision. However, this case went up to the Court of Appeal whereby the decision was overruled. On appeal, the COA found that the High Court decision on the irrelevancy of the identification of the relevant market was wrong as this is well embedded in any deemed provision. It is pertinent to identify the relevant market before MyCC can evaluate the anti-competitive nature of any particular conduct. The High Court Judge's finding on determination of relevant market as irrelevant and not a prerequisite in invoking Section 4(2) of the CA 2010 could not be agreed. It is observed in the final decision, the Commission failed `to identify the relevant market'. The only evidence that MyCC relied upon points was the withdrawal in the East Malaysian routes by Firefly (the four routes). However, as found by the CAT, these four routes were taken over by

MAS and they continued to compete with AirAsia on these four routes. In any event, the withdrawal by Firefly was before the coming into force of the 2010 Act. Hence, the collaboration agreement was very clear namely there were no objects to share market neither there any effects arise due to market sharing. As such there was no infringement committed. Even if the clauses in the collaboration agreement were anti-competitive, it was subject to antitrust clearance by MyCC. It was the terms that come into existence before the CA 2010 comes into effect.

Henceforth, identifying the relevant market is a preliminary condition to determine anti-competitive. Ignoring this principle is a blatant mistake of law and would be subject to judicil review.

Determination of relevant market. In addition to the guidelines on the percentage of the combined market share as provided in *Fantasy Ruby Sdn Bhd v. Padiberas Nasional Bhd* [2018] 10 CLJ 385 recourse can be made to what was provided in COA's judgment in *Malaysian Airline System Bhd v. Competition Commission & another appeal* [2022] 1 CLJ 856. The market must be defined with sufficient particularity because the market can cover a broad spectrum in the airline industry. It is not just merely routes as in point of origin and destination. Airlines may cooperate with each other in areas where there would be economy of scale and reduction of cost for example in engineering and maintenance of the airlines, training of pilots and stewards and stewardesses, in-flight food catering and beverages, purchase of fuel and all these could not be treated as deterring competition. The COA referred to the case of *Maersk Air/SAS (Scandinavian Airlines System) Competition Case* and *EasyJet Airline Co Ltd v. Commission* observed product market to be defined according to the O&D method and remarked that the relevant "markets" referred to the providing of passenger air services between the identified route. Only after identification of the relevant market the MyCC can assess the anti-competitive in nature of a particular conduct. If the relevant "market" as assumed by MyCC means the origin/destination pairs in the four routes, there was no carving out of the four routes as in being shared between MAS and AirAsia. Somewhat both parties continued to compete after MAS took over the four routes from Firefly and this is borne out by the evidence of the revenue generated by both MAS and AirAsia for these four routes. Neither was there the surrendering of the four routes to AirAsia by MAS. The truth facts were there was a competition between MAS and AirAsia over the same four routes. It was evident that in order to avoid duplication for the routes the appellants may collaborate with each other on the flight scheduling and timetable of departure. Ultimately the passengers get to choose which flight they want to be in; whether with the MAS full-service airline or the AirAsia LCC airline. Hence, failure to treat the relevancy of market is vital and renders the agreement outside the ambit of the redeemed provisions.

Besides as celebrated by Ramaiah and Hussein (2021) pertaining to cartels agreements, the MyCC is mandated to assess both the actual common intention of the parties and the aims of an agreement, considering the economic context in the market which it operates.

Horrizontal, vertical agreement and abuse of dominant position. "Horizontal agreement" refers to an agreement between enterprises that operates at the same level in the production or distribution chain whereas "vertical agreement" refers to an agreement between enterprises that operates at a different level in the production or distribution chain.

Horizontal agreement. The example of horizontal agreement is best illustrated in the case of *Langkawi Ro-Ro operators v Competition Commission* (2022) Appeal No.: TRP 1-2022, TRP 2-2022, TRP 3-2022, where the Tribunal found the Commission was correct in identifying the Memorandum of Understanding (MOU) between the Ro-Ro operators as a "horizontal agreement between the enterprises". The appellants in this case involved in the business of providing and/or operating ferry services for the transportation of motor vehicles and/or passengers at the jetty known as Dermaga Tanjung Lembung,

Kuah, Langkawi. Upon investigation revealed that there were two MOUs signed by them standardizing the charges for the fares of various types of vehicles using their Ro-Ro ferry services, resulting in a final decision issued by CC to have infringed the anti-competition practices under section 4(1). On appeal to the Tribunal, it was agreed by the Tribunal that they were operating at the same level in providing the said services, hence, such MOUs fall within the meaning of "horizontal agreement".

The horizontal agreement also could be seen in the collaboration agreement entered between MAS and Air Asia. The judicial review was initiated by the MyCC against CAT decision. A collaboration agreement was entered between Malaysian Airlines System (MAS), the second respondent and AirAsia X Sdn Bhd, the third respondent. The parties' business model was to be undertaken through a subsidiary or affiliate. The collaboration agreement also provided for the establishment of a joint collaboration committee, among others, for the purposes of administering and overseeing the said collaboration and to kick start the collaboration process. The MyCC handed down its final decision, MAS and AirAsia had infringed the Act and imposed a penalty of RM 10,000,000. Disappointed, MAS and AirAsia filed their appeal to the Tribunal. The Tribunal reversed the CC decision. The MyCC commenced with the review. The Court had set aside the Tribunal decisions and ruled the decision was tainted with an error of law and unreasonableness. The court reinstated the final decision of the MyCC and held that there was an infringement of Act. MAS and Air Asia appealed to the Court of Appeal. Similar defences and issues were raised inter alia, that: (i) the collaboration agreement was entered prior to the enforcement date of the Competition Act 2010 rendering difficulty to predict with certainty the form of infringements and reliefs that would be offered under s. 4 and 5 of the Act (ii) no guidelines were ever issued by the MyCC on antitrust clearance despite their application for the same and hence the collaboration agreement had yet to be effective. Thereby there was no infringement was committed. The COA held, the appellants were no longer contractually bound by the collaboration agreement. After such a date too, the collaboration agreement would be unenforceable and appellants would not be allowed to enter into a further or fresh agreement which has the object to prevent, restrict or distort competition. The parties may let the status quo subsist before the enforcement date but not maintain it. The burden of proof lies on the MyCC in proving before the supplemental agreement terminating the collaboration agreement was entered, the appellants were actively collaborating and not merely allowing the status quo to remain but MyCC failed to discharge this. It was held that the appellants had abandoned the collaboration agreement on 2 May 2012, by the signing of the supplemental agreement. There was nothing to restrict either MAS or AirAsia from providing services on any routes rather than to provide better flow to consumers and not on avoiding overlapping routes.

Besides, Ramaiah and Hussein (2021) mentioned horizontal agreement would also applied to Horizontal Cartel Agreement (HCA) which pertains to collaboration among competitors operating at the same level of the production chain and within the same line of business. HCAs are classified as particularly detrimental to market competition and consumer welfare when compared to Vertical Cartel Agreements (VCAs). The common forms of HCAs encompass information exchange, joint purchasing agreements, and research and development agreements.

Vertical Agreement. The Court decided in *Fantasy Ruby Sdn Bhd v. Padiberas Nasional Bhd* [2018] 10 CLJ 385 that the broken rice contract 2011 fall under vertical agreement. The plaintiff and the defendant are not enterprises operating at the same level in the production or distribution chain. The defendant is the importer of rice into Malaysia pursuant to its 1996 Concession Agreement with the Government of Malaysia. The plaintiff entered the 2011 contract as the authorized agent of Persatuan Pengusaha Bee Hoon Malaysia (PBH). The principal to the 2011 contract is surely the PBH. However, PBH is an association of bee hoon manufacturers and not an importer of rice as the plaintiff. The 2011 contract is a vertical agreement between the plaintiff and the defendant.

Vertical agreement also will apply to Vertical Carters Agreements (VCAs) which primarily focus on the trading relationships between firms that operate at different levels of the production or supply chain and within distinct markets. Examples include agreements between producers and distributors. Conversely, prevalent types of VCAs include exclusive distribution, franchising, and resale price restrictions (Ramaiah & Hussein, 2021).

Abuse of Dominant Position. An abuse of a dominant position is provided under Section 10 of the Act and it includes directly or indirectly imposing unfair purchase or selling price or other unfair trading condition on any supplier or customer, limiting or controlling production and market access (Ramaiah, 2017). This implies that merely being a dominant entity is not considered an offense under the Act. However, the dominant firm carries specific responsibilities to refrain from actions that could impede competition, such as engaging in exclusionary practices. Unlike anti-competitive behavior under Section 4, Section 10 focuses on regulating unilateral actions by a dominant firm (Rahman, Ahamat, & Abdul Ghadas, 2017).

In the case of *Federation of Sabah Industries & Ors v. Competition Commission & Ors* [2015] 7 CLJ, 101the applicants alleged that the conditional block exemption order (BEO) 2014 allowed the liners operators to maintain their dominant position. The applicants further alleged that the BEO allows the liners to maintain their dominant position, hence reducing competitional effect of the high shipping costs for Sabah. Besides it cause the increase prices of consumer goods in Sabah. The High Court however found and revealed the key facts led to the higher shipping costs were number of vessels registered in Sabah or owned by businesses in Sabah providing shipping services between Sabah and West Malaysia are very minimum and there was very minimum products being exported or transported to West Malaysia from Sabah on the return leg of ships serving between Sabah and West Malaysia.

In *Fantasy Ruby case* the plea of dominant position was denied due to technical and procedural wrong. Failure of the defendant to plea either party or both had dominant positions in the respective markets or had abused their dominant position by entering into 2011 contract is a dynamic breach rule of pleading and evidence as stipulated under Section 103 of the Evidence Act 1950. This might be different if the technical requirement is strictly followed.

In *MyTeksi Sdn Bhd & 2 Ors v Competition Commission* [2022] 8 AMR 341, where the appellants were the sole and majority shareholder, providing various services including “GrabTaxi”, “GrabFood”, “GrabCar”, “GrabExpress” “GrabAds”, “GrabShare” and “GrabForBusiness”. The investigation which was done in 2018 revealed that the Appellant has abused its dominant position by imposing a restrictive clause on its drivers. This clause prevents the drivers from promoting Grab’s current and potential competitors in the e-hailing platforms and transit media advertising. The Commission proposed to impose a penalty of RM86,772,943.76 on the appellants, and a daily penalty of RM15,000 in the event the appellants failed to comply with the MyCC directions. The case went up to appeal proceedings. The Court of Appeal held that the High Court has erred in reaching such a decision and therefore, the leave for judicial review was allowed. Hence, the finding of abusing of dominant position by the CC might not be remain.

However, the Court of Appeal in *Labuan Ferry Corporation Sdn Bhd v. Chin Mui Kien (Trading Under the Name and Style of Econ Focus Enterprise) & Ors and Other Appeals* [2018] 2 CLJ 142 decided that monopoly is not to be associated with an enterprise holding a “dominant position” within the meaning of Section 10(1) of the Act. Monopoly involves no competition at all. This takes the monopoly of essential products services outside the purview of the Act. In this respect, it is advisable to refer and counter check the application of the theory of cempeitive harm.

According to Rahman, Ahamat and Abdul Ghadas (2017) the theory of harm can be extended here with different concept of 'harm to competition' under Section 4. Section 10(2) provides a non-exhaustive list of abusive conduct According to the guidelines issued by MyCC, abusive conduct can be classified into exploitative and exclusionary categories (MyCC, Guidelines on Chapter 2 Prohibition, 2012). Exploitative conduct refers to an enterprise's capability to sustain prices above the competitive level for a certain period without concern that consumers will readily switch to other producers. Exploitative conduct, in this context, involves imposing excessive prices on consumers with the primary aim of gaining higher profits rather than as a result of innovation. When regulating such exploitative behavior, MyCC appears to assess the degree to which the abusive conduct negatively impacts consumers through the imposition of higher prices.

Exclusionary conduct, on the other hand, pertains to the ability of an enterprise to influence the level of competition in a market by impeding new competitors from entering or substantially harming existing, equally efficient competitors, thereby preventing them from effectively competing in the market. According to MyCC Guidelines, the Commission adopts an effect-based approach to assess whether a unilateral conduct is anticompetitive or not.

To evaluate the impact of exclusionary conduct, MyCC employs two primary tests: examining whether the conduct negatively affects consumers and determining whether the conduct excludes competitors that are equally efficient as the dominant firm. According to these guidelines, it can be reasonably inferred that 'harm to competition' in the context of exclusionary conduct refers to harm to the competitive process. This encompasses the impairment of the ability of efficient firms to compete and also harm to consumers (Rahman et. al, 2017).

It is necessary to prevent the use of a dominant position in the market as it will benefit the economy in general and the consumers specifically. This would avoid monopoly by enterprises rendering those in dominancy to control and be at the upper level of providing products and services. Instead, with the provisions in the CA 2010, enterprises would boost their efficiency, productivity and entrepreneurial innovation, promoting productivity, economic growth and employment in a variety and diversified methods. Competition would also drive enterprises and businesses to adopt sustainable business strategies. Competition encourages continuous improvement of the corporation's internal management. Productivity grows in sectors where competition exists as corporations become more efficient. Competition also initiates innovation. The competitors will exert pressure henceforth encouraging improvisation and innovation in products and services. This benefits both the enterprises and consumers from their own context as will definitely lead to a sustainable Malaysian economy and community well-being.

It is noteworthy to provide some limitations of the 2010 Act based on the foregoings provisions and decisions. The Act is silent in addressing issues encountered by small sellers in their dealings with influential buyers. It becomes evident that terms such as monopsony, duopsony, or oligopsony are absent. Besides, the CA 2010 exclusively focuses on market conduct, lacking provisions for regulating market structure. Consequently, the CA 2010 does not encompass ex ante regulation of mergers involving monopsonists or influential buyers. Similarly the explicit prohibition of the acquisition of supply by a single purchaser or a few powerful purchasers is not articulated eventhough the provisions may implicitly address such purchasers. It is essential to distinguish between conduct involving multiple powerful buyers, falling under the concept of an anti-competitive agreement, and unilateral monopsony conduct, falling under the notion of abuse of a dominant position. Although there is potential for addressing such practices indirectly, particularly if they adversely affect smaller sellers, the absence of explicit provisions may pose challenges for MyCC in taking direct action (Ahamat, Rahman, & Anshori 2020).

Defences

The Exemptions

Section 5 of the CA 2010 provides for relief from infringement if it can be proven that the competitive agreement directly causes significant and identifiable technological, efficiency or social benefits. It must also be proven that these benefits could only be provided with the emergence of such anti-competitive agreement (Ramaiah, 2017). Besides the detrimental effect of the anti-competitive agreement must be balanced to the benefits provided. The anti-competitive agreement also must disallow total elimination of competition from the substantial part of the goods and services by the enterprise concerned.

Contrarywise, this would impliedly convey the grounds for an infringement to be submitted by proposing a failure on part of the enterprises to fulfil the requirements mentioned in Section 5. This could be well illustrated and drawn from several grounds for infringements as proposed by the applicants in the case of *Federation of Sabah Industries & Ors v. Competition Commission & Ors* [2015] 7 CLJ, 101. The applicant argued that the block of exemption (BOE) 2014 infringed the CA 2010 in the sense that:- (i) the conditions vis-à-vis the prohibition of price fixing for liner shipping services was internally incompatible and unenforceable; (ii) the absence of benchmark to guarantee the achievement of its objectives; (iii) the absence of the required implementation and enforcement mechanism as mandated by s. 16(d) of the Competition Act, hence unenforceable; (iv) it supported anti-competition measures; (v) it permitted participants to engage in collusive conduct. Above all, the High Court Judge held that as the applicants failed to produce any statistical evidence to show the BEO 2014 had resulted in anti-competitive practices which increased the prices of consumer goods in Sabah. The applicant also failed to discharge the burden in proving the conditions set out in paras. 5 of the BEO 2014 were irrational or perverse.

Under the CA 2020, exemptions are of two types, individual and block as follows:

Individual Exemption. Individual exemption reflects exemption of a particular agreement provided all the criteria in Section 5 are fulfilled (Individual & Block Exemption, n.d.). The exemption may be granted subject to conditions, obligations and for a limited duration (Section 7). An individual exemption can be canceled or varied if there is a material change of circumstances or there is a breach or non-compliance with an imposed condition.

Block Exemption. Block exemption (Individual & Block Exemption, n.d.) may be granted by the MyCC to a particular category of agreements such as distribution agreements in a particular industry (Section 18). This could be seen in agreements involving liners shippers pertaining to their vessels sharing agreements. There was a joint application made requesting a block exemption for a period of five years under Section 4 of the Act pertaining to "Vessel Sharing Agreements ('VSA')" and "Voluntary Discussion Agreement ('VDA')" entered by liner shippers relating to the entire transport chain, including intramodal transport services (*Federation of Sabah's case*).

Block exemption is advantageous in the sense that similar agreements can be examined simultaneously hence overall evaluation on anti-competitive impact could be conveyed effectively by the MyCC. In addition, this relieves enterprises from submitting separate applications (Individual & Block Exemption, n.d.).

Before granting any of block exemption the MyCC must provide details of the proposed block exemption. A minimum of thirty (30) days period from the date of publication must be given to the public for any intended submission pertaining to the proposed block exemption. Due consideration must be given for any submission made as in Section 9. A right to commence an action under this section would arise if applicants can prove a real and genuine interest over the proposed exemption. In *Federation of Sabah's case* it was alleged that the respondent failed to adhere to Section 9 (b) on 30 days requirement when they held a 30 days public consultation. The appellant contended that they would only have 21 days to reply hence rendering the conditional BEO 2014 is null and void. Nonetheless, it was held that a thirty (30) days submission date would be calculated from the first date of submission made. When the applicants had by a letter dated 28 March 2013 made their first submission and on 18 September 2013 made their second submission, this was held to be clear that the required 30 days of submission dates for the proposed block exemption. The exemption block remains valid.

Besides, the applicant in challenging the block exemption is not required to demonstrate any violation of private rights or the existence of special damage. This rule is laid down in *Federation of Sabah* – the applicants contended infringement of public interest concerning an equitable playing field, competition, reasonable pricing, elevated shipping and logistics expenses. All these could influence consumer prices and the cost of living in Sabah.

Similar to an individual exemption, a block exemption can be canceled if there is a material change of circumstances or there is a breach or non-compliance of an imposed condition laid down in Section 8 (5) of the CA 2010. This is in line with the principles laid down by Stephen Chung J in *Federation of Sabah.* The MyCC as the first respondent can cancel the block exemption for non-compliance of any matter dealt under Section 5(5)(b) of the BEO 2014.

The COA in *Malaysian Airline System Bhd v. Competition Commission & another appeal* [2022] 1 CLJ 856 laid down the following rules on the exemptions: any party liable for infringement of the prohibition may endeavour to show and apply for the exemptions. These exemptions are often called as the net economic benefit ("NEB") exclusion in the language of competition law. Specifically pertaining to airlins, the court proceeded, that airlines often enter into cooperation or alliances with one another and they may amongst others agree on the schedule, price, sales and marketing, service policies and other related matters to improve quality, the service offered to passengers on their existing routes. Since our CA 2010 is not against collaboration, joint ventures, cooperation and alliances, there is a place for competitive collaboration and cooperation or collaborative competition that would confer benefits on the consumers. Not all collaboration is anti-competition and indeed cases in other jurisdictions involving exemptions have resulted in their competition tribunals' findings that there are significant NEB for the exemptions to apply. Since the collaboration agreement was a comprehensive specialisation agreement intended not only to operate cost-effective and efficient networks but also to foster cooperation in a wide range of other aspects relating to the air service industry, it was decided that these fall within the ambit of Section 5(a) as benefiting the consumers by ensuring maximum connectivity, optimizing geographical coverage and broader network and passengers' convenience. The benefits would flow to the consumers in the form of a better schedule of flight timings, increased frequency, capacity coordination and connectivity. Without the collaboration agreement, the increase in capacity would not likely occur.

The provided law on the exemption is important to create a fair competition regulation for a country's economy (Ramaiah, 2015). Malaysian competition law reflects the acceptance of free competition in their market. As such the provisions on exemption confers the importance of rights towards properties, the essential of economic efficacy and optimal allocation of resources. Besides, the exemption also caters to enterprises' transparency and international competitiveness in products or service enhancement.

It facilitates entrance and penetration into markets. All these reasons secure the sustainability of the economy and the well-being of the community, especially the consumers.

Commission Competition (CC), Competition Appeal Tribunal (CAT), and Civil Courts Review

Section 14 CA 2010 provides for Investigation by the Commission basically on two grounds. First is when the MyCC has reason to suspect that any enterprise has infringed or is infringing any prohibition under this Act. Second is when they suspect any person has committed or is committing any offence under this Act. Upon completion of investigation, MyCC may propose to make a decision whether the anti-competition practices under Part II have been infringed and give the notice to inform the suspected enterprise to make a representation (Section 36(a)). In addition, MyCC also is permitted to propose a financial penalty or any remedial action as provided in Section 36(2)(b). However, such a decision by MyCC is merely a proposed decision, hence, it is not conclusive and has yet to have any effect. It is not a final decision where the suspected enterprise still can make a representation, either oral or written, to the Commission, including the opportunity to mitigate the proposed penalty.

On top of that, the MyCC's decision is subject to a review by CAT which is established under Section 44 of the Act. The CAT shall have exclusive jurisdiction to review decision made by the Commission. This is enshrined in Sections 35, 39 and 40.

Skrine - Advocates & Solicitors (n.d.) explained, once an inquiry is instigated under the Competition Act, whether it is initiated through an ex-officio investigation pursuant to Section 14 or is a result of a complaint under Section 15, the MyCC retains the authority to unilaterally conclude the investigation. However, should the MyCC determine, post-completion of the inquiry, that any violations of the Competition Act have occurred, it is obligated to issue a proposed decision according to Section 36. This decision includes a notice that outlines: (i) The rationale behind the proposed decision in adequate detail, allowing the concerned enterprise to comprehensively and effectively provide comments on an informed basis, (ii)The monetary fines or corrective measures the MyCC intends to impose, (iii) Notification that the enterprise is entitled to submit written and oral representations to the MyCC.

After the enterprise has submitted its written and/or oral representations concerning the proposed decision, the MyCC is subsequently empowered to render a determination of non-infringement in accordance with Section 39 of the Competition Act or establish a finding of infringement as outlined in Section 40 of the Competition Act. In the case of an infringement, the MyCC may mandate the cessation of the infringement, stipulate the necessary measures the enterprise must undertake to terminate the infringement, and/or levy a financial penalty (Skrine - Advocates & Solicitors, n.d.).

In the event of a determination of non-infringement under Section 39 of the Competition Act or a finding of infringement under Section 40 of the Competition Act, any aggrieved party or a party whose interests are adversely affected retains the right to challenge the MyCC's decision by filing an appeal with the Competition Appeal Tribunal. Depending on the circumstances, this could involve either the complainant or the entity accused of infringement appealing the decision. Upon initiation of the appeal process, the Competition Appeal Tribunal is tasked with re-examining the matter. Pursuant to Section 58(2) of the Competition Act, the Tribunal holds the authority to either uphold or overturn the MyCC's decision made under Section 39 or Section 40 of the Competition Act (Skrine - Advocates & Solicitors, n.d.).

One interesting case to review pertaining the jusrisdiction of MyCC in this matter is *MyTeksi Sdn Bhd & Ors v Competition Commission* [2022] 6 MLJ 76. This case stems from the well-publicized 2018 merger between Uber Malaysia Sdn Bhd and Grabcar Sdn Bhd, commonly referred to as the Grab-Uber merger. Following the merger, the MyCC, received numerous complaints from the public. Prompted by these complaints, the MyCC initiated an investigation into the conduct of MyTeksi Sdn Bhd, Grabcar Sdn Bhd, and Grab Inc, collectively known as "Grab." On October 3, 2019, the MyCC issued a proposed decision under Section 36 of the Competition Act. The MyCC determined that Grab had abused its dominant position as per Section 10 of the Competition Act by imposing a restrictive clause on its drivers. This clause effectively prevented Grab's drivers from promoting competitors in e-hailing platforms and transit media advertising. In the proposed decision, the MyCC proposed a financial penalty of RM86,772,943.76 on Grab and had instructed Grab to permanently remove the restrictive clause from its terms and conditions, supplement terms of use and code of conduct, and notify all drivers of the removal of the restrictive clause. MyCC also proposed a daily financial penalty of RM15,000.00 on Grab from the date of the proposed decision's service if Grab fails to comply with the remedial direction. In response to the MyCC's proposed decision, Grab initiated a judicial review leave application at the High Court. Among other requests, Grab sought an order for certiorari to annul the proposed decision and a declaration that the MyCC's decision to impose a penalty retroactively before determining an infringement under Section 40 of the Competition Act was ultra vires (Skrine - Advocates & Solicitors, n.d.)..

The Grab judicial review takes an interesting turn as Grab filed its judicial review leave application against the proposed decision under Section 36 of the Competition Act while the proceedings before the MyCC were still ongoing. At that juncture, neither a finding of non-infringement under Section 39 nor a finding of infringement under Section 40 had been reached. Traditionally, the established position has been that there is no decision to review in such circumstances (Skrine - Advocates & Solicitors, n.d.)..

In response, the MyCC opposed Grab's judicial review leave application based on two key arguments: prematurity of Grab's aApplication: The MyCC contended that Grab's judicial review application was premature since the proposed decision was not final, and Grab had not exhausted the internal appeal process outlined in the Competition Act; and lack of full and frank disclosure: The MyCC argued that Grab failed to make full and frank disclosure, specifically regarding Grab's filing of written representations and a notice informing the MyCC of its intention to make oral representations. Grab countered these arguments by asserting amenability of proposed decision to judicial review and there was no alternative remedy available, as there was no right of appeal against a proposed decision under Section 36 of the Competition Act to the Competition Appeal Tribunal. Grab also asserted that the proposed decision was tainted with illegality, providing a basis for commencing the judicial review leave application without exhausting the internal remedy mechanism (Skrine - Advocates & Solicitors, n.d.).

Ultimately, the High Court ruled in favor of the MyCC and dismissed Grab's judicial review leave application on the grounds, the proposed decision was not considered a final decision, supported by the absence of a provision for an appeal to the Competition Appeal Tribunal. It is a requirement to exhaust to internal remedy even in the hypothetical scenario of a finding of non-infringement under Section 39 or a finding of infringement under Section 40, the aggrieved party would be obligated to exhaust the internal remedy through an appeal to the Competition Appeal Tribunal (Skrine - Advocates & Solicitors, n.d.).

Grab appealed to appeal to the Appeal Court. The COA, upon considering Grab's appeal, made a notable decision by allowing it. Consequently, the matter was remitted back to the High Court specifically for the hearing of the substantive judicial review application (Skrine - Advocates & Solicitors, n.d.). This turn of events implies that the COA found merit in Grab's arguments or identified legal issues that warranted a closer examination of the case. The decision to remit the matter back to the High Court indicates that the COA believed there were valid grounds for Grab to have its substantive judicial review application heard and considered in more detail. This step is essential for a comprehensive examination of the case and the specific issues raised by Grab in its judicial review.

The decision of the the COA on October 1, 2022, made a groundbreaking decision that could significantly impact the way competition law cases are litigated in Malaysia. In this landmark ruling, the COA held that a proposed decision under Section 36 of the CA 2010 is subject to judicial review (Skrine - Advocates & Solicitors, n.d.). Hence the binding effect took place. This marks a noteworthy development because a proposed decision under Section 36 of the Competition Act is not considered final and is merely a component of the preliminary stages aimed at determining whether an enterprise has engaged in an anti-competitive agreement, constituting an infringement under Section 4 of the Competition Act, or has abused its dominant position, constituting an infringement under Section 10 of the Competition Act. The court's recognition of the amenability of such a decision to judicial review introduces a novel dimension to the legal landscape surrounding competition law in Malaysia (Skrine - Advocates & Solicitors, n.d.).

The COA, in essence, determined that despite being labeled as a proposed decision, the imposition of a daily financial penalty starting from the date of service of the proposed decision, in the event of non-compliance with the remedial direction, carried a final and decisive impact (Skrine - Advocates & Solicitors, n.d.). This recognition by the COA suggests that the ongoing accrual of the daily financial penalty had tangible and conclusive consequences, effectively treating the proposed decision as having a substantial, rather than provisional, effect. In making this determination, the COA likely considered the practical and financial implications of the daily penalty, acknowledging that it had the potential to significantly impact Grab even before a final decision on infringement had been reached. This interpretation emphasizes the substantive consequences associated with the proposed decision and underscores the need for a judicial review of the matter.

In addition to the above, the High Court in *Competition Commission v. Competition Appeal Tribunal & Ors* [2019] 6 CLJ 623 ruled, it is well settled in judicial review that both the decision-making process and the merits of the decision could be reviewed. An award could be reviewed for substance as well as for process. A judicial review also could be made on a decision involving an error of law. Hence judicial review will stand to indict all errors of law made by the administrative bodies and inferior courts unless there are special circumstances governing a particular case. This is so regardless of any private clause to deny the effect.

However, the MAS case the COA ruled MyCC's jurisdiction and powers are pertaining to the regulation of economic and commercial matters relating to the civil aviation industry, including issues relating to competition. However with the coming into effect of the MAVCOM Act, MyCC jusrisdiction had come to an end. This was nothing less due to the amendment to the First Schedule of the CA 2010, where the matters under the MAVCOM Act were excluded from MyCC. The jurisdiction over civil aviation ever since that date vested with MAVCOM. As such, since the judicial review application by MyCC at the High Court was filed on 3 May 2016, a date after the enforcement date, MyCC no longer had the capacity to file the appeal against the CAT's decision. From the powers and functions of MyCC, it was clear the same was a quasi-judicial body. A quasi-judicial body like MyCC cannot review the decision of its own appellate body, in this case, CAT. Section 40 of the CA 2016 provides that after MyCC made a finding, in respect of the appeal against its decision to be heard by the CAT, it would become functus officio and would not have any interest in such save to assist CAT to arrive at a fair and just decision.

Further, due to their positions, MyCC must give due reverence and respect to CAT's decision and must abide by it. For the MyCC to ignore or challenge the CAT's decision, would be tantamount to administrative insubordination of a kind repugnant to the whole statutory scheme of the CA 2010. Based on this reasoning, MyCC could not be a person adversely affected by the CAT's decision within the meaning of Order 54 rule 2(4) of the Rules Of Courts, and thus, it could not apply for a judicial review against the CAT's decision.

Based on the foregoing decisions, it is crucial in understanding the process of judicial review and the underlying principles pertaining it. Judicial review is a crucial judicial power that serves as a safeguard for the rule of law, protection of fundamental rights, and the promotion of good governance. Rooted in the supervisory jurisdiction of the high courts, this power is foundational for a democratic country. The effectiveness of judicial review is intricately tied to the independence of the judiciary. The constitution lays the groundwork for the general power of the judiciary, and a comprehensive understanding of the court's authority to exercise judicial review necessitates a reference to other legislations, primarily the Courts of Judicature Act 1964, Rules of Court 2012, Interpretation Act 1948 and 1967, and their respective regulations (Aziz, Mangsor, Rahmat, Nasrun & Ristawati 2023).

These legal frameworks provide the necessary guidelines and parameters within which the courts can conduct judicial reviews, ensuring a systematic and fair application of this essential judicial function. By allowing the courts to review and potentially invalidate executive or legislative actions that may contravene the constitution or infringe upon individual rights, judicial review serves as a check and balance mechanism in a democratic system. It reinforces the accountability of government actions and helps maintain the delicate balance between the three branches of government—executive, legislative, and judicial. Overall, the proper functioning of judicial review is crucial for upholding the principles of democracy, ensuring justice, and preserving the rule of law (Aziz et al., 2023).

In Malaysia, the practice of judicial review involves the process by which the courts exercise their supervisory jurisdiction to assess the actions of public authorities that are alleged to have exceeded their powers (Aziz et al., 2023). This process is a fundamental aspect of administrative law and is crucial for ensuring that government actions adhere to the rule of law and do not infringe on the rights of individuals or entities.

In Malaysia, the mechanism through which judicial control of administrative action is exercised by judges is known as judicial review. This process allows the courts, particularly the High Court, to supervise and scrutinize the actions, decisions, or omissions of administrative or public bodies to ensure they adhere to the rule of law and do not exceed their legal powers. The legal framework governing judicial review in Malaysia is primarily outlined in Order 53 of the Rules of Court 2012 (O 53 RHC 2012). the role of judicial review is paramount in upholding the concept of constitutional supremacy. It serves as a crucial mechanism to ensure that the actions of the legislature and the executive adhere to constitutional principles and do not violate the rule of law. In systems where constitutional supremacy is a foundational principle, such as in Malaysia, the judiciary acts as a check and balance on the other branches of government (Aziz et al., 2023).

In the case of *Wira Swire Sdn Bhd v. Ketua Pengarah Hasil Dalam Negeri* [2019] 1 LNS 1026, High Court Judge Nordin Hassan affirmed that the principles governing judicial review are firmly established. According to him, the court is empowered to scrutinize a decision made in the discharge of a public duty or function, focusing on grounds such as illegality, irrationality, or procedural impropriety. a) Illegality: Illegality in decision-making involves the requirement that the decision-maker accurately comprehends the governing law that directs their authority and must duly adhere to it. Determining whether this has occurred is inherently justiciable—a matter to be resolved, in the event of a disagreement, by those vested with judicial power, namely the judges overseeing the judicial functions of the state. b) Irrationality:

Irrationality, commonly known as 'Wednesbury unreasonableness' (refer to Associated Provincial Picture Houses Ltd v. Wednesbury Corp. [1948] 1 KB 223), pertains to a decision that is so patently unreasonable, defying logic or accepted moral standards, that a reasonable person who has diligently considered the matter at hand could not possibly have arrived at the same conclusion. c) Procedural Impropriety: Procedural impropriety involves an assessment of whether there has been any infringement of the prescribed procedures outlined in the Constitution, legislation, or regulations governing the decision-making process. This aspect of judicial review focuses on ensuring that the correct procedural steps are followed in arriving at a decision (Aziz et al., 2023).

The significance of judicial review becomes particularly evident in safeguarding the rights of individuals. Courts play a pivotal role in reviewing and potentially overturning decisions made by legislative or administrative bodies that have overstepped their designated powers (Aziz et al., 2023). This underscores the crucial role of the judiciary in upholding the rule of law and protecting the rights and interests of the people against actions that exceed legal boundaries

The role of the courts in reviewing executive action is confined to verifying that the exercise of executive power adheres to legal limits and follows a process that upholds natural justice for the parties affected. However, the courts are not equipped to assess the desirability of valid policies or invalidate decisions that are reasonably made in alignment with legitimate policies. Courts are apt for determining and upholding individual rights, but they are not well-suited to settling administrative policies that must consider the diverse interests of the entire community (Aziz et al., 2023).

Hence, reversing to My Teksi's case or the Grab case, the judicial review was taken on the proposed decision only, not yet commencing under the relevant procedures of Section 39 and Section 40. What more the review was carried on and skiped the CAT jurisdiction as lays down in Section 44. What was done by the MyCC was deemed procedurally and theoretically correct. In case it was wrong, appeal can be done to CAT. Hence one might consider and argue that such review was procedurally incorrect dan legally wrong. Despite, to date it remains binding. In the MAS cse also since the judicial review application by MyCC at the High Court was filed after the enforcement date of MAVCOM Act, MyCC no longer had the capacity to file the appeal against the CAT's decision. MyCC also as a quasi-judicial body cannot review the decision of its own namely CAT. This review upholds the principles that MyCC must adheres to its legal limits.

Hence, it is worthy to note that the provisions on the establishment of the Competitive Commission as well as the Competition Appeal Tribunal are vital as both functions are preservative and safeguarding in nature specifically on the process of free and fair competition in commercial markets for the benefit of consumer welfare, efficiency of enterprises and the development of the economy as a whole. The same goes to the judicial review power vested in the Civil Courts. This would ensure the sustainability of the economy and the well-being of a nation. Our law on judicial review emphasizes the need for effective, accountable, and inclusive institutions. Courts play a crucial role in ensuring justice and upholding the rule of law by reviewing executive actions within legal boundaries. Besides, by focusing on natural justice and legal boundaries, it reduces inequalities and ensures that executive actions are within legal limits towards contribution to a more equitable and just society. The courts, by limiting their review to legality and natural justice, contribute to stable and effective institutions, fostering partnerships and collaborations by respecting the diverse interests within the community.

CONCLUSION

Competition between enterprises is desirable for economic enhancement. The markets with a high degree of competition rises rival firms strive hard in order to attract buyers by offering quality products at attractive prices. Enterprises also strive to innovate in an attempt to offer products that are superior to their competitors. However, there are some limitations and lacunas that emerges form the CA 2010. One of it is mergers control (Ramaiah, 2017; Skrine - Advocates & Solicitors, n.d.).It is proposed for the insertion of merger control, suggesting a recognition of the importance of regulating mergers within the context of competition law. Cartels are often considered serious violations in competition law due to their potential to harm fair competition and consumer welfare. However, enterprises may sometimes use mergers as a strategy to avoid being labeled as engaging in cartel behavior. In an administrative structure, the MyCC was argued not to possess an independent status of an enforcement agency, that is a fortiori independent, and vice versa. Hence, it is the investigations, decisions and transparency of processes of an enforcement agency that determine MyCC independence. Besides, the question arises as to whether the guidelines on market definition in the CA, by incorporating the definition of the term "market" in the manner they do, have potentially distorted what is essentially an economic concept, leading to a legal debate. Ramaiah (2017) recommended to establish and strengthen competition laws scope and coverage. The competition implications of various policies and regimes that determine market entry must also be considered. This will ensure adequate coordination among the competition law agency and other agencies. As Malaysian Competitive Law is still at the infancy level, yet with excellent development, many more must be done in order to ensure the excellence of this law in the future.

ACKNOWLEDGMENT

We have no conflict of interest to disclose.

Hatijah Mohamed Salleh https://orcid.org/0000-0001-5526-8520

Khairunnisa Ishak https://orcid.org/0000-0002-8378-4829

REFERENCES

Ahamat, H., Rahman, N. A., & Anshori, M. R. A. (2020). Monopsony, powerful buyers and small sellers: Analysis of Malaysian competition law and lessons learnt from Indonesia. *International Journal of Globalisation and Small Business*, *11*(3), 241–257. doi:10.1504/IJGSB.2020.109548

Aziz, N. A., Mangsor, M. M., Rahmat, N. E., Nasrun, M., & Ristawati, R. (2023). An Overview of Judicial Review in The Malaysian Court. *International Journal of Academic Research in Business & Social Sciences*, *13*(1), 336–352.

Competition Commission v. Competition Appeal Tribunal & Ors [2019] 6 CLJ 623.

Fantasy Ruby Sdn Bhd v. Padiberas Nasional Bhd [2018] 10 CLJ 385.

Fayaz, M. (2023). Human Rights Law and Police Interrogation: A Doctrinal Analysis of Anti-Terrorism Legislation of UK and Pakistan. [JLSS]. *Journal of Law & Social Studies*, *5*(3), 468–479.

Federation of Sabah Industries & Ors v. Competition Commission & Ors [2015] 7 CLJ, 101.

Grappling with the issues: Can a proposed decision under the Competition Act 2010 be subject to judi. (n.d.). Skrine - Advocates & Solicitors. https://www.skrine.com/insights/alerts/january-2023/grappling-with-the-issues-can-a-proposed-decision-

Honda Giken Kogyo Kabushiki Kaisha (Also Known As "Honda Motor Co, Ltd") v. Dnc Asiatic Holdings Sdn Bhd & Ors and Another Suit [2018] 9 CLJ 229.

Hutchinson, T., & Duncan, N. (2012). Defining and describing what we do: doctrinal legal research. *Deakin law review*, *17*(1), 83-119.

Labuan Ferry Corporation Sdn Bhd v. Chin Mui Kien (Trading under the Name and Style of Econ Focus Enterprise) & Ors and Other Appeals [2018] 2 CLJ 142.

Langkawi Ro-Ro operators v Competition Commission, Appeal No.: TRP 1-2022, TRP 2-2022, TRP 3-2022. https://www.kpdn.gov.my/en/corporate-info/department/deputy-secretary-general-domestic-trade-development/competition-appeal-tribunal/93-trp/pengumuman-trp/1453-6-grounds-of-decision-langkawi-ro-ro-ferry-services-sdn-bhd-4-others-vs-competition-commission-appeal-no-trp-1-2-3-2022

Malaysian Airline System Bhd v Competition Commission & Anor [2022] 1 CLJ 856.

Malaysia Competition Commission (MyCC). (n.d.). *Individual & block exemption*. https://www.mycc.gov.my/individual-block-exemption

MyTeksi Sdn Bhd & 2 Ors v Competition Commission [2022] 8 AMR 341.

Rahman, N. A., Ahamat, H., & Abdul Ghadas, Z. (2017). The theory of harm under the Malaysian Competition Act 2010. *Pertanika Journal of Social Science & Humanities*, *25*, 155–166.

Ramaiah, A. K. (2015). Competition law and exemption policy in Malaysia: When, why and why not. *Int J Bus Econ Law*, *8*(4).

Ramaiah, A. K. (2017). Innovation, Intellectual Property Rights and Competition Law in Malaysia. *South East Asia Journal of Contemporary Business. Economics and Law*, *14*, 60–69.

Ramaiah, A. K., & Hussein, S. M. (2021). Cartel Prohibitions and Relevance for Exclusion under the Competition Law in Malaysia and Singapore. *Asian Journal of Law and Governance*, *3*(1), 1–21.

SAL Agencies Sdn Bhd & 4 Ors v Competition Commission, Appeal No.: TRP 2-2021. https://www.mycc.gov.my/sites/default/files/pdf/decision/Alasan%20Keputusan%20kes%20SAL%20Agencies%20Sdn%20Bhd%20%26%204%20yang%20lain%20v%20Suruhanjaya%20Persaingan%20%281%29.pdf

Wira Swire Sdn Bhd v. Ketua Pengarah Hasil Dalam Negeri [2019] 1 LNS 1026

KEY TERMS AND DEFINITIONS

Abuse of Dominant Position: The committing of any act as stipulated under s. 10 (2) Competition Act 2010 .

Anti Competition Practices: A fair process of competition. The protection and promotion of competition by avoiding the anti-competition agreement or the use of a dominant position.

Block Exemption: Exemption of a particular category of agreements from anti competition conducts in compliance with s.5 of the Competition Act 2010.

Competition Appeal Tribunal: The Appeal Tribunal established under Part V of the Competition Commission Act 2010.

Competition Commission: The Commission established under Part III and Part IV of the Competition Commission Act 2010.

Competition Law: The competition law as practised in Malaysia based on the enshrined provisions of the Competition Act 2010 and other related statutary provisions.

Individual Exemption: Exemption of a particular agreement from anti competition conducts in compliance with s.5 of the Competition Act 2010.

Chapter 9
Competition Law and Community-Based Sustainable Development:
A Case Study of Selected Homestays in the Kalimpong District of West Bengal, India

Tanwir Arshed
Presidency University, Kolkata, India

Soma Dey Sarkar
North Bengal University, India

ABSTRACT

In 2015, member states of the United Nations Organizations (UNO) pledged to achieve the goal of peace and prosperity for people and the planet, which became famous as the '2030 Agenda for Sustainable Development- a blueprint of 17 Sustainable Development Goals (SDGs),' to achieve an inclusive and sustainable vision for the world. Governmental as well as nongovernmental organizations across the globe have embraced it as the new paradigm of development and have since been striving hard to achieve these goals for "The Future We Want." This chapter talks about the application of competition laws in one such sector in the sub-Himalayan region of India and tries to project that how its applicability has helped in creating an alternative, sustainable and eco-friendly model of regulatory practices in the region- community based homestays.

BACKGROUND

In 2015, member states of the United Nations Organizations (UNO) pledged to achieve the goal of peace and prosperity for people and the planet, which became famous as the '2030 Agenda for Sustainable Development- a blueprint of 17 Sustainable Development Goals (SDGs), to achieve an inclusive and sustainable vision for the world. Governmental as well as nongovernmental organizations across the

DOI: 10.4018/979-8-3693-0390-0.ch009

Copyright © 2024, IGI Global. Copying or distributing in print or electronic forms without written permission of IGI Global is prohibited.

globe have embraced it as the new paradigm of development and have since been striving hard to achieve these goals for the "The Future We Want". Institutions and legal-political bodies with and beyond the borders have vowed to pursue and accomplish such goals for a better future and one such platform is through the application and enforcement of a strong competition law, which seeks to curb down all form of monopolist trade tendency and promote indigenous and innovative sustainable ideas. This paper talks about the application of competition laws in one such sector in the sub-Himalayan region of India and tries to project that how its applicability has helped in creating an alternative, sustainable and eco-friendly model of regulatory practices in the region- community based homestays.

The sub-Himalayan region of West Bengal is well known for its 3-T-s: Tea, Tourism and Timber and for a very long time these industries, especially 'tourism'. With the inbound of colonial presence and since independence these pristine landscapes have been monopolised and dominated by big private players leading to a wholesale exploitation of the natural resources and indigenous and eco-friendly livelihood patters of the region. From railways to dam, multi-storeyed buildings to malls over concretization and cartelised forms of control have totally dismantled the ecological balance and the innovative vigour of and within the region. One such sector which got severely affected due to such lopsided and monopolistic polices of trade and investment is the hotel and hospitality industry. As per a report published in Times of India, (December 8, 2017) the unfettered and unaccountable tourism policy of mushrooming hotels industries in the sub Himalayan region has not only affected the climate of the region but has severely impacted on the natural resources like tea and others. This has also invariably and indirectly affected on the question of employability, gender dichotomy, health, sanitisation, innovation and economic indifference with the native people in and around the region. This trend has gained momentum with the havoc created since the outbreak of COVID-19 pandemic.

In this backdrop, the present empirical research paper compiled by the findings received from filed work conducted in the Kalimpong District of West Bengal is an attempt to study the role of one such non-state institution (homestays), which believes in the principle of a community-based environment-friendly and balanced sustainable approach and has been off-late an increasingly important alternative strategy for achieving the SDGs, especially in the non-western country like India. The region has been selected due to two main reasons- firstly owing to its pristine biodiversity and landscape and sharing its borders with Sikkim and dooars off-late Kalimpong has been the most preferred tourist destination of the region after Darjeeling, making it a lucrative tourism economy site; secondly despite the high influx of tourist and visitors the manner in which the community-owned developmental projects like homestays have been flourishing in the district has discouraged over-concretisation and simultaneously proving as a potential actor to deliver its commitment in achieving the global goals like gender parity, poverty alleviation, inclusive and sustainable economic growth and ecosystem leading an example of our Prime Minister Modi's vision of an Atmanirbhar Bharat or self-reliant India. This paper seeks to evaluate the possibilities of introducing a circular economy (as promoted by OECD Competition Committee) in the hospitality and tourism industry flourishing in North Bengal, with reference to the Kalimpong District of North Bengal and putting the services provided by the local homestays in achieving the SDGs in perspective.

LITERATURE REVIEW

To assess the possibilities of a strong community let eco-friendly entrepreneurships like homestays how competition law is playing an exceptional role, this chapter before proceeding for an empirical study in the select homestays of the sub-Himalayan region of Kalimpong Districts in West Bengal moves with the review of the exiting literatures, thematically. Although most of these works have tried to deal with the question of completion law and sustainable development from normative point of view however despite that, these have been extremely useful in shaping the overview and the research design in an inventive way. Like, the works by Tomislav (2018), where the authors have traced the evolution of the concept of sustainable development. This books explain the challenges and opportunities for sustainable development in the less economically developed regions of the world and narrate how an increasingly globalised world has brought new challenges to achieving a sustainable approach. Jeffrey Sachs and Joseph Stiglitz and the more radical critiques of globalization articulated by Greg Buckman and George Monbiot have discussed the correlation that exists between globalisation and sustainable development, which helped the researchers to frame our understanding of the chapter in the context of homestays.

The works of Rashed Al Mahmud Titumir on Sundarbans and its Ecosystem Services Traditional Knowledge, Customary Sustainable Use and Community Based Innovation; Stephen M. Wheeler's Sustainability in community development; Community-based tourism homestays' capacity to advance the Sustainable Development Goals: A holistic sustainable livelihood perspective by Khamsavay Pasanchay and Christian Schott, and Community-based Entrepreneurship and Rural Development Creating favourable conditions for small businesses in Central Europe by Matthias Fink, Stephan Loidl and Richard Lang, one can find attempts to explore the different dimensions of community-owned sustainability approach to frame the purpose of the present research study. Rashed Al Mahmud, talk about the intricacies of the largest surviving mangrove forest in the world by studying the traditional and customary knowledge and rules and beliefs practised by the Traditional Resource Users (TRUs), in order to bring participatory insights of the indigenous people and local communities. Similarly, Wheeler seeks to provide some basic background on the concept of sustainability and how it may apply to both the practice and content of community development and to develop creative strategies and processes that will work within the local context and with its constituencies to improve long-term human and ecological welfare. Schott and Nhem (2018), in their analysis of the impact of community-based development in rural communities, talks about how homestays are a critical CBT component given tourists need lodging and the capacity to involve many village families and are thus making a positive contribution to lifting whole families out of poverty while retaining decision-making within the community, and finally, Lang and Fink (2019) made an attempt to show that how the creation of a favourable environment for small businesses in rural regions is a key issue in creating jobs and increasing quality of life, which helps the proposed research study to get an idea on the importance and vitality of small business in raising the bar of empowerment and employability.

On a same note, Nath (n.d.) and Basak et al. (2021), talk about the recognition of community-based approaches to the management of environment and development and traces the emergence of the concept of "Sustainable Development" and using the Structural Equation Modelling (SEM) sought to look into the connection between sustainable Homestay tourism and tourist's satisfaction in Darjeeling Himalaya and shows how sustainable homestay tourism development is closely related to tourist satisfaction in three ways viz. socio-cultural, economic, and environmental sustainability. Using this as one of the reference points the proposed study gets a fair enough idea of the nature and role of homestays and the way they work for customer satisfaction.

Using these works in the referral point this chapter tries to understand how the spirit of a sustainable development has been used in the present time especially with regard to community based entrepreneurship like homestays in the Kalimpong region of the sub Himalayan landscape. Further, in order to understand how competition has law in the Indian context has promoted and boosted the growth of many such community based eco-friendly entrepreneurship the following works were duly taken in to consideration. Similarly works on Completion law in India like; The Competition Act, 2002 (Bare Act), Universal Publications, gives an in-depth idea about the legislation passed in the Parliament of India to provide, keeping in view of the economic development of the country, for the establishment of a Commission to prevent practices having adverse effect on competition, to promote and sustain competition in markets, to protect the interests of consumers and to ensure freedom of trade carried on by other participants in markets, in India, and for matters connected therewith or incidental thereto.

Vijay Pratap Singh Chauhan, Aakriti Thakur and Shruti Khaitan's work on Competition Law Tackling Sustainability Goals: An Analysis of International Practices and the Challenges Ahead National Law School Business Law Review; looks into the ever-increasing awareness of the climate change and has put the need for a responsive and pro-active competition law regime fostering sustainability into the limelight. It also emphasises that sustainability and the revision of competition framework have gained significant importance in recent times.

Siddiqui and Anand (2022) in their work entitle, Competition Policy and Sustainability: A Difficult Path to Tread; Report submitted to the Competition Commission of India, make a holistic attempt to report how the role of competition law intersects with the overarching aim of sustainability and examine if the competition laws hinder the growth of sustainability initiatives and co-operations in the corporate world. They have also analysed the recent developments in Europe with regards to green transformations and competition authorities, and put forward suggestions on how competition law in India and other places can be conducive to and promote the goal of sustainable development.

Ramappa (2009) in his book, Competition Law in India: Policy, Issues and Developments, discusses the Competition Act, 2002, and subsequent the major amendments to it, in 2006 and 2007. The book makes a detailed study of key issues including anti-competitive agreements, abuse of dominant position, and combinations (acquisitions and mergers). It further analyses the roles of authorities such as the Competition Commission of India, the Director-General and the Competition Appellate Tribunal in enforcing the provisions of the Act.

Holmes et al. (2021) identifies the challenges of integrating environmental considerations into competition analysis presented by the existing framework, whether through cooperation by businesses, practices by dominant companies, or consideration of sustainability efficiencies in merger assessments. Practical examples across various sectors are also provided, alongside agency views from different jurisdictions, to illustrate how competition policy can facilitate a sustainable economy.

Competition Policy and Sustainable Development: Post Workshop Report have endeavoured to find how competition law and sustainable development intersect. The chapters have emphasised on efficient resource allocation, protecting product quality, and promoting technological advancement and innovation. The document stresses that competition authorities will have a considerable influence on the direction of sustainability-related business practices.

Nowag (2020) in his article entitled, Sustainability & Competition Law and Policy – Background Note: This paper explores the interaction between on the one hand competition law and policy and on the other sustainability. It first charts the historical development of sustainability and its three components: the environmental, the economic, and the social. Then, it explores the normative questions of whether sustainability should play a role in competition law and policy. The main part of the paper shows how sustainability features within the more technical questions of the substantive application of competition law, highlighting less and more contentious areas.

RESEARCH OBJECTIVE

The main objective of this empirical research is to access the how the livelihood challenges of the local communities like zero poverty, empowerment, sanitisation, inequalities, decent work and economic growth can be tackled and structurally managed by the popularisation and promotion of the homestay economy in the region supplemented by a strong framework of competitive law of the land. Secondly, the study seeks to objectify how a simple yet effective tool of homestays has been working in a resilient way in the attainment and achievement of community empowerment projects and simultaneously an effective tool to accomplish the Millennium Development Goals (MDGs) making it a perfect example of a sustained, inclusive and sustainable self-sufficient model. The empirical research aimed to test the following four hypothesis while mapping the role of Homestays as spear head institutions for regulating fair competition and assisting in promoting innovation, improving productivity, and reducing the chances of monopolies in the Kalimpong District:

- Firstly: how has the homestays in the region can be a perfect and timely alternative model for a 'development without destruction framework' for the future we aspire for.
- Secondly, an alternative model how has these homestays in the region has been playing an incredible role in conserving, restoring and promoting the rich cultural heritage and environmental land scape against the unfettered model of over-concretisation of the district and non-sensitive hazardous developmental projects.
- Thirdly, how rise of homestays in the region with their novel and innovative ideas have bashed the monopolisation of organised sectors in the hotel and hospitality industry and had paved platform for improve productivity in a more efficiently and cost effective manner.
- Finally, how has these community based environment friendly model of homestays have been able to tackle the livelihood misfortunes and challenges of the region and the inhabitants like unemployment, and gender disparity through a sustained, inclusive and sustainable self-sufficient model.

METHODOLOGY

Based on the extensive literature review, to evaluate the selected indexes or variables like employability, gender, empowerment, sanitisation, and sustainable industrialization a sample of 30 homestays from the three different administrative zones of the District were selected using a probability simple random sampling design. The rational was to get a wider picture of the research area by keeping variable from all zones of the district. The samples (homestays) were selected in a ratio of 10:90, with 10 homestays in each of the three community development blocks- Kalimpong-I, Kalimpong-II & Gorubathan and data were collected from series of in-person to person semi-structured interviews, field notes and verbal communication with the stakeholders, which includes primarily the homestay owners and beneficiaries of such institutions. Finally, based on the collected data the proposed hypothesis (that can community-based development approach spearheaded by homestays be the model approach for attaining and achieving the global goals of sustainable development) was tested.

INTRODUCTION

In the pre-liberalisation era, the human-environment conflict took the globe by storm where it was thought that economic development and environment preservation cannot go hand in hand. However, liberalization and globalization opened a floodgate of thoughts and busted the myth. The Brundtland Report entitled "Our Common Future", highlighted that poverty was a "major cause and effect of global environment problems" (WBCED, 1987) thus it was inevitable to believe that economic development is essential and an inevitable balancing economic development with environment protection and preservation is core to sustainable development. With the opening up of the market economy and privatisation happening during the 1990s, there was a shift of focus. Contributions of private actors to sustainable development became the call of the day. The simultaneous balancing of the three pillars of sustainability, i.e., economics, environment and social equity further implied that economic growth is still possible while preserving the environment and that growth may actually foster ecological protection and social equity. Meanwhile, the United Nations Organisation came up with its UN Resolution 70/1 entitled "Transforming our World: The 2030 Agenda for Sustainable Development" or commonly known as the UN Sustainable Development Goals (SDGs) or 2030 Agenda, by the UN General Assembly, and referred this to a 'plan of action for people, planet and prosperity' (UNCTAD, 2021). This blueprint provides a roadmap which includes 17 sustainable development goals with 169 associated targets to be achieved by countries in realizing sustainable development. Here comes the question of interaction between sustainable development and competition law where more and more private players are part of economic contribution and economic development and climate change is a real crisis. It has been accepted in a workshop on "Competition Policy and Sustainable Development" held on 9 November, 2022 and also published in the post-workshop Report in July 2023 that the participation of business sector has made significant contributions through their commercial know-how, innovation capability and responsible consumption (APEC, 2023). Meanwhile to sustain and supplement such an ecology for a non-competitive space to promote and give platform to innovation and indigenous output completion law came as the legal safeguard.

Competition law, also known as antitrust law, is a set of regulations aimed at promoting fair competition and preventing anti-competitive practices in the marketplace. Its primary goal is to ensure that businesses compete fairly, consumers have choices, and markets remain open and competitive. Common practices that competition law addresses include price-fixing, market sharing, and abuse of dominant market positions, and mergers that could reduce competition. It is pertinent to draw an interface between sustainability and competition law to get a clearer picture. As already discussed previously, Sustainable practices focus on minimizing negative impacts on the environment, promoting social equity, and maintaining economic viability, one way competition law intersects with sustainability is by preventing companies from gaining excessive market power. When a single company or a small group of companies dominate a market, they can exert control over pricing, supply, and innovation. This can stifle competition and hinder the development and adoption of more sustainable practices by limiting the entry of new players or innovative solutions. Competition often encourages companies to innovate to gain a competitive edge. Innovation can lead to the development of more sustainable products, technologies, and processes. For instance, companies may invest in research and development to create environmentally friendly alternatives to existing products, driven by the need to differentiate themselves in a competitive market. Fair competition ensures that consumers have choices and can make informed decisions based on their preferences, including sustainability considerations. When competition is healthy, companies are motivated to offer products and services that align with consumer demand for more sustainable options. While competition law often discourages collaboration between competitors, there are instances where collaboration is allowed to achieve sustainability goals. For example, competitors might collaborate on research projects to develop industry-wide standards for environmentally friendly practices without violating competition rules. Competition law can play a role in preventing ‘Greenwashing’, which is the practice of exaggerating or misrepresenting a company’s environmental efforts. If a company falsely claims to be sustainable to gain a competitive advantage, it could be subject to legal action under competition law. Thus, competition law and sustainability are interconnected in complex ways. While competition law aims to ensure fair markets and prevent anti-competitive behaviour, sustainability considerations emphasize the need for responsible business practices that balance economic, social, and environmental concerns. (Vijay Pratap Singh Chauhan, et al)

The challenge is to find a harmonious balance between these two objectives to create a business environment that promotes innovation, consumer choice, and long-term well-being. In drawing the relation between competition law and sustainability competitive authorities play a critical role in ensuring fair and competitive market and the mandate is that effective communication is made to the stakeholders. This paper makes an evaluation on how the arena of competition law has helped in the attainment and accomplishment of sustainable development goals in one of the districts of the sub-Himalayan region of West Bengal India by promoting an alternative eco system of environment friendly and community based homestays against the over concretisation and unaccountable monopolistic business polices as an offshoot of a capitalist mode of production.

UNDERSTANDING COMPETITION LAW

According to the Competition Act, 2002, enacted by Parliament in the Fifty-third Year of the Republic of India, Competition Law can be called as a legal framework which is used keeping in view of the economic development of the country. They mainly seek to prevent practices that may having adverse effect on competition, to promote and sustain competition in markets, to protect the interests of consumers and to ensure freedom of trade carried on by other participants in markets, in India, and for matters connected therewith or incidental thereto. To put it in a more simplistic way, these legal frameworks helps in bashing the monopolistic trade nexus and gives spaces for indigenous and smaller entrepreneurs in the market. With increased awareness on sustainable development and role of competition law, various governments and blocs have become pro-active in the area of the interplay between competition laws and sustainability. India being one of the fastest growing countries has been putting effort in exploring the means to explore aspects of competition law to bring in sustainability. Competition law in India aims to promote fair competition and prevent anti- competitive practices. By ensuring that markets remain competitive, businesses are encouraged to innovate to gain a competitive edge. This innovation can extend to the development of sustainable products, technologies, and practices. For example, companies might invest in research and development to create environmentally friendly alternatives to existing products, driven by the need to differentiate themselves in a competitive market. Competition law in India and sustainability have interconnected implications. While competition law focuses on maintaining competitive markets and preventing anti-competitive practices, sustainability emphasizes responsible business practices that balance economic, social, and environmental concerns. A harmonious balance between these objectives can lead to an environment where competition drives innovation toward sustainable practices, while ensuring that companies operate fairly and responsibly. Jyoti Jindgar Bhanot, Secretary, Competition Commission of India, drew the attention towards the competition law framework which has an "in-built flexibility to account for sustainable development and climate change" (The Business Line, 6 December, 2022).

THE GENESIS AND SCOPE OF COMPETITION LAWS IN INDIA

The development and objectives of competition law in India are aimed at promoting fair competition, preventing anti-competitive practices, and fostering a competitive market environment. The Competition Act of 2002, along with its subsequent amendments, serves as the legal framework for competition law in India. Overall, the development of competition law in India reflects the country's commitment to creating a level playing field for businesses, protecting consumer interests, and fostering economic growth through fair competition. The law aims to strike a balance between promoting healthy competition and preventing practices that could hinder market dynamics and consumer welfare. The (Competition Bare Act, 2002)

The primary objectives of competition law in India include:

a) Promotion of Competition: The fundamental objective of competition law in India is to promote competition in the market. Healthy competition encourages businesses to strive for excellence, innovate, and provide better products and services to consumers. Prevention of Anti-Competitive Practices: Competition law seeks to prevent practices that hinder or distort competition. Such practices include price-fixing, bid-rigging, market-sharing agreements, and abuse of dominant market positions. By curbing these practices, competition law ensures that markets remain open, competitive, and accessible to all players.
b) Protection of Consumer Welfare: Competition law is designed to safeguard consumer interests by ensuring that consumers have access to a variety of choices and products at competitive prices. Preventing anti-competitive practices helps prevent unfair pricing and manipulation of market conditions that could harm consumers. Promotion of Innovation: Competition stimulates innovation and encourages businesses to develop new products, technologies, and services to gain a competitive edge. By creating an environment where companies need to continually improve to remain competitive, competition law indirectly fosters innovation. Efficient Allocation of Resources: A competitive market environment encourages the efficient allocation of resources, as businesses strive to use resources effectively to maximize their competitiveness. This efficiency can lead to improved productivity and economic growth.

c) Encouraging Small and Medium Enterprises (SMEs): Competition law aims to prevent dominant market players from unfairly squeezing out smaller competitors. This protection of SMEs encourages a diverse business ecosystem and prevents the concentration of economic power.
d) Regulation of Mergers and Acquisitions: Competition law regulates mergers, acquisitions, and other combinations to ensure that they do not significantly reduce competition in the market. The goal is to maintain market diversity and prevent monopolistic tendencies.
e) Consumer Choice: By maintaining competitive markets, competition law empowers consumers with choices. This enables consumers to select products and services that align with their preferences, including sustainability and ethical considerations.
f) Market Advocacy and Education: The Competition Commission of India (CCI) engages in competition advocacy and education to promote competition culture and raise awareness about the benefits of competition among businesses, consumers, and government bodies.
g) Globalization and International Trade: Competition law helps ensure that Indian businesses can compete fairly in the global market. It aligns with international best practices and contributes to India's participation in international trade and commerce.

UNDERSTANDING THE CONCEPT OF ECO-FRIENDLY TOURISM

Eco-tourism is one such area where completion law has had a massive impact. Though Eco- tourism and competition law are two distinct concepts, but they can intersect in various ways, especially considering the promotion of fair competition and sustainable practices within the eco-tourism industry. Eco-tourism involves responsible travel to natural areas that conserves the environment, sustains the well-being of local communities, and provides educational experiences for travellers. It emphasizes minimizing the negative impacts of tourism on the environment, promoting cultural awareness, and supporting local economies. Sustainable practices are at the core of eco-tourism, and they encompass areas such as waste reduction, wildlife conservation, community engagement, and low-impact infrastructure development. Although the idea of sustainable tourism first emerged during the 1970s, (Nowag, 2020) with the declaration of the 17 goals it was soon considered the most viable alternative to the hard tourism sector and a strategy which promotes "development without destruction" (Schrijver; 2010). With its focus on environmental sustainability and viable economic potential for ecologically 'responsible tourism,' (Siddiqui; 2022) this alternative approach of soft tourism has off-late become a popular and effective model not only in natural resource management but catering for the growing demands of society like gender-gap, poverty, sanitisation and sustainable economic model with ecological viable industrialization and innovation. One such institution that has helps us to map the interplay between the ethics of completion law and an environmentally friendly sustainable inclusive developmental model are homestays.

In popular parlance, Homestays are considered to be alternative forms of hospitality and lodging where the visitors share the residence with the local family or host. It not only gives exposure and experience to the everyday life of the indigenous people but also provided a great platform to know witness and embrace the cultural and traditional uniqueness of such communities along with a boost to the socio economic upliftment of such areas. Far away from the mundane cacophony of the urban over concretised high rise and hotels these alternative institutions of hospitality also provided a best way for a nation state to accomplish a model of 'development form below' Stohr and Taylor's (1981) framework for a sustainable and non-competitive zone of promoting and provided spaces for 'locals' in their livelihood.

However the sustenance of such a non-competitive zone and unbiased monopoly order needs a rigid legal safeguard, and in the Indian context such precautionary steps for the promotion of a sustainable and inclusive economy of community based order is promoted by the legal framework of competition law.

ECO-TOURISM, SUSTAINABILITY AND COMPETITION LAW- THE INTERPLAY

One of the major structural and institutional changes that one could witness with the ratification of UN Agenda 2030 was a renewed thrust for community-based sustainable developmental approaches which were led primarily by the concept of sustainable tourism. India's commitment to attaining these goals was invigorated when at the UN Summit for the adoption of the Post-2015 Development Agenda, Prime Minister Narendra Damodardas Modi highlighted India's obligation to the world and envisaged its sheer commitment to prioritising a zero poverty-led sustained, eco-friendly, inclusive and sustainable economy induced by a sustainable consumption model.

Although in Indian context the Competition Act of India primarily focuses on competition-related issues, and its provisions are not explicitly linked to sustainability. Nevertheless, competition law and indigenous business like eco-tourism e.g., homestays, intersect in various ways, especially when it comes to ensuring that indigenous businesses have a fair opportunity to compete in the marketplace. Indigenous businesses, like homestays, often linked to the economic development and self-determination of indigenous communities, can face unique challenges that competition law may address. This framework ensures that eco-tourism operators compete fairly, which can lead to better services and experiences for tourists. It prevents market dominance that might allow a single provider to dictate terms, ensuring that multiple eco-tourism operators can thrive and offer unique sustainable experiences. Competition law promotes consumer choice, which is important in the eco-tourism sector. Tourists seeking eco-friendly and responsible travel options benefit from a competitive marketplace where they can choose from a variety of operators that align with their values. Eco-tourism relies on conveying accurate information about the sustainability practices and impacts of a tour or destination. Competition law can prevent false or misleading advertising, ensuring that eco-tourism providers accurately represent their practices and benefits to consumers (Srivatsa, n.d.). In some cases, eco-tourism providers might collaborate on initiatives to protect local ecosystems or support community development. Competition law considerations come into play to ensure that such collaborations do not cross into anti-competitive behaviour, while still allowing for meaningful sustainable efforts. It goes without saying that competition law and eco-tourism share common goals of promoting fairness and sustainability. Competition law ensures that the eco-tourism industry operates in a way that benefits both tourists and local communities, while sustainable practices and responsible tourism are fundamental to the principles of eco-tourism. A harmonious balance between competition law and eco-tourism practices is essential to foster an industry that provides authentic, environmentally conscious, and socially responsible travel experiences (Srivatsa, n.d.).

Here are some key considerations highlighting the interplay and role which competition law plays in the context of eco-tourism initiatives like homestays:

a) Promoting Fair Competition for Eco-tourism: Competition law aims to create a level playing field in which businesses can compete fairly. This is particularly important for indigenous businesses, which may have historically faced barriers to entry and competition. Ensuring that indigenous businesses have equal opportunities to participate in the marketplace is a fundamental goal of competition law. Section 3 of the Competition Act prohibits agreements, including those with sustainability implications, which have the effect of appreciably preventing, restricting, or distorting competition. For example, agreements among companies to limit the production or sale of eco-friendly products could be challenged under this section.

b) Preventing Anti-Competitive Practices: Competition law prohibits anti-competitive practices that can harm businesses, including indigenous enterprises like eco-tourism involving homestays. This includes practices such as price-fixing, market-sharing agreements, and abuse of market power, which can negatively impact indigenous businesses' ability to compete. Section 4 prohibits enterprises with a dominant position in a relevant market from abusing their market power. If a dominant enterprise engages in practices that hinder the adoption of sustainable technologies or products, it could be scrutinized under this section.

c) Supporting Economic Self-Determination: Indigenous businesses are often seen as a means of achieving economic self-determination and reducing dependence on external economic forces. Competition law helps protect indigenous businesses from anti-competitive behaviour that could undermine their economic viability.

d) Collaboration and Fair Competition: Indigenous businesses may engage in collaborations and partnerships to pool resources and compete effectively. Competition law allows for collaborations that enhance competition while ensuring that they do not harm consumers or unduly restrict competition. Although not directly related to sustainability, Section 5 of the Act addresses mergers and acquisitions that could substantially lessen competition. If such combinations affect industries involved in sustainability, like renewable energy or environmental services through eco-tourism, they may be subject to scrutiny. Eco-tourism providers like homestays may collaborate to implement sustainable practices collectively, such as wildlife conservation or environmental education initiatives. Eco-tourism providers may collaborate to implement sustainable practices collectively, such as wildlife conservation or environmental education initiatives. Competition law allows for collaborations that enhance sustainability efforts without unduly restricting competition. Eco-tourism relies on conveying accurate information about the sustainability and environmental impact of tours and destinations. Competition law can address false or misleading advertising (greenwashing) in the eco-tourism sector, promoting transparency and consumer trust.

e) Protection from Predatory Practices: In order to bring sustainability in small businesses like eco-tourism, often smaller in scale, can be vulnerable to predatory pricing or other anti-competitive tactics by larger competitors. Competition law can protect against such practices (Siddiqui & Anand, 2022).

Competition law and eco-tourism intersect in various ways, especially in promoting fair competition, preventing anti-competitive practices, and supporting the sustainable development of the eco-tourism industry. Here's how competition law can impact and benefit eco-tourism:

a. Eco-tourists often seek authentic and sustainable experiences: Competition law ensures that consumers have a choice by promoting a competitive marketplace where various eco-tourism operators can offer different sustainable experiences, catering to diverse consumer preferences. In some cases, there may be a tension between conservation efforts and competition. For example, limiting the number of visitors to a sensitive ecological area can be seen as necessary for preservation but may restrict competition.

b. Competition law can play a role in finding a balance between these interests. Competition law indirectly incentivizes eco-tourism providers to adopt sustainable practices. In a competitive market, businesses may differentiate themselves by offering eco-friendly options or environmentally responsible tours.
c. Competition law ensures that small eco-tourism operators have equal access to the market and are not disadvantaged by larger competitors. This promotes diversity in the industry and allows smaller operators with unique sustainable offerings to thrive.
d. The Competition Act provides for the power of inquiry, investigation and imposing penalties where the provisions of the Act are violated. Under Section 19, the Competition Commission of India (CCI) can initiate inquiries into anti-competitive agreements and abuse of dominance. If such agreements or practices hinder competition in sectors with sustainability goals, they could be investigated.
e. Also, Section 27 allows the CCI to impose penalties on enterprises found to be in violation of its provisions and the Competition Commission of India (CCI) can impose a penalty of up to 10% of the average turnover of the violating entity for the preceding three financial years. Penalties can be significant and act as a deterrent against anti-competitive practices that could hinder sustainability initiatives. Again, Failure to notify mergers and combinations that meet the prescribed thresholds can result in a penalty of up to 1% of the total turnover or assets, whichever is higher, of the combination.
    1. Section 42 lays down that if an enterprise fails to comply with CCI orders, it can face a penalty of up to 1 crore rupees (10 million INR) or imprisonment for a term of up to three years or both. Section 26 also empowers the CCI to conduct a market investigation and finds violations, it can issue cease-and-desist orders and require the payment of fines as deemed appropriate. (Competition Bare Act, 2002) It's important to note that the specific penalties imposed may vary based on the facts and circumstances of each case. The CCI has the authority to determine the appropriate penalties, taking into account the severity of the violation, the economic harm caused, and other relevant factors.
f. Additionally, the Act also provides for the imposition of penalties on individuals involved in violations, including officers and directors of the enterprise. The Act aims to deter anti-competitive behaviour and ensure that competition is preserved and protected in the Indian marketplace. It has become evident that competition law supports the eco-tourism industry by ensuring that businesses compete fairly, consumers have choices, and sustainable practices are promoted and not undermined by anti-competitive behavior. A competitive eco-tourism marketplace benefits both businesses and tourists, promoting sustainability, transparency, and responsible tourism practices.

To evaluate the credibility of such homestays in achieving the SDGs, this chapter intends to choose the District of Kalimpong located in the sub-Himalayan region of West Bengal as its research area. The region has been selected due to two main reasons- firstly owing to its pristine biodiversity and landscape and sharing its borders with Sikkim and dooars off-late Kalimpong has been the most preferred tourist destination of the region after Darjeeling, making it a lucrative tourism economy site; secondly despite the high influx of tourist and visitors the manner in which the community-owned developmental projects like homestays have been flourishing in the district has discouraged over-concretisation and simultaneously proving as a potential actor to deliver its commitment in achieving the global goals like gender parity, poverty alleviation, inclusive and sustainable economic growth and ecosystem. Homestays, are not only considered as a potential actors in achieving the goals and brand it as a model of tourism which not only promotes community-based eco-friendly 'responsible tourism', but is an indispensable tool for sustained participative entrepreneurship with a strong commitment of providing livelihoods to the locals and an viable alternative to the monopolistic trade polies of the big-business. Today homestays in Kalimpong District have been have been a silent yet an effective player in achieving the Sustainable Development Goals (SDG-1)- poverty, (SDG-2)- zero hunger, (SDG-5)- gender parity, (SDG-6)- clean water and sanitisation, (SDG-8) sustained, inclusive and sustainable economic growth (empowerment), (SDG-9) sustainable industrialization and innovation,(SDG-10) reduce inequality, (SDG-12) sustainable consumption and production and (SDG-15) protect, restore and promote sustainable use of terrestrial ecosystems.

LOCATING THE RESEARCH AREA

The district town of Kalimpong is located in the sub Himalayan region of West Bengal. It shares its borders with the State of Sikkim in the North and the forests of dooars in its south. Historians and scholars have put forward various meanings of the word Kalimpong. Tamsang (1983) who wrote the highly informative book, The Unknown and Untold Reality about the Lepcha's opines that the original name is 'Kalenpung' which in the Lepcha language means "Hillock of Assemblage". He suggests that this name was distorted in the course of time into 'Kaleebung' and later into Kalimpong. The Tibetan translation of the word, Kalimpong, is "The Stockade of King Ministers" from the two Tibetan words 'Kalon' meaning Kings and Ministers and 'Pong' meaning Stockade. Some Tibetan Scholars translate 'Pong' as assembly, in which case Kalimpong would mean "Assembly of Kings and Ministers". The hill people also call Kalimpong as 'Kalibong" or the Black Spurs. However, the meaning that has found the most favour is "Ridges where we play". It is said that Lepcha tribesmen used to organize field sports here when not engaged in agricultural pursuits.(Kalimpong District, History) With a population of 49,403 (2011 Census), Kalimpong is one of the most pristine region in the sub Himalayan region that homes the rarest of flora, fauna in the region. Its impeccable landscape features meditating mountains, exotic plant varieties, terraced fields, breath-taking rivulets and waterfalls have made it as one of the most cherish and sought after destination for tourist across the globe. Kalimpong is blessed with natural beauty, heritage and multiple varieties of ethnicity, culture and hospitality. It is a perfect blend for Homestay tourism.

Historically, Kalimpong was a part of the Sikkimese or 'Donzong' kingdom which basically was inhabited by three major communities – the Lepchas (who called themselves the 'Rong' or the Ravine folk), the Bhutias and the Limbus (Tshongs). The first Chogyal (Divine Ruler) of Sikkim is believed by scholars, to have brought a consolidated rule over the whole of Sikkim which also included the area now known to be Kalimpong. During the colonial rule, it was the Anglo-Bhutan War in 1864 and the Treaty of Sinchula on 11 November 1865 that gave Kalimpong a status of a vital geo-strategic location. Kalimpong became an important centre for trade with Tibet due to the closeness of the town to the Jelepla Pass which allowed access to Central Tibet. The British government decided to open up Kalimpong as an alternative Hill Station to Darjeeling. The coming of the Scottish Missionaries who did significant work for the development of Kalimpong, and The British Government opened up Kalimpong for settlers from other places who came in large numbers and with their hard work and skill made Kalimpong what it is today. In the post-independence era, this area was transferred to the District of Darjeeling. It was only after this that Kalimpong was set on the development track. The economic development of Kalimpong took a back seat following the Chinese aggression in 1962 after which trade through Jelepla was closed.

Today, Kalimpong relies mostly on the business generated by the educational institutes and majorly only through tourism. Finally in the year 2017, with the upgradation of Kalimpong into a district development in the region has taken an altogether differ dimension with a more environment friendly and sustainable approach of balancing bio-diversity and tourism. Due to its diverse and breathtakingly vibrant natural positioning eventually within a shot span of time this district of sub Himalayan region has now been a face of change in the domain of alternative community based model of tourism and hospitality.

Administratively the region is divided in 4 zones: Kalimpong Municipality consists of 23 wards and 3 community development blocks: Kalimpong I, Kalimpong II and Gorubathan consisting of 42-gram panchayats. As of February 2022, there are a total of 402 homestays in the district which are mostly located in the rural / panchayat areas of Kalimpong I, II and Gorubathan blocks. (Kalimpong District, District Profile) To evaluate the indexes or variables like employability, gender, empowerment, sanitisation, and sustainable industrialization was identified and then categorized in a sample size of 30 homestays.

Figure 1. Thana map of Kalimpong District, West Bengal

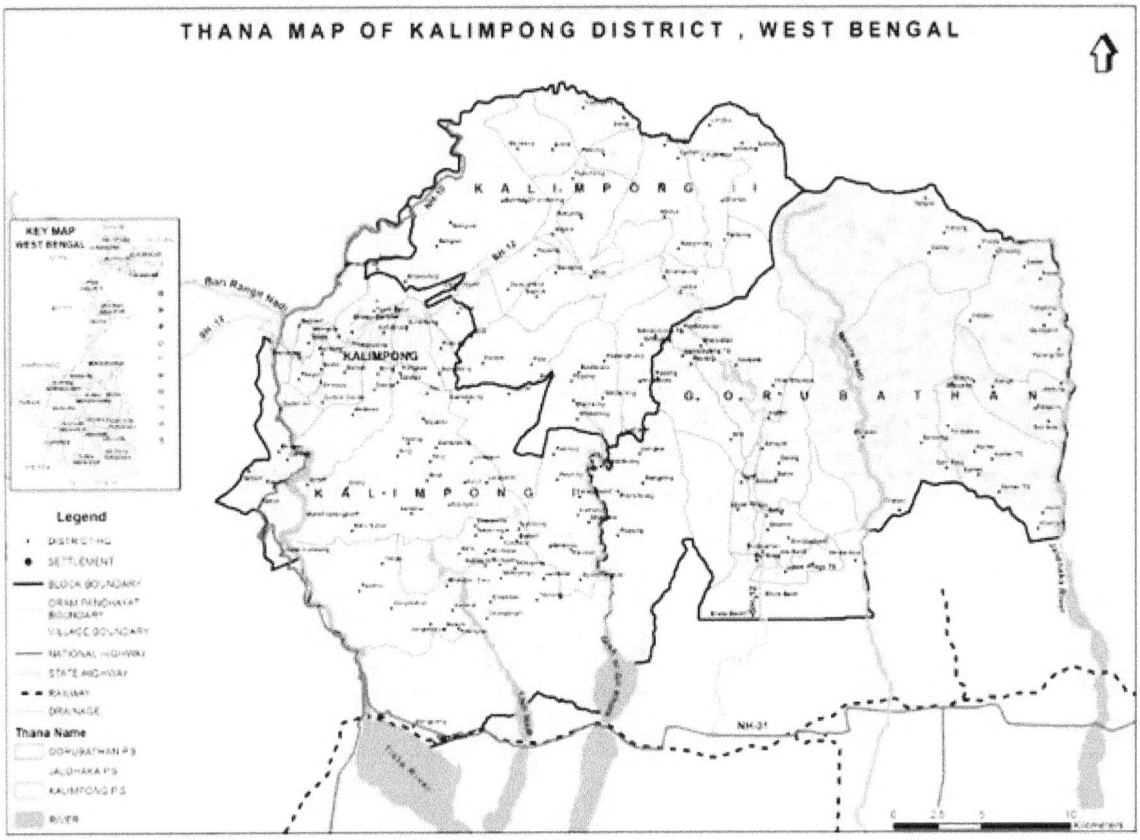

Table 1. List of the homestays those were surveyed

Sl. No	Name of Home Stay	Address	Block
1	Deep Homestay	Upper Gairigaon Jaldhaka Hydel Project, PO + PS Jaldhaka, Dist Kalimpong	Gorubathan
2	Jaldhaka Homestay	Phase -VI II No. P.O. + P.S. Jaldhaka Dist Kalimpong	Gorubathan
3	Karki Homestay	Jhandi, Upper Lungsel, P.O. Fagu, P.S. Gorubathan	Gorubathan
4	Trishna Homestay	Samsing Lower Ghumti Gaon, P.O. Samsing, P.S. Jaldhaka	Gorubathan
5	Rocky Island Homestay	Samsing Lower Ghumti Gaon, P.O. Samsing, P.S. Jaldhaka	Gorubathan
6	Sai Parijat Homestay	Shermali, Dalim GP, P.O. Fagu P.S. Gorubathan Dist Kalimpong	Gorubathan
7	Tempula Inn Homestay	Mandal Gaon km BPO Samsing, P.S. Jaldhaka,	Gorubathan
8	Estikuttum Homestay	Suntalay Busty, Nim GP, P.O. Lava P.S. Gorubathan,	Gorubathan
9	Meeyang Homestay	Upper Gairi Gaon, P.O + P.S Jaldhaka, Dist Kalimpong	Gorubathan
10	Yozonla Homestay	Kumai Naya Busty PO Kumai PS Jaldhaka Dist Kalimpong	Gorubathan
11	Sunrise Homestay	Upper Rabeek, Reshap Busty, P.O. Lava	Kalimpong-II
12	Tshering Homestay	Sillery Gaon, Upper Kashyem, Algarah	Kalimpong-II
13	Mountain View Homestay	Lower Dalap	Kalimpong-II
14	Parijat Eco Huts Homestay	Benda Busty, Kagay Bazar, Pedong	Kalimpong-II
15	Yours Kitchen and Homestay	Dokyong I Pedong	Kalimpong-II
16	Pradhan Homestay	Samdong II Kashyone GP	Kalimpong-II
17	Tshering Choden Homestay	Sillery Busty, Upper Kashyem	Kalimpong-II
18	Sumiksha Homestay	Sillery Busty, Upper Kashyem	Kalimpong-II
19	Sand Valley Homestay	Samdong II Kashyone GP	Kalimpong-II
20	Doon Valley Nature Resort	Lower Doon Loley Gram Panchayat, Block II Kalimpong	Kalimpong-II
21	Amisha Homestay	Burmaik GCP sangsay	Kalimpong-I
22	Chamling Homestay	Ramdhura, Burmaik, Munsong Pin 734315	Kalimpong-I
23	Yankee Homestay	Tagathang Lingsey	Kalimpong-I
24	Dukpa Homesta	Burmaik, Munson	Kalimpong-I
25	Niru I Homestay	Echhey Forest Village, Burmaik P.O, Munsong	Kalimpong-I
26	Mystery Garden	Takna Lolay	Kalimpong-I
27	Jwajalapa Homestay	Lower Lolay	Kalimpong-I
28	Jojolapa Homestay	Rubasta Sangmeer, Munsong Cinchona	Kalimpong-I
29	Little Heaven Homestay	Gitdubling Pakkang	Kalimpong-I
30	Basnet Homestay	Mairong Busty	Kalimpong-I

FINDINGS FROM THE SURVEY OF THE AFOREMENTIONED HOMESTAYS

a) **Viable alternative to monopolisation:** Two major events that changed the socio-economic profile of Kalimpong were- the incoming of Christian missionaries during the colonial period and the dawn of liberalisation in the post 1990s. Within a short span of time Kalimpong turned out to be one of the most popular and sought after destination for tourist and visitors across the globe after Darjeeling in the sub-Himalayan region. This created a wave of concretisation of hotel and hospitality in the region with nucleated settlement mainly centred on the urban spaces. This, where on one hand was beneficial for the rapid rise of the socio-economic parameters of the region on the other hand posed some serious threat to the existential question of sustenance of indigenous culture, tradition, innovation and productivity of the 'locale'. However, now with the incoming of a community based eco-friendly home stay model supplemented with a stringent and inflexible legal framework of competition law, the very basis of the monopolistic competition in the marketplace has been challenged. At present there are around 402 homestays in an around almost all administrative blocks of Kalimpong District creating a viable creative space for to challenge such biased and lopsided market policies of organised hard tourism. With flexible and cost effect policies of the state government and positioned in off beat pristine and surreal locations across the region these homestays have been the preferred option for the majority of the visitors and tourists in the region.

b) **Creating a gender neutral eco-system:** One of major findings that came from the filed on interrogating how these community based eco-tourist platforms are contributing for the greater cause of the society was its potentiality in creating a gender neutral society. It's been observed amongst most of the surveyed variables that the ownership of these homestays are primarily the women. Infant the management, administration and decision making role in majority of the homestays are controlled by the women (house wives or daughters) of the family, which in turn is creating an ecosystem of a gender neural society in Kalimpong. It was been observed that women who have knowledge of formal / informal educations were not only spearheading such ecology of community based empowerment platforms but were also been looked up by the community and society at large as source of inspiration and motivations for others. Due to their active involvement in the socio-economic process their decision making and choices in the family and society has manifested in a considerable manner. These community based homestays are not only bashing the rigidity of a patriarchy society but also creating a balanced framework where the new generations are culturally taught to rethink about and re-creating identities and recognition of roles based on gender lines.

c) **Uplifting the life and well-being:** One of the fascinating aspect the of the field report were the findings which predicted how these community based homestays are paving for a health and good livelihood pattern by uplifting the life and well-being of the people who are directly or indirectly affected by the whole system. These homestays are promoting an organic way of livelihood where not only the primary stake holders but members of the villages are getting benefitted and furthered by such secondary and tertiary activities. It's was been observed across almost all homestays in the region that once the institution starts operating immediately due to the spill over effect there are many small shops, fast food centres, farm fresh products and souvenir outlets comes into existence, which are mostly owned by the local people of that specific village. Thus the exclusivity of benefit which were once restricted in some specific location of the town are now turned into more inclusive in all-encompassing one in a more organic framework. This in a longer run is expected to bring in a radical change in the life and well-being of the people of the region and instead of a top-to bottom approach of allocation and utilisation of resource one could see a completely opposite Gandhian way of bottoms up approach of village based development and well-being.

d) **Empowering through employability:** Although in common parlance Homestays have been defined as an alternative or supplementary mode of accommodational services but while accessing the real implication of these community based homestays during field work it has been observed that they have now been a passive source of employability with the society and amongst the people of the society at large. According to the Centre for Monitoring India Economy (CMIE) reports, unemployment rates in Bengal soared to a record height of 22.1% in June 2021. Although economists argued that it was primarily due to the onslaught of the Covid-19 pandemic, this was an alarm call for academicians and researchers in projecting the possible future of India's stable social-political and economic functionality. In this backdrop homestays are emerging as a viable and most sustainable cost effective mechanism to boost up the ratio of employability in the region along with empowering the stakeholders. The owners of the surveyed homestays consider these alternative mediums of soft tourism as the most convenient way of generating the economic status of the family and the village which in turn help in eradicating the stagnancy of the flow of capital especially at the peripheries.

e) **Environment friendly and affordable model of renewable energy:** Eco-tourism spearheaded by popularisation of homestays in the region are also working as one of the most convenient way in tacking the global concern like climate degradation and eradicating carbon footprint. Almost majority of the homestays believes in the policy of less carbon emission and a sensitive and environment friendly approach to the question of development. Some of the significant and simplistic means to accomplish such objectives those were observed during the field work were usage of solar panels, kitchen gardens, harvesting and conservation of rain water, bio fuels, beautified oil lamps instead of night lamps etc. These simple yet extremely pertinent steps where on one seems to be a brilliant move of cost cutting and efficient managerialism on the same hand is balancing the unaccountable amount of hazardous and environmentally decrepit acts of the organised hard tourism and hospitality sector in the region. This environment friendly and affordable model of renewable energy is now being adopted across the regions as the most popular model and has been successful in mitigating the concerns of climate change.

f) **Sustainable and eco-friendly livelihood pattern:** Last but not the least the homestays in Kalimpong have now surfaced as the face of a sustainable and eco-friendly model of livelihood pattern. Instead of relying of authorities and government resources and polies these eco-huts and the stakeholders have generated a mental revolution amongst the members of the community especially in the peripheries. Participative and accountable governance in managing distributing and allocating the resources have been one of the major structural and operational change that one can witness while accessing the impact of these homestays in the region. Through this not only the goals of the sustainable developmental goals are being pursued but a new form of a self-reliant society is being constructed. In the near future it is expected that this new model of development without destruction and a softer side of hotels and hospitality industry is surely going to usher a new era of a viable ecology and nature friendly healthy structure.

CONCLUSION

Thus one may conclude by arguing that in the near future it is expected that this new model of development without destruction and a softer side of hotels and hospitality industry is surely going to usher a new era of a viable ecology and nature friendly healthy structure. By providing a favourable environment for an eco-friendly home stay culture in the sub-Himalayan regions of Kalimpong District of West Bengal there has been a significant strengthening of the overall growth of the region; not only, towards improving the employment situation but also a sustainable and environment friendly model of local based development. A positive development of such alternative model of a sustainable home stay culture also directly influences the local population's quality of life. On the one hand, for instance, creating jobs increases household incomes as well as living standards and also reduces the number of outward commuters. On the other hand, the increased inflow in taxes increases the financial scope for promotional programmes and infrastructure investment. Ideally, this initiates a positive cycle of development, as the increase in local taxes continuously improves the conditions for the population as well as enterprises and so increases the overall attractiveness of the region.

REFERENCES

APEC; Asia Pacific Economic Cooperation; Competition Policy and Sustainable Development. (2023). Competition Law Tackling Sustainability Goals: An Analysis of International Practices and the Challenges Ahead. *Business Law Review*.

Basak, D., Bose, A., Roy, S., Chowdhury, I. R., & Sarkar, B. C. (2021). Understanding sustainable homestay tourism as a driving factor of tourist's satisfaction through structural equation modelling: A case of Darjeeling Himalayan region, India. Current Research in Environmental Sustainability, 3, 100098.

Holmes, S., Snoep, M., Middelschulte, D., & Ahmad, S. (2021). Competition Law, Climate Change and Environmental Sustainability. (Concurrences)

Kalimpong District. (n.d.). *District Profile*. Kalimpong District. https://kalimpong.gov.in/administrative-map/

Kalimpong District. (n.d.). *History accessed.* Kalimpong District. https://kalimpong.gov.in/history/

Lang, R., & Fink, M. (2019). Rural social entrepreneurship: The role of social capital within and across institutional levels. Journal of Rural Studies, 70, 155-168.

Nath, V. (n.d.). *Critical assessment of community based approaches to environment and sustainable development*. Retrieved from https://www.cddc.vt.edu/knownet/lse-cbd.pdf

Nowag, J. (2020). *Sustainability & Competition Law and Policy – Background Note*. Organisation for Economic Co-operation and Development.

Ramappa, T. (2009). Competition Law in India: Policy, Issues, and Developments. Oxford University Press.

Schott, C., & Nhem, S. (2018). Paths to the market: analysing tourism distribution channels for community-based tourism. Tourism Recreation Research, 43(3), 356-371.

Schrijver, N. (2010). *Development without Destruction: The UN and Global Resource Management (United Nations Intellectual History Project Series)*. Paperback.

Siddiqui, I. (2022). *Competition Policy and Sustainability: A Difficult Path to Tread*. IIT Madras.

Siddiqui, I. & Anand, K. (2022). *Competition Policy and Sustainability: A Difficult Path to Tread*. Available at SSRN 4056805.

Srivatsa, K. R. (n.d.). Competition law fit to assess sustainability, climate action. *The Hindu Business line*.

Stohr, W. B., & Taylor, D. R. (1981). Development From Above or Below? The Dialectics of Regional Planning in Developing Countries. Wiley.

Tamsang, K. (1998). The unknown and untold reality about the Lepchas. Lyangsong Tamsang

Tomislav, K. (2018). The concept of sustainable development: From its beginning to the contemporary issues. Zagreb International Review of Economics & Business, 21(1), 67-94.

UNCTAD. (2021). *United Nations Conference on Trade and Development*. UN.

WBCED. (1987). *Report of the World Commission on Environment and Development: Our Common Future*. WBCED.

KEY TERMS AND DEFINITIONS

Completion Law: They mainly seek to prevent practices that may having adverse effect on competition, to promote and sustain competition in markets, to protect the interests of consumers and to ensure freedom of trade carried on by other participants in markets, in India, and for matters connected therewith or incidental thereto.

Homestays: Usually a private house offering accommodation to paying guests.

Sustainable Development Goals: An aim to achieve an inclusive and sustainable vision for the world.

Chapter 10
Energy Security in Pakistan and Bangladesh:
Questioning the Sustainable Development Goals (SDG)

Debasish Nandy
Kazi Nazrul University, India

ABSTRACT

The issue of energy security has been one of the pertinent issues to the study of international relations. The South Asian states are facing a tremendous energy security crisis due to a lack of conventional energy sources. The high demands for energy and shortage of supply have posed an immense challenge to the states of South Asia. In this chapter, a comparative study will be done between Pakistan and Bangladesh to understand the energy security policy of the two states to address the sustainable development goals. Pakistan and Bangladesh have a huge crisis of energy due to their vast population. A power cut has been very common for both countries. This chapter will attempt to highlight the governmental initiatives to introduce green energy and will also shed light on the administrative lack to fulfill the sustainable development goals (SDGs). The lack of policy implementation by both governments will be investigated in this chapter. The content analysis method will be applied in this chapter.

1. INTRODUCTION

Energy security has become one of the key concerns both for Pakistan and Bangladesh. The shortage of conventional energy sources is very uncertain and limited. The high demand for energy, on the one hand, interrupted the supply chain and created a scarcity of energy security. The issue of apart from the financial aspect, the environment and pollution are two major aspects that impact energy security issues. Based on four parameters, a comparative study will be done on the energy security issue of Pakistan and Bangladesh. Energy security is a multifaceted notion that incorporates a country or region's institutional, legal, and regulatory components as well as its economic, political, and geopolitical dimensions. The first

DOI: 10.4018/979-8-3693-0390-0.ch010

Copyright © 2024, IGI Global. Copying or distributing in print or electronic forms without written permission of IGI Global is prohibited.

aspect is economics which deals with the economic responsibility of energy security. The economy of the importing country and global economic status impact the energy security of a country. The economic aspect addresses the effects of import dependency on unstable energy markets, the diversification of the primary energy mix, and the utilization of local resources, as well as the circular flow of energy. The political economy of energy security, which looks at how nations that export natural gas and crude oil and those that import it interact, is the second dimension. The geopolitics of international relations is the third component. This factor examines the effects and coalition, collaboration, or unilateral action for energy security. The fourth aspect of energy security consists of the legal, and regulatory frameworks in the local, regional, and international context (Taghizadesh-Hesary, et, al. 2019). All of the aspects are interrelated.

The above-mentioned four aspects are related to the SDGs of the United Nations Organizations (UNO). One of the fundamental needs for sustaining social progress is energy. Currently, electricity serves as the foundation for all industrialized nations. The Sustainable Development Goals (SDGs) of the United Nations (United Nations, 2016) are intended to end poverty, safeguard the environment, and ensure the prosperity of all people. Currently, 1.2 billion people worldwide do not have access to modern power, and 2.9 billion must cook with inefficient and polluting fuels like kerosene or firewood. The majority of these people are clustered in a dozen African and Asian nations. Energy security in least-developed countries (LDCs) is a serious issue that requires immediate attention.

The crucial aspect of energy security is projected in a new manner in the era of globalization. Due to the profound effects of globalization, South Asian states have been deeply concerned about their energy security in the twenty-first century (Nandy, 2019). Many steps are being implemented in the region's energy industry to guarantee a stable future. This is crucial to take action to guarantee the region has the energy sources it needs and that they are distributed properly to maintain stable socioeconomic development. The perception of energy security in developed and developing countries differs in various ways. The perception of risk in energy security, the role of the government, the nature of the threat, the supply chain, the fair price of energy, and energy distribution are very important concerns in energy security issues (Bielecki, 2002).

The sources of energy are diversified. The availability of energy resources, which are further quantifiable under the idea of 'diversification' has been inferred by modern discussion on energy security in the literature, generally or in a larger sense. The interpretation of diversity has three components, such as variety, balance, and disparity (Stirling, 2010). Variety measures the economically viable sources of primary energy, whereas balance assesses how much reliance or dominance each source has in the total energy mix. The dependency on energy sources by a recipient country often creates uncertainty. The Middle East region, the hub of the energy supply is always a turmoil region due to war, conflict, and terrorist attacks. So, the dependency on a particular region may interrupt the supply chain. The valuation of the currency is also an important factor in the determination of energy prices. On the subject of energy security, four key factors are crucial: first is the availability of geological resources: the second is access to geopolitical conditions; the third is the affordability of economic conditions; and fourth is the acceptability of environmental and societal conditions (Ang et al. 2015; Cherp & Jewell, 2024; Radovanovi et al., 2017). The next section will deal with the methodological part of this chapter which will lead to the technical aspect of the chapter.

2. RESEARCH OBJECTIVES, RESEARCH QUESTIONS, AND METHODOLOGY

There are three research objectives of this chapter— (1) To investigate the major challenges of energy security of Pakistan and Bangladesh. (2) To delineate the sources of renewable energy in Pakistan and Bangladesh. (3) To search the policy initiatives and policy implementations of Pakistan and Bangladesh towards energy security. This chapter is based on three research questions— (1) What are the key challenges of energy security in both Pakistan and Bangladesh? (2) What is the role of renewable energy sources to mitigate energy sources? (3) What initiatives and policies have been taken to mitigate energy security by both countries? The content analysis method has been applied in this chapter. Both primary and secondary data are used in this chapter. The existing literature has been reviewed and tried to find out the gap.

3. THE EXPERIENCE OF PAKISTAN

This section will highlight the experience of Pakistan on the issue of energy security. Energy security in Pakistan is a very crucial issue. Energy is a vital component of the process of economic expansion. Energy must be available in adequate quantities and continuously to support sustainable economic growth. The key issue with energy security is whether there will be an adequate supply of affordable, reliable electricity to meet future energy demands. The energy supply and demand gap is employed in this study as a stand-in for energy security. Both in the short- and long-term terms, the unidirectional causality goes from the energy demand and supply gap to economic growth. Low energy security in Pakistan halts economic progress, according to this link, which is negative and statistically significant in both the short and long term. The study concludes that the government should concentrate on improving the management of both the supply and demand for energy (Mahamod & Tayyab, 2018). The province of Baluchistan in Pakistan has a big gas reserve. It is the least advanced and industrially backward province. The provincial government could not use energy to advance industrial growth. Due to its geographical proximity to Iran, Pakistan cannot become independent and is dependent on Iran for its oil and gas needs. Pakistan has experienced many social, political, and economic crises as a result of an unbalanced economic policy and improper policy implementation based on natural resources. There is no significant energy policy in Pakistan that could support economic expansion. Due to its excessive reliance on energy imports from the Middle East and the lack of domestic alternative energy-producing technology, it was unable to experience the quickest economic growth. The equal distribution of energy policy has not been implemented domestically. The several aspects of the energy issue of Pakistan will be analyzed in the following sub-sections.

3.1 Major Challenges of Emery Supply in Pakistan

Every year Pakistan imports a huge quantity of energy from abroad to mitigate its demands. As per the data of the State Bank of Pakistan (2018), the total amount of energy imports of Pakistan was worth US $ 14.4 billion in the financial year (FY) 2017-18. In 2016-17 the total amount of energy imports was US $ 10.9 billion. The incensement in energy volume happened in Pakistan due to the rapid hike of energy prices in the world market and the incensement in internal demands.

The question of energy security for an energy-deficient country, like Pakistan depends upon numerous factors which are as follows—

Firstly, the supply chain of energy is often interrupted due to 'price shock'. Secondly, the relational equations between the exporting countries and exporting countries are another key factor in energy security. Thirdly, the volatility of the global financial market and the financial downfall of the importing country impact the energy security of a country. The financial crisis of Pakistan has been accurately shown in 2022 which is responsible for lowering the capacity of payment of imported fuel. Due to the shortage of foreign reserves, the Pakistani government has to face a lot of problems in the payment of imported fuel. Fourthly, the lack of a proper energy policy and the inability to implement the existing policy are also major constraints to the energy security of Pakistan. Fifthly, the political instability, reckless terrorism, and military influence in the decision-making process interrupted the energy crisis in Pakistan. The actual demands, finding new destinations of energy sources, and alternative energy sources have not been searched by the government of Pakistan properly. Sixthly, apart from the deficiency of funds, the bureaucratic lethargy and the lack of facilitating political and monitoring environment stereotypically limit the flow of the foreign direct investment (FDI) in the country (Malik et al., 2019). Being a state-financially crippled and debt-laden country, Pakistan has an additional liability to the donor states and other international funding agencies. The financial profile of the country has been negative. It was on the 'gray list' due to the gross financial irregularities and unregulated economy. Therefore, the external donor widely showed their unwillingness to give further financial assistance to Pakistan which not only barred energy adequacy but also energy security. Eighthly, Pakistan has been facing an acute financial crisis since 2022. Pakistan's most recent attempt to purchase liquefied gas on the world spot market has been unsuccessful. Pakistan is already dealing with an energy crisis. In addition to its political unrest, Pakistan is also dealing with its currency's depreciation, a hefty external debt load, foreign exchange reserves, and an elevated danger of sovereign default (The Economic Times, 2023).

3.2 Conventional Sources of Energy in Pakistan

Pakistan's energy needs are met by several conventional and industrial sources. Over the past few years, the proportion of different primary energy sources in the energy supply mix has stayed at 43.5% for oil, 41.4% for gas, 0.3% for liquefied petroleum gas (LPG), 4.5% for coal, 9.2% for hydroelectricity, and 1.1% for nuclear electricity.

(i) **Natural gas** is more has more demand than other fuels because of advances in technologies for exploration and production, the fact that it produces less harmful combustion products per unit of energy produced, the fact that it has several new applications including transportation fuel and the fact that it is also less expensive. The first natural gas discovery in Pakistan occurred in 1952 near Sui. It is the nation's biggest gas reserve. Out of the original 42.67 MTOE (million or mega tonnes of oil equivalent) of recoverable natural gas reserves, 26.43 MTOE have already been produced, leaving 16.25 MTOE of viable natural gas reserves of natural gas, Pakistan is placed 29th.

(ii) **Oil** is another source of energy in Pakistan. The Ministry of Petroleum and Natural Resources reports that imports of crude oil, high-speed diesel, and fuel oil cover the remaining 82% of overall demand, leaving only 18% for domestic crude oil to satisfy. For $ 4.4 billion, 8.3 million tons of crude oil, and 4.2 million tons of High Speed Diesel (HSD). About 38.3% of the nation's principal commercial energy source comes from oil. The biggest users of oil are the transportation and power industries.

(iii) **Coal** is another important source of energy in Pakistan. Despite the existence of vast coal reserves, coal only makes up 7.6% of the major energy supplies in the nation. In the Tharparkar era, the Southeastern part of Pakistan had 175 billion tons of coal. The coal has a high moisture level of 26% to 55%, although it has low ash and Sulphur concentrations. There is only a coal-fired power plant in Pakistan, 150 megawatts (MW) Lakhra Power Station, and it is currently operating below capacity.

(iv) **Hydropower** is a very effective energy source in Pakistan. Pakistan's energy mix has always included hydropower generation and will continue to do so. Pakistan's energy mix has always included hydropower generation and will continue to do so. In 1960, hydropower accounted for 70% of all electricity produced; by 2004-2005, that number had dropped to 30%. Pakistan has an estimated 40000 MW of hydropower potential of which only 6494 MW, or 16 of the total, have been produced thus far (Uqaili, et, al. 2004). Former Prime Minister of Pakistan, Imran Khan raised US $ 500 million in 2021 to build the US $ 14 billion Diamer-bhasha Dam. The dam is now in the early construction stage and is anticipated to be finished in 2028. The dam will increase the system's hydroelectric output by 4,500 MW. In a similar vein, work on the Mohmand Dam began in 2019, the first year the PTI government was in Office. The capacity of this project will be 800 MW (Siddiqui, 2022).

(v) **Nuclear power** is an alternative energy source in Pakistan. Pakistan generates limited energy through nuclear power. In 1972, Pakistan's first nuclear energy plant started to generate electricity in Karachi with the help of the Canadian government. It could produce 125 MW of electricity during that time. Pakistan currently has two nuclear power plants. Now, the Karachi nuclear power plant can produce 137 MW, and the Chashma nuclear power plant can produce 325 MW of electricity. Only 2.9% of the total generation, or 462 MW, is provided by nuclear power.

3.3 Sources of Green Energy in Pakistan

Some renewable energy sources in Pakistan can be called 'green energy' or 'eco-friendly energy'. The green energy sources of Pakistan are as follows—

(i) **Solar power** is the most popular source of renewable energy. Pakistan has potential sunlight which is available for nine and a half hours daily. After the government implemented a set of support policies to encourage the development of renewable energy, solar power entered Pakistan's energy mix in 2013. According to the Pakistan Economic Survey, six solar power facilities with a combined capacity of 430 MW started operating commercially over the past five years and are presently supplying electricity to the grid. More businesses and industries in Pakistan are resorting to captive solar solutions as a result of increased electricity prices and an unstable grid supply. In the big cities of Pakistan, it has been noticed that many households installed rooftop solar panels. The World Bank provided US $ 100 million to the Sind Solar Energy Project. It will help to produce 400 MW of electricity. Private companies are working on installing solar home systems. The World Bank estimates that Pakistan's current electricity needs could be satisfied by solar photovoltaic power generation on just 0.071% of the nation's land area (World Bank, 2020).

(ii) **Windmill** is a significant source of renewable energy in Pakistan. In the coastal regions of Sindh and Baluchistan, there is significant potential for wind energy use (International Trade Administration, 2022). The southern coastal regions of Sindh and Baluchistan have been turned into a wind energy corridor by the Pakistani government. According to data from Pakistan's Meteorological Department, the country's coastline belt is 60 km (Gharo Keti Bandar) and 180 km long, with a potential for 50,000 MW of wind turbine-based electricity generation. There are 26 private wind farms active in Pakistan which can generate about 1335 MW of electricity.

(iii) **Bioenergy** is a very cheap source of renewable energy in Pakistan. In the country, biomass is thought to produce 50,000 GWh annually. Pakistan's metropolitan areas generate 64,000 tons of municipal solid waste (MSW) every day. 13,900 Gwh of energy are expected to be produced by MSW. Massive biomass reserves may be found in Pakistan's rural areas, which can also generate 12 million m3 of biogas daily.

3.4 Policy Initiative Towards Energy Security in Pakistan

The government of Pakistan has taken several initiatives for energy security. Firstly, the government of Pakistan has adopted a 'renewable energy policy' that aims to generate 60% of all energy from renewable sources by 2023. Renewable energy can help Pakistan to reduce carbon emissions by up to 223.6 million metric tons. Secondly, the government has adopted an energy efficiency and conservation policy. There are several chances in this industry as Pakistan is aiming to save 3 million tons of oil equivalents of energy by 2023 as part of its strategic Plan (2020-2023). Energy efficiency and conservation could allow the nation to conserve up to 10-15% of its primary energy source. Thirdly, by 2030 Pakistan will be a country of 263 million population. The electricity demand will be much higher than at present. The government of Pakistan has initiated to reduce the dependency on expensive imported fossil fuels and move towards renewable energy (Switzerland Global Enterprise, 2021). Fourthly, the government of Pakistan is trying to reduce the emission of greenhouse gases from fossil-based power plants. Fifthly, the government has welcomed foreign investors to invest in the energy sector of Pakistan. Sixthly, Pakistan has enhanced its oil diplomacy with the Gulf countries to get an uninterrupted energy supply.

4. BANGLADESH

This section will discuss various aspects of the energy security of Bangladesh. The extended consequences of energy demand, which has increased dramatically over recent years, are Bangladesh's main energy production challenge. The current energy supply is made up of 53% traditional fuels and the remaining 47% of commercial sources, despite a 400% increase in commercial energy. As a result, commercial energy has displaced traditional energy sources, which have been a hallmark of Bangladesh's energy development since the 1980s. The nation's energy consumption in 2000 and the commercial energy demands predicted by the Gas Demand and Reserve Committee for business-as-usual Gross Domestic Product (GDP) growth rate (4.55) as well as the cumulative natural gas demand for various GDP growth scenarios (3%, 4.55%, 6%, and 7%) up to 2050 have been provided. It has been determined what domestic commercial, noncommercial, and nonrenewable energy sources are available. Energy development strategies for a developing nation like Bangladesh depend on maintaining relationships between energy consumption and economic growth. To guarantee the nation's energy security, a long-term comprehensive policy should be developed along with suitable solutions. The use of renewable energy sources needs to be prioritized, and major research and development programs should be carried out to advance renewable technologies (Nandy, 2019). This section will attempt to delineate various aspects of the energy security of Bangladesh and its challenges.

4.1 Major Challenges of Energy Supply in Bangladesh

The issue of energy security in Bangladesh is very crucial due to having numerous challenges, the majority of Bangladesh's power plants rely primarily on pricy imported fossil fuel energy sources. As a result, the power outage has intensified into a serious issue for the nation and is detrimental to its socioeconomic growth. Secondly, there is a wide gap between the demand and supply of electricity in Bangladesh. It has experienced of long hours loadshedding. According to the information posted PDB website on July 23, 2022, the nation serves fewer than 13,000 MW at the evening peak while having a total installed energy capacity of over 22,000 MW. Thirdly, according to Bangladesh's most recent power generation data, fossil fuels account for over 80% of the total share (Alam et al., 2020). Each year, a sizable number of energy sources like coal, and oil are currently depleting. Natural gas is the key fuel source of Bangladesh which steams power plants (Pranti et al., 2013). Due to the total reliance on natural resources gas is the fuel source for electricity production. The government intends to generate 2900 MW of electricity utilizing coal (Khan, 2009). The coal reserves are limited, which may interrupt the plan of power generation.

Fourthly, the conventional way of power generation is harming the environment which poses a serious threat to air pollution. The amount of emotion of carbon dioxide (CO2) through coal-based power plants is 40%. So, the more coal-based power plant will be dangerous to the environment of Bangladesh (Shrestha et al., 2009). To avoid environmental hazards from the emission of greenhouse gasses, the government of Bangladesh focusing on environmental governance (Nandy, 2023). Fifthly, the growing hike in the price of imported fuel is another challenge to Bangladesh. After starting Russian attacks on Ukraine, the price of petroleum products in the global market has rapidly increased which affects the supply of fuel in Bangladesh. It's because Brent prices at the start of 2022 were around 79 per barrel. Following Russia's invasion of Ukraine in February, the price of oil unexpectedly rose to USD 110 per barrel, the highest level in the previous 14 years (Jamal, 2022). Sixthly, lack of use of renewable energy sources. Seventhly, some other factors led to the energy crisis of Bangladesh in an alarming manner, such as (i) Rapid growth of population, (ii) excessive use of conventional sources of energy, (iii) Lack of consciousness among the people, (iv) inadequacy in running electric vehicles, (v) lack of governmental surveillance on using natural gas for domestic use.

4.2 Sources of Conventional Energy in Bangladesh

There are a few conventional sources of energy in Bangladesh which are as follows—

(i) **Natural Gas** is the key energy source of Bangladesh. About 26 gas fields have been found in the nation as of today, 24 onshore and two offshore, from the first discovery in 1955. Twenty gas fields are currently producing gas; one offshore field was depleted after producing for 14 years, while another offshore was not economically viable due to a limited reserve. 40.09 trillion cubic feet (TCF) was the estimated proved plus probable recoverable resource. 17.79 TCF of gas had previously been produced as of June 2020, leaving only 12.26 TCF of recoverable reserve in the category of proved plus probable. In Bangladesh, approximately 2978 MM cfp of natural gas is produced on average each day.

(ii) **Oil or petroleum** is the key energy source of the transport system of Bangladesh. Deiseal, gasoline, high-octane furnace oil, and other petroleum products make up 20% of the principal commercial energy source in the nation. The fuel is liquid. In Bangladesh, most of the liquid fuel is imported. Only 6% of the entire quantity of liquid fuel consumed is made up of locally generated gas condensate. Bangladesh imports over 4.3 million metric tons (approximately) of refined petroleum products annually in addition to 1.2 million metric tons of crude oil.

(iii) **Coal** is another source of conventional energy. In Bangladesh, 5 coal fields have been found so far, namely Barapukuria, Khalashpir, Phulbari, Jamalgonj, and Dighipara with a total reserve of roughly 31,000 million tons of coal which is comparable to 85 tcf gas. There are ample opportunities to find additional coal mines if nationwide exploration efforts are undertaken. Coal from 4 deposits of the found mines can now be extracted. Due to the depth of the deposits at Jamalganj, production may not be feasible with current technology.

(iv) **Condensate and Natural Gas Liquids (NGL)** are another source of energy in Bangladesh. A significant portion of the gas reserves in Bangladesh's northeastern region contain liquid hydrocarbons. The activity of extracting this liquid, especially value-added byproducts, is expanding.

(v) **Hydropower** is one of the key indigenous sources of energy in Bangladesh. The 230 MW Karnafuli Hydroelectric Power Station's generators were put into service between 1962 and 1988. It is Bangladesh's sole hydroelectric power facility. Although Bangladesh has a large number of rivers, its full potential has not been realized (Islam, et, al, 2020).

(vi) **Nuclear power** is going to be a potential energy source for Bangladesh. Bangladesh is moving towards nuclear energy to mitigate its energy crisis. Bangladesh and China signed a nuclear co-operation pact in 2005. Two 500 MW nuclear reactors were proposed by the Bangladesh Atomic Energy Commission for Rooppur (Choudhury, S.U. S, 2023). Bangladesh is moving on with the construction of its first nuclear plant and the International Atomic Energy Agency (IAEA) is assisting the government of Bangladesh with the safe, secure, and sustainable introduction of nuclear power by its mandate (Fisher, 2021).

4.3 Sources of Green Energy in Bangladesh

The major energy sources of Bangladesh are natural gas, oil, and coal. Apart from this, it has hydel power. But due to the shortage of water and huge consumption of water hydel power is being uncertain. In addition to using a lot of water, fuel production methods pollute water through spills and chemical pollution. Second, energy initiative water management procedures including distribution and purification are required. The energy-food nexus also serves as an input for production as well as a driver of demand (Sarkar et al., 2020). Considering the rapid demand for energy and recurrent power cuts, Bangladesh has been moving towards alternative energy sources. The government of Bangladesh is unable to manage the energy demands for the industrial sector and domestic sector. Moreover, the commitment to abiding SDGs' goal of pollution control is a must. The rapid hike of fuel in the global market also compelled the government of Bangladesh to not only depend on the country's conventional energy sources. There are a few sources of green energy in Bangladesh through which the deficiency of energy is to be mitigated.

(i) **Solar energy** is the key source of renewable energy which generates 39.5% of the total share of renewable energy of the country (Islam, 2009). Solar power-based electricity is connected to a mini-grid system. Basically, to supply electricity in the rural and remote places of the country. These mini-grid system projects are run by the government and private sector. The government is encouraging the people, NGOs, and local administration to set up factories of solar panels to mitigate the demands of rural Bangladesh. Bangladesh has sun radiation that is 4-6.5 kWh/m2, which is higher than many other nations worldwide (Uddin et al., 2019) Solar power is generated through three major methods, such as (1) solar power tower, (2) Solar Parabolic trough, and (3) Solar dish engine.

(ii) **Geothermal energy** is another source of alternative energy and the Bangladesh government has planned to install 200 MGW electricity through this at Thakurgaon area.

(iii) **Windmill** is another effective source of green energy. Bangladesh has a long coastal area of 724 km. where windmills can work effectively. Strong wind blows in the South and Southwestern parts of Bangladesh which is very effective in generating electricity. The government of Bangladesh has slowly implemented windmill-based electricity. Some forthcoming windmill-based power generation projects will be set up at Chittagong (power generation capacity is 50-200 MW), Muhuri dam of Feni (power generation capacity around 15 MW), Mognamaghat, Kepupara, Parky Beach, etc. After the completion of all of these projects, the power cut problem may be resolved at the local level.

(iv) The Bangladesh government has emphasized **bioenergy** through biomass. The biological substance that comes from living things is called biomass. A type of renewable energy called bioenergy is created by using biomass to create electricity. According to Alam et al. (2020), biomass energy is regarded as the first form of energy used by humans in their earliest history. Biomass encompasses all types of organic materials. Biomass is fourth among all energy sources in terms of global energy production. Numerous methods of producing electric energy from biomass are possible. Three types of biomass technologies are used in Bangladesh (a) gasification-based biomass, (b) direct-fired biomass, and (c) biomass co-firing. In Bangladesh, biomass is a substitute for fossil fuels and a long-term renewable energy source (Hassan et al., 2022).

4.4 Policy Initiatives Towards Energy Security in Bangladesh

To enhance and popularize green energy some can take in Bangladesh. Firstly, a political consensus is a must to develop an effective energy policy in Bangladesh because of its political clashes. The issue of reform of energy policy is subject to the convergence of thoughts of political parties for the greater interests of the country. Secondly, the distribution of energy in all districts and socio-economic groups is to be ensured. Thirdly, the conservation of energy is to be initiated through advanced technology. Through social sensitization and awareness, the government should take an active role at the local level in alarming people about the importance of energy security and the prospects of green energy. Fourthly, the judiciary and administration can jointly give directives to the people to ban the old vehicles and can promote electric vehicles which will not only be helpful for the environment but also for reducing over-dependency on conventional fuels. Fifthly, emphasize indigenous energy sources and explore potential energy sources of the country. Bangladesh has a modest reserve of natural gas. About 26 natural gas fields have been identified in Bangladesh. Sixthly, popularizing renewable green energy sources, such as biomass, solar power, and windmills can be the best way to mitigate the energy crises. Seventhly, the

Bangladesh government should form an agency that shall be working on different types of renewable energy sources and technology. An independent Energy Regulatory Commission must be established. Eighthly, to strengthen abilities in the energy sector, proper planning and management of energy sector programs are to be installed. Ninthly, the government should encourage research institutions and universities to research energy security and green energy. Tenthly, A contract for the establishment of FSRU has been linked with Singapore's Excelerate Energy. A floating LNG terminal has already been set up in the Maheshkh adjacent area of Cox's Bazar. Excelerate Energy currently adds 500 MM cups per day of re-gasified LNG to the national grid. Lastly, the government can conduct training programs on energy security to enable the people and technical people.

4.5 Towards Regional Cooperation of Bangladesh on Energy Security

The importance of regional cooperation on energy security has been highlighted in this section. Undoubtedly Energy is an imperative factor in the economic and social welfare of a country. But to cope with the increasing security concern regarding Energy, regional cooperation is a must. Bangladesh is strategically located in between two great geo-economic areas, namely South and South-East Asia, bordering India to the north, west, and north-east, Myanmar to the east, and the Bay of Bengal to the south. So, exchanging energy with these neighboring countries makes very much sense. Here we shall discuss the following factors on Energy security from Bangladesh's perspective

With Bangladesh gaining a strong presence within South Asia, India has also sought to increase energy cooperation with Bangladesh. This is evident from the Modi-Hasina summit in September last year and India's aim to expand cooperation and dialogue amongst the BBIN countries (Bangladesh, Bhutan, India, and Nepal). India is supplying surplus electricity to Bangladesh (Nandy, 2020). In terms of having access to energy, the nations in the BBIN subregion lag substantially behind their counterparts in wealthier nations. Bhutan, one of the nations in the BBIN area, had the greatest per capita power usage in 2014 with 2,600 kWh/capita, followed by India with 957 kWh/capita.

One of the main factors contributing to Bhutan's high per capita energy usage is its small population in comparison to other BBIN member nations. The Bangladeshi government is exploring a plan to swap electricity across international borders with India via the Indian Energy swap. The action will formalize the electricity trading and broaden the scope of the two nation's electrical exchange. Through this exchange program, the Indian government will be financially benefited by selling surplus power. Bangladesh's need for Indian power is growing, as seen by the country's 17.31% increase in energy imports from India in 2020-21, totaling 4712.91 Taka (about Rs. 4,150.99). Currently, the IEX is used by Nepal and Bhutan to transact power sales and purchases with India. Each party can trade by their supply and demand positions at a certain time by joining the exchange (Dasgupta, 2022).

In Bangladesh, both government and private sectors generate electricity. The private sector usually generates electricity through diesel. Bangladesh will now receive 748 MW of electricity thanks to the commissioning of India's premier MNC, Adani Power Ltd.'s first 800 MW ultra-super-critical thermal power production complex at Godda in India's Jharkhand province (Mint, 2023). So, this is clear that to mitigate the energy supply the government of Bangladesh is allowing private electrification from the BBIN region. Cooperation at the level of sub-regional level is a must for Bangladesh to mitigate the growing electricity demand. Bangladesh experienced consistent hour-long power outages in the second half of 2022 due to a daily deficit of 1000-1500 MW of electricity (Kumar, 2023). The most recent implementation of this concept was the recent opening of the India-Bangladesh Friendship Pipeline (IBFPL).

The 131.5 km pipeline connecting Siliguri in West Bengal, India with Parbatpur in the Dinajpur district of Bangladesh would deliver one million metric tons of diesel to the seven districts in north Bangladesh per year (Kumar, 2023).

The economy of Bangladesh is one of the fastest-growing economies in the world. The thousands of garments, Frood processing factories, fertilizer factories, and readymade factories are dependent upon electricity. So, through regional energy connectivity, the government of Bangladesh is trying to ensure an uninterrupted power supply.

A fantastic source of energy is hydropower, which is the production of power using the gravitational force of falling flowing water. Water-based GBM (Ganga, Brahmaputra, Megna) regional cooperation has enormous potential. Nepal and Bhutan can serve as the sellers of hydropower and Bangladesh can be the buyer. With relation to the development of power, India has already reached an agreement with Bhutan and Nepal. Nepal has an 83,000 MW hydropower potential, but it only produces 800 MW and imports electricity from India during the winter, resulting in a serious power shortage.

5. THE ENVIRONMENTAL AND SOCIETAL IMPACTS OF ENERGY SECURITY ISSUES

The energy security issue is impactful in the environmental and societal milieu. Both Pakistan and Bangladesh have witnessed the effects of energy security. Despite Pakistan's abundant natural gas, renewable energy sources, and coal supplies, the country has become entirely reliant on imported fossil fuels, as noted by Ichord (2020). This dependence has had a detrimental impact on the nation's economy and natural resources. Arshad and Shamshad (2022) have opined that the reduced capacity utilization in several key industries, resulting in load-shedding, has disrupted economic activity. The fertilizer industry has been particularly affected, with gas supply delays leading to closures in various locations. Despite having the potential to produce over a million tonnes of exportable surplus urea annually, Pakistan must now purchase urea to meet its fertilizer sector needs due to the energy crisis. The reputation of Pakistan within the international community has been adversely affected by the persistent issues of gas and electricity load-shedding, as well as the scarcity of oil for transportation. The unpredictable nature of these essential resources has resulted in a multitude of psychological challenges among the population. The unannounced load-shedding practices in Pakistan have further exacerbated these problems, leading to widespread frustration among the majority of individuals.

The impact of energy difficulty in the society of Bangladesh has been manifested in various ways. The power cut is very common in Bangladesh because of the demand-supply gap. Due to gross-power-cut, societal dissatisfaction has been reflected in the electoral campaign in Bangladesh. The traditional fuel generates most of the electricity in Bangladesh. The uncontrolled pollution of Bangladesh resulted in health-related hazards. Islam et al. (2021) argued that the attainment of universal access to electricity is contingent upon the establishment of a comprehensive national energy policy, notwithstanding the notable strides made by the energy sector in recent times. For the nation to achieve its objectives in terms of sustainable development, the formulation and implementation of a well-coordinated national energy policy is imperative. To effectively tackle the energy predicament, it is crucial to identify priorities for action and establish an energy regulatory framework. Furthermore, expediting progress in the energy sector necessitates the adoption of long-term planning strategies and the mobilization of private funding.

6. ENVIRONMENTAL GOVERNANCE IN PAKISTAN AND BANGLADESH: THE SDGS GOAL

The energy security issue is closely related to environmental governance. Environmental governance refers to understanding the implementation of rules, regulations, and mechanisms to save the environment and control pollution. Both Bangladesh and Pakistan have failed to protect the environment through environmental governance due to over-dependency on traditional energy uses. The sustainability of Bangladesh's natural resource base and environmental health is a pressing issue, particularly due to its high population density and location in an ecologically vulnerable deltaic region. Ahmed (2019) argues that the state of environmental governance in Bangladesh and highlights significant gaps in the government's progress towards achieving the Sustainable Development Goals and Millennium Development Goals. There are several challenges, including inadequate resource mobilization, ineffective enforcement of laws and regulations, an uncoordinated and unresponsive organizational structure, and a lack of balance between economic growth and environmental conservation. These issues require urgent attention from the government to ensure the long-term sustainability of Bangladesh's natural resources and environmental health. The environmental governance of Pakistan has not been implemented properly due to a lack of administrative efficiency. The state of Pakistan has witnessed democratic deficiency, corruption, and violence. In 2016, Pakistan showcased its dedication to the 2030 Plan for Sustainable Development by wholeheartedly embracing the Sustainable Development Goals (SDGs) as its national development plan. The country is diligently striving to establish institutional frameworks that align with the principles and objectives outlined in the 2030 Agenda. The SDGs have not been achieved by Pakistan on the issue of environmental protection.

7. CONCLUSION

In the concluding part, the scarcity of energy in Pakistan and Bangladesh has been discussed and common areas of convergence have been highlighted. In January 2023, a rolling wave of blackouts that started in Baluchistan and Sindh provinces but quickly spread to nearly the entire country, including the densely populated cities of Karachi, Lahore, and Rawalpindi, occurred as a result of Pakistan's chronic fuel shortage problem. Due to a lack of funding to rebuild its deteriorating infrastructure, Pakistan has regular power outages. If Pakistan does not resolve its power problem, it will harm its industrial output and the daily lives of the households at a time when it is already experiencing one of the biggest economic crises the country has experienced in recent years aimed at declining foreign exchange reserves (Business Standard, 2023). Pakistan could not benefit from regional or sub-regional levels of energy security. Pakistan could maintain a good relationship with India and could benefit from getting electricity like Bangladesh. The proposed tri-lateral pipeline from Iran-Pakistan-India (IPI) is still pending due to the U.S. economic sanctions on Iran (ET Energy World, 2017). Since the beginning, the government of Pakistan has been spending more budget on military-headings. The energy sector is not only boosting the industrial development of the country but also the socio-economic progression. So, more budget is to be allotted by the government of Pakistan in the energy sector. Nationwide corruption is also responsible for interrupted service of energy supply. The government of Pakistan should give priority to developing indigenous energy sources.

According to Ahmed et al. (2001), the policy should guarantee that all available energy sources are exploited, that there is sufficient energy for all uses, and that everyone in society has equitable access to renewable energy. There may be viable plans for the expansion of the energy sector of the Bangladesh government. Both long-term and short-term agreements with the regional collaborators for the expansion of the energy industry. The term 'energy conservation' refers to an attempt to lower energy use. So, the government of Bangladesh is improving technology, switching to different fuel sources, maintaining and using current equipment, or other changes in end-user behavior. Although there is legislation requiring energy conservation and there is good potential to offset energy demand by energy conservation, in the past there has been no success because there have not been any sincere efforts. Commercial energy should take the place of traditional energy sources. Bangladesh is moving towards utilizing renewable energy sources, such as solar, wind, biogas, and biodiesel, among others. In addition to these, it has built a nuclear power plant to provide electricity. Energy as a strategic input for socioeconomic development. Security of the economy, access to food, and environmental sustainability are all directly impacted by energy. The issue of energy security must be seen from the perspective of sustainable human development for developing nations like Pakistan and Bangladesh. It would be required to take the nation's energy needs into account from a long-term perspective to maintain energy security for sustainable development.

The shortage of electricity is a common factor for both Pakistan and Bangladesh. The political obstacles in the political-making process are also similar feature in both countries. Bangladesh has been liberated from Pakistan in 1971. During the Pakistani rule, no such steps had been taken by the Pakistani federal government for the electrification of East Pakistan and ensuring energy security. The initial infrastructure of East Pakistan has been developed for a long time. Bangladesh has experienced financial crisis and political turmoil over the years. Additionally, the rapid growth of the population created a burden for Bangladesh. The impressive growth of the economy of Bangladesh is possible by ensuring an uninterrupted energy supply. Considering the commitment to abiding by the SDGs goal Bangladesh is trying to limit the pupylation and implement sustainable development programs. Conventional energy sources are responsible for harming the environment. So, Bangladesh is moving towards green energy to keep its commitment to following the SDGs. However, environmental governance will have to play a significant role in this regard.

REFERENCES

Ahmad, Q. K. et, al. (eds.). (2001). *Ganges-Brahmaputra-Meghna: Region: A Framework for Sustainable Development*. Dhaka: University Press Limited.

Ahmed, B. (2019). Environmental governance and sustainable development in Bangladesh: Millennium development goals and sustainable development goals. *Asia Pacific Journal of Public Administration*, *41*(4), 237–245. doi:10.1080/23276665.2019.1698930

Alam, T, et, al. (2020). Energy Security in Bangladesh through Renewable Energy Generation. *Journal of Alternative and Renewable Energy*, *6*(3), 27–40.

Ang, B., Choong, W. L., & Ng, T. S. (2015). Energy security: Definitions, dimensions, and indexes. *Renewable & Sustainable Energy Reviews*, *42*, 1077–1093. doi:10.1016/j.rser.2014.10.064

Arshad, F., & Shamshad, M. (2022). Energy Crisis in Pakistan: Socio-Economic Implications and the Way Forward. *Annals of Social Sciences and Perspective*, *3*(1), 105–115. doi:10.52700/assap.v3i1.69

Bielecki, J. (2002). Energy Security: Is the Wolf at the Door? *The Quarterly Review of Economics and Finance*, *42*(2), 235–250. doi:10.1016/S1062-9769(02)00137-0

Business Standard. (27 January 2023). Pakistan's power crisis lingers and paralyzes economic activities. https://www.business-standard.com/article/international/pakistan-s-power-crisis-lingers-paralyses-economic-activities-123012701230_1.html

Cherp, A., & Jewell, J. (2014). The concept of energy security: Beyond the four As. *Energy Policy*, *75*, 415–421. doi:10.1016/j.enpol.2014.09.005

Choudhury, S. U. S. (18 April 2023). Bangladesh Needs to Initiate Nuclear Power Plants. *The Geopolitics*. https://thegeopolitics.com/bangladesh-needs-to-initiate-nuclear-power-plants/

Dasgupta, S. (21 April 2022). India and Bangladesh are set to formalize the electricity-sharing system. *The Times of India*, https://timesofindia.indiatimes.com/articleshow/90969950.cms?utm_source=contentofinterest&utm_medium=text&utm_campaign=cppst, accessed on 13 August 2023.

ET Energy World. (2017). India should revive Iran-Pakistan-India gas pipeline: Parliamentary Panel. ET Energy World. https://energy.economictimes.indiatimes.com/news/oil-and-gas/india-should-revive-iran-pakistan-india-gas-pipeline-parliamentary-panel/57725094

Fisher, M. (2021). *Bangladesh nuclear reactor construction progresses ahead of planned 2023 start-up*. International Atomic Energy Agency (IAEA). https://www.iaea.org/bulletin/bangladesh-nuclear-reactor-construction-progresses-ahead-of-planned-2023-start-up

Hassan, M. Y. (2022). Sustainable energy sources in Bangladesh: A review on present and prospects. *Renewable and Sustainable Reviews*, *155*. https://www.sciencedirect.com/science/article/abs/pii/S1364032121011370

Ichord, R. F. (2020). Transforming the Power Sector in Developing Countries: Geopolitics, Poverty and Climate Change in Pakistan. *Atlantic Council*, 1-19. http://www.jstor.com/stable/resrep23545

International Trade Administration. (2022). *Pakistan: Country Commercial Guide*. ITA. https://www.trade.gov/country-commercial-guides/pakistan-renewable-energy

Islam, A., Hossain, M. B., Mondal, M. A. H., Ahmed, M. T., Hossain, M. A., Monir, M. U., Khan, M. F. H., Islam, K., Khandaker, S., Choudhury, T. R., & Awual, M. R. (2021). Energy challenges for a clean environment: Bangladesh's experience. *Energy Reports*, *7*, 3373–3389. doi:10.1016/j.egyr.2021.05.066

Islam, M. (2020). An Overview of the Hydropower Production Potential in Bangladesh to Meet the Energy Requirements. *Environmental Engineering Research*, *26*(6), 200514. doi:10.4491/eer.2020.514

Islam, M.R. (2009). Effective Solar Photovoltaic Activities in Bangladesh. *International Energy Journal*, *10*(1), 29-36. http://www.rericjournal. ait.ac.th/index.php/relic/article/view/578

Jamal, E. O. (31 October 2022). How can Bangladesh circumvent the global oil war? *The Daily Star*. https://www.thedailystar.net/opinion/views/the-overton-window/news/how-can-bangladesh-circumvent-the-global-oil-war-3157136

Khan, S. (2009). PDB plans big for six coal-fired power plants. *The Daily Star*. https://www. thedailystar.net/news-detail-91772

Kumar, I. (10 April, 2023). Bangladesh's quest for energy security opens up new regional opportunities. *South Asia Monitor*. https://www.southasiamonitor.org/spotlight/bangladeshs-quest-energy-security-opens-new-regional-opportunities.

Mahmood, T., & Ayaz, M. T. (2018). Energy Security and Economic Growth in Pakistan. *Pakistan Journal of Applied Economics*, *28*(1), 47–64.

Malik, S. M. et, al. (2019). *Energy Security in Pakistan: A Quantitative Approach to a Sustainable Energy Policy*. ADBI Working Paper 1024. Tokyo: Asian Development Bank Institute. https://www.adb.org/publications/energy-security-pakistan-sustainable-energy-policy

Malik, S., Qasim, M., Saeed, H., Chang, Y., & Taghizadeh-Hesary, F. (2020). Energy security in Pakistan: Perspectives and policy implications from quantitative analysis. *Energy Policy*, *144*, 111552. doi:10.1016/j.enpol.2020.111552

Mint. (9 April 2023). Adani's Godda plant starts power supply to Bangladesh. *Mint*. https://www.livemint.com/industry/energy/adanis-godda-plant-starts-power-supply-to-bangladesh-11681048727204.html.

Nandy, D. (2019). *Energy Security and Economic Growth in South Asia: An Alternative Policy Option. Handbook of Research on Economic and Political Implications of Green Trading and Energy*. IGI Global. doi:10.4018/978-1-5225-8547-3.ch022

Nandy, D. (2020). Revisiting India's Post Cold War Foreign Policy: Since 1991 to Present Day. Memari: Avenel Press.

Nandy, D. (2023). The Impact of Pollution and Economic Growth on the Maldives and Bangladesh: Interrogative Economic Development and Environmental Governance. In M. Pal (Ed.), *The Impact of Environmental Emissions and Aggregate Economic Activity on Industry: Theoretical and Empirical Perspectives*. Emerald, Publishing. doi:10.1108/978-1-80382-577-920231018

Pranti A. S. (2013). Current Energy Situation and Comparative Solar Power Possibility Analysis for Obtaining Sustainable Energy Security in South Asia. *International Journal of Scientific and Technology Research*, *2*(8). https://www.ijstr.org/paper

Radovanović, M., Filipović, S., & Pavlović, D. (2017). Energy security measurement: A sustainable approach. *Renewable & Sustainable Energy Reviews*, *68*, 1020–1032. doi:10.1016/j.rser.2016.02.010

Sarkar, et, al. (2020). *Role of Regional Cooperation and Integration in Improving Energy Insecurity in South Asia*. ADBI Working Paper Series-1120, Tokyo: Asian Development Bank Institute.

Shrestha, R. M., Anandarajah, G., & Liyanage, M. H. (2009). Factors affecting CO2 emission from the power sector of selected countries in Asia and the Pacific. *Energy Policy*, *37*(6), 2375–2384. doi:10.1016/j.enpol.2009.01.032

Siddiqui, S. (28 December 2023). Pakistan's foray into renewable energy. *The Express Tribune*. https://tribune.com.pk/story/2393075/pakistans-foray-into-renewable-energy

State Bank of Pakistan. (2018). *Annual Report 2017–2018*. The State of Pakistan's Economy.

Stirling, A. (2010). Multi-criteria Diversity Analysis: A Novel Heuristic Framework for Appraising Energy Portfolios. *Energy Policy*, *38*, 1622–1634. doi:10.1016/j.enpol.2009.02.023

Switzerland Global Enterprise. (2021). Market Snapshot: Renewable Energy in Pakistan. https://www.s-ge.com/en/article/export-knowhow/20213-c5-pakistan-renewable-energy?ct, Switzerland Global Enterprise.

Taghizadeh, H. (2019). Introduction. In Farhad T. et, al. (eds.) Achieving Energy Security in Asia: Diversification, Integration, and Policy Implications. Singapore: World Scientific.

The Economic Times. (21 June 2023). Cash-starved Pakistan fails to secure LNG supply as no company responds to its tender. *The Economic Times*. https://economictimes.indiatimes.com/news/international/world-news/cash-starved-pakistan-fails-to-secure-lng-supply-as-no-company-responds-to-its-tender/articleshow/101162096.cms?from=mdr,

Uddin, M. N., Rahman, M. A., Mofijur, M., Taweekun, J., Techato, K., & Rasul, M. G. (2019). Renewable energy in Bangladesh: Status and prospects. *Energy Procedia*, *160*, 655–661. doi:10.1016/j.egypro.2019.02.218

United Nations. (2016). *The Sustainable Development Goals Report 2016*. United Nations.

Uqaili, M. A. (2004). Hydel Power Generation in Pakistan: Past Trends, Current Status and Future Projections. *Mehran University Research Journal of Engineering and Technology*, *23*(3), 207–216.

World Bank. (2020). Expanding Renewable Energy in Pakistan's Electricity Mix. *World Bank*. https://www.worldbank.org/en/news/feature/2020/11/09/a-renewable-energy-future-for-pakistans-power-system

KEY TERMS AND DEFINITIONS

Bangladesh: Bangladesh is the younger republic of South Asia which achieved independence from Pakistan in 1971. It is a highly popular country with a huge demand for energy. However, Bangladesh is facing an energy crisis and searching for a way out for energy security.

Energy Security: Energy security is the security of fossil fuels, like coal, diesel, petrol, kerosene, nuclear energy, hydel energy, etc. There are two types of energy, such as conventional energy, and renewable energy (wind power, solar energy, biomass, etc.) Cost-effective energy access plays a crucial role in modern industry and civilization. The majority of energy required to fuel companies, transportation networks, and residential heating is derived from fossil fuels. On a global scale, we consume an amount of energy equivalent to 200 million barrels of oil daily. However, it is important to note that a significant portion of this energy is also sourced from nuclear power, natural gas, and coal.

Geothermal Energy: is a vital source of alternative energy and the Bangladesh government has planned to install 200 MGW of electricity through this.

Pakistan: Pakistan is a South Asian state which gained independence in 1947. It is an economically challenged country with an acute shortage of fuel.

Pollution: Apart from causing detrimental living conditions and devastating ecosystems, various forms of pollution such as air pollution, lead exposure, toxic substances, and improper disposal of electronic waste can lead to fatal illnesses. The release of pollutants into the atmosphere contributes to air pollution, which in turn triggers climate change and respiratory problems. Water pollution, caused by the discharge of waste and chemicals into water bodies, poses risks to both aquatic life and human health. Additionally, the heavy reliance on fossil fuels for energy generation has resulted in severe pollution issues in Pakistan and Bangladesh.

Sustainable Development Goals (SDGs): The Sustainable Development Goals (SDGs) serve as the United Nations' blueprint for achieving a more sustainable future for all. These goals were established to address pressing global concerns such as water security, climate change, sustainability, and environmental degradation. In 2015, the World Business Council for Sustainable Development, the UN Global Compact, and the Global Reporting Initiative introduced the SDG compass and published a report titled "Business Reporting on the SDGs: An Analysis of the Goals and Targets." Since then, the CDP has played an active role in advancing the SDG agenda.

Windmill: It is another effective source of green energy. Bangladesh has a long coastal area of 724 km. where windmills can work effectively. Strong wind blows in the South and Southwestern parts of Bangladesh which is very effective in generating electricity.

Chapter 11
Gender Discrimination in the Workplace:
A Gloomy Picture of the Indian Economy

Shrabanti Pal
https://orcid.org/0000-0002-5837-3286
Fakir Chand College, India

ABSTRACT

The present chapter is an attempt to highlight and address the issue of gender disparities and the socio-economic problems of women in India. Indian society is patriarchal and driven by men's ideology where women are restricted to being the part of formal workforce, and also experience a high level of domestic violence. The status of Indian women is primarily dependent on various factors like demographic location, basic education, social status, etc. Indian women are restricted in various aspects like access to health facilities, proper education, lessening decision-making power, etc. Despite political reservations, women are hindered to be political participants at local, national, and international levels. Indian government frames various policies for women's welfare and empowerment. However, there is significant gap exists between the framing and execution of such policies. Hence, the main focus of the chapter is to examine the various issues faced by Indian women to achieve economic development and gender equality.

1. INTRODUCTION

Globalization and liberalization accelerate the economic growth of India at the cost of the exploitation of labours, especially female labour. Liberalization enables India to accomplish the phenomenon of economic growth but with unequal distribution of wealth and gender discrimination. The two main features of the Indian labour market are inequality and informality. Inequality exists in terms of wages, working conditions, job specification and job security till the present time (Kundu and Mohanan, 2009). The heterogeneous nature of the Indian labour market in terms of nature, skill and gender biases leads to enormous inequity and the government has failed to address this never-ending problem with differ-

DOI: 10.4018/979-8-3693-0390-0.ch011

Copyright © 2024, IGI Global. Copying or distributing in print or electronic forms without written permission of IGI Global is prohibited.

ent reformation and liberal policies. Indian economy immensely depends on the informal sector and it expanding rapidly in recent decades as it provides employment and livelihood to a generous portion of the Indian population (Mosse, 2018). The informal sector requires low or no skilled workers and a major part of these workers are self-employed or casual in nature and such informal sector is also lack of social and legal protection and employment benefits. Out of total non-agricultural Indian workforce, about 86.3 percent of workers in 1999-00 and 90 percent of workers were absorbed in the informal sector [NSSO (1999-00); NSSO (2004-05)]. The contribution of the informal sector to the Indian economy is very significant. The contribution is accounting for 40 percent of the total industrial output and 35 percent of total export (Bairagya, 2018). In contrast formal employment is created through contractual agreement to provide business, legal and social benefits to the employees.

Gender discrimination is one of the main problems in the Indian informal sector which affect the socio-economic development of the country. Gender discrimination is not determined biologically but socially in India. The denial of equal rights to education, and job opportunities and suppression of any legitimate right in any form based on gender is gender discrimination. Indian society is mainly male dominant and gender discrimination occurred habitually here. Such discrimination creates talent scarcity in the economy which leads to negative consequences. Above all, certain social, religious, and cultural taboos kept women out of economic affairs. It causes a deficiency in the economic, social, and political empowerment of Indian women (Berta Esteve-Volant, 2004). The implementation of different measures to enhance the socio-economic status of women in terms of income generation cannot pave a path to equalizing the economic status of women in employment (United Nations, 1997; Devi, 1999; Dixon, 1982; A.K.Sen, 1999). The Indian government has adopted the principle of 'Sabka Sath, Sabka Vikas' ('Together with all, Development for all') in recent times. It appeals to Indians to work together toward eradicating poverty, gender inequality, and lack of sanitation. It enables the upper class and urban women section to take advantage which facilitates greater access to education and employment of this section.

However, the women belonging to the lower class and lower-middle class face extreme deprivation. These underprivileged women are primarily depending on male members of the family for their livelihoods. Such a patriarchal structure of society hinders women to be an active part of the workforce. However, women from upper-class and urban areas are free to be part of the workforce. It suggests the U-shaped relationship between female labour participation and economic development of a country. Basically, certain social norms impede women to enter into labour market (Choudhry and Elhorst, 2018). Indian women are fond of being part of white-collar jobs where no social stigma exists.

Gender inequality in the workplace is practiced in many forms for instance unequal pay, disparity in promotion, sexual harassment, and racism. Indian women are facing gender biases in the working place on a large canvas. Historically, Indian women have been denied many opportunities for the sake of social norms which lead to gender biases in the domestic arena and beyond the household also. In spite of having all qualities, they are unable to move up into higher positions quickly as compared to men (Beniwal, 2013). In India, due to certain illogical myths, some organizations are not very keen to give responsible positions to their female employees rather they de-motivate them to participate in the competition with male employees (Patrick and Kumar, 2012). Gender disparity has become a serious issue and has a direct impact on labour market outcomes in regard to women's participation in economic activities. According to the latest Periodic Labour Force Survey Report (PLFS, 2020-2021), the estimated Workforce Population Ratio (WPR) on usual status basis for aged 15 years and above for male and female workers was 73.5% and 31.4% respectively (Ministry of Labour & Employment, 2022).

Women empowerment is one of the best ways to eradicate gender disparity at a large scale. Thus to achieve sustainable development goals women's empowerment and gender equality are indispensable. Against the backdrop of gender disparity and suppression of women's rights in the workplace, the present study is an endeavor to focus on the factors that are responsible for gender inequality in India and analyze those facts based on facts and data. Apart from that the study aims to find out the social and economic issues faced by Indian women in the workplace. The study also tries to suggest the necessary measures to overcome the problem of different shades of gender disparity and gender bias in women's employment.

The paper is organized as follows: the next section discusses a brief overview of related literature. Section three presents a comparative study between education level and occupational distribution in the workplace. Section four discusses the consequences of gender inequalities in economic growth and additional discussion of policies undertaken by government for welfare of women. Section five gives a brief description of women's empowerment to achieve sustainable growth goals and the paper concludes with overall findings of status of Indian women.

2. REVIEW OF LITERATURE

Gender discrimination in workplace is one of the most controversial and a debatable matter around the world and gender disparity is highly rampant in developing countries compared to developed countries (Ahmed, et.al., 2001). Discrimination leads to financial losses and also lessens the innovation scope, growth potential and competitiveness of firms and countries (Cornejo, 2007; Dipboye and Colella, 2005). The women empowerment is one of the best ways to eradicate gender disparity at large scale. The empowerment of women indicates the "woman's ability to make strategic life choices where that ability had been previously denied them" (Malhotra, et.al, 2009). At present gender equality has become most significant aspect where rights, responsibilities and opportunities will be uniformly accessible to both men and women. All human beings are free to develop their personal abilities without any restrictions set by strict gender rules. The ultimate goal of gender equality is to reduce the discrimination on the basis of one's gender (Warth and Koparanova, 2012; Alvarez and Lopez, 2013).

The reality of gender disparity in India is very complicated and diversified issue which hindered the achievement of sustainable goal. Thus, to accomplish sustainable development goal women empowerment and gender equality is indispensible. Indian society has defined different norms for men and women. Sociologically, the definitions of men and women are predetermined and according to that their roles in the society is also pre-assigned. The society has imposed lots of restrictions on girls since their birth. The girls are treated as 'Paraya Dhan' in society and therefore families are reluctant to spend money on their formal education, health, and overall wellbeing. Basically they are treated as 'reproductive machine' (Desai, 1994). Indian society is mainly driven by man-determined factors. The society is multifaceted and patriarchy in nature where women are 'objectified' and face various hindrance to have their legitimate constitutional rights. They are experiencing high-rated domestic violence, low health condition and less or no access to education. In one word, Indian women are likely to be prisoner in home and are compelled to take care of family members. Since childhood Indian girls are advised to stay at home and perform household chores. Despite of women reservation women are restricted to be the part of politics. The condition of women is being influenced by various factors like geographical and social belonging, socio-economic status, and proper and equal education opportunities like men. Indian government has taken various initiatives to reduce gender discrimination but a significant gap exists between policy advancement and actual practice at ground level (Bhat, 2014).

Gender inequality is evident in many spheres. The women of India are confined in specific convention and face the economic drawbacks in organized and unorganized sector. It creates income and wealth gap and put the majority of women in poverty (United Nations 2015). The women are playing vital role in economic development. The existence of gender disparity in education and employment impose high cost to the entire society. A number of government initiatives reduce the gender gap exists in education but a pervasive gap subsist in employment. Women are facing structural barriers to enter into labour market. A negative relation persists between gender inequality and economic growth of a country. The reduction of gender disparity in education and employment can promote sustainable development goals (Klasen and Lamanna, 2009).

During the pre-liberalization era there was a clear segregation between domestic and child care work and other types of work where male are forming the active participation in labour market and women to perform domestic duties. This disparity leads to vulnerability and economical dependency of women on men and it wipes out men participation in household chores. However, the labour market scenario is changed during industrialization when women began to participate in the labour market. They are intensified to focus on the economic activities as a whole. But patriarchal system of the society led to economic inequality in terms of opportunities and choice in labour market (Hartmann, 1976). Prevalence of unequal wages in different types of jobs, regional differences and sector wise differences show disparity in wage payments to men and women. In spite of having same skill, education and experience women are less paid than men. This type of discrimination leads to gender biasness at large scale (Lama & Majumdar, 2018, Majumdar, 2011). A study shows gender disparity in Indian labour market by using NSSO (National Sample Survey Organization) data for 1999-00 and 2009-10 (Despande et. al.; 2015).

A substantial number of Indian women are moving into domain of 'household duties' that resulting into less active labour force participation and the rate of participation is declining at an alarming rate during the last decade (Fletcher, et.al., 2017). In India merely 22 percent of women are forming part of labour market out of those 70 percent are associated with informal work with little remuneration and less social protection (Mehrotra, et. al., 2014). The majority of women work force is engaged in informal labour force which tends to be invisible and unrecognized in Indian economic activities. The marginalization of informal female worker iss intensified in the Indian labour market because of socio-economic position of them in the society. They are engrossed in unpaid domestic chores in form of cooking, cleaning, taking care of well-being of family members (Patel, 2019). On an average, across the world men spent 83 minutes in unpaid domestic work while women spent 265 minutes for the same work. However, in India women are spending 297 minutes to discharge 'domestic duties' whereas the Indian men only spent 31 minutes for such duties (Addati, et.al., 2018). The gender biasness in discharging domestic unpaid duties abides by a set of social norms and conservatism promotes insight regarding 'national division' of household duties. The basic problem of 'unpaid work is not being counted as economic activities and rather exacerbate the economic burden of the country (Dong and An, 2015). Although the women constitutes half of the population but their contribution to economy is not up to the mark as compared to men. Indian women tends to spend more times 'on average two to ten times' on domestic unpaid care activities which creates "double burden" of work for women compared to men (Ferrant et.al.; 2014). Indian women spend around 57.7 percent more time than men on household chores; compared internationally at least 40 percent more time than South Africa or Chinese women (OECD, 2021)

The basic objective of the study is to highlight the restrictions on Indian women according to certain weird social norms. It hinders their entry to work force which not only affects the socio-economic status of the women but also the country is lagging behind the economic benefits with such wastage of human resources. The study is also discussed the gender inequality in workplace and its impact on Indian society as a whole.

Apart from that women are marginalized and their condition is being worsened gradually in terms of education, health, income and overall wellbeing in the society. Gender inequality is 'intersectional', in that it is strengthen and intensified by other factors (Kabeer, 2010). Many research shows inverse relation between gender inequality and economic growth (Galor and Weil, 1996; Lagerlof, 2003). The 'feminism of poverty' is a prominent indicator of women's engagement in ill/unpaid occupation (Uppal, 2007). India has witnessed a huge gender gap in formal and informal labour market. Indian labour market is experiencing three types of inequality namely gender inequality, socio-religious and intra-socio-religious gender disparity (Chakraborty, 2016). Majority of Indian women are employed in unorganized sector where they are neither entitled maternity leave nor overtime pay or a safe and dignified working environment (ILO, 2013). However, the gender gap in India is slowly narrowed down. A significant improvement around 68 percent is being observed across the sectors like education, politics, health, etc (Ministry of Human Development, 2018). The possible reason for more girls in school may be withdrawal from household care work or advancement of agricultural process where less female workers are needed (Krishna, et.al, 2016; Verick, 2018).

3. A COMPARATIVE STUDY BETWEEN EDUCATION LEVEL AND OCCUPATIONAL DISTRIBUTION

Gender discrimination in labour market reduces the available talent in an economy and it leads to negative impact on economic system of a country. The labour market in India is highly fragmented and exhibits a high percentage of gender inequality. The perception of gender discrimination in India is the result of many social practices which leave women out of economic main stream. Such practices of gender disparity have a large number of economic consequences and it also restrains the society to take advantages of talent inherent in women. Gender discrimination has myriad of negative consequences like social, psychological, political and religious apart from economic consequences. Gender discrimination has found in different form in developed and developing countries. The differences in wage rate between male and female workers has been found in developed countries while differential access to wage employment is practiced in developing countries (Collier, 1994).

There are certain socio-cultural norms in India which restrict women to enter into labour market. The northern part of India shows relatively less women participation rate in labour market compared to southern part of India because northern region of India is more patriarchal and feudal while women in southern region enjoy more freedom of rights, speech and prominent presence in society. However, the cultural restrictions disallow the Indian women from labour market participation in formal economy (Dunlop & Velkoff, 1999; Nihila, 1999). The women participation rate in India is different in different states. The rural female labour force participation has been increased from 19.7 percent in 2018-19 to 27.7 percent in 2020-21. The overall female labour force participation rate has gone up to 25.1 percent in 2020-21 from 18.6 percent in 2018-19. It is a great relief for Indian government that both the labour markets rural and urban have recovered beyond pre-Covid levels with decreasing rate of unemployment of 5.8 percent in 2018-19 to 4.2 percent in 2020-21.

The middle class women from Indian society are not very keen to take part in labour market while poor women are quite over-burdened with household work, thus, cannot afford engagement in labour force. Though, the urbanized upper class women are enjoying freedom to enter into economic activities at a large scale. It indicates U-shaped relationship between development and female labour participation as evident from study of Goldin (1994). The study shows that Indian women are more interested to engage in white collar job because of non-existence of social stigma, rather to join another kind of job where strict social norms are present.

Historically, women have been denied many opportunities due to deep rooted social norms. Consequently, it leads to gender inequality in labour market. This gender inequality not only limited to domestic area but extends beyond the household. There are certain underline factors which may create gender inequality such as sex ratio at birth, life expectancy at birth, infant mortality rate, the maternal mortality rate, nutritional deprivation, inequality in literacy rate and gender gap at the highest level of political decision making. These types of practice directly affect the women participation in economic activities. Despite of having equal education level and skill women are denied to be promoted to higher responsible force which leads to significant difference in wage payment, status of work, et cetra.

Nevertheless, the pandemic attack also affects the Indian labour market significantly. The outbreak of COVID-19 leads to gender discrimination and severe downturn in economic activities of informal workers, particularly women working at a lower wage rate. They were out of job for a significant time period and after that faces severe wage cut. There is a still huge gender gap which shows only 18 percent of women are employed while 47 percent of men are engaged in employment. It has been observed that the women are mostly engaged in low skilled, low paid work under precarious working environment.

Table-1 and figure-1 show the percentage of illiterate, and literacy rates of men and women in India. It is clear from the table than illiteracy rate is quite higher in case of women compared to men. In contrast the percentage of women in upper-Primary (77%) is high than men (62%). However, the picture is not same for higher education. The percentage of men (38%) is more than the percenge of women (23%) in India.

Table 1. Education level of working women compared to men in India

Participants	Illiterate (%)	Upper-Primary (%)	Secondary & Higher Secondary (%)
Men	19	62	38
Women	42	77	23

Source: Author's Calculation from NSS Data

Table 2. Occupational distribution of women in employment

Participant	Self-Employed (%)	Casual (%)	Regular Salaried (%)
Women	53	25	22

Source: Author's Calculation from NSS Data

Figure 1. Education level of working women compared to men in India

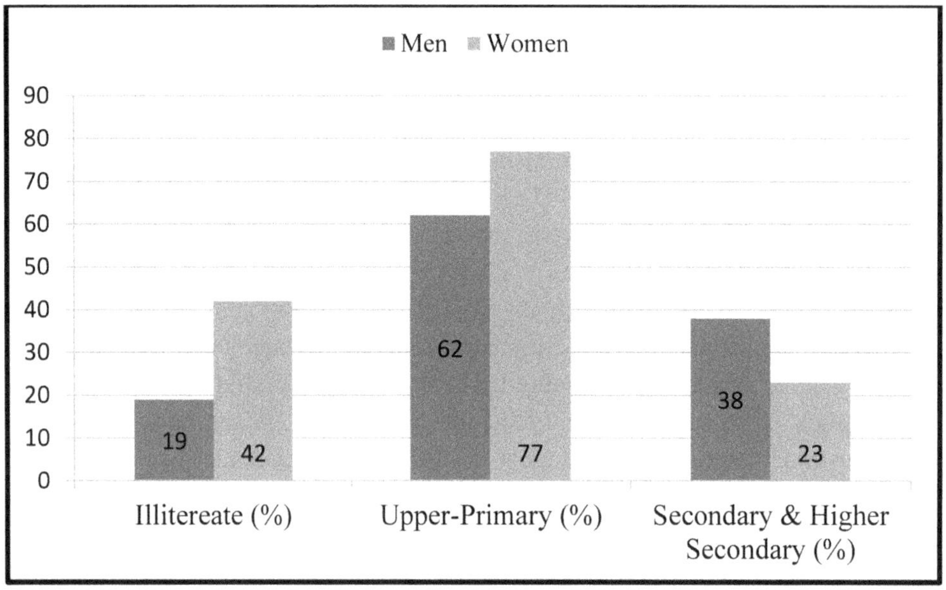

Figure 2. Occupational distribution of women in employment

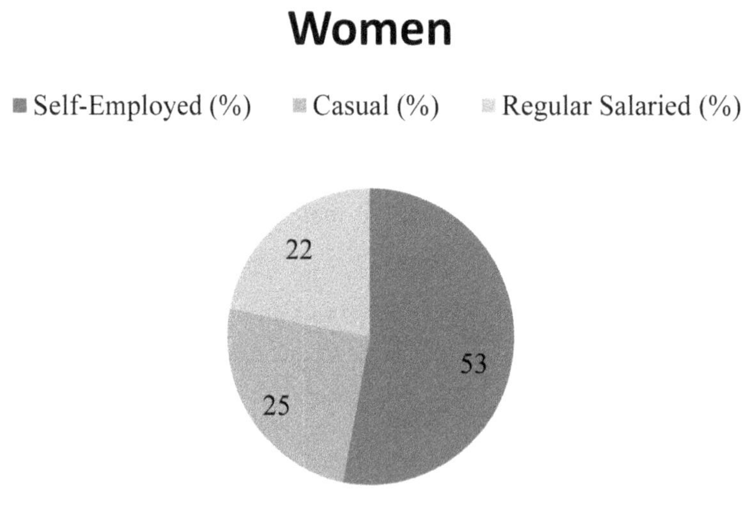

Table-2 and Figure-2 show the occupational distribution of gender. It is clear from the table that the women are relatively more involved than in low paid elementary occupation, such as, domestic help, cleaners, street vendors, garbage collector, etc. Women participation in labour market plays a vital role to achieve UN sustainable development goals efficiently and effectively. The full active and equal participation in decision making and policy development is essential to create and maintain the way to attain SDG.

4. CONSEQUENCES OF GENDER INEQUALITIES IN ECONOMIC DEVELOPMENT

India has witnessed significant growth in the past two decades. In spite of this phenomenal economic development gender inequality exist in many parts of India at a large scale which affects the nation's GDP (gross domestic product) adversely. Gender inequality is the basic hurdle to economic progress. A nation's economy is determined by employment, income and poverty rates. The economic growth of a nation is highly and negatively affected by gender inequality. Indian societies always put some restrictions for the sake of social norms on female children. Across India, girls are always limited to unequal opportunities, and they used to experience different treatment compared to boys during adolescence. The boys of India enjoy more freedom than girls while the girls tend to face extensive limitations.

Gender inequality goes hand-in-hand with macroeconomic and financial stability. It can stimulate economic growth, and the performance of the public and private sector, and reduces income inequality. Gender discrimination is used to reduce the availability of talent inherent in women in an economy which has negative economic consequences on country's economy. Indian economy is expected to be 5 trillion in coming years while economic development is limited by extensive gender inequality. Indian women are restricted to being part of the formal economy and their talents often are devalued in working place and society as a whole. It is very unfortunate that entering of Indian women into the formal sector is falling down during the post-pandemic time. Indian women are holding back due to certain weird social norms and are restricted to be the part of workforce which can influence the country's development in a negative way. Women empowerment not only enables women to take part in leadership and decision-making roles but also makes them aware of their rights and power.

India is on the path of economic development but declining workforce participation of women in formal and informal workforce has become cause of concern. NFHS data reveals that the health and education status of Indian women are improved while the economic, cultural, and political aspects lag behind. Women empowerment plays a crucial role in economic growth and social prosperity. In the changing dynamics of society, women empowerment is very much relevant and vital. The constitution of India prohibits discrimination against women and encourages women empowerment. Article-14 refers to equality before law or equal protection of the laws within the territory of India while Article 15 of Indian constitution forbids discrimination on grounds only of religion, race, caste, gender, or place of birth. However, Article 15 (3) makes it possible for the state to create special provisions to protect the interests of women and children. The indicators of the empowerment process are an enrichment of knowledge, self-confidence, and awareness of gender equality. Indian women are facing a mound of challenges and barriers for decades which make them more forbearance, perseverance, and stronger. Over the past decades, women professionals are working exuberantly with more talent, skill, devotion, and dedication. They contribute a substantial part to the nation's economic growth and prosperity. In the year 2022, there are 432 million women of working age in India, out of which 343 (79.4% approx) million are employed in the informal sector. The contribution of women to India's GDP was 18 percent approx in 2018, reflecting the fact that only 25 percent of India's labour force is female (Mckinsey Global Institute Report, 2018).

Despite social, and ancestral exclusion, Indian women are now more interested to create their own identity and accomplish financial independence. In the wake of the empowerment process, women are indulging themselves in new start-ups. The Panchayat system offers 50 percent reservation to rural women and also conducts certain national programmes like 'National Rural Livelihood Mission' which provides them with leadership opportunities. Apart from that 'Swatch Bharat Mission' and 'Mahatman Gandhi National Rural Employment Guarantee Act' have provided a 'supervisory role' to the women workforce. The mental and financial support is the most important need of the hour to support new women entrepreneurs.

Economic empowerment is a double-edged weapon that not only increases women's employment opportunities but also reduces the double burden of unpaid care work for women. The urgent need is to adopt the 3R approach which involves Recognizing, Reducing, and Redistribution unpaid care work done by women in all areas of policy-making. The industrial sector and CII National Committee on women empowerment are working together to enhance women's participation in the economic sphere and community affairs to attain the aim of gender equality and prevention of sexual harassment in the workplace. Women's empowerment with gender equality is the key to fundamental human rights which can help to achieve sustainable development goals. Working status is playing a decisive role to ascertain the status of women in society. The neoclassical theory predicts the increase in women's education leads to a rise in the workforce participation rate of women.

Table-3 and figure-3 show that LFPR and WPR are increasing for both rural and urban women and unemployment rate is on decreasing trend which creates the positive impact on the nation's economic growth.

Table 3. Trend of women labour force participation rate (LFPR), work participation rate (WPR) and unemployment rate (UR)

PARTICULARS	PLFS (2017-18)		PLFS (2018-19)		PLFS (2019-20)	
	RURAL	URBAN	RURAL	URBAN	RURAL	URBAN
LFPR	18.2	15.9	19.7	16.1	24.7	18.5
WPR	17.5	14.2	19	14.5	24	16.8
UR	3.8	10.8	3.5	9.9	2.6	8.9

Source: Periodic Labour Force Survey (PLFS) 2019-20

Figure 3. Graphical presentation of women labour force participation rate (LFPR), work participation rate (WPR) and unemployment rate (UR)

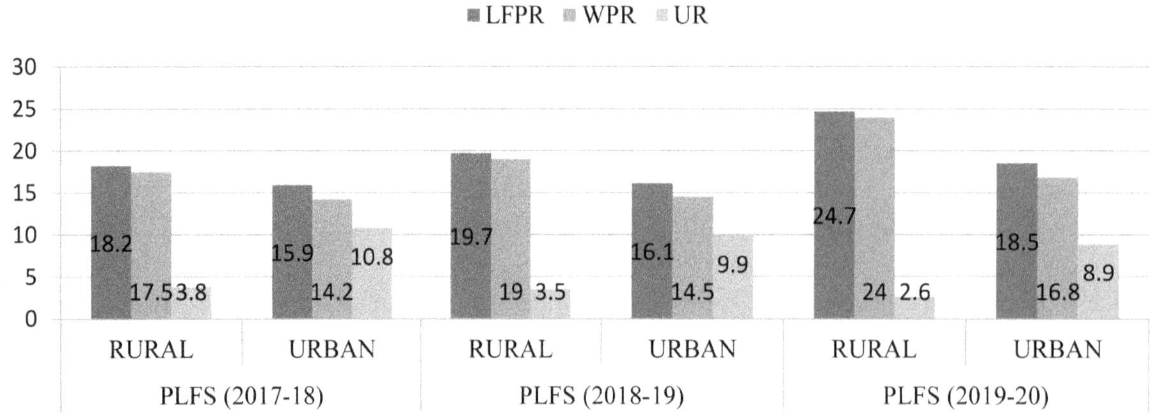

4.1 Government Initiatives for Women Empowerment

The Ministry of Women and Child Development is introducing various programmes to bringing women into main stream and include them in various economic activities.

1. *Swadhar Greh Scheme*: It is a centrally sponsored scheme for women who are victims of different circumstances. The Indian government takes initiative to provide institutional support so that they could survive in society with dignity.
2. *Ujjawala Scheme*: It is being implemented as centrally sponsored scheme for prevention of women trafficking and for Rescue, Rehabilitation, Reintegration, and Repatriation of victims of trafficking for commercial sexual exploitation.
3. *Beti Bachao Beti Padhao (BBBP):* This scheme is introduced by Indian government in 2015 with an aim to address the issue of women discrimination in the society, prevention of gender biased sex selective elimination and ensuring survival and protection of girl child through education.
4. *Mahila Shakti Kendra (MSK):* This centrally sponsored scheme was initiated in November, 2017 with a view to empowering rural women through community participation. This scheme is funded by central and state government with a cost sharing ratio 60:40. But such cost sharing ratio is different for North-East and Special Category States where the funding ratio is 90:10. For Union Territories Central contributes 100 percent fund.
5. *Pradhan Mantri Matru Vandana Yojana (PMMVY):* This scheme was introduced in 2017 by Hon'ble prime Minister of India to provide cash and maternity benefit to the pregnant and lactating mother belongs to unorganized sector. The women who are in regular job of central and state government or public sector undertaking can not avail the benefits of the scheme. The basic objective of this particular scheme is to provide nutrition and health benefits to the women by giving Rs.5000 in three installments to the beneficiaries during pregnancy period.
6. *Working Women Hostel:* This initiative is implemented by government with a view to provide safe and conveniently located accommodation for working women. This facility is also accompanied by daycare facility for their children (where possible) and it iis available to urban, semi-urban and rural areas where opportunities for employment for women exists.

Apart from above schemes, Indian government also take up certain initiatives like Janani Suraksha Yojana (JSY), One Stop Centre and Universalization of Women Helpline, etc. to encourage and strengthen women to pave path towards gender equalization.

5. WOMEN EMPOWERMENT AND SUSTAINABLE GROWTH GOALS

The full and equal participation of Women at all levels of decision making and policy development ensures the effective pursuit of sustainable development. Gender biasness restricts the opportunities for women to access desired, education, employment, leisure and political affairs. In the pre-industrialization era men are more 'specialized' to work in formal workforce while women mostly concentrated in domestic and unpaid care work. This types of separation shows vulnerability and economic dependency of women and children on men and men become non-participant of household chores. According to UNESCO, approximately 132 million girls are unable to get basic school education. In a broad canvas of gender stereotypes and inequalities women are often discourage to pursue the science, technology, engineering and mathematics (STEM) studies. This type of restriction leads to low representation of women participants in critical sectors. The economic gender gap remains significant in India till today. According to UN women, women perform three times as much as unpaid care and domestic work as men. Hence, women empowerment is a need of time in India to increase the women participation in socio-economic and political activities (Ferrant et.al, 2014).

Women empowerment is the most debatable issue in India for decades. It is a process that enables the women to make better control over their own life and take their own decision regarding their livelihood and well-beings. Women empowerment can lead to socio-political-economic growth, improved health issues and greater gender equality. The Indian women are facing significant challenges regarding discrimination, lack of access to education and employment and gender based violence. Women empowerment is one of the key factors to attain the sustainable development goal. The equitable distribution of resources is the primary requirement of sustainable development and one country can only achieve such development with gender equality (Bayeh, 2016). Sustainable development is broadly defined as development which meets the requirements of the present without compromising the ability of future generation to meet their own needs. The sustainable development growth should be based on balanced economic growth, highly competitive social market economy and price stability. Against the backdrop of sustainable development goals women empowerment plays a imperative role in global environmental movement. Despite of full and active participation women are restricted to be the part of decision making process in relation to environmental development in local, national and international perspective.

The Indian government has taken initiatives toward the achievement of gender equality on the basis of a report submitted by a committee on the status of women in India in 1974. However, women continued to be 'beneficiaries' till Seventh Five Year Plan (FYP) [1987-92]. The government undertook different plans and programmes to raise the economic and social status of women in the Eighth FYP. Since then, the planning process has successfully included 'women empowerment' in various forms. It is evident from the fact that no government programme can be effectively implemented until patriarchal stereotypes eliminates from society as a whole.

5.1. Challenges Face by Indian Women

5.1.1 Gender Based Disparity

Indian women are facing abundant number of discrimination beyond the household. In spite of of having same skill and technical knowledge women are limited to be the part of labour market and often are denied to be promoted to higher and responsible post in the workplace. A well deserving female candidate is always penalized due to gender inequalities in household and in workplace also.

5.1.2 Lack of Access to Education and Employment

The female child in India is often forced to sacrifice their basic education for household work. They are denied or restricted to go to school due to certain social norms in many areas in India. The female education rate of India is 65.6 percent which is significantly lower than the world average 79.7 percent. The situation is more critical in rural areas. Where fewer girls go to school compared to boys and the dropout rate is also very alarming among girls. The burden of household work on Indian girls is a spiraling crisis for India. According to a report by Mckinsey Global Institute (2015) on gender inequality in India found that Indian women perform nearly 10 times the unpaid care work as men. The report of 2018 found that Indian women spend more than 85 percent of their time for unaid household work. Another main issue of women is poverty, lack of social consciousness among women, lack of lady teachers, etc. The problem of women education is one of the biggest barriers for nation's development. Due to conservatism, traditionalism, Indian women are often restricted to access primary education. It has been found that the later part of Vedic Period Indian women were culturally and socially denying the right to study Vedas thus half of the population was deprived of one of the most fundamental human rights.

5.1.3 Gender Based Violence

It is one of the major problems prevailing in India right now. The women from rural area economically are still dependent on men which creates utter nuisance in the society. As Indian society is male dominated thus women of India becomes like a bonded unpaid labour and the crime against the women is gradually increasing day by day. The National Crime Records Bureau reports that in 2021, there were over 428,278 reported cases of violence against women in India. It included physical and sexual harassments, dowry-related violence and female infanticide (Pandey, 2022).

To overcome such hurdles women empowerment is the best option to be practiced. The positive outcomes of women empowerment includes economic independency, socio-economical and political participation, better control over own life, health, well-being, future and greater gender equality. Empowering women can lead to enhance self-esteem, physical and mental health. It may seem to women as blessing for improvement overall quality of life.

5.2 Women Empowerment and Gender Equality

A developed nation can only be possible when women empowerment becomes prime and foremost issue for government. Women empowerment can make the women most proficient in decision making role. Societies must challenge and change the patriarchal norms and attitudes that consider women less capable of handing leadership and responsible position (Kelkar, 2013). A cultural shifting towards recognizing and appreciating the abilities of women is quite significant for inclusion of women in key roles which can influence the change. Nevertheless, considering women in leadership role hs become more challenging and burning issue for the nation., Therefore, all the concerned i.e. societies, government, global organizations and individuals must participate to put the right person at the right place without any gender biasness. These efforts can create an equitable, prosperous and sustainable world.

The UN Sustainable Development Goals (SDGs) are a universal call to action to end poverty, protect planet and ensure peace and prosperity for all. It is to be remembered that the elimination of gender inequality is not a standalone goal but can act as facilitator to accomplish other sustainable development goals. According to UN World Survey (2014) on the "Role of Women in Development 2014" there are proven synergies between women's empowerment and economic, social and environmental sustainability. At the present time women are required to be 'empowered' to narrow down the 'gender gap' and to create equal opportunities for both men and women to attain gender equality.

Women empowerment ensures active participation of women in decision making process and equal distribution of natural resources in human development which can priorities female education, net wealth, nutrition, employment and social protection. The increasing trend of female education can lower down the child mortality rate and improve women health. It also helps to increase the women participation in labour force. The augmentation of women earnings can affect children education, nutrition and education prospect in a positive way.

The "rights, responsibilities and opportunities of individuals will not depend on whether they are born male or female". Gender equality seems like a pillar of democracy which leads to goal governance and inclusive sustainable development (Bayeh, 2016). The gender inequality and gender biased social norms discrimination male and female and marginalize female from benefits of socio-economic and political changes. Women empowerment can be achieved through sustainable development which broadly depends on the equitable distribution of resources and can not be attainted without gender equality. Gender equity refers to fairness of treatment of men and women according to their respective needs. In contrast, 'Gender Equality' means equal outcomes for everyone irrespective of gender. 'Gender Equity is a process to achieve 'Gender Equality'.

Figure 4.

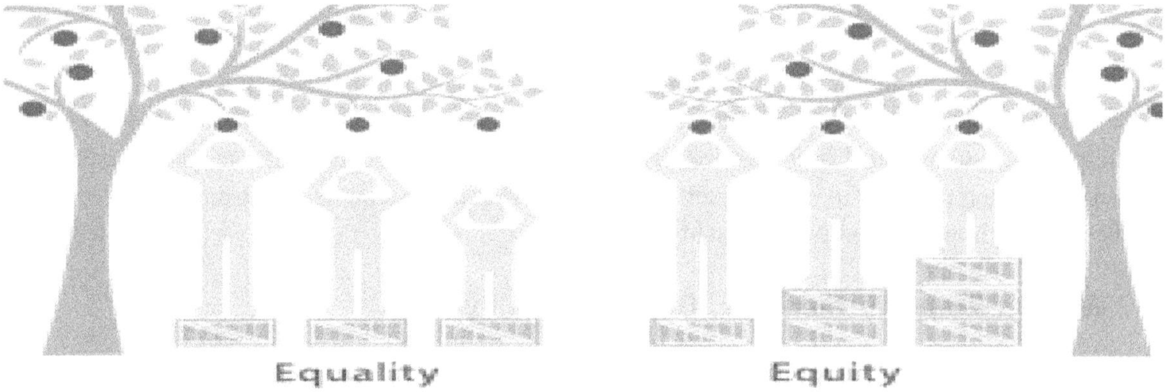

6. MANAGERIAL IMPLICATIONS AND CONCLUSION

6.1 Managerial Implications

The findings of the present study have significant managerial implication for development of gender equality in Indian labour market. The main aim of the study is to identify the gender equality in Indian society and its socio-economic impact on economic growth of the country. The findings also establish the implicit relation between gender discrimination and status of women in the society. The Indian labour market shows a huge gender gap which leads to deprivation of women employees in many respects. On receiving of unequal treatment in household and beyond household the female members are developing frustration and stress which in turn reduce their work ability. This worsens the productivity and self confidence of women and eventually cast a shadow on their work satisfaction. The women empowerment is very essential aspect to build up their confidence and make them functional and rich human labour force. If the women working force is getting gender neutral approach in the labour market then they will assume themselves valuable, empowered, unambiguously confident and indispensible part of the society as a whole. The findings of the study emphasizes practices of wiping out gender inequality establish gender parity in labour market to achieve sustainable economic development. The Government of India plays a vital role in uprooting the gender disparity through implementation of various social reforms.

Indian government need to be forthcoming towards the restructuring various traditional social norms which pull down the status of Indian women. Few suggestive measures are given below:

1. **Women Rights Preservation**: Women form an integral part of the Indian workforce. Thus the rights of women towards equality, dignity, and respect for private life, better social conditions, better access to primary education and health, no domestic violence and cruelty must be ensured. Indian government should incorporate certain strict legal measures to protect women's liberty against domestic violence, mental and physical torture, and cruelty, inhuman and degrading treatment. The women must have control over their private life decision-making and reproductive matters. The constitution of India confers equal rights to everybody without ender disparity but there is a wide gap between theories and real practices. In a patriarchal society, men are always superior to women which results in discrimination, injustice, and dishonor. Thus, the Indian government should look after the proper implementation of legal measures to make sure that violation of such rights may lead to criminal offenses.
2. **Reduction of Unpaid care and household chores**: Indian women are predominantly engaged in household chores which are used to keep them out of 'economic activities'. However, Indian females are forced to contribute to unpaid domestic work for well beings of the family. Indian women are marginalized in the neo-liberal paradigm of the economy and their participation is declining significantly. The disproportionate of burden domestic duties accompanied by mobility and safety concerns results in women forgoing their employment. A generous part of the educated women population is engaged in household chores. A recent NITI Aayog report confirms that Indian women are spending 9.8 times more than men on unpaid domestic care work. Indian women are restricted from making j decision ob decisions due to deep-rooted social norms and a lack of agency. A report by SBI, 2023 states that the total contribution of unpaid women to the economy is approximately 7.5 percent of GDP. Hence, constraints in relation to social stigma and religious norms must be removed so that Indian women can make their own career choices. The active participation of women in the labour market force can only be achieved through the active involvement of women across the formal economic ecosystem. More participation in the formal workforce significantly improves the economy of the country. This will include reducing, redistributing, and rewarding unpaid care work.
3. **Women Leadership in socio-economic-political environment:** Indian women are facing unique challenges and hindrance to get a leadership position due to gender inequality and biased society norms. These challenges range from systematic biasness and cultural expectations to personal barriers and self doubt. Despite of having reservation Indian women are not very much interested to become a politician. Indian government and corporate must support their female employees to break stereotype customs. Indian women suffer mental agony while they put into situation to choose between family and career. If they can be offered flexile working environment then they can strike a better balance between professional and personal life. Sometimes invisible barriers (breaking glass ceilings) prevent the women to take active leadership position in labour market. Apart from that the competent female employees frequently face payment inequality, discrimination in promotion, not having responsible position in the office, etc. The lack of women participation in Indian politics is owing to patriarchal society structure with a so-called communal prejudice that 'politics

is men's job and unsuitable for women'. To evict such ill-conception and assured gender equality Indian government introduce 'women reservation bill' where 33 percent of seats of any election is reserved for women and they will get financial assistance from government to run the campaign. Indian government also provides financial support to the rural and poor women to become independent. Despite of these positive movements India has a long way to go to attain women's parity with men.

6.2 Conclusion

The present paper shows the gender disparity at all levels of Indian society. Unless the government is taking initiatives to address the deep gender inequalities issue prevailing in India transformative changes cannot take place properly. Women empowerment is closely related to the economic development of a nation. The empowerment of women leads to decision-making freedom of women which directly and positively affects the economic growth of a country. Gender equality is integral to sustainable development. The sustainable development goals are 'aspirational global targets' that can be adjusted for 'national circumstances'. Gender inequality leads to constraining the economic growth of a country by limiting the proper use of the women workforce. In many cases Indian women are restricted to being the part of formal labour force because of certain social stigmas. Such exploitation of human resources on the basis of gender is holding back the sustainable economic growth of the country.

It is an indisputable fact that gender equity is vital for human development. Human development is the way to generate economic welfare and distribute the benefits equitably. Sustainable human development is pro-poor, pro-nature, and pro-woman. It helps in growth with employment, growth with environment, growth with empowerment, and growth with equity. A nation is not capable to attain sustainable human development goals without minimizing gender disparities. Being a politically driven country India must enhance the opportunity for women to the arena of politics and decision-making. If women can take part in political decision-making then the desired sustainable economic growth can be achieved in a short span of time. In the backdrop of women empowerment, the Indian government is trying to increase the women's reservation in Parliament up to 50 percent.

The government of India has realized the necessity of women's equal participation in political leadership is the need of the hour. It is an acceptable fact that without the equal and full participation of women in the power structure and decision-making the goals for equity, development, and peace cannot be achieved. Despite the progress in some states of India, serious and persistent obstacles still constrain the empowerment of women and their participation in the political decision-making process. Apart from that there are certain basic barriers like poverty, lack of equal access to basic education, and training, cultural barriers, political and institutional hindrances, the impact of armed conflict and natural disasters that have contributed a large to gender discrimination and lower participation of women in labour force. Hence, women should be more strategic and dignified with self-esteem and confidence in the workplace to make a rightful place in society. They must challenge the traditional gender disparities and male chauvinism for sharing of domestic responsibilities with other family members.

To be 'pro-woman' one does not need to be 'pro-man'. Now, it is the time to change the mindset of women which can minimize the gender gap and enhance gender equality in society. Articles 14, 15, and 16 of the Indian constitution provide equal rights to Indian women before the law, protection, and opportunity to work without discrimination relating to caste, religion, creed, and gender. To eliminate the evil of gender discrimination one should change the state of mind. Historically, women have been playing a dominant role in the socio-economic development of a country. In ancient India, women were enjoying a high status during the Vedic era but such status was diminishing during the later part of the era. The former Prime Minister of India, Pandit Jawahar Lal Neheru once said "You can tell the state of a nation by looking at the condition of the women there". Hence the government should need to address the concern on an urgent basis. As an emerging economy, India must frame the policy which needs to be a comprehensive understanding of what derives gender inequalities in its varied manifestation.

REFERENCES

Addati, L., Cattaneo, U., Esquivel, V., & Valarino, I. (2018). Care work and care jobs for the future of decent work. International Labour Organization.

Ahmed. (2001). *Gender Issues, Population and Development in Ethiopia: In-depth Studies from the 1994 Population and Housing Census in Ethiopia*. Italian Multi-bi Research Project ETH/92/P01.

Alvarez, M. L. (2013, February). From Unheard Screams to Powerful Voices: A Case Study of Women's Political Empowerment in the Philippines. In *12th National Convention on Statistics (NCS) EDSA*, Mandaluyong City.

Bairagya, I. (2018). Why Is Unemployment Higher among the Educated? *Economic and Political Weekly*, *53*(7), 43–51.

Bayeh, E. (2016). The role of empowering women and achieving gender equality to the sustainable development of Ethiopia. *Pacific Science Review B. Humanities and Social Sciences*, *2*(1), 37–42.

Beniwal, A. (2013). Gender Discrimination and Empowerment of Women in India: A View. *Indian Journal of Poultry Science*, *74*(1), 27–38.

Bhat, Z. A. (2014). Gender Bias and Socio-Economic Problems of Women in India. *Abhinav National Monthly Referred Journal of Research in Arts and Education*, *3*(4), 8–13.

Chakraborty, S. (2016). Occupational Sex Segregation: An Inquiry into Indian Job Market. *Journal of Regional Development and Planning*, *5*(2), 1–17.

Choudhry, M. T., & Elhorst, P. (2018). Female labour force participation and economic development. *International Journal of Manpower*, *39*(7), 896–912. doi:10.1108/IJM-03-2017-0045

Collier, P. (1994). Gender Aspects of Labor Allocation during Structural Adjustment: Theoretical Framework and the Africa Experience in Labor Markets in an era of adjustment. World Bank.

Cornejo, J. M. (2007). *An examination of the relationships among perceived gender discrimination, work motivation, and performance*. UMI No. 3377804.

Desai, S. (1994). *Gender Inequalities and Demographic Behaviours: India*. The Population Council, Inc. doi:10.31899/pgy1994.1003

Deshpande, A., Goel, D., & Khanna, S. (2015). Bad Karma or Discrimination? Male-FemaleWage Gaps Among Salaried Workers in India. *IZA Discussion Paper No. 9485*. doi:10.2139/ssrn.2690733

Devi, S. U. (1999). Visions for 21st century. In K. Ahooja-Patel, S. U. Devi, & G. A. Tadas (Eds.), *Women and development* (pp. 21–43). Har-Anand Publications.

Dipboye, R. L., & Colella, A. (2005). *Discrimination at work: The psychological and organizational bases*. Lawrence Erlbaum.

Dixon, R. B. (1982). Mobilizing women for rural employment in South Asia: Issues of class, caste, and patronage. *Economic Development and Cultural Change*, *30*(2), 373–390. doi:10.1086/452562

Dong, X. Y., & An, X. (2015). Gender patterns and value of unpaid care work: Findings from China's First Large-Scale Time Use Survey. *Review of Income and Wealth*, *61*(3), 540–560. doi:10.1111/roiw.12119

Esteve-Volart, B. (2004). Gender discrimination and growth: theory and evidence from India. *LSES-TICERD Research Paper No. DEDPS 42*. file:///C:/Users/imib/Downloads/SSRN-id1127011.pdf

Ferrant, G., Pesando, L. M., & Nowacka, K. (2014). *Unpaid Care Work: The missing link in the analysis of gender gaps in labour outcomes. Boulogne Billancourt*. OECD Development Center.

Fletcher, E., Pande, R., & Moore, C. M. (2017) Women and work in india: descriptive evidence and a review of potential policies. *HKS working paper no. RWP18-004*. Center for International Development Harvard University, Cambridge.

Galor, O., & Weil, D. N. (1996). The Gender Gap, Fertility, and Growth. *The American Economic Review*, *86*(3), 374–387.

Hartmann, H. (1976). Capitalism, Patriarchy, and Job Segregation by Sex. *Signs (Chicago, Ill.)*, *1*(3, Part 2), 137–169. doi:10.1086/493283

ILO. (2013). Women and men in the informal economy: A statistical picture (second edition) / International Labour Office – Geneva: ILO. International Labour Organisation.

Kabeer, N. (2010). Women's empowerment, development interventions and the management of information flows. *IDS Bulletin*, *41*(6), 105–113. doi:10.1111/j.1759-5436.2010.00188.x

Kelkar, G. (2013, December). *At the Threshold of Economic Empowerment: Women, Worker and Gender Regimes in Asia.* ILO Asia-Pacific working paper series, 2227-4391. https://www.ilo.org/wcmsp5/groups/public/---asia/---ro-bangkok/---sro-new_delhi/documents/publication/wcms_233096.pdf

Klasen, S., & Lamanna, F. (2009). The impact of gender inequality in education and employment on economic growth: New evidence for a panel of countries. *Feminist Economics*, *15*(3), 91–132. doi:10.1080/13545700902893106

Krishna, K. L., Erumban, A. A., & Kusumdas, D. (2016). Structural Changes in Employment in India, 1980–2011. *Centre for Development Economics, Delhi School of Economics.*

Kundu, A., & Mohanan, P. C. (2009, April). Employment and inequality outcomes in India. In *Joint Seminar on Employment and Inequality, organized by the Employment* (Vol. 8, pp. 1–43). Labour and Social Affairs Directorate and Development Centre.

Lagerlöf, N.-P. (2003). Gender Equality and Long-Run Growth. *Journal of Economic Growth*, *8*(4), 403–426. doi:10.1023/A:1026256917489

Lama, S., & Majumder, R. (2018). Gender inequality in wage and employment in Indian labour market. *Journal of Academic Research in Economics, 10*(3), 482–500.

Majumder, R. (2011). Female labour supply in india: proximate determinants - Munich Personal RePEc Archive. *Uni-Muenchen.de.* https://doi.org/https://mpra.ub.uni-muenchen.de/43250/1/MPRA_paper_43250.pdf

Malhotra, A., Schulte, J., Patel, P., & Petesch, P. (2009). *Innovation for women's empowerment andgender equality.* International center for research on women (ICRW).www.icrw.org/wp-content/uploads/2016/10/Innovation-for-Womens-Empowerment.pdf

Mckinsey Global Institute. (2018) *McKinsey Global Institute.* McKinsey & Company. https://www.mckinsey.com/~/media/mckinsey/industries/public%20and%20social%20sector/our%20insights/outperformers%20high%20growth%20emerging%20economies%20and%20the%20companies%20that%20propel%20them/mgi-outperformers-full-report-sep-2018.pdf

Mehrotra, S., Parida, J., Sinha, S., & Gandhi, A. (2014). Explaining Employment Trends in the Indian Economy: 1993–94 to 2011–12. *Economic and Political Weekly, 49*(32), 49–57.

Ministry of Human Development. (2018). *Annual Report of the Ministry of Human Development.* MSDE. https://www.msde.gov.in/sites/default/files/2020-09/Annual%20Report%202018-2019%20%28English%29.pdf

Ministry of Labour & Employment. (2021). *Women Participation in Workforce.* Ministry of Labour and Employment. https://labour.gov.in/sites/default/files/pib1843397.pdf

Mosse, D. (2018). Caste and development: Contemporary perspectives on a structure of discrimination and advantage. *World Development, 110*, 422–436. doi:10.1016/j.worlddev.2018.06.003

NSSO. (2005). *2007-09 unit level data, 68th round, Employment Unemployment survey, NSSO Ministry of Statistics and Program Implementation.* Government of India.

OECD. (2021). *Time Use.* Oecd.org. https://stats.oecd.org/Index.aspx?datasetcode=TIME_USE

Pandey, G. (2022, September 13). Rising crimes against Indian women in five charts. *BBC News: Delhi* Edition: https://www.bbc.com/news/world-asia-india- 62830634#:~:text=in%20five%20charts.-The%20rising%20graph,from%20338%2C954%20cases%20in%202016

Patel, L. (2019). Gender: Toward gender equality and poverty reduction. Handbook of Social Policy and Development, (pp. 71-88).

Patrick, H. A., & Kumar, V. R. (2012). Managing Workplace Diversity: Issues and Challenges. *SAGE Open, 2*(2). Advance online publication. doi:10.1177/2158244012444615

Sen, A. (2014). Development as Freedom (1999). *The Globalization and Development Reader: Perspectives on Development and Global Change, 525.*

UN Women. (2014). *The World Survey on the role of women in development 2014: Gender equality and sustainable development.* UN Women. https://www.unwomen.org/en/digital-library/publications/2014/10/world-survey-2014

Unit Level Data Of Periodic Labour Force Survey (PLFS). (2019). MOSPI. https://mospi.gov.in/unit-level-data-periodic-labour-force-survey-plfs-july-2019-june-2020

United Nations Development Programme. (2015). *Human development report 2015. Rethinking work for human development*. UN. https://hdr.undp.org/sites/default/files/2015_human_development_report.pdfC

Uppal A, 2007, Gender Discrimination in Quality of Employment and Wages in Unorganized Manufacturing Sector of India: Paper presented in Gender Issues and Empowerment of Women Platinum Jubilee of Indian Statistical Institute 1-2 February 2007.

Verick, S. (2018). Female Labour Force Participation and Development. The Institute for the Study of Labour (IZA) Germany. *IZA World of Labor: Evidence-Based Policy Making*, *87*(2). Advance online publication. doi:10.15185/izawol.87.v2

Warth, L., & Koparanova, M. (2012). Empowering Women for Sustainable Development. Discussion Paper Series, No. 2012.1. United Nations Economic Commission For Europe, Geneva, Switzerland.

KEY TERMS AND DEFINITIONS

Economic Liberalization: It refers to the relief of government restrictions within the area of social, political, and economic policies. To facilitate private participation and support free trade in the country, the government withdraws certain government restrictions. It reduces the direct interference of government on both internal and international transactions and gives the direction of moving towards a free market economy.

Gender Bias: It is gender based perceptions of behavior where women are differentiated from men in rights and dignity. Generally, gender bias refers to implicit or unconscious bias. It has a tendency to prefer or show certain favoritism towards one gender over another. It indicates unequal treatment of a person or group of people due to gender-based prejudice. Gender bias is a social convention that degrades women as a whole.

Gender Equality: Gender equality refers to the same outcomes for all irrespective of gender. It implies all women, men, girls, and boys have same human rights and same value. It is the principle that indicates that human beings must enjoy equal rights, equal access to resources, freedom, and opportunities despite their biological differences.

Gender Equity: It is a process which implies the fairness of treatment for both male and female according to their respective requirements. Generally it means equal participation of men and women in all aspects of social life. Equity ensures that men, women, boys and girls have equal chance at the starting point as well as reaching the finishing line. It refers to the fair and just treatment to all human beings irrespective of sexes.

Globalization: It is a process of integrating the economic, religious, social, political, and cultural systems among different countries around the world. Economic globalization promotes international free trade which converts the whole world into a single marketplace. It also promotes better cooperation, integration, and interaction between different companies, individuals, and governments with the objective of building strong alliances that are mutually beneficial to everybody.

Informal Worker: It refers to the workers who are engaged in employment without social, legal, and job security. They used to work in precarious working environments for long periods without proper wages. In general, informal workers are insufficiently covered by existing labour legislation. There is a lack of formal employer-employee relationships as well as socio-economic and political benefits.

Sustainable Development: Sustainable development refers to development that meets the requirements of the present without depleting the natural resources It is used to strike a socio-economic-environmental balance between the present and future by conserving and retaining the undue damages of natural resources. Rather it sustains the balance between present and future needs without compromising the natural resources.

Women Empowerment: Women empowerment can refer to a social, cultural, political, and economic process that encourages the rights of women to have equal opportunity as men to make strategic life choices on their own, the right to influence social changes to develop self-esteem and self-worth. It is a process that enables women to attempt personal, social, and economic activities to raise their status in society and acquire the power to take part in the decision-making process.

Chapter 12
Sustainable Development Goals and European Two-Tier Corporate Governance Framework as a Model for Limited Liability Partnerships

Ravindran Nadarajan
Universiti Tunku Abdul Rahman, Malaysia

Hamizah Abdul Rahman
Universiti Sultan Zainal Abidin, Malaysia

ABSTRACT

A two-tier model of corporate governance is perceived to be suitable for the corporate governance of liability partnerships (LLP) in Malaysia because the ownership and management of LLPs are both asserted on the partners, and there is the absence of a board of directors (unlike a company). As such, there is a need for a body to supervise the members/partners to ensure good governance for an LLP. All the corporate governance theories – namely agency theory, ethical theory, stakeholder theory, and corporate social responsibility (CSR) – are also relevant to LLPs in ensuring a good corporate governance framework. As such, the legal justifications and theories to support a corporate governance framework for LLPs should be similar to a company. However, due to the internal regulations of LLPs (which have overlaps between ownership, management, and decision-making structures), this chapter would propose a two-tier model of corporate governance with perceptive view on sustainability's development goals to be adopted for LLPs.

DOI: 10.4018/979-8-3693-0390-0.ch012

Copyright © 2024, IGI Global. Copying or distributing in print or electronic forms without written permission of IGI Global is prohibited.

INTRODUCTION

The aim of this paper is to determine a better corporate governance framework for Limited Liability Partnership (hereinafter referred as "LLP") in Malaysia based on the existing corporate governance framework for companies. Limited Liability Partnerships are a new vehicle that can be beneficial to protect a partner's liability in business. LLP enable expansion of businesses through the sharing of capital, expertise, and many other aspects that are minimal in sole proprietorship, or conventional partnership businesses. LLP have been introduced in Malaysia, and have the legal status of a body corporate, under the Limited Liability Partnership Act 2012 (Abdul Rahman & Nadarajan, 2021). This legal treatment of LLP is similar with Singapore, India, and the United Kingdom. The governance of LLP is important to ensure ethical business conduct - similar to other types of business (Abdul Rahman & Nadarajan, 2021). At present there is no governance framework for LLP. As a hybrid business vehicle, LLP require a special governance framework, different than companies, because despite having the status of a body corporate, the internal legal framework of LLP is based upon partnership agreements, which are akin to partnership laws (Abd Ghadas & Abdul Rahman, 2020). This research aims to propose a tailored corporate governance framework for Malaysian LLP. There are three important research objectives: firstly to identify who are the stakeholders of an LLP, and what are their rights and duties are in an LLP; secondly, to analyses the internal and external regulations of LLP; and thirdly, to propose a framework of corporate governance for LLP. This research found that the Europe Two-Tier framework that are relevant to designing a suitable LLP governance framework. It is proposed that a two-tier framework is suitable for the corporate governance of LLP in Malaysia. The framework indicates that the LLP should set-up a Corporate Governance Supervisory Board that consists of stakeholders other than the partners, and also independent individuals or business experts. This is to ensure that the supervisory board has partners that are impartial from the LLP management board, and do not hold any personal interest in the corporate governance process.

They must be able to provide concrete advice to the management board on how to implement proper governance in managing the LLP. The Second-Tier is the Management Board that is comprised of the LLP partners. None of the management board shall become partners of the corporate governance supervisory board. The role of this board is to provide information to the supervisory board on the LLP's business practices, and to ensure compliance with all corporate governance standards (Abd Ghadas & Abdul Rahman, 2020). The separation of powers and impartiality of the parties in the LLP governance framework is important to avoid any misconduct by the partners - such as corruption or fraud, to manage any disputes between the partners, and to manage any liability issues in any cases of any changes to the makeup of the partners, or LLP dissolutions. This will ensure the effectiveness of governance is fair to all members of the LLP (Abd Ghadas & Abdul Rahman, 2020).

METHODOLOGY

This research's methodology is doctrinal in nature, whereby existing laws, rules, and regulations that are relevant to the establishment of the LLP are referred to; and secondary information is gathered from the literature to determine the best LLP governance framework for Malaysia. This research also applies conceptual analyses of theories of stakeholder primacy, co-determination and managerialism for the European two-tier model.

CORPORATE GOVERNANCE STRUCTURE FOR LLP

The corporate governance is a term normally associated with companies, which is the predominant business structure. However, an LLP, like a company, is a body corporate, and good corporate governance practices are as important for an LLP as they are for the company.

Overview of LLP in Malaysia

Before the introduction of LLP to Malaysia, the frequently used business vehicles were: (i) sole proprietorships; (ii) partnerships; and (iii) companies or corporations. All of these business vehicles are confined to their own statutory legislations, and are separately treated due to their distinguishing features. Sole proprietorships are subjected to certain requirements from the Companies Commission of Malaysia (SSM). Business vehicles in the form of partnerships are bound to follow the Partnerships Act 1961, and companies or corporations are mandated to follow the Companies Act 1965.

The first form of LLP in Malaysia was introduced in the Federal Territory of Labuan, in 1997, as Labuan Limited Partnerships. They were soon followed by the introduction the Limited Liability Partnerships Act 2010 in January of that year. Both of the Acts were only enforceable in the Federal Territory of Labuan. They were not enforceable throughout Malaysia. This means that prior to 2012, LLP could only be established in the Federal Territory of Labuan.

According to Salim (2013), there was an increasing demand to recognise the needs of small businesses in Malaysia. This led to the development of a new form of business vehicle, and it was therefore necessary to introduce LLP into the Malaysian legal framework. The Consultative Document on Limited Liability Partnerships in Malaysia was completed by the Corporate Law Reform Committee. These Consultative Documents provided a proposal for the introduction of LLP throughout Malaysia, proposing a model of LLP that could be used in Malaysia, and the structure for LLP. The Corporate Law Reform Committee claimed that the proposed LLP was complementary to the other existing business vehicles in Malaysia. It is crucial to have LLP, in order to provide wider options for the establishment of businesses, and make businesses more flexible and competitive. In 2012 the Limited Liability Partnership Act 2012 (hereinafter referred as "LLPA 2012") was passed by the Malaysian Parliament. With the LLPA 2012 LLP officially became a form of business vehicle that could be incorporated in Malaysia. Labuan Limited Partnerships and Limited Liability Partnerships Act 2010 remains applicable to the Federal Territory of Labuan, as the Malaysian offshore business centre.

According to Abd. Ghadas (2009), the LLPA 2012 has the potential to increase of the establishment of businesses in Malaysia, either from local or international players. The main contributory source for the LLPA 2012 was the active role of the SSM as the main authority in regulating business vehicles in Malaysia. Even though the LLPA 2012 was passed in 2012, it only enforceable in Malaysia from 2014. The delay was due to the need for improvement to be carried out by the SSM in matters of administration and registration of LLP throughout Malaysia.

Overview of Corporate Governance in LLP in Malaysia

In terms of corporate governance, LLP in Malaysia are required to adhere to certain principles and practices to ensure transparency, accountability, and effective management. The main components of corporate governance consist of the tasks of strategic management, social mechanisms at a lower level, and quality control mechanisms applied by the top management. In the long term, corporate governance is a multi-functional and multi-faceted development of strategies for implementing, monitoring, and controlling the success of an organisation (Deliu, 2019). Corporate governance has an important role in protecting stakeholder interests. Corporate governance refers to the structures and processes for the direction and control of businesses and the relationships among the management, board of directors, controlling shareholders, minority shareholders, and other stakeholders (Ghazali, 2010).

Based on the assumption that good governance is able to boost the development of an economy through the enhancement of business performance in the long term, it is important for companies to establish good corporate governance structures, including within LLP (Rahman, 2018). The corporate governance structures that provide descriptions of the roles and responsibilities of the key persons, the rules and regulations, the standard operating procedures, and corporate affairs (Agarwal, 2009).

Since the internal regulations of LLP are different from those of a company, the application of existing corporate governance is not compatible with LLP. Having the internal regulations of a partnership, LLP partners play active roles in decision-making in the LLP (Rahman, 2018). With full control over the firm, the possibility of a partner committing an infraction is higher due to the lack of structure and protection; for instance, there are no audit requirements for LLP (Rahman, 2018). Without proper accounting management and auditing requirements, it is difficult for LLP to create trust with creditors, and this leads to the question of an LLP's credibility in carrying out business (Aguilera, 2006). The existing law alone is not enough to ensure that partners follow the rules and regulations; however, it is essential that LLP do follow the proper monitoring or governance bodies in order to create transparency and accountability for LLP (Armour, 2001). A governance structure is important to monitor and control the management of an LLP from any abusive decisions taken against the stakeholders, including employees, creditors, suppliers, and others. In terms of liability, limited liability status will be conferred on an LLP, which positions it markedly apart from conventional partnership law, which imposes joint and several liabilities on conventional partnerships for all tortuous acts of their co-partners acting within the scope of their actual or apparent authority (Alnasser, 2012).

Furthermore, in an LLP, partners are accorded limited liability in respect of tort and contractual claims, which means that individual partners will not be liable for the contracts, debts, obligations, and liabilities of the LLP, nor will they have personal liability for the conduct, wrongful acts, omissions, negligence, or other tortuous conduct of an employee, staff member, or co-partner (if carried out during the course of business) (Armour, 2001). The personal assets of partners will not be at risk for such acts or matters. In the event that the LLP becomes insolvent, a partner's liability is limited to the amount of his capital contribution to the limited liability partnership existing at the time (Armour, 2001). Although limited liability status in LLP is partial (partners may be personally liable in some situations), it can still result in unfair and unjust outcomes for stakeholders due to the lack of protections, particularly for the third parties (since the partner's liability is limited to the amount of their agreed contribution in cases of insolvency) (Paul, 2023). In this situation, partners might forge documents or agreements to avoid liability. Without proper monitoring, third parties might suffer losses without any right to recover the money from LLP partners. There needs to be proper regulation on this issue since LLP have very unique attributes when compared to other business entities (Paul, 2023).

Thus, in order to resolve the main problems between stakeholders and an LLP's management team, a theoretical analysis of corporate governance theory is used to design an appropriate governance structure for sharing responsibilities and decision-making. Stakeholder Theory explores the perception that corporations need effective governance in order to achieve success (Salim, 2013). The governance structure will establish the enactment of a code of conduct, strategies, and decision management for the organisation. These include important components of a corporate governance structure: stakeholders, a board of directors, the characteristics of the board, board committees, the management team, and the various protocols of engagement and communication (Salim, 2013).

It is important for the business community (including LLP) to realise that corporate governance is not only applicable to companies; it is also about good decisions being made by the right people to ensure that a business is on the right track and that there are no issues of tortious misconduct that will affect the performance and future of an LLP business (Aguilera, 2006). If there are no governance practices in an LLP, there is a high chance that the business will not be able to grow or expand in the long run due to these issues surrounding the LLP. In order to cater for these issues, it is important for the LLP to have a good corporate governance model to protect the rights of the stakeholders and ensure the transparency and accountability of the business (Aguilera, 2006).

Importance of Transparency and Accountability in LLP

The transparency and accountability play a crucial role in the functioning and success of Limited Liability Partnerships (LLP). By adopting and promoting transparency and accountability, LLP can achieve several benefits (Abd Ghadas & Abdul Rahman, 2020). Firstly, transparency ensures that all stakeholders, including partners, investors, and employees, have access to accurate and timely information about the LLP's operations, financial performance, and decision-making processes (Abd Ghadas & Abdul Rahman, 2020). This transparency fosters trust and confidence among stakeholders, which is essential for the smooth functioning of the LLP.

Secondly, accountability ensures that partners in an LLP are responsible for their actions and decisions (Salim, 2013). It helps in promoting ethical behavior, as partners are aware that their actions will be scrutinised and they will be held accountable for any misconduct or negligence. This accountability also extends to financial matters, ensuring that partners are accountable for the proper management and utilization of the LLP's resources (Abd Ghadas & Abdul Rahman, 2020). Furthermore, transparency and accountability in LLP contribute to the overall governance and compliance of the entity. By maintaining transparent practices, LLP can comply with legal and regulatory requirements, thereby avoiding legal issues and penalties. It also helps in preventing conflicts of interest and promoting fair and equitable treatment of all stakeholders (Abd Ghadas, & Abdul Rahman, 2020).

In summary, transparency and accountability are vital in LLP as they promote trust, ethical behavior, and compliance with legal requirements. By upholding these principles, LLP can enhance their reputation, attract investors, and ensure the long-term success of the partnership (Yetty Komalasari, 2021). Overall, transparency and accountability are essential for LLP to establish trust, manage risks, maintain ethical conduct, attract investors, comply with regulations, and build a positive reputation. By prioritizing these principles, LLP can enhance their overall performance and long-term sustainability, which can be especially beneficial for legal professional businesses looking to sustain and enhance their business (Yetty Komalasari, 2021).

SUSTAINABLE DEVELOPMENT GOALS (SDGS)

Overview of Sustainable Development Goals (SDGs)

The Sustainable Development Goals (hereinafter referred as "SDGs") are a set of 17 global goals established by the United Nations in 2015. These goals aim to address various social, economic, and environmental challenges faced by countries worldwide, with the ultimate objective of achieving sustainable development by 2030 (United Nation, 2023). The SDGs cover a wide range of interconnected issues, including poverty eradication, quality education, gender equality, clean water and sanitation, affordable and clean energy, decent work and economic growth, industry innovation and infrastructure, reduced inequalities, sustainable cities and communities, responsible consumption and production, climate action, life below water, life on land, peace, justice, and strong institutions, and partnerships for the goals. Each goal has specific targets and indicators to measure progress and guide actions at the national and international levels. The SDGs emphasise the importance of leaving no one behind and ensuring that development efforts are inclusive, equitable, and sustainable (United Nation, 2023).

Relevance of Sustainable Development Goals (SDGs) to LLP

The Sustainable Development Goals (SDGs) are a set of global objectives established by the United Nations to address various social, economic, and environmental challenges. While the SDGs are typically associated with governments and international organizations, they are also relevant to limited liability partnerships (LLP) for several reasons (Ordonez-Ponce, 2021).

Firstly, LLP have the potential to contribute to the achievement of the SDGs through their business operations (Ordonez-Ponce, 2021). By aligning their strategies and practices with the SDGs, LLP can actively work towards addressing issues such as poverty, inequality, climate change, and sustainable consumption. For example, an LLP can adopt sustainable production methods, promote gender equality within its workforce, or support community development initiatives.

Secondly, integrating the SDGs into their operations can enhance the reputation and competitiveness of LLP. Many consumers, investors, and stakeholders are increasingly conscious of sustainability issues and prefer to engage with businesses that demonstrate a commitment to social and environmental responsibility (De Oliveira, 2023). By incorporating the SDGs into their business practices, LLP can attract socially conscious customers, investors, and partners, thereby gaining a competitive advantage.

Furthermore, LLP can collaborate with other stakeholders, including governments, non-profit organizations, and communities, to collectively work towards achieving the SDGs. Partnerships and collaborations can leverage the expertise, resources, and networks of different entities to address complex sustainable challenges more effectively (De Oliveira, 2023). In summary, the SDGs are relevant to LLP as they provide a framework for addressing social, economic, and environmental issues. By aligning their operations with the SDGs, LLP can contribute to sustainable development, enhance their reputation, and collaborate with other stakeholders to achieve shared goals.

Significance of SDGs With European Two-Tier Corporate Governance Framework in LLP

The Sustainable Development Goals (SDGs) provide a global framework for addressing social, economic, and environmental challenges. While the SDGs are not specifically designed for corporate governance frameworks, they can certainly influence and guide the practices of various business entities, including Limited Liability Partnerships (LLP). In the context of European two-tier corporate governance framework, which typically consists of a management board and a supervisory board, the SDGs can contribute to the sustainable and responsible business practices of LLP. Here are a few ways in which the SDGs can be relevant:

a) Environmentally Sustainable: The SDGs emphasise the need for businesses to adopt sustainable practices that minimise their environmental impact. LLP can align their operations with SDG targets related to climate action (SDG 13), resource efficiency (SDG 12), and biodiversity conservation (SDG 15). This may involve implementing green initiatives, reducing carbon emissions, and promoting sustainable supply chains.
b) Social Responsibility: The SDGs also highlight the importance of social responsibility, including promoting gender equality (SDG 5), decent work (SDG 8), and inclusive growth (SDG 10). LLP can integrate these goals into their corporate governance framework by ensuring diversity and inclusion in their boards, promoting fair labor practices, and supporting local communities through responsible business practices.
c) Ethical Business Conduct: The SDGs call for businesses to operate ethically and with integrity. LLP can incorporate ethical principles into their corporate governance framework by establishing codes of conduct, implementing robust compliance programs, and promoting transparency and accountability in their decision-making processes by disclosing information about their operations, including their environmental and social impact. This can help build trust with stakeholders and ensure that the LLP is held accountable for its actions.

It is important to note that while European two-tier corporate governance framework provides a solid foundation for LLP, the integration of the SDGs requires a proactive approach from the LLP themselves. By voluntarily aligning their practices with the SDGs, LLP can contribute to sustainable development and demonstrate their commitment to responsible business conduct (Is, M. S., & Saputra, J. A. 2021). Overall, the SDGs can serve as a guiding framework for LLP within European two-tier corporate governance model, helping them to integrate sustainable, social responsibility, and ethical practices into their operations and decision-making processes (Khayesi, 2021).

A TWO-TIER MODEL OF CORPORATE GOVERNANCE FRAMEWORK

Explanation of the Two Tiers System

Figure 1 shows that at the first-tier level (the supervisory board), the LLP should set up a corporate governance supervisory board that consists of stakeholders other than the partners and also independent individuals or business experts (Jungmann, 2006). This is to ensure that the supervisory board is impartial to the LLP partners on the management board and does not have any personal interests in the corporate governance process. They must be able to provide concrete advice to the management board on how to implement proper governance for managing the LLP (Mueller, 2006).

Figure 1 also indicates the second-tier is the management board, which comprises the LLP partners (Jungmann, 2006). None of the management board members should join the corporate governance supervisory board. The main role of this board is to provide information to the supervisory board on the LLP business practices and conduct the business affairs in compliance with all corporate governance standards (Jungmann, 2006).

Figure 1. First and two tiers system model

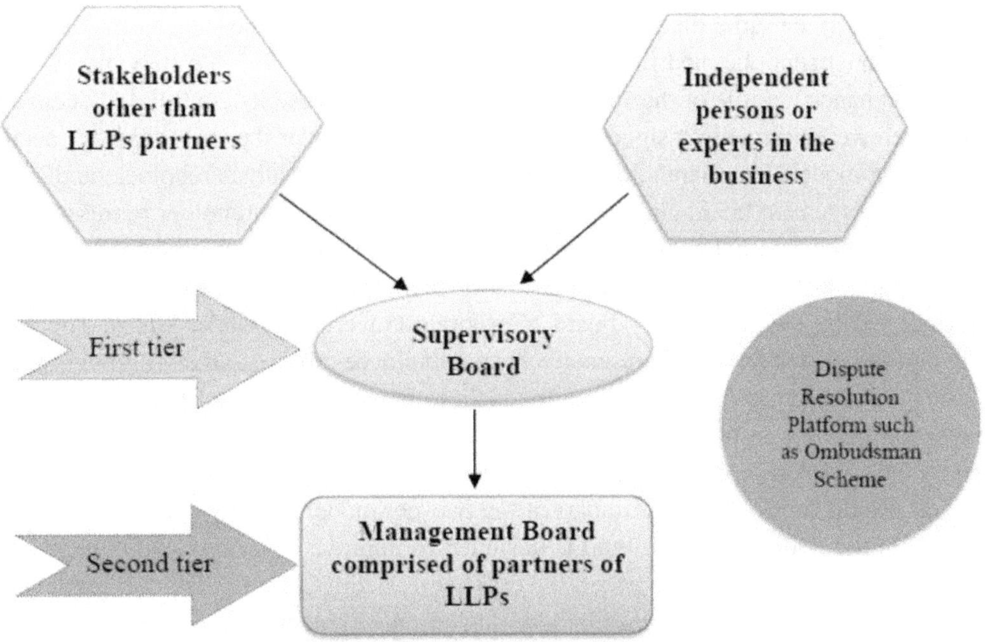

The separation of powers, and the impartiality of the Supervisory Board are very important to avoid any misconduct by the business partners, such as corruption or fraud. It also helps to manage any disputes between the LLP's partners, and to manage any liability issues, in any cases where there is a change of partners, or in the event of the LLP's dissolution (Nordberg, 2021).

LLP require corporate governance frameworks to guarantee that the formation of an LLP proceeds smoothly and with minimum confusion regarding the duties and obligations of the firm owners or partners (Mansor, 2022). Because governance may help the business, it's worth thinking about how to set up tools and procedures to execute a two-tier corporate governance structure that's best suited to LLP (Mansor, 2022). There are certain significant characteristics of corporate governance that LLP may learn from firms in terms of creating excellent governance structures: i) LLP should carefully define a governance structure that achieves its political, cultural, performance, and strategic objectives; ii) LLP should have competent partners that have key characteristics embodying a wide range of skills, and greater experience and knowledge; iii) LLP should be guided by their core functions, such as oversight, fiduciary duties, strategic, and legal obligations; iv) LLP partners should be carefully selected on the basis of best practice, and the nature, needs, sise, and state of development, of the business; and v) LLP's management should be given the room to function effectively, but not without proper supervision and control by the partners (Pomeranz & Stedman, 2020).

A Two-Tier Model of Corporate Governance in Other Countries

In European nations, such as Germany, the two-tier model has a distinctive structure (Jungmann, 2006). The two-tier board structure is made up of a management board, which is made up of corporate executives, and a supervisory board, which is made up of employee and shareholder representatives (Gazioglu, 1992). The two boards are completely separate, and no one may serve on both the management and supervisory boards at the same time. The number and membership of the supervisory board are statutorily mandated and cannot be modified by shareholders (Gazioglu, 1992). In Italy, the two-tier model is designed to enhance the role of the supervisory board and increase its control and decision-making functions, which were originally assigned to the board of directors or the shareholders' meeting in the traditional Italian model. The shareholders' meeting is composed of all shareholders and approves the actions of the management board and the supervisory board, elects shareholder representatives of the supervisory board and external auditors of the enterprise, passes resolutions related to corporate legal principles, and passes the consultation resolution on the approval of the remuneration management system formulated by the supervisory board (Corporate Governance Code, 2020). The supervisory board is composed of shareholder representatives and employee representatives, appoints and removes members of the management board, and has the right to request approval of major transactions while the management board is responsible for the daily operation and management of the enterprise and is appointed by the supervisory board (Provasi & Riva, 2015). The nomination committee, remuneration committee, and audit committee are also part of the two-tier model in Italy. The Italian two-tier model is different from the traditional model and is designed to improve efficiency and enhance the role of the supervisory board (Li, 2021). Moreover, the two-tier model in China the two-tier model is designed to balance the interests of different stakeholders, such as shareholders, employees, and creditors. The supervisory board is responsible for overseeing the management board and ensuring that the company is operating in compliance with laws and regulations while the management board is responsible for the day-to-day operations of the company and implementing the strategies and policies set by the supervisory board (OECD, 2023). Germany has a well-established history with the two-tier model, which has been in use for a long time, while Italy introduced it as an optional model to improve efficiency, and China is establishing its own two-tier corporate structure based on its own conditions and learning from the world's experience with the model, highlighting the different experiences of these countries with the two-tier corporate governance model (Li, 2021).

The two-tier model is also applied in Indonesia (one of Malaysia's closest business allies) as a result of the adoption of Dutch law in Indonesian corporate law. The first tier is made up of the Board of Directors, who are in control of the company's management. The Board of Commissioners, at the second tier, is responsible for supervising the Board of Directors in administering the firm in the best interests of the company (Beritelli, 2007). To support the appropriate fulfilment of its supervisory obligations, the Board of Commissioners has certain authorities and the authority to request any information that they believe essential to adequately supervise the manner the Board of Directors conducts the operations of the corporation (Gazioglu, 1992). In an LLP with corporate body status, the partners who own the LLP have the sole discretion in decision-making and management power. The decision-making body and the ownership structure are inextricably linked. LLP structures reflect the family business companies' structure, where there is an inter-association between ownership and management structures (Anglo, 2023). To enforce the principles of corporate governance, in particular transparency and integrity, there should be a supervisory body to monitor the management (Pomeranz & Stedman, 2020). However, diverging from the two-tier corporate governance model, LLP' supervisory bodies should not involve the partners and should only comprise other stakeholders of the LLP, such as representatives of employees and also independent parties that have expertise and knowledge in the business. This combination should assist to guarantee that the LLP's management follows good governance standards in corporate governance, while also ensuring that the supervisory board does not interfere with the partners' decision-making and management abilities (Pomeranz & Stedman, 2020).

RECOMMENDATION

In the context of limited liability partnerships (LLP), the two-tier model of corporate governance framework is not typically applicable. The two-tier model is commonly associated with the governance structure of corporations, particularly those with a dual-board structure, such as German Aktiengesellschaft (AG) companies (Du Plessis, 2017). In an LLP, the governance structure is typically simpler and more flexible compared to corporations. LLP are often governed by a partnership agreement, which outlines the rights, responsibilities, and decision-making processes of the partners. The partners themselves usually have the authority to make decisions collectively or delegate specific responsibilities to designated partners. Since the ownership and administration of LLP are both placed on the partners, and there is no board of directors (unlike a company), a two-tier model of corporate governance is deemed appropriate for the corporate governance of LLP in Malaysia (Rahman, 2018). As such, there is a need for a body to supervise the members and partners to ensure good governance for an LLP.

However, it is worth noting that LLP may still adopt certain governance practices to ensure transparency and accountability. For example, they may establish a management committee or designate partners to oversee specific functions or areas of the business. These practices can help distribute responsibilities and ensure effective decision-making within the LLP.

All established corporate governance concepts, notably shareholder rights and fair treatment, stakeholder interests, decision-maker roles and duties, integrity, and ethical behaviour, are regarded relevant for LLP in order to provide strong governance systems. All corporate governance theories, including agency theory, ethical theory, stakeholder theory, and corporate social responsibility (CSR), are applicable to LLP in ensuring a good corporate governance framework (Yin, 2023). As such, the legal justification and theories to support a corporate governance framework for LLP should be similar to those of a company. However, due to the internal regulations of LLP (which have overlaps between ownership, management, and decision-making structures), it is proposed that a two-tier model of corporate governance be adopted for LLP rather than the more common model, i.e., the Anglo-Saxon Model (Colemn, 2008).

By implementing a two-tier model of corporate governance framework in LLP, with a management board and a supervisory board, transparency and accountability can be enhanced. This structure ensures that decision-making is carried out by a competent management board while providing independent oversight through the supervisory board, ultimately promoting the interests of stakeholders and the long-term success of the LLP.

CONCLUSION

Due to their comparable legal position as a body corporate, the suggested corporate governance model for LLP in Malaysia emphasises that the concepts, theories, and reasons for corporate governance may be applied to Malaysian LLP with a body corporate status. However, because partners in LLP have both decision-making power and ownership of the business, the two-tier model of corporate governance (with some modifications to the composition of partners in the supervisory committee) has been found to be more appropriate for LLP in order to ensure effective good governance for LLP businesses.

The European two-tier model of successful corporations which is employed in Austria, Indonesia, and Germany, might be used as a model for Malaysian LLP. The suitability and application of the proposed model may raise some concerns regarding the restricted liability, which may interfere with an LLP's capacity to obtain financial services or resolve any disputes between partners or other parties. A more in-depth examination of the two-tier corporate governance model should be conducted so that the suggested model of corporate governance framework may be further investigated for Malaysian LLP.

REFERENCES

Agarwal, S. (2009) *Limited liability partnership: Law and practice*. LexisNexis Butterworths: Wadhwa Nagpur.

Aguilera, R. V., Williams, C. A., Conley, J. M., & Rupp, D. E. (2006). Corporate governance and social responsibility: A comparative analysis of the UK and the US. *Corporate Governance*, *14*(3), 147–158. doi:10.1111/j.1467-8683.2006.00495.x

Alnasser, S. (2012). What has changed? The development of corporate governance in Malaysia. *The Journal of Risk Finance*, *13*(3), 269–276. doi:10.1108/15265941211229271

Armour, D. (2001). *Limited Liability Partnership*. LexisNexis.

Beritelli, P., Bieger, T., & Laesser, C. (2007). Destination governance: Using corporate governance theories as a foundation for effective destination management. *Journal of Travel Research*, *46*(1), 96–107. doi:10.1177/0047287507302385

Carsten, J. (2006). The Effectiveness of Corporate Governance in One-Tier and Two-Tier Board Systems–Evidence from the UK and Germany–. *European Company and Financial Law Review*, *3*(4), 426–474. doi:10.1515/ECFR.2006.019

Coleman, P. T., Fisher-Yoshida, B., Stover, M. A., Hacking, A. G., & Bartoli, A. (2008). Reconstructing ripeness II: Models and methods for fostering constructive stakeholder engagement across protracted divides. *Conflict Resolution Quarterly*, *26*(1), 43–69. doi:10.1002/crq.223

Corporate Governance Code. (2020). Borsa Italiana. https://www.borsaitaliana.it/comitato-corporate-governance/codice/2020eng.en.pdf

De Oliveira, U. R., Menezes, R. P., & Fernandes, V. A. (2023). A systematic literature review on corporate sustainability: Contributions, barriers, innovations and future possibilities. *Environment, Development and Sustainability*. doi:10.100710668-023-02933-7 PMID:36687736

Deliu, D. (2019). Empathetic leadership–Key element for inspiring strategic management and a visionary effective corporate governance. *Journal of Emerging Trends in Marketing and Management*, *1*(1), 280–292.

Dewi, Y. K. (2021). The need to adopt a limited liability partnership for the legal profession in the partnership law: A critical review from Indonesia's perspective. *Cogent Social Sciences*, *7*(1), 1999005. doi:10.1080/23311886.2021.1999005

Du Plessis, J. J., Großfeld, B., Luttermann, C., Saenger, I., Sandrock, O., Casper, M., & Sandrock, O. (2017). An overview of German business or enterprise law and the one-tier and two-tier board systems contrasted. *German corporate governance in International and European context*, 1-16.

Gazioglu, S. (1992). *Monetarisation of the Budget Constraint: Two Country Model for the European Economic Community (EEC) and the Semi-industrial Country (SIC) Blocks*. University of Strathclyde, Department of Economics.

Ghazali, N. A. M. (2010). Ownership structure, corporate governance and corporate performance in Malaysia. *International Journal of Commerce and Management*, *20*(2), 109–119. doi:10.1108/10569211011057245

Hamizah, A. R., Nor Razinah, M. Z., Zuhairah Ariff, A. G., Tengku Adida, T. Z. M., Nurul Syahira, O., Ghazali, O., Muhammad Syafiq, H., & Ravindran, N. (2021). An Analysis on Nature of Limited Liability Partnerships in Malaysia. *The Journal of American Science*, *18*(1), 268–277.

Is, M. S., & Saputra, J. A. (2021). The Legal concept of limited liability company based on Social-Justice through corporate social responsibility. *Jurnal Cita Hukum*, *9*(2), 339–354. doi:10.15408/jch.v9i2.16525

Khayesi, M. (2021). What is the ethical reflection of the sustainable development goals? *Sustainability and Climate Change*, *14*(3), 138–144. doi:10.1089cc.2020.0073

Li, S. (2021). Comparative analysis of development paths within the framework of the two-tier corporate governance model in Germany, Italy, and China. *Corporate Law & Governance Review*, *3*(1), 17–28. doi:10.22495/clgrv3i1p2

Mansor, F., Ahmad, S. H., Hamzah, H. C., & Hussain, S. F. (2022). A capability Framework for Analyzing Corporate Social Responsibility Performance. [MJSSH]. *Malaysian Journal of Social Sciences and Humanities*, *7*(8), e001708–e001708. doi:10.47405/mjssh.v7i8.1708

Morse, G. (2011). *Limited Liability Partnership Law*. Sweet & Maxwell.

Mueller, D. C. (2006). The Anglo-Saxon approach to corporate governance and its applicability to emerging markets. *Corporate Governance, 14*(4), 207–219. doi:10.1111/j.1467-8683.2006.00503.x

Nigeria, C. G. (2020). COVID-19 pandemic: emerging board and governance considerations. *COVID-19 Pandemic: Emerging Board and Governance Considerations.*

Nordberg, D. (2020). *The Cadbury code and recurrent crisis: A model for corporate governance?* Springer Nature. doi:10.1007/978-3-030-55222-0

OECD. (2023). *G20/OECD Principles of Corporate Governance 2023.* OECD Publishing. doi:10.1787/ed750b30-

Ordonez-Ponce, E., Clarke, A., & MacDonald, A. (2021). Business contributions to the sustainable development goals through community sustainability partnerships. *Sustainability Accounting. Management and Policy Journal, 12*(6), 1239–1267. doi:10.1108/SAMPJ-03-2020-0068

Pomeranz, E. F., & Stedman, R. C. (2020). Measuring good governance: Piloting an instrument for evaluating good governance principles. *Journal of Environmental Policy and Planning, 22*(3), 428–440. doi:10.1080/1523908X.2020.1753181

Provasi, R., & Riva, P. (2015). The Italian two-tiers model. Evidence and comparison with some other countries. *Corporate Ownership & Control, 12*(3–3), 388–396. doi:10.22495/cocv12i3c3p9

Rahman, H. A., & Ghadas, Z. A. A. (2018). The evolution of partnership structure; Special reference to governance legal framework for LLPs. *PROCEEDINGS–ICLG, 2018*, 511.

Salim, M. R. (2013). Limited liability partnership in Malaysia: A corporate governance perspective. *This material was first published by Thomson Reuters (Professional) UK Limited in Mohammad Rizal Salim, "Limited Liability Partnership in Malaysia: A Corporate Governance Perspective"[2013]. ICCLR, 24*(12), 421.

Sharma, J. K. (2020). Limited Liability Partnership as a Better Alternative to Incorporation. *Jus Corpus LJ, 1*, 440.

United Nation. (2023). *The Sustainable Development Goals Report Special edition Towards a Rescue Plan for People and Planet.* UN. https://unstats.un.org/sdgs/report/2023/The-Sustainable-Development-Goals-Report-2023.pdf

Yin, X. (2023). The Analysis of Accounting Firms' Organization Types and Reasons for Switching the Organization Types. *Academic Journal of Business & Management, 5*(12), 77–81.

Zuhairah Ariff, A. & Hamizah, A. (2020). Governance issues in Malaysia limited liability partnerships (LLP). *International Journal of Psycho social Rehabilitation, 24*(6), 12242-12255.

KEY TERMS AND DEFINITIONS

Corporate Governance: The framework that directs and controls businesses which the corporate management is the responsibility of their boards of directors. The shareholders' duty is to choose directors and auditors and to ensure that an appropriate structure for governance is in place.

Limited Liability Partnership (LLP): A type of general partnership where every partner has a limited personal liability for the debts of the partnership.

Sustainable Development Goals: Known as the Global Goals, were adopted by the United Nations in 2015 as a universal call to action to end poverty, protect the planet, and ensure that by 2030 all people enjoy peace and prosperity. The 17 SDGs are integrated—they recognise that action in one area will affect outcomes in others, and that development must balance social, economic and environmental sustainability.

Two-Tier Model of Corporate Governance: A dual board or two-tier system is a corporate structure system that consists of two bodies i.e. the Council of Delegates to govern the Board of Directors and the Board of Directors to manage a corporation. The roles and relationships between the two bodies vary across countries.

Compilation of References

A. P. E. C., & the Law Group. (2023). *Competition Policy and Sustainable Development.* Bangkok: Trade Competition Commission of Thailand. https://www.apec.org/docs/default-source/publications/2023/7/223_ec_competition-policy-and-sustainable-development.pdf?sfvrsn=cfd2c2f9_2

Abalansa, S., El Mahrad, B., Icely, J., & Newton, A. (2021). Electronic waste, an environmental problem exported to developing countries: The GOOD, the BAD and the UGLY. *Sustainability (Basel)*, *13*(9), 5302. doi:10.3390u13095302

ACCA. (2018, May 24). *ACCC re-authorises Tyre Stewardship Scheme.* ACCA. https://www.accc.gov.au/media-release/accc-re-authorises-tyre-stewardship-scheme

AdamsJ. M. Non-Compete Agreements: A Review of the Literature. December 31, 2019; Available from: https://ssrn.com/abstract=3513639orhttp://dx.doi.org/10.2139/ssrn.3513639

Addati, L., Cattaneo, U., Esquivel, V., & Valarino, I. (2018). Care work and care jobs for the future of decent work. International Labour Organization.

Adilla, F. (2022, April 18). Lazada unveils campaign to support sustainable practices in e-commerce. *New Straits Times.* https://www.nst.com.my/business/2022/04/789773/lazada-unveils-campaign-support-sustainable-practices-e-commerce

African Development Bank Group. (2023). *Tanzania.* ADBG. https://www.afdb.org/en/countries/east-africa/tanzania

Agarwal, S. (2009) *Limited liability partnership: Law and practice.* LexisNexis Butterworths: Wadhwa Nagpur.

Aguilera, R. V., Williams, C. A., Conley, J. M., & Rupp, D. E. (2006). Corporate governance and social responsibility: A comparative analysis of the UK and the US. *Corporate Governance*, *14*(3), 147–158. doi:10.1111/j.1467-8683.2006.00495.x

Aguirre, M., & Ibikunle, G. (2014). *Determinants of renewable energy growth: A global sample analysis.* Energy Policy. doi:10.1016/j.enpol.2014.02.036

Agyeman, S. D., & Lin, B. (2023). Electricity industry (de) regulation and innovation in negative-emission technologies: How do market liberalization influences climate change mitigation? *Energy*, *270*, 126863. doi:10.1016/j.energy.2023.126863

Ahamat, H., Rahman, N. A., & Anshori, M. R. A. (2020). Monopsony, powerful buyers and small sellers: Analysis of Malaysian competition law and lessons learnt from Indonesia. *International Journal of Globalisation and Small Business*, *11*(3), 241–257. doi:10.1504/IJGSB.2020.109548

Ahmad, Q. K. et, al. (eds.). (2001). *Ganges-Brahmaputra-Meghna: Region: A Framework for Sustainable Development.* Dhaka: University Press Limited.

Ahmed. (2001). *Gender Issues, Population and Development in Ethiopia: In-depth Studies from the 1994 Population and Housing Census in Ethiopia.* Italian Multi-bi Research Project ETH/92/P01.

Ahmed, B. (2019). Environmental governance and sustainable development in Bangladesh: Millennium development goals and sustainable development goals. *Asia Pacific Journal of Public Administration*, *41*(4), 237–245. doi:10.1080/23276665.2019.1698930

Aker, J. C., & Mbiti, I. M. (2010). Mobile Phones and Economic Development in Africa. *The Journal of Economic Perspectives*, *24*(3), 207–232. doi:10.1257/jep.24.3.207

Akib, M., Sumarja, F., & Heryandi. (2019). Environmental Law Policy as an Approach to Achieve Sustainable Development and Prosperity in an Era of Regional Autonomy. *Environmental Policy and Law*, *49*(1), 83–87. doi:10.3233/EPL-190130

Akman, P. (2022). A Web of Paradoxes: Empirical Evidence on Online Platform Users and Implications for Competition and Regulation in Digital Markets. *Virginia Law and Business Review*, *16*(2), 217.

Alam, S., & Nurhidayah, L. (2017). The international law on transboundary haze pollution: What can we learn from the Southeast Asia region? *Review of European, Comparative & International Environmental Law*, *26*(3), 243–254. doi:10.1111/reel.12221

Alam, T, et, al. (2020). Energy Security in Bangladesh through Renewable Energy Generation. *Journal of Alternative and Renewable Energy*, *6*(3), 27–40.

Albors-Llorens, A. (2002). *EC competition law and policy*. Willan Pub.

Ali, H., Phoumin, H., Suryadi, B., Farooque, A. A., & Yaqub, R. (2022). Assessing ASEAN's Liberalized Electricity Markets: The Case of Singapore and the Philippines. *Sustainability (Basel)*, *14*(18), 11307. doi:10.3390u141811307

Alisjahbana, A. S., & Busch, J. M. (2017). Forestry, forest fires, and climate change in Indonesia. *Bulletin of Indonesian Economic Studies*, *53*(2), 111–136. doi:10.1080/00074918.2017.1365404

Alnasser, S. (2012). What has changed? The development of corporate governance in Malaysia. *The Journal of Risk Finance*, *13*(3), 269–276. doi:10.1108/15265941211229271

Alvarez, M. L. (2013, February). From Unheard Screams to Powerful Voices: A Case Study of Women's Political Empowerment in the Philippines. In *12th National Convention on Statistics (NCS) EDSA,* Mandaluyong City.

Amenta, C., Aronica, M., & Stagnaro, C. (2022). Is more competition better? Retail electricity prices and switching rates in the European Union. *Utilities Policy*, *78*, 101405. doi:10.1016/j.jup.2022.101405

Amornkitvikai, Tham, S. Y., Harvie, C., & Buachoom, W. W. (2022). Barriers and Factors Affecting the E-Commerce Sustainability of Thai Micro-, Small- and Medium-Sized Enterprises (MSMEs). *Sustainability (Basel)*, *14*(14), 8476. doi:10.3390u14148476

Amy McKenna. (n.d.). German East Africa: Former German dependency, Africa. In *Britannica*. https://www.britannica.com/place/German-East-Africa

Ang, B., Choong, W. L., & Ng, T. S. (2015). Energy security: Definitions, dimensions, and indexes. *Renewable & Sustainable Energy Reviews*, *42*, 1077–1093. doi:10.1016/j.rser.2014.10.064

APEC; Asia Pacific Economic Cooperation; Competition Policy and Sustainable Development. (2023). Competition Law Tackling Sustainability Goals: An Analysis of International Practices and the Challenges Ahead. *Business Law Review*.

Arinaldo, D., Prasojo, H., Tampubolon, A. P., Simamora, P., Kurniawan, D., Marciano, I., & Adiatma, J. C. (2021). *Indonesia Energy Transition Outlook 2021*. IESR. file:///C:/Users/hp/Downloads/IETO%20-%202021_IESR.pdf

Aris, H., Mohd Zawawi, I. S., & Jørgensen, B. N. (2020). The Philippines' and Singapore's Journeys towards Liberalised Electricity Supply Industries—Takeaways for Malaysia. *Energies*, *13*(14), 3514. doi:10.3390/en13143514

Armour, D. (2001). *Limited Liability Partnership*. LexisNexis.

Arnow-Richman, R. (2019). The new enforcement regime: Revisiting the law of employee competition (and the scholarship of Professor Charles Sullivan) with 2020 vision. *Seton Hall L. Rev., 50*, 1223. doi:10.2139/ssrn.4396108

Arshad, F., & Shamshad, M. (2022). Energy Crisis in Pakistan: Socio-Economic Implications and the Way Forward. *Annals of Social Sciences and Perspective*, *3*(1), 105–115. doi:10.52700/assap.v3i1.69

ASEAN Economic Community. (2015, December 7). ASEAN. https://asean.org/asean-economic-community/

ASEAN Experts Group on Competition (AEGC). (n.d.). ASEAN. https://www.asean-competition.org/aegc

ASEAN. (2020). *Consumer Protection*. Competitive, Innovative and Inclusive Economic Region. https://asean.org/our-communities/economic-community/competitive-innovative-and-inclusive-economic-region/consumer-protection/

Aziz, N. A., Mangsor, M. M., Rahmat, N. E., Nasrun, M., & Ristawati, R. (2023). An Overview of Judicial Review in The Malaysian Court. *International Journal of Academic Research in Business & Social Sciences*, *13*(1), 336–352.

Azmi, R., Maslahat, P., & Wahono, J. W. (2022). *The carbon footprint from the power plant in Indonesia and renewable energy supply for reduce the carbon emission*. NASA.

Bairagya, I. (2018). Why Is Unemployment Higher among the Educated? *Economic and Political Weekly*, *53*(7), 43–51.

Bakhoum, M. (2012). Reflections on the concepts of 'economic freedom', 'free competition' and 'efficiency' from the perspectives of developing countries. In D. Zimmer (Ed.), *The Goals of Competition Law* (pp. 408–440). Edward Elgar. doi:10.4337/9780857936615.00029

Balakrishnan, A., Sundaresan, S., & Zhang, B. (2013, August 30). Browse-and-Switch: Retail-Online Competition under Value Uncertainty. *Production and Operations Management*, *23*(7), 1129–1145. doi:10.1111/poms.12165

Bank of Tanzania. (2019). *Mobile Money Transactions*. Bank of Tanzania.

Baris, K., & Kucukali, S. (2012). Availability of renewable energy sources in Turkey: Current situation, potential, government policies, and the EU perspective. *Energy Policy*, *42*, 377–391. doi:10.1016/j.enpol.2011.12.002

Basak, D., Bose, A., Roy, S., Chowdhury, I. R., & Sarkar, B. C. (2021). Understanding sustainable homestay tourism as a driving factor of tourist's satisfaction through structural equation modelling: A case of Darjeeling Himalayan region, India. Current Research in Environmental Sustainability, 3, 100098.

Bayeh, E. (2016). The role of empowering women and achieving gender equality to the sustainable development of Ethiopia. *Pacific Science Review B. Humanities and Social Sciences*, *2*(1), 37–42.

BBC. (2023, February 5). *Zanzibar Profile*. BBC. https://www.bbc.com/news/world-africa-14115176

Behrens, P. (2018). The Ordoliberal Concept of 'Abuse' of a Dominant Position and its Impact on Article 102 TFEU. In F. Di Porto & R. Podszun (Eds.), *Abusive Practices in Competition Law* (pp. 5–25). Edward Elgar Publishing. doi:10.4337/9781788117340.00008

Bellan, R. (2021, July 9). *EU fines BMW, VW $1B for running emissions cartel since the 90s*. Tech Crunch. https://techcrunch.com/2021/07/08/eu-fines-bmw-vw-1b-for-running-emissions-cartel-since-the-90s/

Belyaev, L. S. (2010). *Electricity market reforms: Economics and policy challenges*. Springer Science & Business Media.

Beniwal, A. (2013). Gender Discrimination and Empowerment of Women in India: A View. *Indian Journal of Poultry Science*, *74*(1), 27–38.

BEREC (Body of European Regulators for Electronic Communications). (2018). *BEREC Report on infrastructure sharing*. BEREC.

Bergkamp, L. (2002). The Privacy Fallacy: Adverse Effects of Europe's Data Protection Policy in an Information-Driven Economy. *Computer Law & Security Review*, 31. doi:10.1016/S0267-3649(02)00106-1

Beritelli, P., Bieger, T., & Laesser, C. (2007). Destination governance: Using corporate governance theories as a foundation for effective destination management. *Journal of Travel Research*, *46*(1), 96–107. doi:10.1177/0047287507302385

Bhat, Z. A. (2014). Gender Bias and Socio-Economic Problems of Women in India. *Abhinav National Monthly Referred Journal of Research in Arts and Education*, *3*(4), 8–13.

Bielecki, J. (2002). Energy Security: Is the Wolf at the Door? *The Quarterly Review of Economics and Finance*, *42*(2), 235–250. doi:10.1016/S1062-9769(02)00137-0

Bishop, S., & Walker, M. (2010). *The Economics of Competition Law: Concepts, Application and Measurement* (3rd ed.). Sweet & Maxwell.

BKA. (2019). *Case B6-22/16 Facebook, Exploitative business terms pursuant to Section 19(1) GWB for inadequate data processing*. BKA. <https://www.bundeskartellamt.de/SharedDocs/ Entscheidung/EN/Fallberichte/Missbrauchsaufsicht/2019/B6-22-16.html?nn=3600108>

Blake, H. M. (1960). Employee Agreements Not to Compete. *Harvard Law Review*, *73*(4), 625–691. doi:10.2307/1338051

Blazquez, J., Fuentes-Bracamontes, R., Bollino, C. A., & Nezamuddin, N. (2018). The renewable energy policy Paradox. *Renewable & Sustainable Energy Reviews*, *82*, 1–5. doi:10.1016/j.rser.2017.09.002

Blechman, J., Odhiambo, F., & Roberts, S. (2017). Competition Dynamics in Mobile Money Markets in Tanzania. Centre for Competition, Regulation and Economic Development, Centre for Competition, Regulation and Economic Development.

Bojnec, Š., & Križaj, A. (2021). Electricity markets during the liberalization: The case of a European Union country. *Energies*, *14*(14), 4317. doi:10.3390/en14144317

Botta, M., & Wiedemann, K. (2019). Exploitative Conducts in Digital Markets: Time for a Discussion after the Facebook Decision. *Journal of European Competition Law & Practice*, *10*(8), 465–478. doi:10.1093/jeclap/lpz064

Botta, M., & Wiedemann, K. (2019). The Interaction of EU Competition, Consumer and Data Protection Law in the Digital Economy: The Regulatory Dilemma in the Facebook Odyssey. *Antitrust Bulletin*, *64*(3), 428–446. doi:10.1177/0003603X19863590

Brisimi, V. (2014). *The Interface between Competition and the Internal Market: Market Separation under Article 102 TFEU*. Bloomsbury Publishing.

Bruneckienė, J., Pekarskienė, I., Guzavičius, A., Palekienė, O., & Šovienė, J. (2015). *The impact of cartels on national economy and competitiveness: A Lithuanian case study*. Springer International Publishing. doi:10.1007/978-3-319-17287-3

Brynjolfsson, E., & Smith, M. D. (2000, April 1). Frictionless Commerce? A Comparison of Internet and Conventional Retailers. *Management Science*, *46*(4), 563–585. doi:10.1287/mnsc.46.4.563.12061

Business Standard. (27 January 2023). Pakistan's power crisis lingers and paralyzes economic activities. https://www.business-standard.com/article/international/pakistan-s-power-crisis-lingers-paralyses-economic-activities-123012701230_1.html

Butt, S., Lyster, R., & Stephens, T. (2015). *Climate change and forest governance: Lessons from Indonesia*. Routledge. doi:10.4324/9781315735351

Büyüközkan, G., Karabulut, Y., & Mukul, E. (2018). A novel renewable energy selection model for United Nations' sustainable development goals. *Energy*, *165*, 290–302. doi:10.1016/j.energy.2018.08.215

Byrne, J., & Mun, Y. M. (2003). Rethinking reform in the electricity sector: Power liberalization or energy transformation. Electricity reform: Social and environmental challenges, pp. 48–76.

C2ES. (2020). *Global Emissions*. C2ES. https://www.c2es.org/content/international-emissions/

Cadwalladr, C., & Graham-Harrison, E. (2018, March 17). Revealed: 50 million Facebook profiles harvested for Cambridge Analytica in major data breach. *The Guardian*. https://www.theguardian.com/news/2018/mar/17/cambridge-analytica-facebook-influence-us-election

Canada Minister of Justice. (2023, October 5). *Competition Act (R.S.C., 1985, c. C-34)*. Justice Laws Website. https://laws.justice.gc.ca/eng/acts/C-34/index.html

Carsten, J. (2006). The Effectiveness of Corporate Governance in One-Tier and Two-Tier Board Systems–Evidence from the UK and Germany–. *European Company and Financial Law Review*, *3*(4), 426–474. doi:10.1515/ECFR.2006.019

Case, M., Ardiansyah, F., & Spector, E. (2007). Climate change in Indonesia: Implications for humans and nature. In Climate change in Indonesia: Implications for humans and nature. (p. 13). World Wide Fund for Nature, UK (WWF).

CGAP. (2015, March). *Tanzania's Mobile Money Revolution*. CGAP. https://www.cgap.org/research/infographic/tanzanias-mobile-money-revolution

Chakraborty, S. (2016). Occupational Sex Segregation: An Inquiry into Indian Job Market. *Journal of Regional Development and Planning*, *5*(2), 1–17.

Chapman, A. J., & Itaoka, K. (2018). Energy transition to a future low-carbon energy society in Japan's liberalizing electricity market: Precedents, policies, and factors of a successful transition. *Renewable & Sustainable Energy Reviews*, *81*, 2019–2027. doi:10.1016/j.rser.2017.06.011

Charter of Fundamental Rights of the European Union. (2010). *Official Journal of the European Union, C*, *83*(02).

Chen, J. (2021, March 6). *China guides e-commerce sector to greener path of development*. EN. http://en.people.cn/n3/2021/0306/c90000-9825820.html

Chen, X., Luo, Z., & Wang, X. (2017). Impact of efficiency, investment, and competition on low carbon manufacturing. *Journal of Cleaner Production*, *143*, 388–400. doi:10.1016/j.jclepro.2016.12.095

Cherp, A., & Jewell, J. (2014). The concept of energy security: Beyond the four As. *Energy Policy*, *75*, 415–421. doi:10.1016/j.enpol.2014.09.005

Chong, S. (2023, July 4). E-Commerce Contribution To Malaysia's GDP Rises To 13%, Said Fahmi. *Business Today*. https://www.businesstoday.com.my/2023/07/04/e-commerce-contribution-to-malaysia-gdp-rises-to-13-said-fahmi/#:~:text=The%20Minister%20Of%20Communications%20And,2020%20to%2013.0%25%20in%202021

Chong, D. K. (2021). The times they are a-changin'. *AJOPS*, *4*(1), 6–8. doi:10.34239/ajops.v4n1.298

Choudhry, M. T., & Elhorst, P. (2018). Female labour force participation and economic development. *International Journal of Manpower*, *39*(7), 896–912. doi:10.1108/IJM-03-2017-0045

Choudhury, S. U. S. (18 April 2023). Bangladesh Needs to Initiate Nuclear Power Plants. *The Geopolitics*. https://thegeopolitics.com/bangladesh-needs-to-initiate-nuclear-power-plants/

Cifuentes-Faura, J. (2022). European Union policies and their role in combating climate change over the years. *Air Quality, Atmosphere & Health, 15*(8), 1333–1340. doi:10.100711869-022-01156-5 PMID:35035604

Clark, J. (1925). What is Competition? *The University Journal of Business, 3*(3), 217–240. JSTOR.

CMA. (2019). *Expects Facebook and eBay to tackle sale of fake reviews*. UK Gov. https://www.gov.uk/government/news/cma-expects-facebook-and-ebay-to-tackle-sale-of-fake-reviews

CNBC. (2023, January 2). Perppu Jokowi! Angin Segar Perusahaan Batu Bara: Setoran 0%. *CNBC Indonesia*. https://www.cnbcindonesia.com/news/20230102012111-4-401887/perppu-jokowi-angin-segar-perusahaan-batu-bara-setoran-0

Coleman, P. T., Fisher-Yoshida, B., Stover, M. A., Hacking, A. G., & Bartoli, A. (2008). Reconstructing ripeness II: Models and methods for fostering constructive stakeholder engagement across protracted divides. *Conflict Resolution Quarterly, 26*(1), 43–69. doi:10.1002/crq.223

Collier, P. (1994). Gender Aspects of Labor Allocation during Structural Adjustment: Theoretical Framework and the Africa Experience in Labor Markets in an era of adjustment. World Bank.

Commerce, A. M. (2006). *Public Submission for the Proposed U.S.-Malaysia Free Trade Agreement (USMFTA)*. Bilaterals. https://www.bilaterals.org/IMG/pdf/003eb926-8a8a-49e8-9901-700353a31e93.pdf

Communications Authority of Kenya. (2023). *Third Quarter Sector Statistics Report for the Financial Year 2022/2023 (1st January – 31st March 2023)*. Communications Authority of Kenya. https://www.ca.go.ke/sites/default/files/2023-06/Sector%20Statistics%20Report%20Q3%202022-2023.pdf

Competition Commission v. Competition Appeal Tribunal & Ors [2019] 6 CLJ 623.

Cooter, R., & Ulen, T. (2008). *Law and Economics*. Pearson.

Cornejo, J. M. (2007). *An examination of the relationships among perceived gender discrimination, work motivation, and performance*. UMI No. 3377804.

Corporate Governance Code. (2020). Borsa Italiana. https://www.borsaitaliana.it/comitato-corporate-governance/codice/2020eng.en.pdf

Council Directive 93/13/EC of 5 April 1993 on Unfair Terms in Consumer Contracts [1993] OJ L 95/29.

Cozzolino, Corbo, L., & Aversa, P. (2021). Digital platform-based ecosystems: The evolution of collaboration and competition between incumbent producers and entrant platforms. *Journal of Business Research, 126*, 385–400. doi:10.1016/j.jbusres.2020.12.058

Craven, M. (2015). Between law and history: The Berlin Conference of 1884-1885 and the logic of free trade. *London Review of International Law, 3*(1), 31–59. doi:10.1093/lril/lrv002

Cremer, J., de Montjoye, Y., & Schweitzer, H. (2019). Competition policy for the digital era *(European Commission Report No. 30)*. https://ec.europa.eu/competition/publications/reports/kd0419345enn.pdf

Crémer, J., Montjoye, Y.-A. d., & Schweitzer, H. (2019). *Competition Policy for the digital era*. European Commission.

Crippa, M., Guizzardi, D., Muntean, M., Schaaf, E., Solazzo, E., Monforti-Ferrario, F., Olivier, J., & Vignati, E. (2020). *Fossil CO2 emissions of all world countries*. European Commission.

Cseres, K. (2006). The controversies of the consumer welfare standard. *Competition Law Review, 3*(2), 121–173.

Cuofano, G. (2023, November 6). *How does Shopee Make Money? The Shopee Business Model in A Nutshell.* Four Week MBA. https://fourweekmba.com/shopee-business-model/#:~:text=Shopee%20employs%20a%20typical%20marketplace,of%20ancillary%20and%20complimentary%20services

Das, D., Sarkar, A., & Debroy, A. (2022). Impact of Covid-19 on changing consumer behaviour: Lessons from an emerging economy. *International Journal of Consumer Studies*, *46*(3), 692–715. doi:10.1111/ijcs.12786 PMID:35602666

Dasgupta, S. (21 April 2022). India and Bangladesh are set to formalize the electricity-sharing system. *The Times of India*, https://timesofindia.indiatimes.com/articleshow/90969950.cms?utm_source=contentofinterest&utm_medium=text&utm_campaign=cppst, accessed on 13 August 2023.

Daskalova, V. (2015). Consumer welfare in EU competition law: what is it (not) about? *The Competition Law Review, 133.*

de Araujo, R. C., & Nogueira, J. M. (2020). Environmental law & competition law: Conflicts & complementarities from an environmental economics perspective. *Direito e Desenvolvimento*, *11*(1), 92–105. doi:10.26843/direitoedesenvolvimento.v11i1.1220

De Oliveira, U. R., Menezes, R. P., & Fernandes, V. A. (2023). A systematic literature review on corporate sustainability: Contributions, barriers, innovations and future possibilities. *Environment, Development and Sustainability.* doi:10.100710668-023-02933-7 PMID:36687736

De StefanoG. (2020). Measurable environmental protection as a necessity for competition law. SSRN 3533499. doi:10.2139/ssrn.3533499

Declaration On The Asean Economic Community Blueprint. (2003, October 7). ASEAN. https://www.asean.org/wp-content/uploads/images/archive/5187-10.pdf

Del Río, P., & Kiefer, C. P. (2022). Which policy instruments promote innovation in renewable electricity technologies? A critical review of the literature with a focus on auctions. *Energy Research & Social Science*, *89*, 102501. doi:10.1016/j.erss.2022.102501

Deliu, D. (2019). Empathetic leadership–Key element for inspiring strategic management and a visionary effective corporate governance. *Journal of Emerging Trends in Marketing and Management*, *1*(1), 280–292.

Department of Economic and Social Affairs. (2023). *Sustainable Development.* UN. https://sdgs.un.org/goals/goal9

Dermawan, A., & Hospes, O. (2018). When the state brings itself back into GVC: The case of the Indonesian Palm Oil Pledge. *Global Policy*, *9*(S2), 21–28. doi:10.1111/1758-5899.12619

Desai, S. (1994). *Gender Inequalities and Demographic Behaviours: India.* The Population Council, Inc. doi:10.31899/pgy1994.1003

Deshpande, A., Goel, D., & Khanna, S. (2015). Bad Karma or Discrimination? Male-FemaleWage Gaps Among Salaried Workers in India. *IZA Discussion Paper No. 9485.* doi:10.2139/ssrn.2690733

Devaraj, S., Fan, M., & Kohli, R. (2002, September 3). Antecedents of B2C Channel Satisfaction and Preference: Validating e-Commerce Metrics. *Information Systems Research*, *13*(3), 316–333. https://www.jstor.org/stable/23015740. doi:10.1287/isre.13.3.316.77

Devi, S. U. (1999). Visions for 21st century. In K. Ahooja-Patel, S. U. Devi, & G. A. Tadas (Eds.), *Women and development* (pp. 21–43). Har-Anand Publications.

Dewi, Y. K. (2021). The need to adopt a limited liability partnership for the legal profession in the partnership law: A critical review from Indonesia's perspective. *Cogent Social Sciences*, *7*(1), 1999005. doi:10.1080/23311886.2021.1999005

Deyo, F. C. (2013). Addressing the development deficit of competition policy: the role of economic networks. In J. G. Michael W. Dowdle, & I. Maher (Eds.), Asian Capitalism and the regulation of Competition: Towards a Regulatory Geography of Global Competition Law (pp. 283-300). Cambridge: Cambridge University Press. doi:10.1017/CBO9781139226349.018

Diaz-Rainey, I., Tulloch, D. J., Ahmed, I., McCarten, M., & Taghizadeh-Hesary, F. (2021). *An energy policy for ASEAN? Lessons from the EU experience on energy integration, security, and decarbonization.*

Digital Commerce 360. (2023, February 17). *US ecommerce in 2022 tops $1 trillion for first time.* Digital Commerce 360. https://www.digitalcommerce360.com/article/us-ecommerce-sales/

Dipboye, R. L., & Colella, A. (2005). *Discrimination at work: The psychological and organizational bases.* Lawrence Erlbaum.

Directive 2005/29/EC of the European Parliament and of the Council concerning unfair business-to- consumer commercial practices in the internal market, (Unfair Commercial Practices Directive) [2005] OJ L 149/22.

Directive 2019/2161/EU amending Council Directive 93/13/EEC (unfair contract terms) and Directives 98/6/EC (price indications), 2005/29/EC (unfair commercial practices) and 2011/83/EU (consumer rights) as regards the better enforcement and modernisation of EU consumer protection rules.

Dixon, R. B. (1982). Mobilizing women for rural employment in South Asia: Issues of class, caste, and patronage. *Economic Development and Cultural Change, 30*(2), 373–390. doi:10.1086/452562

Dkhil, I. B. (2014). *Regulation and Investment in Telecom Network Infrastructure Facilities: The Recent Developments and Debates* [MPRA Paper No. 72910]. MPRA. https://mpra.ub.uni-muenchen.de/72910/1/MPRA_paper_72910.pdf

DolmansM. (2021). Sustainability Agreements and Antitrust–Three Criteria to Distinguish Beneficial Cooperation from Greenwashing. *Available at* SSRN 3920369. doi:10.2139/ssrn.3920369

Domazet, S. (2013). Environmental Protection and Competition Law of the European Union: Complementary or Conflicting Goals? *Agriculture in Serbia and Portugal: Recent*, 208.

Dong, X. Y., & An, X. (2015). Gender patterns and value of unpaid care work: Findings from China's First Large-Scale Time Use Survey. *Review of Income and Wealth, 61*(3), 540–560. doi:10.1111/roiw.12119

Douglas, E. (2021). Digital Crossroads: The Intersection of Competition Law and Data Privacy. *Temple University Legal Studies Research Paper No. 2021-40.*

Dresang, D. L., & Sharkansky, I. (1973). Public Corporations in Single-Country and Regional Settings: Kenya and the East African Community. [JSTOR.]. *International Organization, 27*(3), 303–328. doi:10.1017/S0020818300003520

Du Plessis, J. J., Großfeld, B., Luttermann, C., Saenger, I., Sandrock, O., Casper, M., & Sandrock, O. (2017). An overview of German business or enterprise law and the one-tier and two-tier board systems contrasted. *German corporate governance in International and European context*, 1-16.

Economic Planning Unit. (2021). *Malaysia Voluntary National Review Report.* Sustainable Development United Nations. https://sustainabledevelopment.un.org/content/documents/285982021_VNR_Report_Malaysia.pdf

Economic Planning Unit. (n.d.). *SDG Roadmap Phase 1 2016-2020.* Economic Planning Unit. www.ekonomi.gov.my: https://www.ekonomi.gov.my/sites/default/files/2021-05/SDG_Roadmap_Phase_I_2016-2020.pdf

Economides, N., & Jeziorski, P. (2017). Mobile Money in Tanzania. *Marketing Science, 36*(6), 815–837. doi:10.1287/mksc.2017.1027

Economides, N., & Lianos, I. (2021). Restrictions On Privacy and Exploitation In The Digital Economy: A Market Failure Perspective. *Journal of Competition Law & Economics, 17*(4), 765–847. doi:10.1093/joclec/nhab007

Edwards, S. (2014). *Toxic aid: Economic collapse and recovery in Tanzania* (1st ed.). Oxford University Press. doi:10.1093/acprof:oso/9780198704423.001.0001

Elhauge, E., & Geradin, D. (2011). *Global Competition Law and Economics* (2nd ed.). Hart Publishing.

Elvidge, A. M., & Martucci, J. (2003). Telecommunications Network Total Cost of Ownership and Return on Investment Modelling. *BT Technology Journal, 21*(2), 184–190. doi:10.1023/A:1024467706446

Elzinga, K. G., & Mills, D. E. (2015). Predatory Pricing. In R. D. Blair & D. D. Sokol (Eds.), *The Oxford handbook of international antitrust economics* (pp. 40–61). Oxford University Press. doi:10.1093/oxfordhb/9780199388592.013.0002

EPA. E. (2022). *Inventory of U.S. Greenhouse Gas Emissions and Sinks: 1990-2020. U.S. Environmental Protection Agency* (EPA 430-R-22-003). Environmental Protection Agency. https://www.epa.gov/system/files/documents/2022-04/us-ghg-inventory-2022-main-text.pdf

Esayas, S. (2019). Data Privacy in European Merger Control: Critical Analysis of Commission Decisions Regarding Privacy as a Non-Price Competition. *European Competition Law Review, 40*(4).

Esteve-Volart, B. (2004). Gender discrimination and growth: theory and evidence from India. *LSESTICERD Research Paper No. DEDPS 42.* file:///C:/Users/imib/Downloads/SSRN-id1127011.pdf

ET Energy World. (2017). India should revive Iran-Pakistan-India gas pipeline: Parliamentary Panel. ET Energy World. https://energy.economictimes.indiatimes.com/news/oil-and-gas/india-should-revive-iran-pakistan-india-gas-pipeline-parliamentary-panel/57725094

European Commission. (2009). Guidance on the Commission's Enforcement Priorities in Applying Article 82 of the EC Treaty to Abusive Exclusionary Conduct by Dominant Undertakings. *Official Journal of the European Union, C, 45*(7).

European Commission. (2009, February 24). *Guidance on the Commission's enforcement priorities in applying Article 82 of the EC Treaty to abusive exclusionary conduct by dominant undertakings.* EC. https://eur-lex.europa.eu/legal-content/EN/ALL/?uri=CELEX%3A52009XC0224%2801%29

European Commission. (2015, December 15). *Agreement on Commission's EU data protection reform will boost Digital Single Market [Press release].* EC. https://ec.europa.eu/commission/presscorner/detail/en/IP_15_6321

European Commission. (2019). *Factual Summary of the Contributions Received during the Public Consultation on the Evaluation of the Two Block Exemption Regulations and the Guidelines on Horizontal Cooperation Agreements.* EC. https://ec.europa.eu/competition/publications/reports/kd0419345enn.pdf

European Commission. (2021, July 8). *Antitrust: Commission fines car manufacturers €875 million for restricting competition in emission cleaning for new diesel passenger cars [Press Release].* EC. https://ec.europa.eu/commission/presscorner/detail/en/ip_21_3341

Ewing, K. P. (2006). *Competition rules for the 21st century: Principles from America's experience* (2nd ed.). Kluwer Law International.

Ezrachi, A. (2016). *Sponge. Journal of Antitrust Enforcement, 1, Ezrachi, A., & Stucke, M. (2016). Virtual Competition.* Harvard University Press.

Ezrachi, A. (2021). *Competition and antitrust law: A very short introduction* (1st ed.). Oxford University Press. doi:10.1093/actrade/9780198860303.001.0001

Fantasy Ruby Sdn Bhd v. Padiberas Nasional Bhd [2018] 10 CLJ 385.

Fayaz, M. (2023). Human Rights Law and Police Interrogation: A Doctrinal Analysis of Anti-Terrorism Legislation of UK and Pakistan. [JLSS]. *Journal of Law & Social Studies*, *5*(3), 468–479.

Federation of Sabah Industries & Ors v. Competition Commission & Ors [2015] 7 CLJ, 101.

Ferrant, G., Pesando, L. M., & Nowacka, K. (2014). *Unpaid Care Work: The missing link in the analysis of gender gaps in labour outcomes. Boulogne Billancourt*. OECD Development Center.

Ferrari, V. (2022). The platformisation of digital payments: The fabrication of consumer interest in the EU FinTech agenda. *Computer Law & Security Report*, *45*, 45. doi:10.1016/j.clsr.2022.105687

Fisher, M. (2021). *Bangladesh nuclear reactor construction progresses ahead of planned 2023 start-up*. International Atomic Energy Agency (IAEA). https://www.iaea.org/bulletin/bangladesh-nuclear-reactor-construction-progresses-ahead-of-planned-2023-start-up

Fisher, E. (2017). *Environmental law: A very short introduction*. Oxford University Press. doi:10.1093/actrade/9780198794189.001.0001

Fisse, B. (2019). Facilitating the SDGs by Competition and Consumer Law and Policy Reform: Aspirations and Challenges in Papua New Guinea. In J. Walker, A. Pekmezovic, & G. Walker (Eds.), *Sustainable Development Goals: Harnessing Business to Achieve the SDGs through Finance, Technology, and Law Reform*. John Wiley & Sons Ltd. doi:10.1002/9781119541851.ch18

Flanagan, A. (2018). Authorization and Licensing. In I. Walden (Ed.), *Telecommunications Law and Regulation* (5th ed., pp. 285–380). Oxford University Press. doi:10.1093/oso/9780198807414.003.0009

Fletcher, E., Pande, R., & Moore, C. M. (2017) Women and work in india: descriptive evidence and a review of potential policies. *HKS working paper no. RWP18-004*. Center for International Development Harvard University, Cambridge.

Forgioni, P. A. (2013). *Os fundamentos do antitruste*. Editora Revista dos Tribunais.

Fox, E. M. (2008). Antitrust, Economic Development and Poverty: The Other Path. In G. L. Hassan Qaqaya (Ed.), The Effects of Anti-competitive Business Practices on Developing Countries and Their Development Prospects (p. 179). Geneva: United Nations.

Fox, E. (2014). Monopolization and abuse of dominance: Why Europe is different. *Antitrust Bulletin*, *59*(1), 129–152. doi:10.1177/0003603X1405900106

Franklin, S. L. Jr. (2015). Investment decisions in mobile telecommunications networks applying real options. *Annals of Operations Research*, *226*(1), 201–220. doi:10.100710479-014-1672-9

Frederiksson, T., & Korka, D. (2017). *Harnessing E-Commerce for Sustainable Development*. OECD.

Frieden, R. (2015). Ex Ante Versus Ex Post Approaches to Network Neutrality: A Comparative Assessment. *Berkeley Technology Law Journal*, *30*(2), 1561–1612. doi:10.15779/Z386Z81

Fritzsche, H., & Phillips, M. (2017). Electromagnetic Radiation. In *Encyclopaedia Britannica*. https://www.britannica.com/science/electromagnetic-radiation

Gal, M., & Fox, E. (2014). Drafting Competition Law for Developing Jurisdictions: Learning from Experience. *Contracts & Commercial Law eJournal*.

Gal, M. S., & Aviv, O. (2020). The Competitive Effects of the GDPR. *Journal of Competition Law & Economics*, 1.

Galor, O., & Weil, D. N. (1996). The Gender Gap, Fertility, and Growth. *The American Economic Review*, *86*(3), 374–387.

Garcia, J. M., & Kelly, T. (2015). *The Economics and Policy Implications of Infrastructure Sharing and Mutualisation in Africa*. World Bank Publications.

Garner, B. A. (2004). *Black's Law Dictionary* (8th ed.). West Publishing Co.

Gavil, A. I., Kovacic, W. E., Baker, J. B., & Wright, J. D. (2022). *Antitrust law in perspective: Cases, concepts, and problems in competition policy* (4th ed.). West Academic Publishing.

Gazioglu, S. (1992). *Monetarisation of the Budget Constraint: Two Country Model for the European Economic Community (EEC) and the Semi-industrial Country (SIC) Blocks*. University of Strathclyde, Department of Economics.

Gehring, M. W. (2006). Competition for sustainability: Sustainable development concerns in national and EC competition law. *Review of European Community & International Environmental Law*, *15*(2), 172–184. doi:10.1111/j.1467-9388.2006.00519.x

Gelvanovska, N., Rogy, M., & Rossotto, C. M. (2014). *Broadband Networks in the Middle East and North Africa: Accelerating High-Speed Internet Access*. World Bank Publications.

Geradin, D., & O'Donoghue, R. (2005). The Concurrent Application of Competition Law and Regulation: The Case of Margin Squeeze Abuses in the Telecommunications Sector. *Journal of Competition Law & Economics*, *1*(2), 355–425. doi:10.1093/joclec/nhi009

Gerbrandy, A. (2019). Rethinking competition law within the European economic constitution. *Journal of Common Market Studies*, *57*(1), 127–142. doi:10.1111/jcms.12814

Gerpott, T. J., & Berends, J. (2022, June 14). Competitive pricing on online markets: A literature review. *Journal of Revenue and Pricing Management*, *21*(6), 596–622. doi:10.105741272-022-00390-x

Ghazali, N. A. M. (2010). Ownership structure, corporate governance and corporate performance in Malaysia. *International Journal of Commerce and Management*, *20*(2), 109–119. doi:10.1108/10569211011057245

Giocoli, N. (2014). *Predatory pricing in antitrust law and economics: A historical perspective*. Routledge. doi:10.4324/9781315832692

Gjersø, J. F. (2015). The Scramble for East Africa: British Motives Reconsidered, 1884–95. *The Journal of Imperial and Commonwealth History*, *43*(5), 831–860. doi:10.1080/03086534.2015.1026131

Glass, K. E. (2014). *I speak for the trees": An exploration of environmental advocacy and speaker credibility in Dr. Seuss'" The Lorax*. San José State University. doi:10.31979/etd.3r4c-qhxm

Global Data. (2020, September 8). *COVID-19 accelerates e-commerce growth in Malaysia, says GlobalData*. Global Data. https://www.globaldata.com/media/banking/covid-19-accelerates-e-commerce-growth-malaysia-says-globaldata/

Goldfarb, A., & Tucker, C. (2017). *Digital Economics*. NBER Working Paper No. 23684.

Gorecka, A. (2020). A confusing relationship between privacy and competition law — a way forward for EU competition law and algorithms pricing. Indi*an Journal of AI and Law, 7.*

Gorecka, A. (2020). Is "Privacy" a Means to Protect the Competition or Advance Objectives of Innovation and Consumer Welfare? In M. Tzanou (Ed.), *Personal Data Protection and Legal Developments in the European Union*. IGI Global. doi:10.4018/978-1-5225-9489-5.ch006

Goyder, J., & Albors-Lloren, A. (2009). *Goyder's EC Competition Law* (5th ed.). Oxford University Press.

Grappling with the issues: Can a proposed decision under the Competition Act 2010 be subject to judi . (n.d.). Skrine - Advocates & Solicitors. https://www.skrine.com/insights/alerts/january-2023/grappling-with-the-issues-can-a-proposed-decision-

Grenfell, D. M. (2023, March 16). *Can we protect the environment and keep the benefits of competition?* Economist Impact. https://impact.economist.com/sustainability/resilience-and-adaptation/can-we-protect-the-environment-and-keep-the-benefits-of-competition

GSMA. (2012). *Mobile Infrastructure Sharing*. GSMA.

GSMA. (2013). *Tanzania Mobile Money Infographic*. GSMA. https://www.gsma.com/mobilefordevelopment/wp-content/uploads/2014/03/Tanzania-Mobile-Money-infographic-GSMA-MMU.pdf

Guerci, E., Rastegar, M. A., & Cincotti, S. (2010). Agent-based modeling and simulation of competitive wholesale electricity markets. Handbook of power systems II, 241-286.

Guliyev, F. (2023). Renewable Energy Targets and Policies in Traditional Oil-Producing Countries: A Comparison of Azerbaijan and Kazakhstan. *Journal of Eurasian Studies*.

Hafner, M., & Raimondi, P. P. (2020). Priorities and challenges of the EU energy transition: From the European Green Package to the new Green Deal. *Russian Journal of Economics*, *6*(4), 374–389. doi:10.32609/j.ruje.6.55375

Haidar, A. M., John, P. N., & Shawal, M. (2011). Optimal configuration assessment of renewable energy in Malaysia. *Renewable Energy*, *36*(2), 881–888. doi:10.1016/j.renene.2010.07.024

Hajighasemi, A., Oghazi, P., Aliyari, S., & Pashkevich, N. (2022). The impact of welfare state systems on innovation performance and competitiveness: European country clusters. *Journal of Innovation & Knowledge*, *7*(4), 100236. doi:10.1016/j.jik.2022.100236

Haldorai, A., & Kandaswamy, U. (2019). *Intelligent Spectrum Handovers in Cognitive Radio Networks*. Springer Nature Switzerland AG. doi:10.1007/978-3-030-15416-5

Halkos, G. E., & Tsirivis, A. S. (2023). Electricity Prices in the European Union Region: The Role of Renewable Energy Sources, Key Economic Factors and Market Liberalization. *Energies*, *16*(6), 2540. doi:10.3390/en16062540

Hamizah, A. R., Nor Razinah, M. Z., Zuhairah Ariff, A. G., Tengku Adida, T. Z. M., Nurul Syahira, O., Ghazali, O., Muhammad Syafiq, H., & Ravindran, N. (2021). An Analysis on Nature of Limited Liability Partnerships in Malaysia. *The Journal of American Science*, *18*(1), 268–277.

Handayani, K., Filatova, T., Krozer, Y., & Anugrah, P. (2020). Seeking for a climate change mitigation and adaptation nexus: Analysis of a long-term power system expansion. *Applied Energy*, *262*, 114485. doi:10.1016/j.apenergy.2019.114485

Hang, T. T., & Huy, N. D. (2022). Non-compete agreement in labor relations according to the regulations of some countries and recommendations for Vietnam. Journal of Science and Technology Development – Economics. *Law and Management*, *6*(3), 3118–3127.

Hansard Parliament Malaysia. (2023, October 13). *DEWAN RAKYAT PARLIMEN KELIMA BELAS PENGGAL KEDUA MESYUARAT KETIGA*. Portal Rasmi Parlimen Malaysia. https://www.parlimen.gov.my/files/hindex/pdf/DR-13102023.pdf

Harlow, B. (2003). The Scramble for Africa. In B. Harlow & M. Carter (Eds.), Archives of Empire: Volume 2. The Scramble for Africa (pp. 1–9). Duke University Press.

Hartmann, H. (1976). Capitalism, Patriarchy, and Job Segregation by Sex. *Signs (Chicago, Ill.)*, *1*(3, Part 2), 137–169. doi:10.1086/493283

Hassan, M. Y. (2022). Sustainable energy sources in Bangladesh: A review on present and prospects. *Renewable and Sustainable Reviews*, *155*. https://www.sciencedirect.com/science/article/abs/pii/S1364032121011370

Hawthorne, R. (2018). The effects of lower mobile termination rates in South Africa. *Telecommunications Policy*, *42*(5), 374–385. doi:10.1016/j.telpol.2018.02.007

Hazlewood, A. (1965). The Territorial Incidence of the East African Common Services1. *Bulletin of the Oxford University Institute of Economics & Statistics*, *27*(3), 161–176. doi:10.1111/j.1468-0084.1965.mp27003001.x

Healy, P. (1992). The Effect of Changes in Corporate Control of Firms Performance. In T. A. Kochan & M. Useem (Eds.), *Transforming Organizations* (pp. 61–79). Oxford University Press. doi:10.1093/oso/9780195065046.003.0005

Heffron, R. J., Körner, M.-F., Sumarno, T., Wagner, J., Weibelzahl, M., & Fridgen, G. (2022). How different electricity pricing systems affect the energy trilemma: Assessing Indonesia's electricity market transition. *Energy Economics*, *107*, 105663. doi:10.1016/j.eneco.2021.105663

He, Y., Xu, Y., Pang, Y., Tian, H., & Wu, R. (2016). A regulatory policy to promote renewable energy consumption in China: Review and future evolutionary path. *Renewable Energy*, *89*, 695–705. https://www.mordorintelligence.com/industry-reports/malaysia-power-market. doi:10.1016/j.renene.2015.12.047

Hieu, T. (2020). Restraint of business clauses in employment contracts: experience from some countries. *VNUHCM Journal, 4.* . doi:10.32508/stdjelm.v4i2.619

HM Government Gazette. (n.d.). *COMPETITION ACT 2010 THE MyCC GUIDELINES ON INTELLECTUAL PROPERTY RIGHTS AND COMPETITION LAW.* MyCC Guidelines. https://www.mycc.gov.my/sites/default/files/pdf/newsroom/WJW013224%20Teks%20%282%29.pdf

Hoffmann-La Roche v Commission, [1979] European Court of Justice, Case 85/76. (European Court of Justice).

Holmes, S., Snoep, M., Middelschulte, D., & Ahmad, S. (2021). Competition Law, Climate Change and Environmental Sustainability. (Concurrences)

Holmes, S. (2020, July). Climate change, sustainability, and competition law. *Journal of Antitrust Enforcement*, *8*(2), 354–405. doi:10.1093/jaenfo/jnaa006

Honda Giken Kogyo Kabushiki Kaisha (Also Known As "Honda Motor Co, Ltd") v. Dnc Asiatic Holdings Sdn Bhd & Ors and Another Suit [2018] 9 CLJ 229.

Hovenkamp, H. (2016). *Federal Antitrust Policy: The Law of Competition and Its Practice* (5th ed.). West Group.

Howells, G., & Weatherill, S. (2005). *Consumer Protection Law*. Routledge.

Hudzaifi, N. N. (2023, March 29). Membedah Skenario Praktik Monopoli Kendaraan Listrik di RI. *CNBC*. https://www.cnbcindonesia.com/opini/20230329173428-14-425586/membedah-skenario-praktik-monopoli-kendaraan-listrik-di-ri

Hunter, E. (2015). *Political Thought and the Public Sphere in Tanzania*. Cambridge University Press. doi:10.1017/CBO9781316104620

Hunt, S. D., & Morgan, R. M. (1995). The Comparative Advantage Theory of Competition. *Journal of Marketing*, *59*(2), 1–15. doi:10.1177/002224299505900201

Hurić-Larsen, J. F., & Münch, A. (2016). Competition and Environmental Policy in the EU: Old Foes, New Friends? *Journal of Industry, Competition and Trade*, *16*(2), 137–153. doi:10.100710842-015-0201-0

Husnina, N., & Kevin, W. (26 May 2023). *The Extent and The Applicability of Non-Compete Clause in Employment Agreement.* Kevin Wu & Associates. https://www.mondaq.com/contract-of-employment/1320820/the-extent-and-the-applicability-of-non-compete-clause-in-employment-agreement-

Hutchinson, T., & Duncan, N. (2012). Defining and describing what we do: doctrinal legal research. *Deakin law review, 17*(1), 83-119.

Iansiti, M. (2021). The Value of Data and Its Impact on Competition. Harvard Business School, 1 - 26.

Ichord, R. F. (2020). Transforming the Power Sector in Developing Countries: Geopolitics, Poverty and Climate Change in Pakistan. *Atlantic Council*, 1-19. http://www.jstor.com/stable/resrep23545

IESR, I. (2021). *Hitting Record-Low Solar Electricity Prices in Indonesia.* Institute for Essential Service Reform. file:///C:/Users/hp/Downloads/IESR-Solar%20Final%20-%20Digital.pdf

Igini, M. (2022, December 15). *The Truth About Online Shopping and Its Environmental Impact.* Earth.org. https://earth.org/online-shopping-and-its-environmental-impact/

Iimura, A., & Cross, J. S. (2018). The impact of renewable energy on household electricity prices in liberalized electricity markets: A cross-national panel data analysis. *Utilities Policy, 54*, 96–106. doi:10.1016/j.jup.2018.08.003

Ilić-Petković, A., & Ilić-Krstić, I. (2016). The role of environmental law in the implementation of sustainable development. *Safety Engineering, 6*(2), 99–105. doi:10.7562/SE2016.6.02.07

Iliffe, J. (1979). In A Modern History of Tanganyika (African Studies, pp. I-Vi). Cambridge: Cambridge University Press.

ILO. (2013). Women and men in the informal economy: A statistical picture (second edition) / International Labour Office – Geneva: ILO. International Labour Organisation.

Inderst, R., & Thomas, S. (2023). Competition Policy and the Environment. *Annual Review of Resource Economics*, 15.

Interaction between Trade and Competition Policy. (n.d.). World Trade Organisation. https://www.wto.org/english/tratop_e/comp_e/comp_e.htm

International Trade Administration. (2022). *Pakistan: Country Commercial Guide.* ITA. https://www.trade.gov/country-commercial-guides/pakistan-renewable-energy

Irwansyah, I. (2016). What do scientists say on climate change? A study of Indonesian newspapers. *Pacific Science Review B. Humanities and Social Sciences, 2*(2), 58–65.

Islam, M.R. (2009). Effective Solar Photovoltaic Activities in Bangladesh. *International Energy Journal, 10*(1), 29-36. http://www.rericjournal. ait.ac.th/index.php/relic/article/view/578

Islam, A., Hossain, M. B., Mondal, M. A. H., Ahmed, M. T., Hossain, M. A., Monir, M. U., Khan, M. F. H., Islam, K., Khandaker, S., Choudhury, T. R., & Awual, M. R. (2021). Energy challenges for a clean environment: Bangladesh's experience. *Energy Reports, 7*, 3373–3389. doi:10.1016/j.egyr.2021.05.066

Islam, M. (2020). An Overview of the Hydropower Production Potential in Bangladesh to Meet the Energy Requirements. *Environmental Engineering Research, 26*(6), 200514. doi:10.4491/eer.2020.514

Is, M. S., & Saputra, J. A. (2021). The Legal concept of limited liability company based on Social-Justice through corporate social responsibility. *Jurnal Cita Hukum, 9*(2), 339–354. doi:10.15408/jch.v9i2.16525

Itaoka, K., Chapman, A., & Farabi-Asl, H. (2022). Underpinnings of consumer preferences and participation in Japan's liberalized energy market. *Utilities Policy, 76*, 101379. doi:10.1016/j.jup.2022.101379

Jamal, E. O. (31 October 2022). How can Bangladesh circumvent the global oil war? *The Daily Star*. https://www.thedailystar.net/opinion/views/the-overton-window/news/how-can-bangladesh-circumvent-the-global-oil-war-3157136

Jamasb, T., & Pollitt, M. G. (2011). Electricity sector liberalization and innovation: An analysis of the UK's patenting activities. *Research Policy*, *40*(2), 309–324. doi:10.1016/j.respol.2010.10.010

Jarvenpaa, Tractinsky, N., & Vitale, M. (2000). Consumer trust in an Internet Store. *Information Technology and Management*, *1*(1/2), 45–71. doi:10.1023/A:1019104520776

Jensen, K. (2020, March 23). Water at Heart of Climate Action. *The Jakarta Post*. https://www.thejakartapost.com/academia/2020/03/23/water-at-heart-of-climate-action.html

Johari, A., SitiHafshar, S., Hashim, H., & Ramli, M. (2013). Feed-in-Tariff (FiT) concept to promote the usage of renewable energy in Malaysia. *International Journal of Energy and Power*, *2*(2), 33–37.

Jones, A. (2011). *Identifying an Unlawful Margin Squeeze: The Recent Judgments of the Court of Justice in Deutsche Telekom and TeliaSonera. Cambridge Yearbook of European Legal Studies, 13, 161–193*. Cambridge Core. doi:10.5235/152888712801752942

Jones, A., Sufrin, B., & Dunne, N. (2019). *EU Competition Law: Text, Cases and Materials* (7th ed.). Oxford University Press.

Jong, H. N. (2020). Indonesia Won't Sacrifice Economy for More Ambitious Emissions Cuts. *Mongabay Series: Jokowi Commitments*. Https://News.Mongabay.Com/2020/04/Indonesia-Emissionsreduction-Climate-Carbon-Economy-Growth/Philips-Meltzer

Joskow, P. L. (2022). From hierarchies to markets and partially back again in electricity: Responding to decarbonization and security of supply goals. *Journal of Institutional Economics*, *18*(2), 313–329. doi:10.1017/S1744137421000400

Kabeer, N. (2010). Women's empowerment, development interventions and the management of information flows. *IDS Bulletin*, *41*(6), 105–113. doi:10.1111/j.1759-5436.2010.00188.x

Kabeyi, M. J. B., & Olanrewaju, O. A. (2022). Sustainable energy transition for renewable and low carbon grid electricity generation and supply. *Frontiers in Energy Research*, *9*, 1032. doi:10.3389/fenrg.2021.743114

Kafker, S. L. (1993). Golden handcuffs: Enforceability of non-competition clauses in professional partnership agreements of accountants, physicians, and attorneys. *American Business Law Journal*, *31*(1), 31–58. doi:10.1111/j.1744-1714.1993.tb00674.x

Kahn, A. (2023). *Distinguishing Genuine Sustainability Agreements from Disguised Cartels under Article 101 (3) TFEU*.

Kalimpong District. (n.d.). *District Profile*. Kalimpong District. https://kalimpong.gov.in/administrative-map/

Kalimpong District. (n.d.). *History accessed*. Kalimpong District. https://kalimpong.gov.in/history/

Kamiński, M. (2021). Energy Transition Enhanced by the European Green Deal-How National Competition Authorities Should Tackle This Challenge in Central and Eastern Europe? [YARS]. *Yearbook of Antitrust and Regulatory Studies*, *14*(23), 101–121.

Kang, H., & Fleming, L. (2020). Non-competes, business dynamism, and concentration: Evidence from a Florida case study. *Journal of Economics & Management Strategy*, *29*(3), 663–685. doi:10.1111/jems.12349

Kauzya, J.-M. (2011). Comparative Perspectives of the Challenges and Prospects of the Civil Services Reforms in Kenya, Tanzania and Uganda. In A. Massey (Ed.), *International Handbook on Civil Service Systems* (pp. 178–224). Edward Elgar Publishing. doi:10.4337/9781781001080.00015

Kelkar, G. (2013, December). *At the Threshold of Economic Empowerment: Women, Worker and Gender Regimes in Asia.* ILO Asia-Pacific working paper series, 2227-4391. https://www.ilo.org/wcmsp5/groups/public/---asia/---ro-bangkok/---sro-new_delhi/documents/publication/wcms_233096.pdf

Kemp, K. (2020). Concealed data practices and competition law: Why privacy matters. *European Competition Journal, 16*(2-3), 628–672. doi:10.1080/17441056.2020.1839228

Kerber, W. (2016). Digital Markets, Data and Privacy: Competition Law, Consumer Law and Data Protection. *MAGKS Joint Discussion Paper Series in Economics, No. 14-2016*. https://www.econstor.eu/bitstream/10419/144679/1/850599016.pdf

Kerber, W., & Specht-Riemenschneider, L. (2020). *Synergies Between Data Protection Law and Competition Law.* Bundesverband. https://papers.ssrn.com/sol3/papers.cfm?abstract_id=3977039

Kerber, W., & Zolna, K. K. (2022). The German Facebook case: The law and economics of the relationship between competition and data protection law. *European Journal of Law and Economics, 54*(2), 217–250. doi:10.100710657-022-09727-8

Khan, S. (2009). PDB plans big for six coal-fired power plants. *The Daily Star.* https://www. thedailystar.net/news-detail-91772

Khayesi, M. (2021). What is the ethical reflection of the sustainable development goals? *Sustainability and Climate Change, 14*(3), 138–144. doi:10.1089cc.2020.0073

Khemani, R. S. (n.d.). *Objectives of Competition Law.* OECD. https://www.oecd.org/regreform/sectors/aframeworkforthedesignandimplementationofcompetitionlawandpolicy.htm

Khoo, K., & Sng, A. (2019). Singapore's competition regime and its objective: The case against formalism. *Singapore Journal of Legal Studies, 1*, 67–107. https://law1.nus.edu.sg/sjls/articles/SJLS-Mar-19-67.pdf

Kim, Kim, M., Im, S., & Choi, D. (2021, October 19). Competitiveness of E Commerce Firms through ESG Logistics. *Sustainability (Basel), 13*(20), 1–15. doi:10.3390u132011548

Kimmelman, G., & Cooper, M. (2017). *A Communications Oligopoly on Steroids—Why Antitrust Enforcement and Regulatory Oversight in Digital Communications Matter.* Equitable Growth. https://equitablegrowth.org/research-paper/communications-oligopoly-steroids/

Kimmelman, G., & Cooper, M. (2015). Antitrust and Economic Regulation: Essential and Complementary Tools to Maximize Consumer Welfare and Freedom of Expression in the Digital Age. *Harvard Law & Policy Review, 9*(2), 403–436.

Kingston, S. (2021). Introduction to Competition Law, Climate Change and Environmental Sustainability. UCD Working Papers in Law, Criminology & Socio-Legal Studies Research Paper.

Kira, B., Sinha, V., & Srinivasan, S. (2021). Regulating digital ecosystems: Bridging the gap between competition policy and data protection. *Industrial and Corporate Change, 30*(5), 1337–1360. doi:10.1093/icc/dtab053

Kitchen, T., & Oreilly, P. (2016). Energy poverty amidst abundance in Malaysia: Placing energy in multidimensional poverty. *Development in Practice, 26*(2), 203–213. doi:10.1080/09614524.2016.1133562

Klasen, S., & Lamanna, F. (2009). The impact of gender inequality in education and employment on economic growth: New evidence for a panel of countries. *Feminist Economics, 15*(3), 91–132. doi:10.1080/13545700902893106

Kloosterhuis, E., & Mulder, M. (2015). Competition law and environmental protection: The Dutch agreement on coal-fired power plants. *Journal of Competition Law & Economics, 11*(4), 855–880. doi:10.1093/joclec/nhv017

Krishna, K. L., Erumban, A. A., & Kusumdas, D. (2016). Structural Changes in Employment in India, 1980–2011. *Centre for Development Economics, Delhi School of Economics.*

Kroes, N. (2009, October 8). Tackling cartels – a never-ending task. *Speech*. Brasilia. https://ec.europa.eu/commission/presscorner/detail/en/SPEECH_09_454

Kumar, I. (10 April, 2023). Bangladesh's quest for energy security opens up new regional opportunities. *South Asia Monitor*. https://www.southasiamonitor.org/spotlight/bangladeshs-quest-energy-security-opens-new-regional-opportunities.

Kumar, M., Poudineh, R., & Shamsuddin, A. (2021). *Electricity supply industry reform and design of competitive electricity market in Malaysia* (No. 44). OIES Paper: EL.

Kundu, A., & Mohanan, P. C. (2009, April). Employment and inequality outcomes in India. In *Joint Seminar on Employment and Inequality, organized by the Employment* (Vol. 8, pp. 1–43). Labour and Social Affairs Directorate and Development Centre.

Kuzminac, M. (2022). *Non-competes in employment contracts: (Un)justified restrictions on the freedom to work*. Glasnik Advokatske komore Vojvodine. . doi:10.5937/gakv94-36244

Kwon, H., & Izaguerri, A. (2023). *Competition and Consumer Protection Policies for Sustainability*. United Nations.

Labuan Ferry Corporation Sdn Bhd v. Chin Mui Kien (Trading under the Name and Style of Econ Focus Enterprise) & Ors and Other Appeals [2018] 2 CLJ 142.

Lagerlöf, N.-P. (2003). Gender Equality and Long-Run Growth. *Journal of Economic Growth*, *8*(4), 403–426. doi:10.1023/A:1026256917489

Lamadrid, A. (2017). Competition law as Fairness. *JIPLP, 147*.

Lama, S., & Majumder, R. (2018). Gender inequality in wage and employment in Indian labour market. *Journal of Academic Research in Economics*, *10*(3), 482–500.

Lambrecht, A., & Tucker, C. E. (2017). Can Big Data Protect a Firm from Competition? *CPI, 3*. https://www.competitionpolicyinternational.com/can-big-data-protect-a-firm-from-competition/

Lancieri, F., & Sakowski, P. M. (2021). *Competition in Digital Markets: A Review of Expert Reports*. Standford Journal of Law, Business & Finance.

Langkawi Ro-Ro operators v Competition Commission, Appeal No.: TRP 1-2022, TRP 2-2022, TRP 3-2022. https://www.kpdn.gov.my/en/corporate-info/department/deputy-secretary-general-domestic-trade-development/competition-appeal-tribunal/93-trp/pengumuman-trp/1453-6-grounds-of-decision-langkawi-ro-ro-ferry-services-sdn-bhd-4-others-vs-competition-commission-appeal-no-trp-1-2-3-2022

Lang, R., & Fink, M. (2019). Rural social entrepreneurship: The role of social capital within and across institutional levels. Journal of Rural Studies, 70, 155-168.

Lazada. (2023, August 28). *LazadaForGood*. Lazada. https://pages.lazada.com.my/wow/camp/lazada/dailycampaign/my/donation/lazadaforgood

Lebow, S. (2021, August 19). *Worldwide ecommerce continues double-digit growth following pandemic push to online*. Insider Intelligence. https://www.insiderintelligence.com/content/worldwide-ecommerce-continues-double-digit-growth-following-pandemic-push-online

Leese, M. (2022). Privacy, data protection, and security studies. *Research Handbook on Privacy and Data Protection Law: Values, Norms and Global Politics*, 214.

Lesirma, S. (2016). Effect of Environmental Laws on Protection of Ecosystem. *International Journal of Environmental Sciences*, *1*(1), 29–40.

Lestari, S., Sova, S., & Njatrijani, R. (2017). Implementation of non-competition clause as the basis of trade secret protection in indonesia. *Implementation Of Non-Competition Clause As The Basis Of Trade Secret Protection In Indonesia.*, *17*(3), 320–327. doi:10.20884/1.jdh.2017.17.3.1278

Levenstein, M. C., & Suslow, V. Y. (2015). Cartels and Collusion: Economic Theory and Experimental Economics. In R. D. Blair & D. D. Sokol (Eds.), *The Oxford Handbook of international antitrust economics* (pp. 442–463). Oxford University Press. doi:10.1093/oxfordhb/9780199388592.013.0018

Levin, H. J. (2013). *The Invisible Resource: Use and Regulation of the Radio Spectrum*. Routledge. doi:10.4324/9781315064574

Li, S. (2021). Comparative analysis of development paths within the framework of the two-tier corporate governance model in Germany, Italy, and China. *Corporate Law & Governance Review*, *3*(1), 17–28. doi:10.22495/clgrv3i1p2

Littlechild, S. (2021). *The evolution of competitive retail electricity markets. Handbook on Electricity Markets*. Edward Elgar Publishing Limited.

Lorenz, M. (2013). *An Introduction to EU Competition Law*. Cambridge University Press. doi:10.1017/CBO9781139087452

Love, L. (2000). *The single-buyer model: A dangerous path toward competitive electricity markets.* OpenKnowledge. https://openknowledge.worldbank.org/server/api/core/bitstreams/b13421df-1bf3-5207-9d99-001284177404/content

Luo, Z., Chen, X., & Wang, X. (2016). The role of co-opetition in low carbon manufacturing. *European Journal of Operational Research*, *253*(2), 392–403. doi:10.1016/j.ejor.2016.02.030

Lynskey, O., & Da Costa Cabral, F. A. (2017). Family Ties: The Intersection between Data Protection and Competition in EU Law. *Common Mkt L Rev, 11*.

Mahmood, T., & Ayaz, M. T. (2018). Energy Security and Economic Growth in Pakistan. *Pakistan Journal of Applied Economics*, *28*(1), 47–64.

Mahn, K. (2017, August 9). *Navigating the E-Commerce Ecosystem for Growth Opportunities.* Smart Trust. https://www.smarttrustuit.com/whitepaperspost/navigating-the-e-commerce-ecosystem-for-growth-opportunities/

Majumder, R. (2011). Female labour supply in india: proximate determinants - Munich Personal RePEc Archive. *Uni-Muenchen.de.* https://doi.org/https://mpra.ub.uni-muenchen.de/43250/1/MPRA_paper_43250.pdf

Malaysia - eCommerce. (2019, August 19). Export.gov. https://www.export.gov/apex/article2?id=Malaysia-E-Commerce

Malaysia Competition Commission (MyCC). (n.d.). *Individual & block exemption.* https://www.mycc.gov.my/individual-block-exemption

Malaysia country profile. (n.d.). Malaysia Competition Commission. https://www.mycc.gov.my/files/advocacy/Malaysia-UNCTADPaper.pdf

Malaysiakini. (2021, July 23). *Lazada steps up support for frontliners and Malaysians in need.* Malaysiakini. https://www.malaysiakini.com/announcement/584188

Malaysian Airline System Bhd v Competition Commission & Anor [2022] 1 CLJ 856.

Malaysian Parliament Hansard. (2010). *Official Parliament Hansard Third Session First Meeting on 20.4.2010.* Parliament Malaysia. https://www.parlimen.gov.my/files/hindex/pdf/DR-20042010.pdf

Malhotra, A., Schulte, J., Patel, P., & Petesch, P. (2009). *Innovation for women's empowerment andgender equality*. International center for research on women (ICRW).www.icrw.org/wp-content/uploads/2016/10/Innovation-for-Womens-Empowerment.pdf

Malik, S. M. et, al. (2019). *Energy Security in Pakistan: A Quantitative Approach to a Sustainable Energy Policy*. ADBI Working Paper 1024. Tokyo: Asian Development Bank Institute. https://www.adb.org/publications/energy-security-pakistan-sustainable-energy-policy

Malik, S., Qasim, M., Saeed, H., Chang, Y., & Taghizadeh-Hesary, F. (2020). Energy security in Pakistan: Perspectives and policy implications from quantitative analysis. *Energy Policy*, *144*, 111552. doi:10.1016/j.enpol.2020.111552

Malinauskaite, J. (2022). Competition Law and Sustainability: EU and National Perspectives. *Journal of European Competition Law & Practice*, 336 - 348.

Malinauskaite, J. (2022, July). Competition Law and Sustainability: EU and National Perspectives. *Journal of European Competition Law & Practice*, *13*(5), 336–348. doi:10.1093/jeclap/lpac003

Mansor, F., Ahmad, S. H., Hamzah, H. C., & Hussain, S. F. (2022). A capability Framework for Analyzing Corporate Social Responsibility Performance. [MJSSH]. *Malaysian Journal of Social Sciences and Humanities*, *7*(8), e001708–e001708. doi:10.47405/mjssh.v7i8.1708

Manyele, A., & Moyo, D. (2019). Impacts of the Tanzanian 2013—2017 Glide Path Implementation Phase on Telecom Voice Call Pricing. *International Journal of Scientific and Engineering Research*, *10*(6), 1–5.

Marquis, M. (2017). Competition law in the Philippines: Economic, legal, and institutional context. *Journal of Antitrust Enforcement*, *6*, 79–122. doi:10.1093/jaenfo/jnx014

Marty, F. (2021). Is Consumer Welfare Obsolete? A European Union Competition Perspective. *Prolegómenos*, *24*(47), 55–78. doi:10.18359/prole.4722

Marx, M. (2018). Reforming non-competes to support workers. *Policy Proposal, 4*.

Marx, M. (2011). The Firm Strikes Back. *American Sociological Review*, *76*(5), 695–712. doi:10.1177/0003122411414822

Marx, M., & Fleming, L. (2012). Non-compete Agreements: Barriers to Entry...and Exit? *Innovation Policy and the Economy*, *12*, 40–64. doi:10.1086/663155

Marx, M., Singh, J., & Fleming, L. (2014). Regional disadvantage? Employee non-compete agreements and brain drain. *Research Policy*, *44*(2), 394–404. doi:10.1016/j.respol.2014.10.006

Matthäus, D. (2020). Designing effective auctions for renewable energy support. *Energy Policy*, *142*, 111462. doi:10.1016/j.enpol.2020.111462

Maulidia, M., Dargusch, P., Ashworth, P., & Ardiansyah, F. (2019). Rethinking renewable energy targets and electricity sector reform in Indonesia: A private sector perspective. *Renewable & Sustainable Energy Reviews*, *101*, 231–247. doi:10.1016/j.rser.2018.11.005

Mawenya, A. (1997). Regulating the Communications Sector in Tanzania: Experiences and Lessons. In M. Mwandosya, G. Mbowe, & P. Young (Eds.), *Competition policy and utility regulation* (pp. 111–124). Centre for Energy, Environment, Science and Technology.

Mayer-Schönberger, V., & Ramge, T. (2018). *Reinventing Capitalism in the Age of Big Data*. Basic Books.

McIntyre, D. P., & Srinivasan, A. (2017, January). Network, platforms, and strategy: Emerging views and next steps. *Strategic Management Journal*, *38*(1), 141–160. doi:10.1002mj.2596

Mckinsey Global Institute. (2018) *McKinsey Global Institute.* McKinsey & Company. https://www.mckinsey.com/~/media/mckinsey/industries/public%20and%20social%20sector/our%20insights/outperformers%20high%20growth%20emerging%20economies%20and%20the%20companies%20that%20propel%20them/mgi-outperformers-full-report-sep-2018.pdf

Mcmahon, C., & Eustace, A. (2023). Nothing to Lose but Their Restraints of Trade: Lessons for Employment Non-Compete Clauses from EU Competition Law. *Industrial Law Journal, 52*(2), 409–450. doi:10.1093/indlaw/dwac025

McNulty, P. J. (1968). Economic Theory and the Meaning of Competition. *The Quarterly Journal of Economics, 82*(4), 639. doi:10.2307/1879604

Measey, M. (2010). Indonesia: A vulnerable country in the face of climate change. *Global Majority E-Journal, 1*(1), 31–45.

Mehrotra, S., Parida, J., Sinha, S., & Gandhi, A. (2014). Explaining Employment Trends in the Indian Economy: 1993–94 to 2011–12. *Economic and Political Weekly, 49*(32), 49–57.

Menon, J. (2017, December). Government-Linked Companies: Impact on the Malaysian Economy. *Policy IDEAS*(No 45). https://www.ideas.org.my/wp-content/uploads/2017/12/PI45-Government-Linked-companies-and-its-Impacts-on-the-Malaysian-Economy-V4.pdf

Mfungahema, R. (2006, October 3). *Policy and Regulatory Approach on The Next Generation Networks: The Case of Tanzania.* ITU-Regional Workshop on the Next Generation Networks (NGN), Markham Suite Hotel, Dar es Salaam. https://www.itu.int/ITU-T/worksem/ngn/200610/presentations/npr-p2.pdf

Michelin, V. (1983). *Commission, [1983] European Court of Justice, Case 322/81.* European Court of Justice.

Michon, A., & Hyppolite, P.-A. (2018, December 13). Data Portability: An Antitrust Weapon for the Digital Economy? *Le Monde.* https://www.fondapol.org/en/the-foundation/medias-en-en/data-portability-an-antitrust-weapon-for-the-digital-economy/

Micklitz, H. W., Schiefke, N., Liedtke, C., Kenning, P., Specht-Riemenschineider, L., & Baur, N. (2020). *E-commerce and the trade-off between consumer protection and sustainability.* Advisory Council for Consumer Affairs.

Minister of Energy and Mineral Resources Regulation No. 15/2010, 15 (2010). https://gunungbale.co.id/v2/wp-content/uploads/2015/04/1201-RMEMRRI-Amendments-to-the-regulations-Minister-of-Energy-and-Mineral-Resources.pdf

Ministry of Economy. (n.d.). *SDG Roadmap Phase 1 2016-2020.* Ministry of Economy. https://www.ekonomi.gov.my/sites/default/files/2021-05/SDG_Roadmap_Phase_I_2016-2020.pdf

Ministry of Economy. (n.d.). *Sustainable Development Goals.* Ekonomi. https://www.ekonomi.gov.my/en/sustainable-development-goals

Ministry of Human Development. (2018). *Annual Report of the Ministry of Human Development.* MSDE. https://www.msde.gov.in/sites/default/files/2020-09/Annual%20Report%202018-2019%20%28English%29.pdf

Ministry of Labour & Employment. (2021). *Women Participation in Workforce.* Ministry of Labour and Employment. https://labour.gov.in/sites/default/files/pib1843397.pdf

Ministry of Transportation. (1997). *National Telecommunications Policy.* Government Printers.

Ministry of Works, Transportation and Communications. (2016). *National ICT Policy.* Ministry of Works, Transportation and Communications.

Mint. (9 April 2023). Adani's Godda plant starts power supply to Bangladesh. *Mint.* https://www.livemint.com/industry/energy/adanis-godda-plant-starts-power-supply-to-bangladesh-11681048727204.html.

Mishan, E. (1975). The Folklore of the Market: An Inquiry into the Economic Doctrines of the Chicago School. *Journal of Economic Issues*, *9*(4), 681–752. https://www.jstor.org/stable/4224459. doi:10.1080/00213624.1975.11503319

Monti, G. (2007). *EC competition law*. Cambridge University Press. doi:10.1017/CBO9780511805523

Morse, G. (2011). *Limited Liability Partnership Law*. Sweet & Maxwell.

Moss, D. L., & Kwoka, J. E. Jr. (2010). Competition policy and the transition to a low-carbon, efficient electricity industry. *The Electricity Journal*, *23*(7), 6–15. doi:10.1016/j.tej.2010.06.018

Mosse, D. (2018). Caste and development: Contemporary perspectives on a structure of discrimination and advantage. *World Development*, *110*, 422–436. doi:10.1016/j.worlddev.2018.06.003

Mothobi, O. (2017). The Impact of Telecommunication Regulatory Policy on Mobile Retail Price in Sub-Saharan African Countries. *ERSA Working Paper 662*.

Mpapalika, J. (2014, February 11). A Market Led Approach to Digital Dividend Review for Financing Digital Broadcasting Migration. *9th Annual Digital Switchover Forum Africa*. 9th Annual Digital Switchover Forum Africa, Arusha, Tanzania.

Mueller, D. C. (2006). The Anglo-Saxon approach to corporate governance and its applicability to emerging markets. *Corporate Governance*, *14*(4), 207–219. doi:10.1111/j.1467-8683.2006.00503.x

Muhammad, R. (2022, September 22). Menteri ESDM Ungkap Penyebab Surplus Listrik PLN. *Bisnis Indonesia*. https://ekonomi.bisnis.com/read/20220922/44/1580299/menteri-esdm-ungkap-penyebab-surplus-listrik-pln

Munadiya, R. (2022). Isu Keberlanjutan dan Persaingan Usaha: Kapan Otoritas Harus Campur Tangan? *Jurnal Persaingan Usaha*, *2*(2), 127–137. doi:10.55869/kppu.v2i2.66

Murshed, M. (2020). Are Trade Liberalization policies aligned with Renewable Energy Transition in low and middle-income countries? An Instrumental Variable Approach. *Renewable Energy*, *151*, 1110–1123. doi:10.1016/j.renene.2019.11.106

Mustafa, M., Ghazali, F., & Yuniza, M. E. (2022). Governance interventions in providing affordable, reliable, sustainable, and modern energy in the ASEAN region (Goal 7). In Good Governance and the Sustainable Development Goals in Southeast Asia (pp. 84-97). Routledge.

MyCC Guidelines. (n.d.). *MyCC Guidelines on Abuse of Dominant Position*. MyCC. www.mycc.gov.my: https://www.mycc.gov.my/guidelines

MyCC v CAT, AirAsia and MAS, WA-25-82-05/2016 (High Court 2016). https://www.mycc.gov.my/sites/default/files/pdf/decision/wa-25-82-05%282016%29%20competition%20commission%20v%20competition%20appeal%20tribunal%20and%20mas%20berhad%20and%20airasia%20berhad.pdf

MyCC v Dagang Net Technologies Sdn Bhd, 700–2/2/003/2015 (MyCC February 16, 2021). https://www.mycc.gov.my/case

MyCC v General Insurance Association of Malaysia (PIAM) and 22 others, 700-2.1.3.2015 (MyCC September 14, 2020). https://www.mycc.gov.my/sites/default/files/pdf/decision/Public%20Version%20Decision%20PIAM%20%26%2022%20Members_28.2.2021_2.pdf

MyCC. (2011). *MyCC Annual Report*. Kuala Lumpur: MyCC. https://www.mycc.gov.my/sites/default/files/pdf/newsroom/MyCC-AR-2011-English.pdf

MyCC. (2023, March 22). MyCC stands firm with the public on Touch n Go. *The Star*. https://www.thestar.com.my/news/nation/2023/03/22/mycc-stands-firm-with-the-public-on-touch-n-go

MyCC. (n.d.). *MyCC Advocacy Programmes.* MyCC. www.mycc.gov.my: https://www.mycc.gov.my/programmes-events?page=1

MyTeksi Sdn Bhd & 2 Ors v Competition Commission [2022] 8 AMR 341.

Nadiyya, A. (2021). Analisis Pengaturan Klausul Non-Kompetisi dalam Perjanjian Kerja: Studi Perbandingan Indonesia, Malaysia, dan Singapura. *Hukum dan Masyarakat Madani, 11*(2).

Najm, S., & Matsumoto, K. I. (2020). Does renewable energy substitute LNG international trade in the energy transition? *Energy Economics, 92*, 104964. doi:10.1016/j.eneco.2020.104964

Nandy, D. (2020). Revisiting India's Post Cold War Foreign Policy: Since 1991 to Present Day. Memari: Avenel Press.

Nandy, D. (2019). *Energy Security and Economic Growth in South Asia: An Alternative Policy Option. Handbook of Research on Economic and Political Implications of Green Trading and Energy*. IGI Global. doi:10.4018/978-1-5225-8547-3.ch022

Nandy, D. (2023). The Impact of Pollution and Economic Growth on the Maldives and Bangladesh: Interrogative Economic Development and Environmental Governance. In M. Pal (Ed.), *The Impact of Environmental Emissions and Aggregate Economic Activity on Industry: Theoretical and Empirical Perspectives.* Emerald, Publishing. doi:10.1108/978-1-80382-577-920231018

Nath, V. (n.d.). *Critical assessment of community based approaches to environment and sustainable development.* Retrieved from https://www.cddc.vt.edu/knownet/lse-cbd.pdf

Nerini, F. F., Tomei, J., To, L. S., Bisaga, I., Parikh, P., Black, M., & Milligan, B. (2018). Mapping synergies and trade-offs between energy and the Sustainable Development Goals. *Nature Energy, 3*(1), 10–15. doi:10.103841560-017-0036-5

Newbery, D., Pollitt, M. G., Ritz, R. A., & Strielkowski, W. (2018). Market design for a high-renewables European electricity system. *Renewable & Sustainable Energy Reviews, 91*, 695–707. doi:10.1016/j.rser.2018.04.025

Nicholas, K. (May 12, 2022). *Can You Work for Competitors in Malaysia After Leaving Your Company?* Althr. https://althr.my/resources/can-you-work-for-competitors-in-malaysia

Nicolli, F., & Vona, F. (2019). Energy market liberalization and renewable energy policies in OECD countries. *Energy Policy, 128*, 853–867. doi:10.1016/j.enpol.2019.01.018

Nigeria, C. G. (2020). COVID-19 pandemic: emerging board and governance considerations. *COVID-19 Pandemic: Emerging Board and Governance Considerations.*

Nikolinakos, N. T. (2006). *EU Competition Law and Regulation in the Converging Telecommunications, Media and IT Sectors.* Kluwer Law International B.V.

Nogueira, J. M., & de Araujo, R. C. (2020). Environmental Law & Competition Law: Conflicts & Complementarities from an Environmental Economics Perspective. *Direito e Desenvolvimento, 11*, 93.

Nordberg, D. (2020). *The Cadbury code and recurrent crisis: A model for corporate governance?* Springer Nature. doi:10.1007/978-3-030-55222-0

Novitz, T. (2021). Gig work as a manifestation of short-termism: Crafting a sustainable regulatory agenda. *Industrial Law Journal, 50*(4), 636–661. doi:10.1093/indlaw/dwab027

Nowag, J. (2020, December 1). *Sustainability & Competition Law and Policy – Background Note.* OECD. https://one.oecd.org/document/DAF/COMP(2020)3/En/pdf

Nowag, J. (2022). Competition Law's Sustainability Gap? Tools for an Examination and a Brief Overview. Nordic Journal of European Law Issue 2022(1) 149-165. doi:https://dx.doi.org/10.2139/ssrn.3484964.

Nowag, J. (2020). *Sustainability & Competition Law and Policy – Background Note*. Organisation for Economic Co-operation and Development.

Nowag, J. (2021). *Sustainability & Competition Law and Policy - Background Note*. OECD.

NSSO. (2005). *2007-09 unit level data, 68th round, Employment Unemployment survey, NSSO Ministry of Statistics and Program Implementation*. Government of India.

Nugroho, A. W. (2020). What students know about climate change? A case study of high school students in Samboja. *Indonesia*, *487*(1), 012001.

Nyerere, J. K. (1977). *The Arusha Declaration Ten Years After*. Government Printer.

O. E. C. D. Law and Policy. (2023, March 20). *Digital challenges for competition policy explained in 9 minutes. Budapest, Central Hungary, Hungary*. [Video]. YouTube. https://www.youtube.com/watch?v=0cN9gkrUuVw

OECD. (2000). *Guidelines for Consumer Protection in the Context of Electronic Commerce*. OECD Publishing.

OECD. (2008). Global Forum on Competition: The Interface between Competition and Consumer Policies. OECD.

OECD. (2014). *OECD Review of Telecommunication Policy and Regulation in Colombia*. OECD Publishing.

OECD. (2018). *Implications of e-commerce for competition policy*. OECD. www.oecd.org/daf/competition/e-commerce-implications-for-competition-policy.htm

OECD. (2018). *Rethinking Antitrust Tools for Multi-Sided Platforms*. OECD.

OECD. (2020). *Sustainability and Competition*. OECD.

OECD. (2021). *Data Portability, Interoperability and Digital Platform Competition.* OECD. https://oe.cd/dpic

OECD. (2021). *Ex-Ante Regulation and Competition in Digital Markets – Note by BEUC*. OECD Publishing. https://one.oecd.org/document/DAF/COMP/WD(2021)66/en/pdf

OECD. (2021). *Time Use*. Oecd.org. https://stats.oecd.org/Index.aspx?datasetcode=TIME_USE

OECD. (2022). *Handbook on Competition Policy in the Digital Age.* OECD Publishing. https://www.oecd.org/daf/competition-policy-in-the-digitalage

OECD. (2023). *G20/OECD Principles of Corporate Governance 2023*. OECD Publishing. doi:10.1787/ed750b30-

OECD. (2023). *The Consumer Welfare Standard - Advantages and Disadvantages Compared to Alternative Standards, OECD Competition Policy Roundtable Background Note.* OECD. https://www.oecd.org/daf/competition/consumer-welfare-standard-advantages-and-disadvantages-to-alternative-standards-2023.pdf

OECD. (n.d.). *OECD COVID-19 Competition policy actions for governments and competition authorities.* OECD. https://www.oecd.org/competition/competition-policy-responses-to-covid-19.htm

OECD. O. (2021). *Environmental Considerations in Competition Enforcement* [OECD Competition Committee Discussion Paper]. OECD. https://www.oecd.org/daf/competition/environmental-considerations-in-competition-enforcement-2021.pdf

Ohm, P. (2013). Branding Privacy. *Minn. L. Rev., 907.*

Olivier, J. G., Schure, K., & Peters, J. (2017). Trends in global CO2 and total greenhouse gas emissions. *PBL Netherlands Environmental Assessment Agency*, *5*, 1–11.

Orbach, B., & Avraham, R. (2015). Squeezing Claims: Refusal to Deal, Essential Facilities, and Price Squeezes. In R. D. Blair & D. D. Sokol (Eds.), *The Oxford Handbook of international antitrust economics* (pp. 120–131). Oxford University Press. doi:10.1093/oxfordhb/9780199388592.013.0006

Ordonez-Ponce, E., Clarke, A., & MacDonald, A. (2021). Business contributions to the sustainable development goals through community sustainability partnerships. *Sustainability Accounting. Management and Policy Journal*, *12*(6), 1239–1267. doi:10.1108/SAMPJ-03-2020-0068

Ottow, A. T. (2014, April). Erosion or innovation? The institutional design of competition agencies—A Dutch case study. *Journal of Antitrust Enforcement*, *2*(1), 25–43. doi:10.1093/jaenfo/jnt016

PackinN. G. (2021). Show Me the (Data About the) Money! *University of Chicago Law Review*, 1277. / doi:10.26054/0D1VS8WMM3

Panda, A., & Patel, A. (2011). Competition law and competition issues affecting the energy sector in India. *Journal of Infrastructure Development*, *3*(2), 107–115. doi:10.1177/097493061100300201

Pandey, G. (2022, September 13). Rising crimes against Indian women in five charts. *BBC News: Delhi* Edition: https://www.bbc.com/news/world-asia-india- 62830634#:~:text=in%20five%20charts.-The%20rising%20graph,from%20338%2C954%20cases%20in%202016

Pandit, S., & Singh, G. (2017). Spectrum Sharing in Cognitive Radio Networks: Medium Access Control Protocol Based Approach. Springer International Publishing Imprint: Springer. doi:10.1007/978-3-319-53147-2

Papadopoulou, M., Papasolomou, I., & Thrassou, A. (2022). Exploring the level of sustainability awareness among consumers within the fast-fashion clothing industry: A dual business and consumer perspective. *Competitiveness Review*, *32*(3), 350–375. doi:10.1108/CR-04-2021-0061

Paryono, P., Absori, A., Dimyati, K., Basri, M., & Rismawati, S. D. (2020). Liberalization and electricity policy changes: Problems and challenges in the electricity sector in Indonesia. *International Journal of Energy Economics and Policy*, *10*(1), 170–177. doi:10.32479/ijeep.8636

Pasquale, F. (2013). Privacy, Antitrust, and Power. *Geo. Mason L. Rev., 1009.*

Patel, L. (2019). Gender: Toward gender equality and poverty reduction. Handbook of Social Policy and Development, (pp. 71-88).

Patrick, H. A., & Kumar, V. R. (2012). Managing Workplace Diversity: Issues and Challenges. *SAGE Open*, *2*(2). Advance online publication. doi:10.1177/2158244012444615

Pauw, W. P., König, M., Sadikhova, K., & Stutzmann, T. (2021). *Financing Low-Carbon and Climate Resilient Development: Do countries integrate Article 2.1 (c) of the Paris Agreement in their long-term strategies?* Frankfurt School- UNEP Centre. https://dspace.library.uu.nl/bitstream/handle/1874/417005/Pauw_et_al_2022_Financing_Low_carbon_and_Climate.resilient_development_final.pdf?sequence=1&isAllowed=y

Peeperkorn, L. (2009). Price Discrimination and Exploitation. In B. E. Hawk (Ed.), *International Antitrust Law & Policy: Fordham Competition Law 2008* (pp. 611–634). Juris Publishing, Inc.

Penz, E., & Hogg, M. K. (2011, February 15). The role of mixed emotions in consumer behaviour: Investigating ambivalence in consumers' experiences of approach-avoidance conflicts in online and offline settings. *European Journal of Marketing*, *45*(1/2), 104–132. doi:10.1108/03090561111095612

Pepermans, G. (2019). European energy market liberalization: Experiences and challenges. *International Journal of Economic Policy Studies*, *13*(1), 3–26. doi:10.100742495-018-0009-0

Petinrin, J., & Shaaban, M. (2015). Renewable energy for continuous energy sustainability in Malaysia. *Renewable & Sustainable Energy Reviews*, *50*, 967–981. doi:10.1016/j.rser.2015.04.146

Pettitpierre, A. (2015). *Environmental Law in Switzerland*. Kluwer Law International.

Phelps, J., Nowag, G., & Ferrell, E. (2000). Privacy Concerns and Consumer Willingness to Provide Personal Information. *Journal of Public Policy & Marketing*, *19*(1), 27–41. doi:10.1509/jppm.19.1.27.16941

Pietzcker, R. C., Stetter, D., Manger, S., & Luderer, G. (2014). Using the sun to decarbonize the power sector: The economic potential of photovoltaics and concentrating solar power. *Applied Energy*, *135*, 704–720. doi:10.1016/j.apenergy.2014.08.011

Politt, M. G. (2012). The role of policy in energy transitions: Lessons from the energy liberalization era. *Energy Policy*, *50*, 128–137. doi:10.1016/j.enpol.2012.03.004

Pomeranz, E. F., & Stedman, R. C. (2020). Measuring good governance: Piloting an instrument for evaluating good governance principles. *Journal of Environmental Policy and Planning*, *22*(3), 428–440. doi:10.1080/1523908X.2020.1753181

Ponce, P., Oliveira, C., Álvarez, V., & del Río-Rama, M. D. L. C. (2020). The liberalization of the internal energy market in the European Union: Evidence of its influence on reducing environmental pollution. *Energies*, *13*(22), 6116. doi:10.3390/en13226116

Popov, A. (2021, March 15). *How COVID-19 triggered the digital and e-commerce turning point*. UNCTAD News. https://unctad.org/news/how-covid-19-triggered-digital-and-e-commerce-turning-point#:~:text=As%20lockdowns%20became%20the%20new,to%20about%2017%25%20in%202020

Porter, E. (2021). *The Consumer Citizen*. Oxford University Press. doi:10.1093/oso/9780197526781.001.0001

PosnerE. (2019). The Antitrust Challenge to Covenants Not to Compete in Employment Contracts. [S.l.]: SSRN. https://ssrn.com/abstract=3453433. . doi:10.2139/ssrn.3453433

Pramudya, E. P., Hospes, O., & Termeer, C. (2018). Friend or foe? The various responses of the Indonesian state to sustainable non-state palm oil initiatives. *Asian Journal of Sustainability and Social Responsibility*, *3*(1), 1–22. doi:10.118641180-018-0018-y

Pranti A. S. (2013). Current Energy Situation and Comparative Solar Power Possibility Analysis for Obtaining Sustainable Energy Security in South Asia. *International Journal of Scientific and Technology Research*, *2*(8). https://www.ijstr.org/paper

Prasad, R., Sridhar, V., & Bunel, A. (2016). An Institutional Analysis of Spectrum Management in India. *Journal of Information Policy, 6*, 252–293. doi:10.5325/jinfopoli.6.2016.0252

Provasi, R., & Riva, P. (2015). The Italian two-tiers model. Evidence and comparison with some other countries. *Corporate Ownership & Control, 12*(3–3), 388–396. doi:10.22495/cocv12i3c3p9

Putri, A. M. H. (2023, June 23). Deforestasi dan Hasrat Eropa "Membunuh" Sawit Indonesia. *CNBC Indonesia*. https://www.cnbcindonesia.com/research/20230620072029-128-447429/deforestasi-dan-hasrat-eropa-membunuh-sawit-indonesia

Qaqaya, H., & Lipimile, G. (2008). *The effects of Anti-competitive Business Practices on Developing Countries and their Development Prospects*. United Nations.

Qawaya, H., & Lipimile, G. (2008). *The effects of anti-competitive business practices on developing countries and their development prospects*. UNCTAD.

Rachinger, Rauter, R., Müller, C., Vorraber, W., & Schirgi, E. (2019). Digitalization and its influence on business model innovation. *Journal of Manufacturing Technology Management*, *30*(8), 1143–1160. doi:10.1108/JMTM-01-2018-0020

Radovanović, M., Filipović, S., & Pavlović, D. (2017). Energy security measurement: A sustainable approach. *Renewable & Sustainable Energy Reviews*, *68*, 1020–1032. doi:10.1016/j.rser.2016.02.010

Rahman, H. A., & Ghadas, Z. A. A. (2018). The evolution of partnership structure; Special reference to governance legal framework for LLPs. *PROCEEDINGS–ICLG*, *2018*, 511.

Rahman, N. A., & Ahamat, H. (2021). *Competition Law in Malaysia* (2nd ed.). Sweet & Maxwell.

Rahman, N. A., Ahamat, H., & Abdul Ghadas, Z. (2017). The theory of harm under the Malaysian Competition Act 2010. *Pertanika Journal of Social Science & Humanities*, *25*, 155–166.

Raitt, G. (2019). *The Metaphysics of Market Power: The Zero-sum Competition and Market Manipulation Approach*. Bloomsbury Publishing. doi:10.5040/9781509928101

Raj, V., & Gohain, M. (2021). Impact of Covid-19 on Malaysian E-Commerce. *International Journal on Recent Trends in Business and Tourism*, 8 - 10.

Ramaiah, A. K. (2019). Competition in Digital Economy: Fate of Consumer Welfare in Malaysia. Malaysian Journal of Consumer and Family Economics, 22, 223-245.

Ramaiah, A. K. (2015). Competition law and exemption policy in Malaysia: When, why and why not. *Int J Bus Econ Law*, *8*(4).

Ramaiah, A. K. (2017). Innovation, Intellectual Property Rights and Competition Law in Malaysia. *South East Asia Journal of Contemporary Business*. *Economics and Law*, *14*, 60–69.

Ramaiah, A. K., & Hussein, S. M. (2021). Cartel Prohibitions and Relevance for Exclusion under the Competition Law in Malaysia and Singapore. *Asian Journal of Law and Governance*, *3*(1), 1–21.

Ramappa, T. (2009). Competition Law in India: Policy, Issues, and Developments. Oxford University Press.

Razak, A. A. (2019). Competition Act 2010 (Act 712). In *The Annotated Statutes of Malaysia*. Lexis Nexis.

Regulation (EU) 2016/679 of the European Parliament and of the Council of 27 April 2016 on the protection of natural persons with regard to the processing of personal data and on the free movement of such data, and repealing Directive 95/46/EC (General Data Protection Regulation).

Regulation (EU) 2022/1925 of the European Parliament and of the Council of 14 September 2022 on contestable and fair markets in the digital sector and amending Directives (EU) 2019/1937 and (EU) 2020/1828 (Digital Markets Act) (Text with EEA relevance). Official Journal of the European Union, L 265, 12.10.2022.

Report of the World Commission on Environment and Development: Our Common Future. (1987). United Nations Digital Library. https://digitallibrary.un.org/record/139811

Revinova, S. (2021). E-Commerce effects for the sustainable development goals. *SHS Web of Conferences*, 1 - 8.

Richter, H. (2023). The public interest dimension of the single market for data: Public undertakings as a model for regulating private data sharing. *European Law Journal*, eulj.12476. doi:10.1111/eulj.12476

Ritter, L., & Braun, W. D. (2005). *European Competition Law: A Practitioner's Guide*. Kluwer Law International B.V.

Riyandanu, M. F. (2022, August 16). PLN Diminta Tak Monopoli Hak Serifikat Energi Baru dan Terbarukan. *Katadata*. https://katadata.co.id/agustiyanti/ekonomi-hijau/62fae83983b4f/pln-diminta-tak-monopoli-hak-serifikat-energi-baru-dan-terbarukan

Robb, G., Paelo, A., & UNU-WIDER. (2020). *Competitive dynamics of telecommunications markets in South Africa, Tanzania, Zambia, and Zimbabw*. UNU-WIDER. doi:10.35188/UNU-WIDER/2020/840-5

Ronald, J. G. (1999). The Legal Infrastructure of High Technology Industrial Districts: Silicon Valley, Route 128, and Covenants not to Compete. *New York University Law Review*, *74*(3), 575–629.

Rwanda Utilities Regulatory Authorities. (2022). *Annual Report 2021-2022*. RURA. https://rura.rw/fileadmin/Documents/docs/report/Annual_Report_for_2021-2022.pdf

Ryan, J. K., Sun, D., & Zhao, X. (2012, March 11). Competition and Coordination in Online Marketplaces. *Production and Operations Management*, *21*(6), 997–1014. doi:10.1111/j.1937-5956.2012.01332.x

Saini, M., & Rajagopal, D. (2022, October 13). *Canada's watchdog launches investigation into RBC over climate complaints*. (S. Kuber, Editor) Reuters. https://www.reuters.com/world/americas/canadas-watchdog-launches-investigation-into-rbc-over-climate-complaints-2022-10-12/

SAL Agencies Sdn Bhd & 4 Ors v Competition Commission, Appeal No.: TRP 2-2021. https://www.mycc.gov.my/sites/default/files/pdf/decision/Alasan%20Keputusan%20kes%20SAL%20Agencies%20Sdn%20Bhd%20%26%204%20yang%20lain%20v%20Suruhanjaya%20Persaingan%20%281%29.pdf

Salim, M. R. (2013). Limited liability partnership in Malaysia: A corporate governance perspective. *This material was first published by Thomson Reuters (Professional) UK Limited in Mohammad Rizal Salim, "Limited Liability Partnership in Malaysia: A Corporate Governance Perspective"[2013]. ICCLR*, *24*(12), 421.

Santos, A. Q. O., da Silva, A. R., Ledesma, J. J. G., de Almeida, A. B., Cavallari, M. R., & Junior, O. H. A. (2021). Electricity Market in Brazil: A Critical Review on the Ongoing Reform. *Energies*, *14*(10), 2873. doi:10.3390/en14102873

Sarkar, et, al. (2020). *Role of Regional Cooperation and Integration in Improving Energy Insecurity in South Asia*. ADBI Working Paper Series-1120, Tokyo: Asian Development Bank Institute.

Saura, J. R., Ribeiro-Soriano, D., & Palacios-Marqués, D. (2021). From user-generated data to data-driven innovation: A research agenda to understand user privacy in digital markets. *International Journal of Information Management*, *60*, 60. doi:10.1016/j.ijinfomgt.2021.102331

Schäfer, F., Gebauer, H., Gröger, C., Gassmann, O., & Wortmann, F. (2023). Data-driven business and data privacy: Challenges and measures for product-based companies. *Business Horizons*, *66*(4), 493–504. doi:10.1016/j.bushor.2022.10.002

Schinkel, M. P., & Treuren, L. (2021, March 26). *Green Antitrust: Why Would Restricting Competition Induce Sustainability Efforts?* Promarket. https://www.promarket.org/2021/03/26/green-antitrust-why-would-restricting-competition-induce-sustainability-efforts/

Schmid, D. G., & Koehler, P. (2022, September 19). *Digital Services Act - an overview*. Taylor Wessing. https://www.taylorwessing.com/en/interface/2022/the-eus-digital-services-act/digital-services-act---an-overview

Schott, C., & Nhem, S. (2018). Paths to the market: analysing tourism distribution channels for community-based tourism. Tourism Recreation Research, 43(3), 356-371.

Schrijver, N. (2010). *Development without Destruction: The UN and Global Resource Management (United Nations Intellectual History Project Series)*. Paperback.

Schütze, R. (2018). *European Union Law*. Cambridge University Press. doi:10.1017/9781108555913

Schweitzer, H. (2022). A European Market Investigation: Institutional Setup and Procedural Design. In M. Motta, M. Peitz, & H. Schweitzer (Eds.), *Market investigations: A new competition tool for Europe?* (pp. 90–163). Cambridge University Press. doi:10.1017/9781009072007.003

SDG Knowledge Platform. (2023, August 15). Retrieved from Sustainable Development Goals: https://sdgs.un.org/goals

Sen, A. (2014). Development as Freedom (1999). *The Globalization and Development Reader: Perspectives on Development and Global Change, 525.*

Setyawan, D. (2013). Assessing the current Indonesia's electricity market arrangements and the opportunities to reform. *Int. Journal of Renewable Energy Development*, *3*(1), 2014.

Sharma, J. K. (2020). Limited Liability Partnership as a Better Alternative to Incorporation. *Jus Corpus LJ*, *1*, 440.

Shearer, C., Ghio, N., Myllyvirta, L., Yu, A., & Nace, T. (2017). *Boom and bust 2017: Tracking the global coal plant pipeline*. CoalSwarm, Sierra Club, Greenpeace International. https://apo.org.au/node/75523

Shem, C., Simsek, Y., Hutfilter, U. F., & Urmee, T. (2019). Potentials and opportunities for low carbon energy transition in Vietnam: A policy analysis. *Energy Policy*, *134*, 110818. doi:10.1016/j.enpol.2019.06.026

Shin, K. J., & Managi, S. (2017). Liberalization of a retail electricity market: Consumer satisfaction and household switching behavior in Japan. *Energy Policy*, *110*, 675–685. doi:10.1016/j.enpol.2017.07.048

Shofa, J. N. (2023, September 21). Carbon Tax to Put Indonesia on Track Toward 2030 Climate Goal. *Jakarta Globe*. https://jakartaglobe.id/business/carbon-tax-to-put-indonesia-on-track-toward-2030-climate-goal

Shrestha, R. M., Anandarajah, G., & Liyanage, M. H. (2009). Factors affecting CO2 emission from the power sector of selected countries in Asia and the Pacific. *Energy Policy*, *37*(6), 2375–2384. doi:10.1016/j.enpol.2009.01.032

Siddiqui, I. & Anand, K. (2022). *Competition Policy and Sustainability: A Difficult Path to Tread.* Available at SSRN 4056805.

Siddiqui, S. (28 December 2023). Pakistan's foray into renewable energy. *The Express Tribune*. https://tribune.com.pk/story/2393075/pakistans-foray-into-renewable-energy

Siddiqui, I. (2022). *Competition Policy and Sustainability: A Difficult Path to Tread.* IIT Madras.

Sieber-Gasser, C., Kalra, S., & Sheth, A. V. (2021). Sustainable Development Goals vs Non-Discrimination in WTO Law: Does the End Justify the Means? *Indian J. Int'l Econ. L.*, *13*, 82.

Siksnelyte, I., & Zavadskas, E. K. (2019). Achievements of the European Union countries in seeking a sustainable electricity sector. *Energies*, *12*(12), 2254. doi:10.3390/en12122254

Simon, E. (2015). *Indonesian Pledge Suggests No Increase in Emissions to 2030.* Carbon Brief. https://www.carbonbrief.org/indonesian-pledge-suggests-no-increase-in-emissions-to-2030/

Sims, M., Youell, T., & Womersley, R. (2016). *Understanding Spectrum Liberalisation*. CRC Press.

Singapore Ministerial Declaration. (1996, December 18). Word Trade Organisation. https://www.wto.org/english/thewto_e/minist_e/min96_e/wtodec_e.htm#investment_competition

Smith, A. (1971). *History of the East African Posts and Telecommunications Administration 1837 to 1967* [Doctor of Philosophy, University of Nairobi]. http://erepository.uonbi.ac.ke/handle/11295/26809

Snoep, M. (2023). What is fair and efficient in the face of climate change? *Journal of Antitrust Enforcement*, *11*(1), 1–4. doi:10.1093/jaenfo/jnad001

South African Government. (2021, March 31). *The Competition Act of 1998*. The Competition Commission. https://www.compcom.co.za/wp-content/uploads/2021/03/Competition-Act-A6.pdf

Sovacool, B., & Drupady, I. (2011). Examining the Small Renewable Energy Power (SREP) Program in Malaysia. *Energy Policy*, *39*(11), 7244–7255. doi:10.1016/j.enpol.2011.08.045

Srivatsa, K. R. (n.d.). Competition law fit to assess sustainability, climate action. *The Hindu Business line*.

Stagnaro, C., Amenta, C., Di Croce, G., & Lavecchia, L. (2020). Managing the liberalization of Italy's retail electricity market: A policy proposal. *Energy Policy*, *137*, 111150. doi:10.1016/j.enpol.2019.111150

Starr, E., & Robert, H. (2019). The use, abuse, and enforceability of non-compete and no-poach agreements. *Washington, DC: Economic Innovation Group*. United Nations. https://sdgs.un.org/topics/employment-decent-work-all-and-social-protection

State Bank of Pakistan. (2018). *Annual Report 2017–2018*. The State of Pakistan's Economy.

Statista. (2023). *Contribution of e-commerce to the gross domestic product (GDP) of Malaysia from 2015 to 2021*. Statista. https://www.statista.com/statistics/956908/e-commerce-contribution-to-gdp-malaysia/

Stigler Committee on Digital Platforms. (2019). *Final Report*. Chicago: The University of Chicago Booth School of Business.

Stigler, G. J. (1972). Economic competition and political competition. *Public Choice*, *13*(1), 91–106. doi:10.1007/BF01718854

Stirling, A. (2010). Multi-criteria Diversity Analysis: A Novel Heuristic Framework for Appraising Energy Portfolios. *Energy Policy*, *38*, 1622–1634. doi:10.1016/j.enpol.2009.02.023

Stohr, W. B., & Taylor, D. R. (1981). Development From Above or Below? The Dialectics of Regional Planning in Developing Countries. Wiley.

Stucke, M. E. (2013, April). Is Competition always Good? *Journal of Antitrust Enforcement*, *1*(1), 162–197. doi:10.1093/jaenfo/jns008

Stucke, M. E., & Grunes, A. P. (2016). *Big Data and Competition Policy*. Oxford University Press.

Sukarso, P. (2021). Decarbonizing Electricity in Indonesia. *Opportunity in the Implementation of Rooftop Solar PV.*, *1096*(1), 012098.

Suprobowati, G. D., Apriliana, G. M. C., & Hutami, W. P. (2021). *Indonesian Electric Vehicle Policy, Realization and Development*. 99–102.

Surden, H. (2014). Machine Learning and Law. *Wash. L. Rev.*, *8*.

Suroyo, G., & Munthe, B. C. (2021, November 15). *Indonesia introduces carbon trading policy to reduce emission*. Reuters. https://www.reuters.com/business/cop/indonesia-introduces-carbon-trading-policy-reduce-emission-2021-11-15/

Sutton, J. (1991). *Sunk Cost and Market Structure: Price Competition, Advertising, and the Evolution of Concentration*. MIIT Press.

Switzerland Global Enterprise. (2021). Market Snapshot: Renewable Energy in Pakistan. https://www.s-ge.com/en/article/export-knowhow/20213-c5-pakistan-renewable-energy?ct, Switzerland Global Enterprise.

Taghizadeh, H. (2019). Introduction. In Farhad T. et, al. (eds.) Achieving Energy Security in Asia: Diversification, Integration, and Policy Implications. Singapore: World Scientific.

Taghizadeh-Hesary, F., Rasoulinezhad, E., & Phoumin, H. (2022). Ways to achieve universal access to sustainable electricity in Southeast Asia. *Economic Change and Restructuring*, *55*(4), 2031–2050. doi:10.100710644-022-09386-4

Tamsang, K. (1998). The unknown and untold reality about the Lepchas. Lyangsong Tamsang

Tanga Fresh v FCC, Appeal No 5 of 2014, Fair Competition Tribunal.

Tanzania Telecoms Market Report. (2023). Tanzania Telecoms. https://www.budde.com.au/Research/Tanzania-Telecoms-Mobile-and-Broadband-Statistics-and Analyses#:~:text=Tanzania%27s%20mobile%20market%20enjoys%20effective,has%20struggled%20to%20gain%20subscribers

TCRA. (2010a). *Telecommunications Statistics from 2000 to 2010*. TCRA.

TCRA. (2010b). *Quarterly Telecom Statistics*. TCRA.

TCRA. (2011). 50 Years of Communications in Tanzania. *The Regulator*, 5–10.

TCRA. (2023). *Communications Statistics: Quarter Ending 30th June 2023*. TCRA. https://www.tcra.go.tz/uploads/text-editor/files/Communication%20Statistics%20for%20Q4%202023_1689602781.pdf

TeliaSonera Sverige, Case C-52/09, [2011] ECR I-527

Temu, G. (2021). *Regulation and Enforcement of Competition Law in Tanzania's Telecommunications Sector: Law, Institutional Design and Practice* [PhD Thesis, Bayreuth; Application/pdf]. https://epub.uni-bayreuth.de/id/eprint/5921

The Citizen. (2019). *How telecoms can boost contribution to the economy. The Citizen*. https://www.thecitizen.co.tz/news/1840340-5031780-format-xhtml-xwxxg8/index.html

The Economic Times. (21 June 2023). Cash-starved Pakistan fails to secure LNG supply as no company responds to its tender. *The Economic Times*. https://economictimes.indiatimes.com/news/international/world-news/cash-starved-pakistan-fails-to-secure-lng-supply-as-no-company-responds-to-its-tender/articleshow/101162096.cms?from=mdr,

The Editor. (2012, December 30). *Why the first EA Community collapsed*. Daily Monitor. https://www.monitor.co.ug/OpEd/Letters/Why-the-first-EA-Community-collapsed-/806314-1653726-arwsdy/index.html

The United Nations General Assembly. (2015). *Resolution adopted by the General Assembly on 25 September 2015, A/RES/70/1*. The United Nations. https://documents-dds-ny.un.org/doc/UNDOC/GEN/N15/291/89/PDF/N1529189.pdf?OpenElement

The United Republic of Tanzania (URT), Ministry of Finance and Planning, Tanzania National Bureau of Statistics and President's Office - Finance and Planning, Office of the Chief Government Statistician, Zanzibar. (2022). *The 2022 Population and Housing Census: Administrative Units Population Distribution Report*. National Bureau of Statistics.

The World Bank in Tanzania. (2023). *Overview*. World Bank. https://www.worldbank.org/en/country/tanzania/overview

Thibodeau, P. (2014). The Internet of Things Could Encroach on Personal Privacy. *Computerworld*. https://www.computerworld.com/article/2488949/emerging-technology/the-internet-of-things-could-encroach-on-personal-privacy.htm

Tisdell, C. A. (2013). *Competition, Diversity and Economic Performance: Processes, Complexities and Ecological Similarities*. Edward Elgar Publishing, Inc. doi:10.4337/9781781002391

Tomislav, K. (2018). The concept of sustainable development: From its beginning to the contemporary issues. Zagreb International Review of Economics & Business, 21(1), 67-94.

Tracker, C. A. (2020). *Paris Agreement Compatible Sectoral Benchmarks: Elaborating the decarbonisation roadmap*. Climate Action Tracker. https://climateactiontracker.org/documents/753/CAT_2020-07-10_ParisAgreementBenchmarks_FullReport.pdf

Tracker, C. A. (2021). *Indonesia Policy Action*. Climate Action Tracker. https://climateactiontracker.org/countries/indonesia/

Train, K. (1991). *Optimal regulation: The economic theory of natural monopoly*. MIT Press.

Triana, K., & Wahyudi, A. (2020). Sea level rise in Indonesia: The drivers and the combined impacts from land subsidence. *ASEAN J. Sci. Technol. Dev*, *37*(3), 115–121. doi:10.29037/ajstd.627

Tsai, J., Egelman, S., Cranor, L., & Acquisti, A. (2011). The Effect of Online Privacy Information on Purchasing Behavior: An Experimental Study. *Information Systems Research*, *22*(2), 234–248. doi:10.1287/isre.1090.0260

Turillazi, A., Casolari, F., Taddeo, M., & Floridi, L. (2022). *The Digital Services Act: An Analysis of Its Ethical*. Legal, and Social Implications.

Turner, D. F. (1965). Conglomerate Mergers and Section 7 of the Clayton Act. *Harvard Law Review, 78*(7), 1313–1395. doi:10.2307/1338906

Uddin, M. N., Rahman, M. A., Mofijur, M., Taweekun, J., Techato, K., & Rasul, M. G. (2019). Renewable energy in Bangladesh: Status and prospects. *Energy Procedia*, *160*, 655–661. doi:10.1016/j.egypro.2019.02.218

Uffer, M. (2023). Chapter 9 Competition Law: Sustainability Through Competition and Participation. In B. Peters, & E. J. Lohse, Sustainability through Participation: Perspectives from National, European and International Law. Bril / Nijhoff.

Uganda Communications Commission. (2022). *Market Performance Report 4Q22*. Uganda Communications Commission. https://www.ucc.co.ug/wp-content/uploads/2023/06/UCC-4Q22-Market-Performance-Report-compressed.pdf

UN Department of Economics and Social Welfare. (n.d.). *17th Goals of Sustainable Development*. UN Department of Economics and Social Welfare Sustainable Development. https://sdgs.un.org/goals

UN Women. (2014). *The World Survey on the role of women in development 2014: Gender equality and sustainable development*. UN Women. https://www.unwomen.org/en/digital-library/publications/2014/10/world-survey-2014

UNCTAD. (2016). *United Nations Guidelines for Consumer Protection*. UNCTAD.

UNCTAD. (2019). *Competition issues in the digital economy*. United Nations.

UNCTAD. (2021). *Fifteenth session of the United Nations Conference on Trade and Development (UNCTAD 15)*. UNCTAD. https://unctad.org/meeting/fifteenth-session-united-nations-conference-trade-and-development-unctad-15

UNCTAD. (2021). *The Bridgetown Covenant: From inequality and vulnerability to prosperity for all*. United Nations.

UNCTAD. (2021). *United Nations Conference on Trade and Development*. UN.

UNCTAD. (2021, March 15). *How COVID-19 triggered the digital and e-commerce turning point*. Unctad.org. https://unctad.org/news/how-covid-19-triggered-digital-and-e-commerce-turning-point

UNCTAD. (2023). *Competition and Consumer Protection Policies for Sustainability*. UNCTAD.

Understanding The WTO: Cross-Cutting And New Issues. (n.d.). WTO. https://www.wto.org/english/thewto_e/whatis_e/tif_e/bey3_e.htm

Unit Level Data Of Periodic Labour Force Survey (PLFS). (2019). MOSPI. https://mospi.gov.in/unit-level-data-periodic-labour-force-survey-plfs-july-2019-june-2020

United Nation. (2023). *The Sustainable Development Goals Report Special edition Towards a Rescue Plan for People and Planet*. UN. https://unstats.un.org/sdgs/report/2023/The-Sustainable-Development-Goals-Report-2023.pdf

United Nations Department of Economics and Social Affairs. (n.d.). *Promote sustained, inclusive and sustainable economic growth, full and productive employment and decent work for all*. United Nations Departments of Economics and Social Affairs, Sustainable Development. https://sdgs.un.org/goals/goal8

United Nations Department of Social and Economic Affairs. (2023). SDGs. https://sdgs.un.org/goals/goal9

United Nations Development Programme. (2015). *Human development report 2015. Rethinking work for human development*. UN. https://hdr.undp.org/sites/default/files/2015_human_development_ report.pdfC

United Nations. (2016). *The Sustainable Development Goals Report 2016*. United Nations.

United Nations. (2023). *The Sustainable Development Goals Report* (Special Edition). United Nations.

Uppal A, 2007, Gender Discrimination in Quality of Employment and Wages in Unorganized Manufacturing Sector of India: Paper presented in Gender Issues and Empowerment of Women Platinum Jubilee of Indian Statistical Institute 1-2 February 2007.

Uqaili, M. A. (2004). Hydel Power Generation in Pakistan: Past Trends, Current Status and Future Projections. *Mehran University Research Journal of Engineering and Technology*, *23*(3), 207–216.

Van den Berg, R., & Camesasca, P. (2001). *European Competition Law and Economics: A Comparative Perspective*. Intersentia NV.

Vanberg, V. J. (2011). Consumer Welfare, Total Welfare and Economic Freedom – On the Normative Foundations of Competition Policy. In W. K. Josef Drexl (Ed.), *Competition Policy and the Economic Approach*. Edward Elgar Publishing. https://econpapers.repec.org/bookchap/elgeechap/13786_5f2.htm

Verbong, G. P., & Geels, F. W. (2010). Exploring sustainability transitions in the electricity sector with socio-technical pathways. *Technological Forecasting and Social Change*, *77*(8), 1214–1221. doi:10.1016/j.techfore.2010.04.008

Verick, S. (2018). Female Labour Force Participation and Development. The Institute for the Study of Labour (IZA) Germany. *IZA World of Labor: Evidence-Based Policy Making*, *87*(2). Advance online publication. doi:10.15185/izawol.87.v2

Vestager, M. (2021, September 10). *Competition policy in support of the Green Deal. Speech presented at the 25th IBA Competition Conference*. Europa. https://ec.europa.eu/commission/commissioners/2019-2024/vestager/announcements/competition-policy-support-green-deal_en

Vickers, J. (1995). Concepts of Competition. [JSTOR.]. *Oxford Economic Papers*, *47*(1), 1–23. doi:10.1093/oxfordjournals.oep.a042155

Vijayan, V. (2019). Employment. Chamber Global Practice Guide. http://www.shearndelamore.com/pdfs/Chambers-Global-Practice-Guide-Employment-2019.pdf

Viscusi, W., & Vernon, J. (2005). *Economics of regulation and antitrust* (4th ed.). MIT Press.

Vit, J. (2016, July 1). *Under gov't pressure, palm oil giants disband green pledge*. Mongabay Indonesia. https://news.mongabay.com/2016/07/under-government-pressure-palm-oil-giants-disband-green-pledge/

Vlados, C., Chatzinikolaou, D., & Kapaltzoglou, F. F. (2021). Energy market liberalization in Greece: Structures, policy, and prospects. *International Journal of Energy Economics and Policy*, *11*(2), 115–126. doi:10.32479/ijeep.10804

Vodacom Tanzania Limited v Tanzania Communications Regulatory Authority & Six Telecommunications Company Limited, Fair Competition Tribunal, Appeal No 2/2007.

Vodacom Tanzania PLC v Tanzania Communications Regulatory Authority, Fair Competition Tribunal, Appeal No 8/2018.

Wahyudi, N. A. (2022, June 28). Monopoli Listrik PLN Dinilai Hambat Investasi EBT. *Bisnis.Com.* https://ekonomi.bisnis.com/read/20220628/44/1549029/monopoli-listrik-pln-dinilai-hambat-investasi-ebt

Wai, C. K., & Derek, C. T. Q. (2021). *Contracts in Restraint of Trade in Malaysia.* Low Partners. https://www.lowpartners.com/contracts-restraint-trade-malaysia/

Walden, I. (2018). Access and Interconnection. In I. Walden (Ed.), *Telecommunications Law and Regulation* (5th ed., pp. 435–490). Oxford University Press. doi:10.1093/oso/9780198807414.003.0011

Wang, J., Gao, X., & Wang, Z. (2021, April 8). Sustainable Supply Chain Decisions under E-Commerce Platform Marketplace with Competition. *Sustainability (Basel)*, *13*(8), 1–23. doi:10.3390u13084162

Wang, W. H., Moreno-Casas, V., & Huerta de Soto, J. (2021). A free-market environmentalist transition toward renewable energy: The cases of Germany, Denmark, and the United Kingdom. *Energies*, *14*(15), 4659. doi:10.3390/en14154659

Wang, X., Chen, G., Afshan, S., Awosusi, A. A., & Abbas, S. (2023). Transition towards sustainable energy: The role of economic complexity, financial liberalization and natural resources management in China. *Resources Policy*, *83*, 103631. doi:10.1016/j.resourpol.2023.103631

Warth, L., & Koparanova, M. (2012). Empowering Women for Sustainable Development. Discussion Paper Series, No. 2012.1. United Nations Economic Commission For Europe, Geneva, Switzerland.

WBCED. (1987). *Report of the World Commission on Environment and Development: Our Common Future*. WBCED.

Whish, R., & Bailey, D. (2012). *Competition law* (7th ed.). Oxford University Press.

Whish, R., & Bailey, D. (2021). *Competition Law* (10th ed.). Oxford University Press. doi:10.1093/he/9780198836322.001.0001

White, L. (2015). Monopoly and Dominant Firms: Antitrust Economics and Policy Approaches. In R. D. Blair & D. D. Sokol (Eds.), *The Oxford Handbook of International Antitrust Economics* (Vol. 1, pp. 313–344). Oxford University Press.

Why competition and consumer protection matter. (n.d.). UNCTAD. https://unctad.org/Topic/Competition-and-Consumer-Protection

Wickelgren, A. (2017). A novel justification for legal restrictions on non-compete clauses. *International Review of Law and Economics.*

Wijaya, A., Chrysolite, H., Ge, M., Wibowo, C. K., Pradana, A., Utami, A. F., & Austin, K. (2017). How can Indonesia achieve its climate change mitigation goal? An analysis of potential emissions reductions from energy and land-use policies. *World Resources Institute. World Resour Inst Work Pap*, 1–36.

Wilcox, R. M. (1999). Enforcing lawyer non-competition agreements while maintaining the profession: The role of conflict of interest principles. *Minnesota Law Review*, *84*, 915.

Winkler, K., & Baumgarten, G. (2009). The Framework for Network Access and Interconnection. In C. Koenig (Ed.), *EC competition and telecommunications law* (2nd ed., pp. 421–469). Wolters Kluwer Law & Business.

Winn, J. K., & de Koker, L. (2013). Introduction to Mobile Money in Developing Countries: Financial Inclusion and Financial Integrity Conference Special Issue. *Washington Journal of Law. Technology & Arts*, *8*(3), 155–163.

Wira Swire Sdn Bhd v. Ketua Pengarah Hasil Dalam Negeri [2019] 1 LNS 1026

Wismer, S., Bongard, C., & Rasek, A. (2017, April). Multi-Sided Market Economics in Competition Law Enforcement. *Journal of European Competition Law & Practice*, *8*(4), 257–262. doi:10.1093/jeclap/lpw082

World Bank. (2020). Expanding Renewable Energy in Pakistan's Electricity Mix. *World Bank*. https://www.worldbank.org/en/news/feature/2020/11/09/a-renewable-energy-future-for-pakistans-power-system

World Bank. (2023). *World Bank Data*. World Bank. https://data.worldbank.org/indicator/IT.CEL.SETS.P2?locations=BI

Worldmeters, W. (2016). *Indonesia CO2 Emissions*. Worldmeters. https://www.worldometers.info/co2-emissions/indonesia-co2-emissions/

Wurmnest, W. (2011). Predatory Pricing: From Price/Cost Comparisons to Post-Chicago Thinking. In J. Basedow & W. Wurmnest (Eds.), Structure and effects in EU competition law: Studies on exclusionary conduct and state aid. Kluwer Law International; Sold and distributed in North, Central, and South America by Aspen Publishers.

Yang, D. X., Jing, Y. Q., Wang, C., Nie, P. Y., & Sun, P. (2021). Analysis of renewable energy subsidy in China under uncertainty: Feed-in tariff vs. renewable portfolio standard. *Energy Strategy Reviews*, *34*, 100628. doi:10.1016/j.esr.2021.100628

Yi, C., & Cai, J. (2016). *Market-Driven Spectrum Sharing in Cognitive Radio*. Springer. doi:10.1007/978-3-319-29691-3

Yin, X. (2023). The Analysis of Accounting Firms' Organization Types and Reasons for Switching the Organization Types. *Academic Journal of Business & Management*, *5*(12), 77–81.

Zhang, Y. F., Parker, D., & Kirkpatrick, C. (2008). Electricity sector reform in developing countries: An econometric assessment of the effects of privatization, competition, and regulation. *Journal of Regulatory Economics*, *33*(2), 159–178. doi:10.100711149-007-9039-7

Zipp, A. (2017). The marketability of variable renewable energy in liberalized electricity markets–an empirical analysis. *Renewable Energy*, *113*, 1111–1121. doi:10.1016/j.renene.2017.06.072

Zuhairah Ariff, A. & Hamizah, A. (2020). Governance issues in Malaysia limited liability partnerships (LLP). *International Journal of Psycho social Rehabilitation, 24*(6), 12242-12255.

About the Contributors

Siti Fazilah Binti Abdul Shukor is a Law Lecturer at the Business Department of Faculty of Business and Finance, Universiti Tunku Abdul Rahman. She completed her Bachelor of Law and Commerce from Management and Science Univesity; Master of Comparative Law and Doctor of Philosophy (Law) in the field of Industrial Relations Law from International Islamic University Malaysia. She has been working as a lecturer for almost ten years with specializations in contracts, torts, employment, company, and partnership and consumer law. Her current research area is the Employment and Industrial Relations Law. Besides, her interest areas are on Human Trafficking and Migration law matters, Consumer Protection Law, and any current Issues on the aspect of law matters.

Farahdilah Ghazali is a senior lecturer at School of Business and Economics, University of Putra Malaysia. Previously, she served University of Malaysia Terengganu (UMT) and University of Tenaga Nasional Malaysia (UNITEN). She obtained her PhD in Law from Ahmad Ibrahim Kulliyyah of Laws, International Islamic University Malaysia (IIUM). Her interest areas are Natural Resources Law and Sustainability, particularly related to renewable energy. She has been appointed as a technical member for the enactment of the Malaysian Legal Framework on Seabed Mining in 2019. Being a passionate researcher and academic, she has widely published in peer-reviewed journals and presented papers at several national and international conferences in her areas of interest.

***

Zalina Binti Abdul Halim has been teaching the subjects of Media and the State, Communications and Multimedia Regulation, Law and Society, Research Methodology, Malaysian Legal System and Land Law in the undergraduate, postgraduate, and Bachelor of Jurisprudence external programme. Her focus had been on the development of the law students' appreciation of the impact on law and society and vice versa which she instilled in the course of Law and Society which was reintroduced into the curriculum in 2010. The students visited the Bukit Koman Residents in Pahang, the Orang Seletar in Danga Bay Johor, the Orang Jahut in Jerantut Pahang. The students also visited vulnerable communities on their own to do their research as part of their assessment. Currently, Dr Zalina binti Abdul Halim helms the Research Methodology class under the Master of Criminal Justice and Master of Commercial Law programme at the Faculty of Law, University of Malaya.

Norhoneydayatie Binti Abdul Manap, Ph.D, senior lecturer at the Center for Sharia Studies, Faculty of Islamic Studies, National University of Malaysia (UKM). Completed Bachelor of Laws (LLB), Bachelor of Sharia Law (LLBS), Master of Comparative Law (MCL) at UIAM, and Doctor of Philosophy (Ph.D) at Faculty of Law UKM. Area of expertise is commercial law including contract law, e-commerce, consumer law and competition law.

Adlan bin Abdul Razak is a senior lecturer with the Faculty of Law, Universiti Teknologi MARA (UiTM). He obtained his degree in Business Law from the University of Huddersfield in the United Kingdom. He then continues with an LLM in International Economic Law from the University of Warwick in the UK. He completed his PhD in Competition Law at the Faculty of Law UiTM. Dr Adlan completed his Certificate in Legal Practice and was admitted as an Advocate and Solicitor of the High Court of Malaya in 2003. Dr Adlan was seconded to the Ministry of Domestic Trade and Consumer Affairs to help draft the Competition Act and Competition Commission Act 2010. He also represented Malaysia in various Free Trade Negotiations including the ASEAN Australia New Zealand Free Trade Agreement. He also represented Malaysia at the United Nations Commission on Trade and Development (UNCTAD) International Group of Experts (IGE) conference on Competition Law in Geneva. Dr Adlan was also instrumental in setting up the ASEAN Experts Group on Competition (AEGC) in 2009. He teaches Law and Economics, Competition Law, Torts Law, Remedies (Torts) and Business Law at UiTM. He is also the Executive Director of the Centre for Continuous Legal Education at the Faculty of Law, UiTM. On occasion, Dr Adlan is also a consultant to law firms on trade remedies and competition law.

Ong Tze Chin is a senior lecturer and course coordinator for the Masters of Commercial Law programme at the Faculty of Law, University of Malaya (UM). She is also a research fellow of UM's Malaysian Centre of Regulatory Studies (UMCORs) and a researcher at the ASEAN Competition Research Centre. She holds a PhD in Law and an LLM from the National University of Malaysia (UKM). She graduated in law with an LLB (Hons) from Northumbria University and was called to the Bar as a barrister at Gray's Inn, United Kingdom. In 2022, she was appointed as an expert consultant for Consumer Protection in ASEAN (PROTECT) project in drafting the ASEAN Guidelines for Consumer Protection in E-commerce and is the main expert consultant in ASEAN (PROTECT) II Project in drafting the ASEAN Guidelines on Unfair Contract Terms. She is also the Principal Researcher for a research project on competition law and consumer protection in the digital market under the Fundamental Research Grant Scheme (FRGS) funded by the Malaysian Ministry of Higher Education. Her research interest lies in Consumer Protection Law, ASEAN Comparative Law, Commercial Law, Alternative Dispute Resolution, and E-commerce.

Arletta Gorecka graduated from the University of Stirling in June 2019 with the First Class LL.B. (Hons) and is currently a PhD Candidate at the University of Strathclyde. Arletta has worked at various law firms in Scotland and actively supported international, law, doctoral students. She also acts as a freelance interpreter and provided support for the Vis Moot. She also assists in the delivery of undergraduate modules. Arletta's research interest includes privacy, digital economy, data protection, goals and enforcement of competition law, and Big Data. Arletta's thesis focuses on the impact of privacy and Big Data on the EU competition law goals. It also considers the enforcement of competition law in the Big Data issues and attempts to identify workable and predicable intervention benchmarks and scope of remedies.

Sherin Kunhibava is a Senior Lecturer at the University Malaya Law faculty. Her area of expertise is in commercial law and Islamic finance law. Apart from her fifteen years of teaching experience in academia, Dr. Sherin has also worked at Pacific Bank Bhd., International Shariah Research Academy (ISRA) and Wisdom Management Consultancy Sdn. Bhd. Her working experience has been in the area of commercial law which includes contract law, company law and Islamic finance and banking. Dr. Sherin has also provided training under the LEEP program at University Malaya and for a number of years was the examiner for two external bodies, namely the Malaysian Association of Company Secretaries and the Malaysian Institute of Chartered Secretaries and Administrators. She also sits on the editorial board of the Journal of Malaysian and Comparative Law as a Subject Editor and is the Academic Advisor to the Student Journal of UMLR of the faculty of Law. Since 2018 Dr Sherin has worked on research projects funded by external grants researching on regulatory issues for digital solutions for the financial industry. In particular, blockchain. She was part of a team of researchers who were one of the first to report on regulatory issues in the blockchain space in Malaysia – the report can be viewed here: . Dr. Sherin was Principal Researcher in the team that produced a report on Blockchain sukuk 2021, the report can be viewed here . Currently Dr. Sherin is researching on the use of blockchain in Islamic social finance and its use.

Cynthia Lee Mei Fei is a PhD candidate in law and a graduate research assistant at the University of Malaya (UM) under a research project on competition law and consumer protection in the digital market. The research project is led by Dr Ong Tze Chin and funded under a Fundamental Research Grant Scheme (FRGS) by the Malaysian Ministry of Higher Education. She is also a lawyer practising civil litigation (contractual and tortious) in Kuala Lumpur. She graduated in law from Cardiff University with an LLB (Hons) and has a Master of Commercial Law (MCL) from the University of Malaya. She was called to the Bar as a barrister at Middle Temple, United Kingdom and is an advocate and solicitor of the High Courts of Malaya, Malaysia.

Cenuk Sayekti is an Assistant Professor at School of Postgraduate Program, Airlangga University, Surabaya, Indonesia. The focus of the research field is competition law, law and economic, and international economic law. Currently, she leads as the Director of Renewable Energy Studies and Research Center of Postgraduate Program, University of Airlangga.

Sridevi Thambapillay obtained her LLB(Hons) with an Upper Second Class from the University of Malaya in 1995. She was admitted as an Advocate and Solicitor of the High Court of Malaya in 1996. She completed her Masters in Law (LLM) at the University of Malaya in 1997 and thereafter began her career as a Senior Officer at the Loan Documentation Department in the United Overseas Bank (Malaysia) Berhad. Her passion for teaching law resulted in her joining as a lecturer in HELP Institute in 1998. Wanting to enhance her teaching career in a public university, she was indeed fortunate to be offered a tutor's post at the Faculty of Law, University of Malaya in 2001. She is currently a Senior Lecturer at the same place. Her area of research is in Family Law and Elderly Law and has written various articles and edited various books in this area, individually and jointly. She has also presented papers at various conferences, both locally and at the international level. She received the best paper presenter award at a few of the international conferences. She teaches the following subjects at the Faculty of Law, namely, Administrative Law, Legal Method and Family Law. She was conferred a PhD in Law in 2017 by the University of Malaya.

Suparto Wijaya is a Professor at Airlangga University, School of Postgraduate Program. The main research focuses is environmental Law and administrative law. He also the vice director at School of Postgraduate Program at University of Airlangga, Indonesia.

Index

Recommended Reference Books

IGI Global's reference books are available in three unique pricing formats: Print Only, E-Book Only, or Print + E-Book.

Order direct through IGI Global's Online Bookstore at **www.igi-global.com** or through your preferred provider.

ISBN: 9781799877851
EISBN: 9781799877875
© 2022; 402 pp.
List Price: US$ **215**

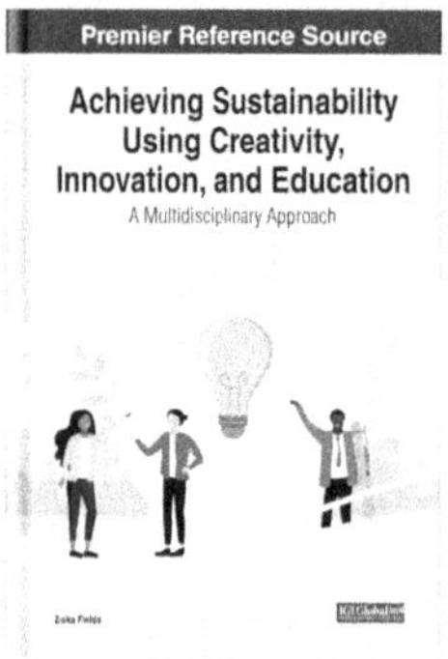

ISBN: 9781799879633
EISBN: 9781799879657
© 2022; 260 pp.
List Price: US$ **240**

ISBN: 9781799890904
EISBN: 9781799890928
© 2022; 307 pp.
List Price: US$ **195**

ISBN: 9781668437063
EISBN: 9781668437070
© 2022; 1,611 pp.
List Price: US$ **1,040**

ISBN: 9781799883395
EISBN: 9781799883418
© 2022; 327 pp.
List Price: US$ **215**

ISBN: 9781799868071
EISBN: 9781799868095
© 2022; 353 pp.
List Price: US$ **215**

Do you want to stay current on the latest research trends, product announcements, news, and special offers?
Join IGI Global's mailing list to receive customized recommendations, exclusive discounts, and more.
Sign up at: **www.igi-global.com/newsletters.**

Publisher of Timely, Peer-Reviewed Inclusive Research Since 1988

IGI Global
PUBLISHER of TIMELY KNOWLEDGE

www.igi-global.com Sign up at www.igi-global.com/newsletters facebook.com/igiglobal twitter.com/igiglobal linkedin.com/igiglobal

Ensure Quality Research is Introduced to the Academic Community

Become an Reviewer for IGI Global Authored Book Projects

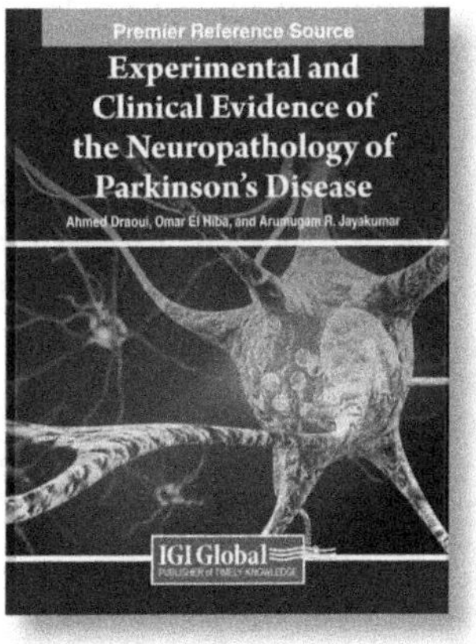

The overall success of an authored book project is dependent on quality and timely manuscript evaluations.

Applications and Inquiries may be sent to:
development@igi-global.com

Applicants must have a doctorate (or equivalent degree) as well as publishing, research, and reviewing experience. Authored Book Evaluators are appointed for one-year terms and are expected to complete at least three evaluations per term. Upon successful completion of this term, evaluators can be considered for an additional term.

If you have a colleague that may be interested in this opportunity, we encourage you to share this information with them.

Submit an Open Access Book Proposal

Have Your Work Fully & Freely Available Worldwide After Publication

Seeking the Following Book Classification Types:

Authored & Edited Monographs • Casebooks • Encyclopedias • Handbooks of Research

Gold, Platinum, & Retrospective OA Opportunities to Choose From

Easily Track Your Work in Our Advanced Manuscript Submission System With **Rapid Turnaround Times**

Double-Blind Peer Review by Notable Editorial Boards (*Committee on Publication Ethics* (COPE) Certified

Publications Adhere to All **Current OA Mandates & Compliances**

Affordable APCs ***(Often 50% Lower Than the Industry Average)*** Including Robust Editorial Service Provisions

Direct Connections with **Prominent Research Funders** & OA Regulatory Groups

Institution Level OA Agreements Available (Recommend or Contact Your Librarian for Details)

Join a **Diverse Community of 150,000+ Researchers Worldwide** Publishing With IGI Global

Content Spread Widely to Leading Repositories (AGOSR, ResearchGate, CORE, & More)

DID YOU KNOW? Retrospective Open Access Publishing

You Can Unlock Your Recently Published Work, Including Full Book & Individual Chapter Content to Enjoy All the Benefits of Open Access Publishing

Learn More

Publishing Tomorrow's Research Today
IGI Global
e-Book Collection

Including Essential Reference Books Within Three Fundamental Academic Areas

Business & Management
Scientific, Technical, & Medical (STM)
Education

- Acquisition options include Perpetual, Subscription, and Read & Publish
- No Additional Charge for Multi-User Licensing
- No Maintenance, Hosting, or Archiving Fees
- Continually Enhanced Accessibility Compliance Features (WCAG)

Over **150,000+** Chapters | Contributions From **200,000+** Scholars Worldwide | More Than **1,000,000+** Citations | Majority of e-Books Indexed in Web of Science & Scopus | Consists of Tomorrow's Research Available Today!

Recommended Titles from our e-Book Collection

Innovation Capabilities and Entrepreneurial Opportunities of Smart Working
ISBN: 9781799887973

Advanced Applications of Generative AI and Natural Language Processing Models
ISBN: 9798369305027

Using Influencer Marketing as a Digital Business Strategy
ISBN: 9798369305515

Human-Centered Approaches in Industry 5.0
ISBN: 9798369326473

Modeling and Monitoring Extreme Hydrometeorological Events
ISBN: 9781668487716

Data-Driven Intelligent Business Sustainability
ISBN: 9798369300497

Information Logistics for Organizational Empowerment and Effective Supply Chain Management
ISBN: 9798369301593

Data Envelopment Analysis (DEA) Methods for Maximizing Efficiency
ISBN: 9798369302552

Request More Information, or Recommend the IGI Global e-Book Collection to Your Institution's Librarian

For More Information or to Request a Free Trial, Contact IGI Global's e-Collections Team: eresources@igi-global.com | 1-866-342-6657 ext. 100 | 717-533-8845 ext. 100

Are You Ready to

Publish Your Research?

IGI Global
PUBLISHER of TIMELY KNOWLEDGE

IGI Global offers book authorship and editorship opportunities across 11 subject areas, including business, computer science, education, science and engineering, social sciences, and more!

Benefits of Publishing with IGI Global:

- Free one-on-one editorial and promotional support.
- Expedited publishing timelines that can take your book from start to finish in less than one (1) year.
- Choose from a variety of formats, including Edited and Authored References, Handbooks of Research, Encyclopedias, and Research Insights.
- Utilize IGI Global's eEditorial Discovery® submission system in support of conducting the submission and double-blind peer review process.
- IGI Global maintains a strict adherence to ethical practices due in part to our full membership with the Committee on Publication Ethics (COPE).
- Indexing potential in prestigious indices such as Scopus®, Web of Science™, PsycINFO®, and ERIC – Education Resources Information Center.
- Ability to connect your ORCID iD to your IGI Global publications.
- Earn honorariums and royalties on your full book publications as well as complimentary content and exclusive discounts.

Join Your Colleagues from Prestigious Institutions, Including:

Australian National University

Massachusetts Institute of Technology

Johns Hopkins University

Harvard University

Tsinghua University 1911

Columbia University in the City of New York

Learn More at: www.igi-global.com/publish

or Contact IGI Global's Aquisitions Team at: acquisition@igi-global.com

Individual Article & Chapter Downloads

US$ 37.50/each

Easily Identify, Acquire, and Utilize Published Peer-Reviewed Findings in Support of Your Current Research

- Browse Over ***170,000+ Articles & Chapters***
- ***Accurate & Advanced*** Search
- Affordably Acquire ***International Research***
- ***Instantly Access*** Your Content
- Benefit from the ***InfoSci® Platform Features***

THE UNIVERSITY of NORTH CAROLINA at CHAPEL HILL

"*It really provides* an excellent entry into the research literature of the field. *It presents a manageable number of* highly relevant sources *on topics of interest to a wide range of researchers. The sources are* scholarly, but also accessible *to 'practitioners'.*"

- Ms. Lisa Stimatz, MLS, University of North Carolina at Chapel Hill, USA

www.ingramcontent.com/pod-product-compliance
Lightning Source LLC
LaVergne TN
LVHW080646011026
849160LV00014B/1333